Carolina Cavalier

Johnston Pettigrew—The Charleston Years
"It is a great pleasure to me, that I have never yet been taken for a
Yankee or a Locofoco." (Pettigrew Family Papers, Southern
Historical Collection, University of North Carolina)

Carolina Cavalier

THE LIFE AND MIND OF

JAMES JOHNSTON PETTIGREW

Clyde N. Wilson

The University of Georgia Press • *Athens and London*

© 1990 by the University of Georgia Press
Athens, Georgia 30602
All rights reserved

Designed by Mary Mendell
Set in Janson Text
Typeset by Tseng Information Systems, Inc.
Printed and bound by Thomson-Shore, Inc.
The paper in this book meets the guidelines for
permanence and durability of the Committee
on Production Guidelines for Book Longevity
of the Council on Library Resources.

Printed in the United States of America

94 93 92 91 90   5 4 3 2 1

Library of Congress
Cataloging in Publication Data

Wilson, Clyde Norman.
Carolina cavalier : the life and mind of
James Johnston Pettigrew / Clyde N. Wilson.
p.   cm.
Includes bibliographical references.
ISBN 0-8203-1201-0 (alk. paper)
1. Pettigrew, James Johnston, 1828–1863.
2. Legislators — South Carolina — Biography.
3. South Carolina. General Assembly —
Biography.   4. Upper classes — South
Carolina — History — 19th century.
5. Generals — Southern States — Biography.
6. Confederate States of America. Army —
Biography.   I. Title.
F273.P53W55   1990
975.7'03'092 — dc20   89-20136 CIP

British Library Cataloging in
Publication Data available

Contents

Preface

"The cult of chivalry, while it imposed limitations on the intellectual life of the South, produced at the same time some fine fruits in manners and behavior. In no other Southerner did romantic ideals show to greater advantage than in James Johnston Pettigrew." These words were published a half a century ago by Clement Eaton, at that time one of the leading historians of the Old South.[1]

I read his words about a quarter of a century ago—half way between the publication of Eaton's book and the publication of mine. The two sentences were only obiter dicta, but I was full of the energy and earnestness of youth and they struck me. I was just learning to be a historian, just beginning to appreciate the excitement and satisfaction involved in the exploration and mastery of documents, and I knew of the huge collections of Pettigrew manuscripts preserved at Chapel Hill and Raleigh.

Of course, it was the late sixties, and it was impossible for me not to be aware at the time that my native country, the South, which had until the day before yesterday seemed so solid, was wracked within and besieged without, was, indeed, the focus of the world's attention. My generation of southerners could not avoid response to this situation.

One of my responses was an investigation, historically framed, of the phenomenon of the South. In this endeavor Eaton had suggested a host of interesting subsidiary questions. What was the "cult of chivalry"? If it did indeed signify in American history, how did American chivalry differ from European? Of what exactly did the "limitations" on the intellectual life of the South which Eaton postulated consist? In what way did they differ from the limitations or lack of limitations found elsewhere, and why? What exactly were the "fine fruits in manners and behavior," certainly not something to be lightly dismissed, that he had suggested? What were the "romantic ideals" that James Johnston Pettigrew exhibited to such advantage, and how did they come to be created and sustained?

Not too long after reading Eaton's remark, in the course of further searching for the best thought that had been offered on the questions that interested me, I encountered an essay of C. Vann Woodward, called "The Southern Ethic in a Puritan World." One passage seemed to speak to and justify a task that I was beginning to conceive for myself as a would be southern historian:

> Social role-playing is a broad mark for satire, but all societies engage in it consciously or unconsciously. The sharpest ridicule is reserved for the unfortunate society that is caught at the height of collective posturing, brought low with humiliating exposure of its pretenses, and forced to acknowledge them—or live with them. The Old South has had its share of exposure along this particular line, and more at this juncture has rather low priority among the pressing tasks of historiography. More needful are analytical appraisals of the social content of the patriarchal, paternalistic, and aristocratic values and the remarkable qualities of leadership they developed.
>
> Also needed are discerning assessments of the skill, conviction, and zest which other players brought to the colorful variety of roles assigned them by the Old Regime.... It is possible that a majority of the players identified completely with their roles as "real life"—as completely perhaps as the saints, prophets, and come-outers in other quarters found identity in their roles. At least the cast for the Old South drama, slaves included, often acted as if they did, and sometimes they put on rather magnificent performances. Study of the institutional setting in which they performed—the patriarchal tradition, the caste system, the martial spirit, the racial etiquette, the familial charisma—all deserve attention from the historian of the Southern Ethic.[2]

By this time I knew enough about James Johnston Pettigrew to know that his life provided an ideal case study for investigation of the questions that Eaton had raised and at least some of the subjects that Woodward had suggested: the patriarchal tradition, the martial spirit, and the familial charisma. In Pettigrew's brief existence "aristocratic values and the remarkable qualities of leadership they developed" were articulately and abundantly displayed and documented. That life certainly exhibited "skill, conviction, and zest" in carrying out a role assigned by the "Old Regime." Miraculously, Pettigrew played the role to the hilt, and yet he was an intelligent man capable of reflecting with detachment on the world in which he was active. While he was not a first-rank historical figure in any sphere, he was a significant second-rank player in multiple aspects of the life of the Old South: intellectual endeavor, politics, and that experience of warfare which characterized the entire existence of the abortive southern nation. Moreover, his career was played out equally in the two Carolinas, sister states who presented variant aspects of the drama of southern history.

This book is a revised version of my first study of Pettigrew completed as a dissertation in 1971. I take a certain wry and ambiguous satisfaction that my treatment of Pettigrew and his world — though definitely out of step at the time it was first outlined — anticipated in some respects the course that scholarship on the Old South has since taken. Quite naturally influenced by the civil rights revolution and the negative feelings and judgments about the Old South that entailed, the central literature of that time emphasized the irrationality and destructiveness of Pettigrew's generation of southerners, the last antebellum generation.

Running rather counter to the prevailing winds and tides, I anticipated, I think, a scholarly treatment of southern intellectual life, which was not then taken seriously but which is now a significant and growing field of study. I anticipated also the interest in "southern honor," then considered no more than hypocrisy and self-delusion but now a major subject in the literature. My study embodied a respect for the Confederate military effort, which then was treated (and still is in some quarters) with a somewhat cheap and superficial condescension despite the fact that it represents the most extensive sacrifice and heroic effort that any large group of Americans has ever been called upon to make. Finally, at a time when James Louis Petigru, an important figure in this study, was being thought of as a modern liberal, I fully developed a portrait of him as, on the contrary, a relic of Federalism, a view that is now generally accepted.[3]

Professor Joel Williamson signed my study of Pettigrew in its original form as a dissertation at the University of North Carolina at Chapel Hill, despite the extent to which I differed from his own views of southern history, proving what nobody ever doubted, that he is a gentleman as well as a scholar. He, along with Anna Brooke Allan, J. Isaac Copeland, and Carolyn Andrews Wallace, taught me everything I know about being a historian, though they should not necessarily be blamed for the uses to which I have put it. M. E. Bradford and W. Kirk Wood never doubted that my biography of Pettigrew ought to be published. Professor Eugene Genovese and Mr. Malcolm Call, director of the University of Georgia Press, made the publication possible.

My approach herein is not primarily analytical — rather it is narrative, though a good deal of analysis is subsumed in the narrative, and the final chapter is explicitly interpretive. The analysis is "critical," I hope, in the sense that it is investigative, but it is not unsympathetic. Rather, my orientation is guided by an observation of Professor Genovese on the central figures of the Old South:

> These men were class conscious, socially responsible, and personally honorable; they selflessly fulfilled their duties and did what their class and society required of them. . . . There is no reason . . . to withhold from such people respect and even admiration. . . . If we blind ourselves to everything noble, virtuous, honorable, decent, and selfless in a ruling class, how do we account for its hegemony? . . . Such hegemony could never be maintained without some leaders whose individual qualities are intrinsically admirable.[4]

My strategy is to present a narrative that conveys with as much immediacy and forcefulness as I can muster an exemplary and articulate life that was lived to the hilt, and that touched on many neglected aspects of that large and not-quite-vanished segment of the American experience that goes under the label the "Old South." Twenty years of practicing and pondering history have convinced me that narrative, when it incorporates within itself the descriptive and analytical functions, is the most difficult form of history to write, probably the most enduring, and possibly the most meaningful.

I have constructed the narrative mainly from primary sources, calling on secondary sources only for factual data, not for interpretations. Interpretations I have supplied and interwoven myself. I have not made reference to a vast body of secondary material treating the interpretation of the Old South in general and the interpretation of many specific events and phenomena in which Pettigrew participated. This does not mean that I am either unaware of or indifferent to this literature, but that I have chosen not to make reference to it.

This choice has been made for a number of reasons. To take account of all the scholarly views that impinge significantly on all the facets of Pettigrew's life (the battle of Gettysburg or the interpretation of the Old South, for instance) would expand the book to too great a length. To most readers the resulting expansion of text and notes would present material with which they were already familiar if they are professional scholars, or in which they are not really interested if they are not. But, most important, it would encumber the freshness of the narrative and its encounter with the raw stuff of history. In general, it seems to me, historians at the present day tend to conceptualize too much at second and third hand, within the frameworks established for them by others, which is a different thing than acknowledging a proper debt to other thinkers. Thus they limit their capacity to think in new directions.

I will be content if my work fulfills the goal outlined for himself by one of the first modern scholars of southern history, William Garrott Brown, who wrote, early in the twentieth century: "It will be something if these papers shall make it plain that my subject is a true body of human life,—a thing, and not a mass of facts, a topic in political science, an object lesson in large moralities. To know the thing itself should be our study; and the right study of it is thought and passion, not research alone."[5]

Chronology of

James Johnston Pettigrew

4 July 1828. Born at Bonarva plantation, Tyrrell County, North Carolina.

1836–1843. Attends Bingham Academy, Hillsborough.

1843–1847. Attends the University of North Carolina. Graduates with a perfect academic record.

1847–1848. Professor at the Naval Observatory under Matthew F. Maury. Studies law in Baltimore.

1849. Takes up residence in Charleston.

1850–1852. In Europe. Receives a degree in civil law from the University of Berlin. Travels extensively in Germany, France, Italy, Spain, and the Austro-Hungarian empire.

1853–1860. Practices law in Charleston as the junior partner of James Louis Petigru. Active in the intellectual and social life of the city and in the militia.

1856–1857. Serves one term in the South Carolina General Assembly. Writes a celebrated report against the reopening of the foreign slave trade.

1859. Returns to Europe and attempts unsuccessfully to enlist in the Sardinian army during the Franco-Austrian war. Travels once more in Spain.

December 1860–April 1861. Commands the South Carolina First Regiment of Rifles in Charleston harbor from secession to the fall of Fort Sumter.

June 1861. Notes on Spain and the Spaniards printed at Charleston.

July 1861–April 1862. Commands Twenty-second North Carolina Regiment on the Potomac.

22 March 1862. Promoted to brigadier general.

31 May 1862. Commands brigade at Seven Pines; wounded and captured. Imprisoned at Fort Delaware until exchanged.

August 1862–April 1863. Pettigrew's Brigade formed; engaged in minor operations in eastern North Carolina.

1 June 1863. Pettigrew's Brigade joins the Army of Northern Virginia on the march to Pennsylvania.

1 July 1863. Pettigrew's Brigade successfully assaults McPherson's and Seminary ridges at Gettysburg, with heavy casualties.

3 July 1863. Commands Heth's division in "Pickett's" charge.

14 July 1863. Wounded for the fifth time, mortally, in a rearguard action on the Potomac; dies 17 July.

Carolina Cavalier

Chapter 1

The Lake

In 1859 the young southerner James Johnston Pettigrew was making his way on muleback across the dusty plains of Spain. This was an unusual activity for an American, but Pettigrew was always one for the unexpected and untried. He dozed in the saddle for a moment, and his thoughts "wandered home to the old plantation. I dreamed myself once more a boy, playing under the noble forest trees that border its lake. Birds sung in their branches, and squirrels skipped playfully about their venerable roots, while a Southern breeze rippled gently over the water."[1] In recording this revery somewhat self-consciously in print, Pettigrew paid a southerner's homage to the homeplace that had nurtured three generations of his family.

According to a prized tradition of that family, the paternal ancestors of James Johnston Pettigrew were French Protestants who emigrated to Scotland in the seventeenth century or perhaps earlier. For services rendered to William III at the Battle of the Boyne, one of the Scottish family was awarded an estate in County Tyrone, and meanwhile he Anglicized his name from "Petigru" to "Pettigrew." From this Irish home James Pettigrew (1713–1784), a younger son of the warrior and thus not in the direct line of inheritance, departed for Pennsylvania in 1740, having first acquired a classical education, a wife, and the displeasure of his parents. From Pennsylvania, James, following the Scotch-Irish track, moved on to the Virginia Piedmont where he prospered as a planter and physician. By 1760 he was established in North Carolina, and about 1768 he made a final removal to the South Carolina upcountry, leaving behind in North Carolina some of the older of his thirteen children.[2]

Among these was Charles Pettigrew (1744–1807), grandfather of James Johnston Pettigrew. Shortly before the Revolution, Charles, having abandoned the Presbyterian faith of his father, made the perilous voyage across the Atlantic required for ordination into the Anglican ministry. By the close of the War of Independence, Charles Pettigrew of Edenton was perhaps the leading clergyman of North Carolina below the fall line. Respected for his learning and eloquent sermons, for his tolerant cooperation with dissenters, and for the zeal with which he traveled about the hinterland ministering to the unchurched, Charles was the natural choice for the first bishop of the North Carolina diocese. To this position he was elected, although he died before his consecration could be arranged.[3]

By his first marriage, to Mary Blount (who died in 1786), Charles was united to the numerous, wealthy, and aristocratic Blount family of New Bern, who in turn were or became related by blood or marriage to other prominent families, including the Philadelphia Biddles. Finding the disestablished post-Revolutionary church an inadequate support for his family, he acquired lands in a fertile, swampy region of eastern North Carolina between Albemarle and Pamlico sounds and devoted part of his attention in later life to planting.[4]

There, Ebenezer Pettigrew, the only surviving son of Charles and Mary and the father of James Johnston Pettigrew, began in the early nineteenth century his career as a planter with the two raw plantations and thirty slaves that were his inheritance. The intellectual powers that Charles Pettigrew had bestowed on the church, Ebenezer turned to the art and science of agriculture, and he became one of the ablest planters to appear in the three centuries of that American vocation. The scene of his labors was a sixty-by-forty-mile peninsula, much of which resembled the Great Dismal Swamp further to the north. Such of this region's land that could be cleared of the dense forests and properly drained was immensely fertile at the beginning of the nineteenth century. In the northern part of the peninsula, situated across what was declared in 1799 to be the border of Washington and Tyrrell counties, is a clear lake, approximately twelve miles long and eight miles wide, formed, some authorities believe, in the crater of a prehistoric meteor which was filled by subterranean springs.[5]

At first called Lake Scuppernong and later Lake Phelps, this body of water, known to the Pettigrews simply as "The Lake," was the center of the world into which James Johnston Pettigrew was born on 4 July 1828. The plantation house of Bonarva in which the birth occurred stood on the northeastern shore of The Lake in Tyrrell County just east of the Washington County line. Belgrade, an older Pettigrew plantation, was eight miles to the west in Washington County. A third plantation, Magnolia, was cleared to the east when James Johnston Pettigrew was a child.[6]

In the eighteenth century a corporation formed by a group of Charles Pettigrew's wealthy Edenton parishioners, among whom Josiah Collins was principal, had acquired title to vast lands in The Lake region and built a canal from The Lake to the Scuppernong River six miles away. Labor for the project was provided by a slave force brought from Africa especially for the purpose and who became the progenitors of many of the nineteenth-century plantation slaves of the region. Completed in 1789, the twenty-foot-wide canal gave the products of the area an easy access to the outside world on rafts floated down the canal to the river and down the river to the little port of Columbia on an inlet of Albemarle Sound. Even more important, The Canal, as it was known, through smaller connecting ditches, permitted both flood control and irrigation. A veritable Nile to the inhabitants, it was not only an aid to agriculture and navigation, but it provided as well a source of power for machinery. Charles Pettigrew's land lay in sight of The Canal and he had the foresight to secure for his heirs rights to its use.[7]

Ebenezer Pettigrew, by constant effort, achieved considerable prosperity. At the time of James Johnston Pettigrew's childhood there were five thousand cleared acres in The Lake region, belonging chiefly to the Pettigrew and Collins families and producing, among other crops, fifteen thousand barrels of corn per year for sale at Charleston. Certainly there were few planters anywhere who produced as great a diversity of cash products as Ebenezer Pettigrew. Besides the huge corn output, his plantations yielded sizable quantities of wheat, rice, and vegetables. His sawmill turned out dressed lumber, barrels, shingles, staves, posts, and ship-building materials in marketable quantities. Profits were made from mulberry bushes, bricks, and the fish in the canal, and wine was produced from the scuppernong grapes abounding in the vicinity. Ebenezer Pettigrew had agents in Charleston, Baltimore, Norfolk, New York, and several small North Carolina ports. There were few times of the year when he did not have a favorable balance on the books of at least some of them. All of this earned the attention and admiration of the noted agricultural reformer Edmund Ruffin.[8]

Ebenezer's slave force numbered on average about one hundred, of whom fifty were "full hands." The semi-industrial enterprises conducted at The Lake and the care and operation of the machinery constantly employed in ditching required the presence of up to a half-dozen white overseers and skilled artisans, whom Pettigrew seems to have treated as friends and associates rather than as hired hands.[9]

The rules of Ebenezer Pettigrew's life were unflagging industry and unflinching rectitude. So respected was he by the yeomanry and lesser gentry of the vicinity that when he reluctantly stood for Congress in 1834 he received the votes of all but three of the seven hundred free men of Tyrrell County. His only indulgences were occasional trips to the North and the collection of a library of three thousand volumes. He strenuously resisted the planter's traditional triple temptations: political ambition, lavish living, and dissipation. Somerset Place, nearby seat of the Collins family, boasted a luxurious mansion and a racetrack. The Pettigrew buildings were comparatively modest and businesslike. The few political offices Ebenezer held were undertaken with genuine reluctance and at the insistence of friends, and, after one term in Washington, nothing could induce him to seek another although reelection was considered certain.[10]

Yet this highly successful, practical man had a disarming streak of sentimentality that approached mysticism. His famous first cousin James Louis Petigru, leading lawyer of South Carolina, whom he did not encounter until both were middle-aged, reacted to their meeting thus:

> So we had two days to become acquainted, which was no great matter for him as he had only such everyday, common-life people as Caroline and myself to understand. But our cousin is a perfect study. His garrulity is immense, his simplicity such that he talks of himself in preference. . . . his feelings are so sensitive, that tears choke his voice in speaking of his brother who died more than 40 years ago. . . . prudence is his guiding star and perseverance his motto. . . . from his neighbors . . . we learned, that in all North Carolina, there is no man, whose opinions on agriculture and everything connected with it, are so much regarded. He

changed his District from Democratic to Whig by his intrinsic popularity as a candidate, and left it as such to his successor.[11]

Ebenezer's marriage to Ann Blount Shepard, daughter of a New Bern merchant, was apparently happy. Still, in 1828 at the age of forty-five Ebenezer could not have been particularly delighted at the birth of another child. Besides two children who had died in infancy, he already had a daughter and four sons, two of whom were sickly and destined not to survive childhood. Perhaps a certain casualness in relaying the news of James Johnston's birth to his best friend was self-defensive. Infant mortality was so high in the low country, particularly in the summer, that it did not pay to become too attached to a baby who might not last the week. Ebenezer's main concern was that his wife had survived the ordeal in good health.[12]

Ann Shepard Pettigrew, however, did not survive her next pregnancy. Within two years, at age thirty-five, she died from the complications of the birth of a daughter. The disconsolate Ebenezer, who never fully recovered from the melancholia induced by the death of his wife, was left with the care of four children, not counting his three older sons who were away at school. As a result, James Johnston Pettigrew (who was always to be called "Johnston") spent much of his first seven years living with his Shepard and Bryan relatives at the eastern North Carolina town of New Bern. Ann Pettigrew's sister, Mary Shepard, had married John Herritage Bryan. A protégé of the state's beloved chief justice William Gaston, Bryan had been elected to Congress when he was twenty-five years old. In 1830, at thirty-two, he was devoting his attention to becoming one of the leading attorneys of North Carolina and to supporting a family which would eventually include fourteen children. All of the Bryan children lived to their majority except two who were killed in the Civil War.[13]

With her husband away on law circuit much of the year, Mrs. Bryan undertook the rearing of the four youngest Pettigrews along with her own huge brood. By all evidence she treated the Pettigrew children as tenderly as her own offspring. Still, there could not have been much time for individual attention. Possibly some of the excessive sensitiveness and pride which marked Johnston Pettigrew throughout his life arose from the awkward circumstances of his motherless childhood. While his two sisters referred to Mrs. Bryan as "Mother" and to the

Bryan children as brothers and sisters, he never did. John Herritage Bryan was in some ways more of a father to him than his own, but after Pettigrew was grown their relations were cool, a condition which Pettigrew attributed to Bryan's resentment that none of his own sons proved as able as the nephew who had been raised in his home.[14]

The Pettigrew children spent most of each year in New Bern with their relatives. Occasionally in winter, when it was considered safe, they visited the swampy plantations. While at The Lake, the child Johnston was usually under the care of one of his brothers, Charles Lockhart or William Shepard, twelve and ten years his senior respectively, who at that time would be on vacation from their academy or from the University of North Carolina.

Ill health was the salient circumstance of Johnston Pettigrew's childhood. Surviving documents mention an "unfortunate exposure" which weakened the child's constitution, although the exact nature of this is impossible to determine. At any rate he was frequently sick and it was lamented that he could stand neither hot weather nor cold. Concern for the child's health predominated in the frequent and full reports that John and Mary Bryan sent to the father and the frequent instructions returned by Ebenezer. The family's fears for Johnston's health were exacerbated by the condition of his brothers, James and Henry Ebenezer, both of whom died in childhood after long and painful illnesses accompanied by recurring paralysis.[15]

It was no doubt his semiorphan status along with delicate health and the restraint it put upon him that caused Pettigrew to reflect later to his brother that his "childhood and boyhood up to my 19th year was detestable, and I never look back to them but with disgust." Still there must have been a pleasant side to his life, at least at The Lake with its opportunities for riding, hunting, and fishing, the huge library, the fascinating and varied activities going on, the close ties to the great outer world of commerce, the beautiful natural setting, and the mild climate.[16]

Alternating melancholy and contentment seemed to run through the life of the Pettigrews at The Lake. The natural setting was one of idyllic beauty: the huge, clear, placid lake situated on a plateau above the surrounding countryside and circled by giant cypresses, water oaks, and elms, with tree-shaded carriage lanes radiating out along the ridges.[17] As always, there was a ghost at the feast. Seasonal fevers disabled for a part of every year those inhabitants that they did not kill. The paradox was not limited to nature.

Ebenezer Pettigrew and his sons Charles and William who succeeded him as planters lived possessed of wealth and power. Yet their lives, while not solitary, were isolated from the diversions, comforts, and amenities of the cities of the world. The management of the vast and varied enterprises of The Lake required of the proprietors not only great effort, initiative, and willpower, but also constituted a relentless emotional drain. Upon their exertions depended not only the maintenance and advancement of their own fortunes and reputations, but also the well-being and control of one hundred slaves who were at the same time the family's treasure and its burden. The latter was inevitably a load on the minds of sensitive men such as the Pettigrews were. Still, this tension was relatively minor. On the whole, except for the ills that flesh is inevitably heir to, life was pleasant for the inhabitants of The Lake.

Johnston Pettigrew's first seven years alternated between New Bern and The Lake. During the next seven years the cycle changed because he was sent to school and because the Bryan family moved upcountry to Raleigh. In his second seven years the boy rotated between school at Hillsborough, his relatives' homes at Raleigh during the shorter holidays, and The Lake during the winter when the upcountry was considered more dangerous to his health than the low.[18]

Johnston had received some preliminary schooling at New Bern and it was there that his exceptional mental capacities became evident to his family. When he was four his uncle John Bryan declared that if the boy's health held out and he received an adequate education "he will become an extraordinary man." Another uncle described the child as a genius.[19]

Johnston's secondary education was entrusted to William James Bingham, whose academy was then the most noted in the state and who had successfully handled three older Pettigrew boys. In 1836 Johnston and his sisters Mary, two years older, and Ann, two years his junior, were sent to Hillsborough where they boarded with respectable families and the girls were given lessons.[20]

Upon examination Bingham found Johnston already in advance in learning of the other boys of his age, so that in the first two years at Hillsborough he was not put into a formal course but was allowed a life of outdoor exercise designed to improve his health and his capacity to withstand extremes of weather. This program was successful, for within a few months the schoolmaster reported that Johnston's appearance and appetite were almost as good as those of an upcountry boy, and at the end of a year his brother found him sturdier than he had ever seen him.[21]

The intellectual side of Johnston's education posed no problem. Bingham's Academy was the best in the state, and the boy took full advantage of it. He started at the head of his class and stayed there except on one occasion when he fell behind because of an unusually long winter stay at The Lake. For a few weeks he mastered an extra lesson a day in private and was soon at the head of his class again. Johnston's reading ranged far beyond what was required. Ebenezer marvelled at the knowledge the boy acquired from perusing the medical books of a physician with whom he boarded for a time at Hillsborough.[22]

As he grew older the boy had a certain amount of freedom about the town, which was small but one of the more important of the rural state, and this proved as educational in its own way as the school. There was much for a spirited boy to do and see: court sessions and political rallies, and occasionally public corporal punishment; the stores and blacksmith shops; the arrival and departure of stagecoaches; nearby woods and fields where frogs were shot with a companion's rifle and cooked and eaten. On a few occasions these adventures led to premature vices such as card playing or swaggering about with a "mannish air" too insolent for his age, and then he was punished by a whipping or by being set to dig stumps.[23]

Bingham was gentle, devout, and thoughtful, and yet he was a vigorous and effective man who seems to have had a large capacity to inculcate both intellectual and moral fundamentals. He took a genuine interest in the future of the boys under his charge, of whom there were approximately eighty-five at the time, and Ebenezer Pettigrew's children he regarded as a special trust. The father and teacher were close friends and frequent correspondents. They agreed on politics, agriculture, and morals, and both felt disdain for fashionable swaggering and love for virtuous industry. Despite his gentleness Bingham was fully capable of meting out punishment when it was required. During a riot in Johnston's time, an older student armed with a pistol locked himself in a building and defied authority. Bingham armed himself, broke open the door, faced the culprit down, and expelled every student who had countenanced the uprising in any way despite the pleas and threats of influential parents. "There is not a kinder woman or man in the world than Mr. and Mrs. Bingham. . . . [But] it is true he will make you study," was the comment of one of Johnston's uncles who had been to school at Bingham's Academy.[24]

The guiding principle of the education the boy received was the intent to instill character, to the end that his wealth, social position, and abilities would be perceived not only as matters of luxury and privilege but also as imperatives to duty and responsibility. The twin axioms of this effort to instill character, reiterated in every letter from father to son and every advice of teacher to pupil, were the avoidance of vice and wastefulness and the cultivation of self-control and humility. Johnston's elders assumed that pride and self-assertion would be strong enough to take care of themselves without encouragement, for it was early noted that the boy was strongly self-willed.[25]

Johnston was constantly reminded that his wealth was due to the labor and self-denial of his father and grandfather and that their substance was to be preserved and increased, not cast away in self-indulgence. Ebenezer allowed himself few luxuries and his first concern was the ceaseless improvement of his property. While others relaxed and lived off their capital, he increased his. When he died there were no debts owed by his huge estate that could not be easily paid off in one season.[26] Ebenezer gave stern lectures, but he was his own best example:

> I was very sorry to learn my dear son that a boy who could learn his lessons so easily should still do something that would subject him to correction [Ebenezer wrote on one occasion]. You think that Mr. Bingham is getting more strict, but my son you are mistaken you are getting more self-willed, and do not know it. . . . to let a boy have his own way, is to ruin him forever. . . . Look at other young men who have been permitted to do as they think proper. Where are they[?] Gone and going to destruction as fast as they can.[27]

Johnston's intellectual powers, his father and teacher stressed, were the gift of God. Rather than a cause for vanity, they were a debt owed to himself, to his family, and to society, a gift to use productively and honorably. "Nature has done a great deal for you," wrote the father, "but what will it avail if your evil propensities are not conquered?" When Johnston spent his pocket money on the scandalous penny paper, the *New York Herald*, he was reprimanded for wastefulness of time and talents. When his superior ability tempted him to slight the preparation of his lessons and rely on quick wits, he was whipped. And when Johnston took the dry pledge under the influence of the Hillsborough temperance society, Ebenezer regarded it as an ungentlemanly departure from the golden mean, that might result in the opposite extreme of drunkenness.[28] The father and teacher were at one in all this, and the father never failed to back up the teacher's discipline.

Like most young men, Johnston Pettigrew desired to go his own way, resented his father's admonitions, and failed to recognize the value of his lessons until he was older and had seen something of the world.[29] Yet the lessons took, and when he became a man he lived by them both reflexively and reflectively. When his father was dead and his teacher left behind, his older brother William and a remarkable old man, James Cathcart Johnston, for whom he had been named, were on hand to remind him of the requirements of duty and honor. In the path Pettigrew cut out for himself, in his relation to his fellows and his country, even in his literary tastes, the moral lessons of the father and the teacher could be seen.

When the boy was thirteen Bingham felt his work was largely done. He wrote Ebenezer:

> You desire my ideas of J. in general, together with any suggestions as to what may be best to do with him? Well, he has the capacity *to be* & *to do what he pleases*. He has not only the capacity but *the inclination* to be a scholar; and unless some malign influence should come over him, he cannot fail in that. He is inclined to think & act for himself, i.e., he has an independent turn of mind — a very valuable trait of character, when properly chastened by correct moral & religious sentiment. Yet he submits very readily to lawful authority. A more submissive and docile pupil no teacher could desire: yet it is necessary he should feel the *justice* as well as the *weight* of the authority exercised over him. His character, standing & success in life depend more on *moral* than *intellectual* influences,

more on the *heart* than on the *head*. With such schooling in morals & common practical sense as his brothers and yourself will give him, I augur well for him.[30]

Growth and the proper mixture of self-reliance and discipline had worked favorably on the sickly, sensitive child in other ways. "I am pleased with Johnston's bearing," the teacher reported. "He exhibits a *manliness & confiding frankness* of manner, the more agreeable because not looked for. You know he was wont to be shy & distant. I think he has *resolved to do his duty*, and hope most sincerely there will be no difficulty in his further management."[31]

Bearing and manners were of great importance in a southern society where personal force counted as much toward success as inherited wealth or acquired institutional status. Without much exaggeration we may say that here is a clue to the southern aristocracy's power within a democratic form of government. Bearing was indispensable to men who aspired to lead. A self-respecting frankness, often remarked as the characteristic of the southern gentry, was the outward badge of an honorable man who desired no unjust advantage, just as a cunning pseudo-affability was the sign of a self-seeking manipulator of men. More and more, people like the Pettigrews were coming to think of this false friendliness as characteristic of their fellow countrymen in the North.

A month before his fifteenth birthday in 1843 Johnston easily passed the entrance examination to the University of North Carolina at Chapel Hill, missing only a few unimportant questions asked by the examining committee. Academically he had been ready a year before, but Bingham had advised that he was too young to be cast into the college.[32]

Ebenezer's main interest of late had been clearing a new plantation, Magnolia, to the east of Bonarva, so that he might leave an agricultural establishment to each of the three sons who survived. The evidence of his youngest son's abilities led him to revise his calculations, however: "I know not what course Johnston may take," he wrote. "He is unequivocally the most talented person of his age that I have ever seen, but like most such seems to have no particular preference to any one profession. . . . books he is constantly diving into, & he knows a good deal of the contents after he gets through one. I am disposed not to make a negro driver of him without it is with his will and desire."[33]

Chapter 2

The University

It is difficult to assess accurately at this distance the impact James Johnston Pettigrew had on the University of North Carolina. Some allowance must be made for the eulogistic tendencies of the post-Confederate era in recounting the recollected impressions of his classmates and teachers. On the other hand, the nineteenth-century university was the place where the bulk of the members of the state's ruling class came together, and these men had considerable capacity for gauging each other's character and ability: their society operated largely on force of personality.

Kemp Battle, postbellum president of the university, who had been a youthful resident of Chapel Hill during Pettigrew's stay at the college, commented in 1907 after more than sixty years of observation that Pettigrew's scholarship had never been excelled, if equalled, at the university. On another occasion he stated, "I have never seen a man with a more penetrating mind than Pettigrew," and at yet another time he said, "He seemed to me the ablest man I ever met." The scientist, Professor Elisha Mitchell, referred to Pettigrew some years after graduation as "the pride of the college." At the commencement of 1862, President David Lowry Swain, having occasion to eulogize the hero lately wounded in battle, spoke of Pettigrew as the most accomplished scholar who ever went forth from the university. Battle, Swain, and Mitchell had ample opportunity for assessing most of the leading men of the state and had no particular motive to single Pettigrew out from other distinguished alumni. A writer who studied Pettigrew's collegiate career plausibly concluded that he was "an ideal student both from the viewpoint of the faculty and from that of the student body."[1]

Theodore Bryant Kingsbury, a freshman when Pettigrew was a

senior, remembered him as having the "finest eye we ever beheld, and a head of rare symmetry and beauty, indicating a high intelligence." Thomas Edward Skinner, a classmate who became a bishop, remembered Pettigrew particularly for his freedom from the customary vice of profanity. "He was thought by some of his acquaintances to be wanting in social qualities," wrote Skinner. "It was true that he had in college but few friends, with whom anything like familiarity existed. This may be accounted for from the fact, that his habits of study and punctuality forbid it."[2] Pettigrew was somewhat retiring and sensitive, and in a society in which education was valued largely to the extent that it was conducive to the successful management of men and affairs, his interest in intellectual activities for their own sake made him stand out from his fellows.

The reputation for stand-offishness came both from sensitivity and from a maturity that placed him above the pranks and debauchery of his classmates. "Johns, . . . I can well imagine too how uninteresting and unsocial and even burdensome to you are sprees of drunkenness and cardplaying of the others," wrote his friend, John Napoleon Daniel of Halifax County, when Pettigrew had to stay at the college during a holiday. Another time Daniel was reminded "of the many times you have saved me from a 'spree[,]' Johns. I recollect them more warmly than you think. . . . You are the only man who ever could exercise an influence of that sort."[3]

Pettigrew's reserved nature and intellectual interests did not prevent him from taking an active part in the life of the college. In his first semester he was admitted to membership in the Philanthropic Literary Society, one of two student self-government organizations. The next semester he was elected librarian of the society, a considerable honor since the Philanthropic and its sister, the Dialectic Literary Society, together owned more books than the university itself. In his sophomore year he was elected supervisor, an office next in importance to president, and while a junior he was elected president. Pettigrew declined the presidency, and this decision was one of the earliest instances of the sensitive pride and contrary independence that throughout his life led him to refuse honors lest he appear to be currying favor with his fellows or superiors.[4]

The societies each had a hall on the third floor of South Building, the main campus building. The students were proud of these halls, which, with their polished desks and portraits of eminent former members, were designed to resemble legislative chambers. The main activity of the societies was speechmaking, in which all members took part. President Battle described the societies as "worthy of all praise. Not only was parliamentary law learned, but the power of extempore speaking and writing compositions, as well as gracefulness in delivery were acquired. The members were proud of their society and afraid of its censure. The habit of self-government, of using their own liberty so as not to interfere with the liberties of others, was inculcated."[5] The societies tried their own members for infractions with scrupulous regard for due process and in this way learned responsible jurisprudence. In teaching respect for legal and parliamentary forms and decision by debate, the societies offered a fit training ground for the ruling class of a republic.

Pettigrew's friend and eulogist, the Charleston scholar William Henry Trescot, found in perusing the records of Pettigrew's college career a key to the later man. These showed

> how great was the superiority of his general preparation, how keen, persistent and vigorous was the ambition which stimulated his labors, and . . . his complete absorption in that mimic public life which, especially in a State institution, goes so far not only to form the character but to shape the fortunes of the rising generations. Knowing him as I did, familiar with many of the hopes and some of the plans of his after-life, I have found a peculiar but sad interest in the traits scattered through these records, written with all the inconsequence, the frankness, the generosity, the vanity of his age, and showing how truly the boy was father of the man.[6]

Among a number of men later notable, the active members of the Philanthropic Society in Pettigrew's time included Matt W. Ransom, later Confederate general, United States senator, and minister to Mexico, who was considered more eloquent than Pettigrew; Bryan Grimes, planter and Confederate major general, a close friend of Pettigrew; and John Pool, later United States senator.[7]

Deliberation and mutual respect were one aspect of the societies, independence and competitiveness were the other. Parliamentary rule for the management of public affairs did not transcend the extralegal imperatives of personal honor that the antebellum southerner felt, as is well indicated by an altercation (seemingly the only one of his college career) Pettigrew had with John Pool. At a Philanthropic meeting Pettigrew was chairman of a committee that reported unfavorably on some proposals made by Pool. Pool returned sharp remarks to Pettigrew. Pettigrew replied in kind. Coolly, Pettigrew waited until after the meeting, then jumped on Pool and fought him until someone separated them. "I believe I should have whipped him, for I have become quite strong in the arms," Pettigrew wrote his brother, "although he was larger and longer-winded than I." When they were pulled apart Pettigrew told the older youth that he would be "at his service" the next day. The next morning Pettigrew attempted unsuccessfully to procure a pistol. Not until later did he learn that a friend was standing by with one if it were needed. He armed himself with a knife and waited. Pool referred the matter to his friends, who took from his shoulders the responsibility for the decision to pursue the matter no further.[8]

In a society in which reputation was considered one's most essential possession and in which there were no ready institutional means of protecting it, the inevitable remedy for insult was direct action. Johnston felt the incident was entirely to his credit: "Our family has a tremendous reputation here. We are considered as the intimate friends of Mr. Clay, worth $300,000, and a perfect set of tigers. This character, together with this little fuss will save me the necessity of any more fights," Pettigrew informed his brother. "I never knew, what it was before to have relatives. William [Bryan] and James [Bryan] stood up to me nicely and so did some of my other friends." Possibly it was because of this incident that Pettigrew asked his sister to send him a pair of pistols and a bowie knife from home, which she refused.[9]

The college curriculum consisted chiefly of Latin, Greek, and pure mathematics, with smaller amounts of modern languages, chemistry, geology, physics, botany, zoology, metaphysics, logic, rhetoric, political economy, and constitutional and international law. More than half of a student's time in four years was spent in languages ancient and modern, mostly ancient; three-fifths in the languages and pure mathematics together.[10] The intent of these studies was to develop the powers of reason, analysis, and perspective, and by familiarity with the classical republics to inspire an understanding and love of American institutions. The curriculum also reflected a highly verbal and personalized society in which fixed status and institutional rigidity had not robbed words of their power to persuade and move.

The reading tastes of Pettigrew's classmates seem to have run chiefly to novels and popularized history—the type of literature represented by the *Arabian Nights* and *Charles O'Malley*. Pettigrew's interests, however, reveal a genuine and broad intellectual curiosity. He read La Rouchefoucauld's *Maxims*—perhaps acquiring there, like many others, a touch of cynicism he never lost and that was compatible with what would later be referred to as his "Latin" temperament—Voltaire, the Greek dramatists, works on composition, encyclopedic collections of knowledge in various fields, the *Edinburgh Review*, congressional debates, and French grammar, among much else.[11]

Mathematics was the subject that attracted Pettigrew's greatest attention. His senior oration, delivered to the assembled college community, was titled "In Defense of the Pure Mathematics." It was recorded that "he was a peerless student. . . . The only trouble the Professor had with him was that he dashed through theorems, corollaries, problems, so rapidly that nothing was left for other members of the class."[12] Cornelia Phillips Spencer, whose father and brother taught Pettigrew mathematics, recalled that

> He seemed to master his text books by intuition. They formed the smallest portion of his studies, for his eager appetite for learning ranged widely over subjects collateral to his immediate tasks. . . . In the class room . . . he appeared in reciting rather to have descended to the level of the lesson, than to have risen up to it. Student as he was, and somewhat reserved in demeanor, he was nevertheless very popular with his fellows, and the object of their enthusiastic admiration. Anecdotes were abundant as to the marvellous range of his acquirements, and the generosity and patience with which he contributed from his stores even to the dullest applicant for aid.[13]

And, when a student languished for weeks with a fatal disease, Kemp Battle recalled, Pettigrew was an able nurse.[14]

The Mexican War caused an increased interest in physical fitness, and Pettigrew excelled in fencing and boxing, sports taught by an army officer. He was considered the best fencer in the college.[15] Characteristically, he was attracted to the kind of sport in which a man of small size and weak constitution but of great determination could excel.

The opportunity to attend parties and balls and to visit young ladies was provided at Raleigh, a day's stage ride from the college. John H.

Bryan, whose law practice was then confined to the state Supreme Court and federal District Court, had moved to the capital and had purchased a mansion with extensive grounds not far from the capitol building. With fourteen Bryan children and innumerable cousins, this home was inevitably a major social center for youth, and typically it was filled with young guests who slept six to a room. Chief Justice William Gaston and other luminaries were frequent visitors. Pettigrew spent many holidays there with the two Bryan sons who were fellow students, and no doors in society were closed to him.[16]

"I know your church-going and beauty-looking-at propensities can be most abundantly gratified during the Christmas," wrote a classmate once when Pettigrew had gone to Raleigh for the holiday. Teasing him about one female interest, Pettigrew's sister wrote, "I hope you and John will never duel on that account, especially before she has decided which shall be killed." Elaborate, carefully laid plans to see one particular young lady alone were continually going awry. "If I could always see her alone when I wished; perhaps she might have an opportunity of throwing me a few feet in the air before commencement," Pettigrew wrote. Evidently this did not happen, for his interest faded after graduation.[17]

There were other attractions at the nearby capital city. One was an introduction to Henry Clay, who visited Raleigh during his presidential campaign of 1844. Clay was the family's political hero and, besides, a friend of Ebenezer since his term in Congress in the 1830s, and Ebenezer came up from The Lake to serve on the reception committee. Another attraction was watching volunteers depart for the Mexican War.[18]

During the summer vacation of 1846, with one companion, Edmund Halsey Norcom, son of an Edenton merchant, Pettigrew made the first of the many trips he was to undertake as frequently as he could the rest of his life. Norcom and Pettigrew bought horses and spent some weeks journeying over the piedmont and mountain regions of the state up to the Tennessee line. As might be expected of a Low Country youth, Pettigrew found the mountain scenery beautiful but the backward North Carolina yeomanry uninspiring.[19] War was to alter the latter opinion.

The sea had held an attraction for Pettigrew since he visited the Norfolk navy yards with Ebenezer when he was ten. He had frequently expressed interest in a naval career and had shown considerable talent for boat-building and sailing at The Lake. During his sophomore year he received his father's reluctant permission to seek an appointment to the recently opened Naval Academy.[20] The reasons he gave indicate the self-knowledge and the ambition which he possessed already at seventeen:

> If Pa should have no objection and should procure one [a midshipman's warrant], I should be very glad and should remain there a year or two at all events. I should wish to make one voyage, so as to see something of the world and to acquire a constitution, which I do not believe, that I now have. Although I am scarcely or never sick, I hardly suppose, that I could pass through a sickly season with impunity. I should like also to acquire a little more brass and affability, than I have, the former of which qualities can be procured in abundance, aboard any ship-of-war, I suspect.[21]

Although Uncle John Bryan leaned strongly toward West Point, where one of his sons had gone, he and other relatives made some overtures about the appointment. A new Democratic administration had just taken office, and the well-known Whig allegiance of the family was considered a bar to success.[22]

Johnston had another expedient. "I find that my size and strength do not increase in proportion to my years, since even in the vacation we are compelled to live, comparatively a sedentary life," he wrote his father in 1845. "I have come to the determination of asking your permission to my taking a trip somewhere this winter." What he had in mind was a voyage to the West Indies, which would not only be good for his health but would give him a chance to improve his French and Spanish. Ebenezer declined to countenance such a frivolity.[23]

The father's censorious tendencies increased with age. He stood at the ready to condemn his son at any evidence that Johnston's academic excellence was creating an undue vanity. Bingham, who stayed in close touch with the university, assured the father that Johnston, according to the faculty, "wears his laurels with wonderful modesty, as if unconscious of his superiority." Ebenezer was also critical of Johnston's expenses, which, as seems to be the rule with college students, rose and rose. The son gave assurances, seconded by Bingham, that he spent less money on clothes and recreation than any youth in the college except the scholarship students. He attempted to counter his father's criticisms and show his freedom from frivolity by sending along a drawing and an explanation of a wheat-threshing machine he had seen, which he knew would interest Ebenezer.[24]

Throughout his career at Chapel Hill Pettigrew was recognized as the academic leader of his class. Among the thirty-six graduates of the class of 1847 he won the valedictory position, having a rating of "excellent" in every subject. Matt W. Ransom was not far behind.[25]

The commencement of 1847 was a week of ceremonies, balls, and speeches. In attendance were President James K. Polk, class of 1818; Secretary of the Navy John Y. Mason, class of 1816; John Branch, class of 1801, former governor of North Carolina and secretary of the navy, in 1847 governor of Florida; and most of the then dignitaries of the state, including Ebenezer Pettigrew and John H. Bryan, who introduced Secretary Mason, his old classmate. Benjamin Peirce, the Harvard mathematician whose text Pettigrew had studied, and Matthew Fontaine Maury of the United States Navy, then at the beginning of his fame as a scientist, were on hand to receive honorary degrees. Johnston Pettigrew, delegated by his class, wrote a graceful letter to Henry Wadsworth Longfellow to request a few lines for the occasion, but Longfellow replied that he was unfit for the task since he did not know the persons and scene firsthand.[26]

The visiting statesmen sat in on the oral examinations of the seniors in constitutional and international law. A special examination in astronomy was arranged for Maury's benefit. President Swain and the professors had already bent Maury's ear about Pettigrew's mathematical genius and wished him to see for himself. Johnston had also the honor of the valedictory address. His text seems not to have been preserved, but Bingham felt that his former pupil acquitted himself admirably.[27]

Prior to the commencement Pettigrew met Mason and his daughter, Lt. Maury, and President Polk's niece at the reception at Uncle John Bryan's mansion in Raleigh. Already showing the mature talent for satire that comforted him throughout his life, Pettigrew reported that "the country people along the rail-road heard the 'President's suite' mentioned frequently and thought that the two young ladies were the 'sweets,' by which name we called them afterwards." These and other light comments in Pettigrew's report to a friend on the commencement week activities revealed that, two weeks before his nineteenth birthday, he was by no means unduly impressed with his own laurels nor with those of the dignitaries he had met. He described the most important result of the week casually:

> Mason and Maury were splendid souls; both ready to hear a joke, the former more so than the latter, however. The celestial man [Maury], as the reporter styles him, enjoys a college yarn with as good a grace as you or I.
>
> Maury is superintendent of the National Observatory. He has six professorships attached whose duty is to be astronomers. He and Mason were kind enough to offer me one. They both repeated the offer three or four times and I believe that I will accept the station for 6 months, provided they are willing to so short a stay. The professors rank with the Lieutenants in the Navy and receive a salary of $1200.00 per annum. . . . The offer . . . was unsolicited, since I did not even know that there was such a thing. The news of it made a great rise at the Hill and two or three people asked me, if Polk had given me some high appointment in the army. . . . Some thought I was to be sent minister to Mexico.[28]

President Swain, the professors, and Bingham all urged acceptance of the appointment, and Johnston consented after consulting with his father. Even Ebenezer Pettigrew had difficulty concealing his pride.[29]

Chapter 3

Stargazing

In the fall of 1847 Matthew Fontaine Maury published wind and current charts that revolutionized the navigation of the Atlantic and brought him fame as an oceanographer. When Johnston Pettigrew joined his staff in Washington in July of that year, however, Maury was better known as an astronomer. The institution which Maury had headed since 1842 had been founded in 1830 and was called interchangeably the National Observatory or the Naval Observatory. The duties of its staff were to draw up maps and navigational charts, furnish correct daily time to the United States, maintain continuous astronomical observation, and develop, inspect, and service astronomical and navigational instruments for the navy.[1]

Since the publication of the first volume of Maury's astronomical observations in 1846, the Observatory had been recognized on both sides of the Atlantic as a competitor of hallowed European observatories and as one of the handful of important scientific centers in North America. Under Maury, it has been said, "the waters, the winds, and the stars yielded up their secrets and multiplied their treasures." The Observatory was situated in a new building at 23d and E Streets NW on a seventeen-acre site which had originally been set aside for a national university. It was a brick structure with three wings, one housing the superintendent's family, and a twenty-three-foot dome containing the instruments of the observatory proper.[2]

Pettigrew's work began immediately on arrival. One of a staff of junior and senior naval officers and civilian professors, he was on duty every day from 9:00 A.M. to 3:00 P.M. doing mathematical calculations. Every clear night he was up most of the night taking turns at celestial observation. This regime allowed little sleep and little leisure. Pettigrew enjoyed the observation and was good at it, but he soon began to tire of the repetitious round and to have concern for the effects of the all-night sessions on his health. "The weather has been provokingly fair, and, of course, the stars are out every night in all their majesty, ready to be criticized by every fellow that can point a telescope at them," he complained to an old Chapel Hill classmate.[3]

Although the greater part of Maury's time was occupied with chart-making, he took an active part in the observations. Two years before, he had begun one of the most ambitious astronomical projects ever undertaken: a complete and definitive catalogue of the position, size, color, and other pertinent information about every star in the heavens then visible by telescope. Although the project was never finished, 100,000 stars were catalogued in ten years. It was this work in which Pettigrew was engaged along with other regular observations. Pettigrew's work contributed to a volume Maury published in 1853.[4]

Pettigrew was invited to Secretary Mason's on Sundays, and once when he was departing President Polk offered him a seat in his carriage. A North Carolina congressman reported to his wife that Pettigrew seemed a promising young man. Pettigrew said that he had in Washington "a very agreeable set of female acquaintances, though few in number; [and] plenty of pocket change. The Washington Eves are quite agreeable also, and the city life, the method of dividing the day . . . suit me precisely." On the other hand it was dreary boarding at Mrs. Voorhees's on 17th Street between H and I, and the sights of the small capital were soon seen.[5]

Pettigrew got on well with his colleagues, who were professional naval officers and civilian mathematicians from all parts of the Union, but he felt no close kinship with them. Their relations were friendly but shallow. As for his male acquaintances in the city, "I do not know whether they are the sons of bakers and butchers, rowdies or gentlemen; and furthermore it is utterly impossible to find out; one thing is certain, the young men about here have heads of the veritable pumpkin order."[6]

The narrowness of his companions and his work chafed the youth with his broad intellectual curiosity. Envying momentarily his brothers' lives as planters whose leisure was free for mental cultivation, Pettigrew wrote: "You cannot imagine how disgusting the men of one profession are; I mean those that have neither the wish nor the intellect to cultivate a taste for reading. The heads of the merchants are continually upon mere monetary affairs; a naval officer thinks a row of buttons confers enviable distinction and the young lawyers, here at least, can talk of nothing but clients." [7]

Undoubtedly Maury was pleased with his recruit. While most of the telescopes were manned by pairs of observers, Pettigrew was given one of his own. He recorded more observations in three months than his predecessor had in nine. Certainly the two men remained good friends for the rest of Pettigrew's life. When Maury's son was court-martialled during the Civil War, he asked Pettigrew to serve as counsel, and Maury many years later was to write that he felt Pettigrew was the man in the Confederacy best qualified to be commander in chief of all the armies. [8]

Still, it would have taken an unreserved zeal for a scientific life, which Pettigrew did not possess, to thrive at the Observatory. Maury, thought by many to be a difficult man, was frequently too carried away by his enthusiasms to be aware of the feelings of his honor-sensitive subordinate. "This office holding is very unpleasant in that it tends to destroy independence. And an apparently large salary produces a very small net income when you are expected to live like a gentleman," Pettigrew wrote. Months later, meeting his former superior after he had left the Observatory, Pettigrew was struck by Maury's changed attitude. "A feeling of independence alters the relations of individuals marvelously. It is better," he concluded, "to starve in freedom, than luxuriate in slavery, and without doubt, if I were to accept any other such station, it would be accompanied by the same frowns." [9]

More important than the chafing of pride, there was simply not much future at the Observatory for a young man who craved distinction above all else in life. Pettigrew's days were spent on mathematical calculations "which do not improve me at all, but . . . have a stultifying effect. You know that it is ruinous for any person who hopes for distinction to spend the early years of his life in close attention to matters of mere drudgery, and thus throw them away," he wrote his father. Assuming that his object was to attain eminence, his only hope as far as astronomy was concerned was to take a year or two's leave of absence for study so that he might acquire "a complete knowledge of the foundation of the science" as well as its operational details. [10]

It was probably with the end in view of surveying the possibilities for advanced scientific study that Pettigrew secured a brief leave in November 1847. He visited Harvard and Yale with letters of introduction to the scientific gentlemen of those places, who received him politely. Professor Denison Olmsted gave him a copy of his latest work. This trip enabled Pettigrew to see for the first time Boston, New York, and Philadelphia. In Philadelphia he spent three days visiting Chapel Hill classmates who were at medical school. The bustling streets, the theaters and restaurants, the riverfront, and other attractions of the metropolis caught the imagination of the plantation youth, and sallying about the streets took on the hue of an adventure for him, although unfortunately, he told his sister, a full purse at that degenerate day was the only weapon required.[11]

Pettigrew's Observatory appointment had been deliberately made for six months so he might leave without prejudice at the end of that time if, as Maury had said, he were not "perfectly rabid" with "the Astronomical mania."[12] As the end of the period grew near Pettigrew made up his mind that the Observatory position was not his life's work.

Pettigrew had behind him, as his friend Trescot later observed, every encouragement to ambition — wealth, family, talents, reputation — all of which "left him free to pursue the even tenor of a life devoted to scientific achievement, or to make his preparation deliberately for a more exciting theatre. He was not long in choosing, for in the vigor of genius he was not exempt from that restlessness which is its almost certain accompaniment until it has found a congenial field for its work."[13]

For once his father approved of Johnston's decision, concerned that the labors of the professorship would bring on a recurrence of his son's childhood sickliness. Ebenezer was so agreeable to Johnston's leaving the Observatory that he went so far as to broach the possibility of study in Europe: "Do you think it would be of use to you & do you think it would not unsettle your mind and be in danger of inflating it above what you can ever realize? These are hard questions to a young man not yet twenty. . . . think on them until I see you, & then answer them."[14]

Ebenezer Pettigrew's offer to send his son to Europe was made on the advice of his best friend "whose judgment I would rely on before any other man I know in the world." James Cathcart Johnston, the man for whom Johnston Pettigrew had been named, had offered to pay for the young man's European study.[15] Henceforward, Mr. Johnston, as he was always known to the Pettigrews, would play an important role in his namesake's life.

The grandnephew of a royal governor; the son of a Revolutionary leader, governor, and United States senator; a wealthy sixty-five-year-old bachelor of broad learning and large and sometimes eccentric charities, J. C. Johnston was the master of many plantations and was possibly the richest man in North Carolina. Hayes, his home plantation near Edenton, boasted an eighteenth-century elegance, was filled with books and works of art, and had sheltered at one time or another almost every famous man in America. In taste and manners a courtly relic of the early Republic, in politics a remnant of the brief eighteenth-century hegemony of North Carolina Federalism, Mr. Johnston was a kind of counterpoint to the ambitious, thrusting, romantic generation of southerners personified by his namesake. James Johnston and Johnston Pettigrew came to love but never to understand each other.[16]

At The Lake during Christmas, the son declined the European offer, much to the father's chagrin. It was then agreed that Johnston would study law, which was the first and obvious avenue to distinction in America. Probably because of a feeling that stagnant North Carolina offered no stage equal to the young man's talents, Baltimore was chosen to be the scene of his endeavors.[17]

A letter was dispatched to James A. Pearce, Ebenezer's Maryland friend with whom he had served in Congress, asking advice. Next young Pettigrew visited Chief Justice Roger B. Taney in Washington, who well remembered both Ebenezer and Mr. Johnston, whom he had often met during vacations at the Virginia springs. It was soon arranged that Johnston would take up the study of law in the office of Taney's son-in-law, James Mason Campbell, in Baltimore. By February 1848 Johnston was established in the city. He was cordially received and offered every courtesy by Campbell and by the household of John Williams, Ebenezer's Baltimore merchant.[18]

At first Johnston was pleased with his situation and read law with enthusiasm. He could see that Baltimore, in the long run, offered promise for distinction and profit at the bar. The younger lawyers of the city he found to be an unpromising lot. A long period of building clientele and waiting for established luminaries to pass from the scene would be required, however.[19]

On one occasion Campbell was so pleased with Pettigrew's answer to a legal query he had given him to research that he showed it to fellow lawyers and wrote some words of praise upon it before handing it back. This Johnston sent along to his father with the request that after reading them he tear off the favorable comments—which Ebenezer did—"for if I wrote such to others, it would be vanity." [20]

The main disadvantage to his circumstances was that his busy mentor had little time to instruct or to answer the questions of his students. After a few months Pettigrew advised his former classmates that if they desired to study law they should do so at the law school at Chapel Hill, for "studying in the City with a person who has a large practice is entirely a farce; you . . . learn nothing except what you ask, and you do not know what to ask. Upon the whole the law is a humbug, but it is the road to wealth and distinction. By proper exertion, one may have here an income of $10,000 . . . which would be very delightful. So hurrah for $10,000 and a splendid country palace." [21]

A talented but inexperienced young man is likely to have a naively exaggerated expectation of the success of his talents. It was a step on the road to maturity when Pettigrew wrote his friend Bryan Grimes on the eve of Grimes's graduation at Chapel Hill:

> You are now . . . about to launch your little bark upon the great water, and before you have been sailing six months, you will be completely overpowered with disgust. You will see vanity without any foundation: ignorance, nothing but ignorance . . . [in] gray, wise and reverend heads. Lawyers, who never poked their noses out of the door without having a precedent, except perhaps to smear on it a little of the mud of politics. Fellows here, aspiring to head a party, who actually did not know that when the election of President devolves upon the H. of Representatives, the votes are by States. . . . And the Baltimore bar think themselves at the head of the country!! [22]

The large half-northern, half-southern city was interesting if not entirely congenial to Pettigrew. The huge, closely built town, with its narrow streets, its few open spaces, and its proletariat, at the same time pitiable and explosive, was oppressive. Pettigrew soon longed for The Lake and for "aunt Gilly's fried chickens." He did not go out in society much, concentrating on his law work in Campbell's office at 27

Lexington Street. In his spare time he heard a speech by General Sam Houston, and, attending a Taylor-for-President rally, was caught in the midst of a riot. Establishing a habit he kept up the rest of his life, Pettigrew undertook a regular program of scholarship, studying higher mathematics on his own and taking German and French lessons.[23]

At the various houses in which he boarded, Pettigrew became acquainted with a number of German and French immigrants and this whetted his appetite for travel. "I have been regretting exceedingly that I did not accept Mr. Johnston's proposition in going to Europe," he wrote. "My residence with these foreigners has taught me, how much I have lost." The Germans were highly excited about the revolution under way in France. The French on the other hand were indifferent or hostile, most of them favoring Louis Philippe.[24]

In May James C. Johnston passed through Baltimore on his annual journey North and found Pettigrew ill with an attack of chills and fever.[25] As he was leaving he handed the young man a note to be opened after he was gone. It contained five hundred dollars and the recommendation that

> a traveling excursion this summer & fall through the Northern States & into Canada and visiting the different watering places would be a great advantage to your health and a great source of mental improvement[.] with your acute observation more may perhaps be acquired by traveling & mixing with men than can be attained altogether fr. books. Anything I can do toward your interest and advancement I will do with the greatest cheerfullness. If agreeable you could make a southern tour next winter & by that means become acquainted with all the United States.
>
> N. B. Any further sum that you may require I will most cheerfully forward to you.[26]

Mr. Johnston was a master of the delicate art of gift giving.

Pettigrew's sensitive pride had previously led him to be stiff with the wealthy family friend for fear that others would construe warmth as currying favor. Now he was inclined, with his father's permission, to accept the fortuitous offer. A second rebuff of generosity would be more dishonorable than acceptance.[27]

Mr. Johnston followed up the offer with a letter expressing fears for his namesake's health if he remained in Baltimore. This letter was a

graceful eighteenth-century essay on the advantages of travel, quoting
Pope that the proper study of Mankind is Man. Pettigrew's mind was
"already better stored with knowledge of books than any young person" Mr. Johnston had "ever met with." It was time to round out his
education by traveling and learning men. By travel he meant, of course,
a leisurely progression allowing the traveler to mingle with society in
various places. Mr. Johnston concluded with some suggestions on determining the route and some shrewd observations on the different
societies to be encountered at Boston, New York, and Philadelphia.[28]

James C. Johnston's opinion of the young man to whom he made his
generous offer is of interest:

> I was very much pleased with your Brother Johnston when I saw
> him in Baltimore [he wrote William S. Pettigrew.] his manners
> are frank without the least presumption or affectation. his con-
> versation when called out displays a great deal of information . . .
> without the least appearance of arrogance, great firmness in main-
> taining his own position without treating his adversary with con-
> tempt and great readiness to listen to advice or the observations of
> those whose experience entitles them to respect[.] His character
> is of the highest order as respects morals and a freedom from all
> those foolish fashionable habits which most young men fall into.
> . . . he . . . is remarkably particular I am told in his associates
> preferring the sedate to the gay and fashionable. I was sorry to
> observe that his health was impaired I think by too much close ap-
> plication & setting up too late at night. I advised him to travel and
> with his talent for observation & acuteness I think he will learn as
> much from men as he would from books. His opinion of men &
> insight into character is very correct.[29]

In June Pettigrew went to Washington to visit his former Observatory colleagues, and there his health improved rapidly. On 8 July 1848
he sailed for Boston to begin the northern tour Mr. Johnston had recommended. On the same day, at The Lake, Ebenezer Pettigrew felt a
severe pain in his chest, went to bed, and died a few hours later. The
news of this event changed Johnston's itinerary.[30]

Some time before his death Ebenezer had put his eldest son, Charles
Lockhart Pettigrew, in possession of Bonarva plantation and a portion of slaves. By terms of the will the second son, William Shep-

ard Pettigrew, received the Belgrade and Magnolia plantations with their Negroes as well as certain bank stock. In return for this bequest William was to pay off Ebenezer's debts (which amounted to only two thousand dollars), and he was to pay fifteen thousand dollars to Johnston and twelve thousand dollars to their sister Mary. These payments were not actionable at law for five years; that is, William was supposed to pay them off gradually (with interest) out of the profits of the plantations, which were not to be broken up to settle the estate. Johnston also received one slave. Charles was to pay twelve thousand dollars to the youngest sister, Ann, out of his inheritance.[31]

That fall William offered Johnston an opportunity to become a planter. He would turn over the Belgrade establishment and slaves in lieu of the fifteen thousand dollars if Johnston wished. Both knew, however, that the younger brother would never be content with a planter's life, and the offer amounted only to a gesture.[32]

Johnston Pettigrew was now, at twenty years of age, a man of independent means and the master of his own fate. He had, eventually, a capital of fifteen thousand dollars to count on. Meanwhile he had the income from the interest on the bequest and from William's hire of his slave, Dimur. Eventually he would also have his share of the proceeds of the sale of New Bern property left by his grandmother and of West Tennessee lands bequeathed by an aunt.[33]

After a decent funeral sojourn at The Lake, Pettigrew traveled to the Virginia springs and then to the North, much to the benefit of his health. In October 1848 he returned to his law studies in Baltimore with the vigor of a man free to meet life on his own terms. Meanwhile his brother Charles, who had recently been in South Carolina, had received a letter that persuaded Johnston that his future might lie in the famous old city of Charleston. There he would go after Christmas holidays at The Lake.[34]

Chapter 4

A City of Knights-errant

The letter that took Johnston to Charleston early in 1849 was from Ebenezer's famous first cousin, James Louis Petigru. It conveyed an invitation to Johnston to join the foremost law firm of South Carolina.[1]

Petigru was the son of one of Bishop Charles Pettigrew's younger brothers who had moved to South Carolina before the Revolution. While a student at South Carolina College, James Louis had changed the spelling of his name back to the supposed original French version. His mother was Huguenot, and there were advantages to a Huguenot name in South Carolina. Petigru was unquestionably the most famous of the Pettigrews. The leading lawyer of South Carolina, one of the first in the nation, he had more than once been mentioned in connection with appointment as a federal Supreme Court justice or attorney general. He had, besides, a literary reputation and a personality of remarkable force and independence. Though a completely unreformed and outspoken Federalist in politics and a leader of the resistance to nullification within the state, he had retained the respect of South Carolina.[2]

Johnston Pettigrew's first impressions, later much revised, of the city whose servant he was to become are worth quoting at length because they convey the young North Carolinian's initial response to South Carolina society, because they make apparent the powers of observation and analysis which were unusually mature in a youth of twenty, and because they reveal his already-developed personality, at the same time ironical and earnest:

Charleston Feb. 5th, 1849

My dear Friend [J. C. Johnston, Hayes, near Edenton]
    I arrived at this City of Knight Errants and Pinks of Chivalry

on Friday last, and the first few days have left any thing but an agreeable impression upon me, though I live on in the hope that it will improve upon acquaintance. Mr. Petigru is all that I expected. He received me very cordially, seems to be perfectly free from the affectation, which generally characterizes those, that dwell in Mr. Calhoun's Plantation, and is very popular in the City and more particularly among his relatives. When I went to his office, it was necessary to wait some half hour, while he was behind the screen, talking with a client, and during this interval I had an opportunity of learning his manner before seeing him. He suspected his clients of unfair dealing and was probing them to discover the truth, and the reception, which they gave to his remarks was proof of his unbounded popularity, and was at the same time very amusing. But, with him, my satisfaction at my change of residence ceased. His family are all extremely fashionable, his daughters more so than his wife, if possible, having the excellencies and defects that belong to those who devote themselves to the world, — gay, witty &c and not filled with "the heart." I find that I can no longer do as I please, without a struggle, and that, I cannot appear in the street with a cap, because it is not fashionable, neither can I live where nor how it suits me best, but that I must reside among the bucks of the city. In short, I anticipate three or four months, at least, of little pleasure or comfort. I am expected to attend somebody's fancy-ball, to spend this week in betting gloves on the races. (the gloves I would not grudge, if my attendance was not required,) and Capt. [Thomas] Petigru gives shortly a "*debut*" party to introduce his daughter, from which I almost despair of escaping. But necessity is the mother of invention, and I may slip out yet. My greatest dependence is upon the opinion, which they have taken up, that I am a great mathematician, and such characters are proverbially unsuited to the gay world. Indeed I do not think that I ever felt so lonely; in a strange place, without one person with whom to sympathize — for Mr. Petigru is too old, and the young men I have seen are too stupid — and with a future still more unpromising than the present, sojourning in a state of disunionists and conceited fellows. Another source of regret, is the opinion which the family here entertain of our wealth, which is so extravagant (and they will not be undeceived) that I am fearful of acquiring the reputation of a miser. These and a great many other causes of disquietude almost cause me to wish, that I was a farmer in *North* Carolina, independent of the world and its inhabitants.

But I suppose this state of things will disappear gradually as I make congenial acquaintances, if I be fortunate enough to find any such.

Many of my troubles I lay to brother Charles, because, by his gaiety, and fondness for society, while here, Mr. Petigru's family have adopted a similar opinion with regard to myself.

Mr. P's sisters and brother are entirely different from his own immediate family. They are very agreeable, unassuming people without the desire of display, either in dress or intercourse, that distinguishes the latter. Charleston presents a different aspect from any other city that I have ever visited. The streets are sandy and unpaved, except a few; but are frequently ornamented by trees peculiar to this southern latitude, such as the "magnolia"; and the residences, with their green blinds and verandas, surrounded by the deep foliage, would contrast favorably with the naked piles of brick and marble that grace New York. Many of the houses, which formerly belonged to the great people of the colony and are situated upon the water, are of great size and somewhat resemble things of past ages. Here, no particular place has been selected by fashion, where her subjects must reside; they are scattered from one end of the city to the other, and in paying half a dozen visits you have an opportunity of seeing the whole place. . . .

Believe me your sincere friend,

J. Johnston Pettigrew

P.S. The Cre-owls are in a flourishing state of vegetation about these parts.[3]

For his part, James Louis Petigru was delighted with his young kinsman. To his sister he confided "that all we have heard of him is below his merit, and that he will certainly, if his health is spared be one of the most considerable men of his age and country." Even before their first meeting Petigru had begun to look on the young man, by report, as the "hope of the family," but he was pleasantly surprised to find him not only talented, but "an amiable and unpretentious youth of charming simplicity." "No circumstance for a great while has been so welcome in the incidents of life to me as James Johnston's visit," he wrote.[4]

Other members of the South Carolina family were equally taken with the newfound relative. Petigru's sister, Mrs. Jane North, and her daughter, Caroline or "Carie" North, the report of whose beauty both of person and personality had been carried to North Carolina by Charles, took a great liking to the "very young looking man not handsome, but very intelligent, [with] a very lofty forehead."[5]

A mutual attraction developed between the two young people and continued for the rest of Pettigrew's life. This was cemented when Pettigrew made a visit that spring to Badwell, the plantation run by the widowed Mrs. North, far upcountry in the Abbeville District. Shortly after his arrival in Abbeville, Pettigrew came down with the measles. The mother and daughter nursed him back to health. Soon Johnston pointed out Carie to his younger sister as the model upon which to mold herself. Carie combined delicate grace, affable manners, and a proper degree of self-respect, he said. Although endowed with natural high spirits, she never allowed any manifestations of pettiness, impatience, or ill humor to escape her, and an atmosphere of equanimity surrounded all her actions.[6]

Pettigrew had often expressed his objections to matrimony, to having "150 pounds of beauty" around his neck in the race through life: "a very fine thing to look at and love . . . but a most costly article of furniture." He presented Carie with a beautiful edition of poetry inscribed "to my charming sister." For Carie's part, she commented: "I have been annoyed at some of the wise ones in the family saying he was 'smitten.' This is altogether a mistake. . . . He . . . [is] quite too wise a person to let any foolish notion take possession of his head. I like him so much and am perfectly frank and kind in my manner because I feel there is not the possibility of any nonsense to *mar* our intercourse."[7]

The source of James Louis Petigru's enthusiasm for his young relative is apparent. Of Petigru's two sons, the eldest, Albert Porcher, had been killed at the age of eight in a fall from a second-story balcony. The other, Daniel Elliott Huger, was a scapegrace who had then recently been saved from a dishonorable dismissal from the army only by the timely mustering out of his regiment. Petigru's grandsons, William Carson and James Petigru Carson, were still children. Of his two sons-in-law, one, William Augustus Carson, husband of Jane Caroline Petigru Carson, was content with a comfortable life as a planter. The other son-in-law (and Petigru's law partner), Henry C. King, was an agreeable fellow who lacked any trace of ambition or brilliance. His exceptional young North Carolina cousin was an obvious heir to the empire of legal and intellectual reputation Petigru had carved out and was the only hope for preserving the family name from descent into mediocrity. Pettigrew himself was well aware of the reasons for the older man's sponsorship.[8]

Even more important, Johnston supplied Petigru with a vicarious satisfaction of unrealized educational ambitions. Left fatherless and without capital at an early age with younger sisters to support, and then saddled with an expanding law practice and a frivolously fashionable wife and daughters, Petigru had postponed beyond possibility of fruition the hopes for study, for travel, and for literary fame he had nourished in his youth as an associate of Stephen Elliott, Hugh Swinton Legaré, and William John Grayson in the *Southern Quarterly Review*.[9]

Thus it was in part a projection of his own lost youth when, less than a week after Johnston's arrival in Charleston, Petigru recommended that his young kinsman study in Europe, "for he is quite too good for the beaten track of education." The plan he proposed was a year or two's study of civil law at the University of Berlin, followed by travel on the Continent. Then Johnston would return to take up law practice with the best possible educational foundation.[10]

The family debate which preceded the implementation of this plan was a confrontation of eras. James C. Johnston, when asked for advice, reacted like a reincarnated Cato of the early Republic and succeeded in postponing the decision for several months. In his view only England and Scotland were fit places for study by an American republican:

> I was not a little surprised at the idea you express of spending a year or two at Berlin to study the civil law. I feel flattered that you should ask my advice on the subject and have no hesitation in giving it. At the present time I think that Berlin or Vienna would be the last places I should think of visiting much less of making a place of residence. . . . For they seem to be the very center of disorganization and civil discord and particularly dangerous for

strangers & those coming fr a country under a republican form of government. . . . *mob law* & *martial law* seem more the order of the day than civil law. . . . I think it very probablematical whether the advantages you would derive . . . would compensate you for the loss of time & other opportunities of acquiring knowledge at home of your own country her laws & institutions. I have very little acquaintance with German literature or science of the present day but it seems to me there is too much refinement too much metaphysics too much sophistry and too little common sense.[11]

To this James Louis Petigru, spokesman of a newer, expansive nineteenth century, replied:

It is a great selfishness to monopolize a common gift, as a youth of genius is to be considered, and I thought it my duty immediately to take the part of a disinterested friend by proposing to our young student a course of travel and the study of the Civil Law. . . . Tho it would be folly for a young man to spend all he has in seeing foreign parts and returning to live upon the friends, that he turned his back upon; the case is very different when a young man has a liberal curiosity and has a fortune that puts it in his power to indulge the thirst for knowledge. . . . With such powers of concentration as Johnston possesses, with his taste for knowledge and aptness to learn, it would indeed be a pity if his faculties were not encouraged to . . . their full growth. . . . [Some people think European study lacks utility] But the great object of Education is to open and enlarge the scope of mental vision. . . . Nor is there any branch of knowledge that never fails to reward its followers more abundantly than the civil law. It is the repository of all the practical philosophy of property. It is impossible for one to know the civil law well, without having an ample store of material for thinking.[12]

Brother William Shepard Pettigrew, with characteristic method and detachment, added up the pros and cons. On the one hand Berlin (1) might turn Johnston into an agnostic and (2) might make him too learned and proud to be of any use for practical business. (William was strongly inclined to suspect the latter would happen.) On the other hand there was (3) the weight of J. L. Petigru's recommendation and

(4) the possibility that European study would fit his brother for some great place in the world. William concluded that he would back up Petigru's idea and promised to endeavor to meet any call that Johnston might make upon him for payment of interest or principal on their father's legacy.[13]

During part of the year 1849 Pettigrew was occupied by the law studies which prepared him for the examination for admission to the South Carolina bar, which he successfully passed before a panel of judges at Columbia as soon as it could be arranged after his requisite twenty-first birthday had passed. Meanwhile he found rooms accessible to the sea breeze and was admitted to the fellowship of the young men of Charleston's highest social circles. He became acquainted with the life of the South Carolina Low Country by a sojourn at Petigru's son-in-law's splendorous rice plantation, Dean Hall, on Cooper River forty miles from the city. The trip to Badwell showed him the uplands, and Petigru introduced him to many of the notable men of the state capital, Columbia. Because the measles left him debilitated he also made a summer trip with Petigru's brother-in-law, Henry Deas Lesesne, to the vacation haven of the South Carolina gentry at Flat Rock in the North Carolina mountains.[14]

The charms of the modish, polished, and intellectual South Carolina society began to have their effect. Although the relentless political mobilization and almost conventional radicalism of the inhabitants of "Mr. Calhoun's Plantation" still shocked the young Whig from North Carolina, he found that in personal relations the South Carolina gentlemen "abate much from that insupportable arrogance" for which they had a reputation. Indeed, they were quite agreeable.[15]

The last week in December 1849, although the thought of his departure threatened Carie North with "a severe attack of all sorts & colours of dull spirits," Pettigrew set out, pausing at The Lake and Edenton to say farewell to his brothers and to Mr. Johnston, who kindly kept their misgivings to themselves.[16]

Caught between boats, Pettigrew spent a dreary Christmas in Norfolk, then pressed on to Washington where his sister Mary was living. He put up at Gadsby's Hotel where he dined at the same table with former Vice-President George M. Dallas and several Supreme Court justices and congressmen. These dignitaries impressed Pettigrew only with their commonplaceness and lack of intellectual interests. Henry

Clay received him politely but begged off writing letters of introduction. Secretary of War George W. Crawford, however, supplied Pettigrew with letters to American representatives abroad. Maury invited him to dine and provided introductions to five of the leading astronomers of the Continent.[17]

At the family factor's in Baltimore Johnston picked up three hundred dollars in cash and a bill of exchange on Liverpool for twelve hundred dollars more. On 9 January 1850, amid snow and fog, he sailed from New York on the steamer *Cambria* bound for England. Pettigrew had means, ability, and learning. He had seen New York, Philadelphia, and Boston. He had moved in the best society of Washington, Baltimore, and all of North and South Carolina. He had partaken of as good as the New World could offer. Cheerfully he looked ahead to the Old.[18]

Chapter 5

Europe, North and South

The winter North Atlantic crossing was lacking in materials of adventure. After a single day's seasickness Pettigrew spent his time below deck playing whist with an American, a German, and a Swede, although he declined to wager. On 22 January 1850 the *Cambria* landed at Liverpool. Pettigrew found this city much like New York, except that the people were rosy-cheeked and more polite.[1]

He spent one day strolling about Liverpool, and "with my moustache, white overcoat, and *independent American bearing*, as Sam Slick would say, created some little sensation, whether favorable or unfavorable, I can not say; at least every lady looked at me." Befriended and given indispensable traveling advice in the London central station by an Englishman and a Belgian, he was able to reach Dover and cross the Channel the next day. He took the train, traveling first class so that everyone took him for either a prince or a fool, and seeing as much as possible of the Belgian and German countryside and cities as he went. On the night of 24 January he reached Cologne and the Rhine, and on the 26th, Berlin.[2]

To a freeborn American republican the encounter of continental authoritarianism stiffened by the recent revolutions was sudden and shocking. The train was met at the Berlin depot by a military guard and a bevy of officials who demanded Pettigrew's passport. This demand was repeated several times in the short trip through the city, and finally the passport was taken and filed at the police station. Fees were required at every turn. At his permanent lodgings at the corner of Louisen and Marien Strassen, Pettigrew found everything locked at all times by government order so that it was necessary to carry a key to the house, a key to his floor, a key to his room, and a key to each of his trunks and boxes. Nevertheless, with some effort and taste applied to decorating and furnishing, Pettigrew's room was soon considered the finest student establishment in Berlin.[3]

Within a month he was well settled into the regime of study and recreation which he followed the first year. He rose at 7:00 A.M. and began studying. At 7:30 he had in his room what Americans would consider an extremely light breakfast since it was without meat. From 11:00 A.M. to noon his teacher of German came in. At 1:30 P.M. he sallied forth and dined at a student café. At first his afternoons were spent reciting, with one other American, to a tutor at the university. After a few months he was able to dismiss his German teacher, dispense with the private sessions, and attend the regular university lectures. He also took French lessons and studied music three days a week. After 5:00 P.M. he was free to explore Romantic Germany.[4]

Naturally Pettigrew was thrown at first into the society of Americans, although later he deliberately detached himself as much as possible from them and made friends among the Germans and the students from other countries. On his first full day in Berlin he met Francis James Child, a Bostonian who was in Germany pursuing the philological studies that were to prepare him for a distinguished career at Harvard. Child was Pettigrew's companion later in Italy and they remained friends until the Civil War.[5]

At a party during his first few weeks, Pettigrew, as the latest arrival, was asked by a "Mister Birney" of Alabama for the political news from home. The Carolinian made some strong remarks about the "Compromise of 1850" controversy then raging and was embarrassed later to learn that Birney was the son of the noted abolitionist James G. Birney. Those of the American community he met who could be considered expatriates permanently attached to the attractions of Europe, such as the son and daughter-in-law of Supreme Court Justice Joseph Story, Pettigrew instantly regarded with distaste as apostates and idlers. Of the approximately twenty American students in Berlin, most were from either Massachusetts or South Carolina, and he found "each division preserving the characteristic of their section; the Yankees being studious, sobersided and a little parsimonious, the others more generous and social."[6]

As was entirely natural, the extracurricular attractions of Berlin occupied more of Pettigrew's energy and attention than his formal studies. The university lectures, mostly a historical exegesis of the Justinian Code, he regarded as something of a "humbug."[7] Before he returned to America Pettigrew acquired a diploma in civil law, ease in writing and speaking German, French, Spanish, and Italian, and a knowledge of the theory of music. His object, however, was preparation for life, not specialized study, and he acquired other experience of greater value. Berlin at this time was probably the greatest center of learning in the world, and Pettigrew might easily be condemned for failing to take advantage of all the opportunities of formal scholarship it offered. His casual and eclectic approach, however, was typically American. A life of specialized learning hardly held out a hope of a livelihood, much less of distinction, in America. Pettigrew's friend Child, after arduous studies at Berlin and Göttingen equalled by no other American, spent twenty-five years grading freshman themes at Harvard before achieving a position equal to his training.[8] And there was only one Harvard.

As soon as the initial cultural shock induced by what in the next century would be referred to as American puritanism had worn off—he was at first surprised that Sunday was a day of recreation rather than of worship and rest—Pettigrew threw himself with delight into the free and adventuresome life of the Continental student. Music of a quantity and quality unheard-of in America was an especial attraction. Pettigrew spent many afternoons in the winter gardens listening to the orchestra performances that were free for the purchase of a little refreshment. In his diary he kept a detailed record of the operas and symphonies which he heard and described the atmosphere and circumstances of Berlin performances.[9]

Pettigrew seems to have enjoyed conventional German student adventures, roving about the streets attempting to strike up an acquaintance with young women or to foment a quarrel. There was perhaps an element of self-satire in his description of the typical student: "He wears generally a little cap, with certain colors upon, to denote the association to which he belongs; a very fierce moustache, considerably heightened in effect by sundry great scars upon his face; the mementoes of various duels." One student activity, drunkenness, held no more attraction for him in Germany than it had at Chapel Hill.[10]

At an evening concert once, Pettigrew noticed a beautiful young woman of dubious status and her several male companions staring at him impertinently and laughing over his clothes. He followed them out, "intending to demand satisfaction," but lost them in the crowd. The failure to rectify this affront enraged him and put him out of temper for several days. It was natural that Pettigrew attracted such attention, for his large, high-domed head over a slight build made him stand out in any crowd. "Some time ago several persons asked Greenwood privately if I were not such & such a political character and could not be persuaded that I was simply an American," he confided to his diary. "I wish to Heaven that I could look like the generality of Mankind, so as not to attract stares at public places. Thayer says that I am taken for a foreign military [officer] . . . because I walk so erect." [11]

The young man had long had an attraction for things military, and he had been stimulated on the Atlantic passage by an acquaintance with an officer who stood out admirably, in Pettigrew's mind, among the company of merchants and tourists. "The most gentlemanly person aboard was the Colonel of a Rifle Brigade," he recorded on the second page of his diary. At some point during his stay in Berlin, Pettigrew made overtures to the authorities, attempting to secure a temporary commission in the Prussian army. The application was turned down on the ground that for an American and a man of republican and antimonarchical views to be an officer in the Prussian army was not permissible. [12]

Pettigrew's attitude toward things military, which occupied more and more of his attention as his life went on, was a curious blend of romantic impulses and realistic perceptions. He was under no illusions about the Prussian army. As an American, he regarded its autocracy as both inefficient and repugnant. But to be the only American ever to serve in the Prussian army would be a considerable distinction and might give one experience and reputation of value in any future wars, foreign or civil, in one's own country.

The vaunted Prussian soldiery, which because of the universal three-year draft was no longer an elite corps, did not impress Pettigrew greatly, although he did note that "military discipline and habit tend to improve the physical quality of the race." The draft violated his American sense of liberty. He remarked that the greatest social problem of Prussia was the interruption of studies and apprenticeships, followed by the release of the conscripts upon the country three years later unfit for normal work. He sympathized with men whose lives were disrupted by the frequent calling out of the reserves for no better reason than some alarm caused by the maneuverings of power politics. The armed presence of the state everywhere about the streets was disagreeable. Once Pettigrew twitted a policeman who demanded his passport by handing him a receipted bill. The policeman perused it gravely before handing it back and sending him on his way. When a lunatic took a shot at the king, Pettigrew was appalled by the automatic rounding up of the leading republicans of the city "without the slightest cause having been assigned. A sweet government this truly!" [13]

On the other hand, he found the revolutionary parties of Europe as distasteful as the autocratic governments. "The democratic parties of Germany, England, and France are completely different from our own democracy," he wrote. "We agree only in that we do not like to be governed by people not of our own choosing." European democratic revolts were easily put down because they were supported by only a small part of the community. Revolution would not succeed until it had the backing of a majority. Despite Mr. Johnston's fears, there was little danger that Pettigrew would be corrupted by either of the European extremes of "mob law" or "martial law." Americans of his generation were taught to revere their own institutions and regard them as a golden mean between the anarchy and tyranny of the Old World. Pettigrew found that Europeans were completely ignorant of American society and principles. Monarchists pointed to the alleged license and dissension in America as an excuse for repression. Democrats held up the alleged beneficent anarchy and equality of America as an excuse for revolution.[14]

The German nobility, archetypes of vested privilege and Old World reaction, particularly repulsed the young American, who ridiculed the pretensions of men who were poor horsemen strutting about in spurs. After observing a group of German princes he wrote:

> My democratic, republican blood boiled over at the bare sight. . . .
> If you desire to imagine how such a personage appears, figure to
> yourself a man of rather larger body than ordinary, a countenance
> not intelligent to say the least, forehead retreating, a military coat,
> with tremendous epaulettes, and his breast covered with ribbands

and stars, which he does not deserve. . . . So many lounging, idle, ugly, worthless people I had never before seen. . . . The more I see of such creatures, the more awfully Republican I become.[15]

The only ruling class Pettigrew could respect was one like the American class to which he belonged (in the eighteenth century the aristocracy of all America; in the nineteenth century the elite that was more and more restricted to the South) or like the Hungarian and Spanish nobility he soon would observe and admire, which justified itself by service and moral force.

Pettigrew made every effort to lay aside his prejudices and understand Europeans even though he found that the Europeans, for their part, were incorrigibly and erroneously opinionated about America. It was not hard to make friends with Germans if one refrained from the boasting that he found the nearly universal fault of both Englishmen and Americans, making them not only disagreeable but also undermining their credibility: "If one will only keep silent about his own country and give due praise to the one he may be in, he becomes quite a favorite at once. Discoursing about America is at all events useless, for if one tells the naked truth he is never believed, nor is it possible to alter by conversation the preconceived ideas of Europeans."[16]

Once, German friends became incensed at press reports of the hanging of some of their countrymen in New York for a trifling theft. Pettigrew despaired of explaining that under Anglo-American law burglary was a capital crime regardless of the amount stolen. The other Americans became apologetic, which only rendered the Germans angrier. Pettigrew concluded the discussion by stating that the report was probably not true, but if it were the incident should teach Germany not to send thieves to America.[17]

James Warley Miles, a Charleston clergyman, had entrusted Pettigrew with a copy of his work *Philosophic Theology* to present to Augustus Neander of Berlin, then one of the noted church historians of the world. Delivery of the book netted several invitations to the home of the elderly Neander, who seemed almost a caricature of the eccentric, near-sighted scholar and whom Pettigrew was unable to disabuse of an exaggerated conception of the religiosity of Americans. Once, at Neander's, a theology student accosted Pettigrew with a scheme of emancipation. The southerner replied in his terse manner that the plan would require the planters to beggar themselves, thus presuming that they were angels, not men. To this the German commented in all seriousness that German philosophers had recently proved that there was no difference between men and angels.[18]

Far more impressive to Pettigrew than Neander or the astronomer Johann Franz Encke or Alexander von Humboldt, among the famous scholars with whom he came in contact in Berlin, was the geographer Karl Ritter, whom he probably met while carrying out one of the several scientific missions that Maury had entrusted to him. Ritter he described as "a philosopher of commanding intellect and thorough information, coupled with the most unassuming simplicity and absence of [the usual German] political rabidness."[19]

Berlin was reputed very unhealthy in the fall, so Pettigrew planned to spend his first summer and fall on an extended continental tour. This plan was disrupted by an attack of ague and fever which prostrated him for a month at a spa near Frankfurt under the care of a doctor, "a man of very high cultivation" with whom he made friends and who became his traveling companion upon recovery. Getting a late start, he visited many of the cities of the Rhine valley, which he found a welcome relief in two respects. Their free and hedonistic atmosphere offered pleasant respite from Prussian militarism, and their historical charm, bringing the Middle Ages forcefully home to Pettigrew's imagination, contrasted happily with the modern, official city of Berlin. In addition to Frankfurt, Pettigrew visited Hamburg, Weimar, Kassel, Göttingen, and Dresden. (He had earlier made short trips to Wittenberg, Leipzig, Halle, Brandenburg, Magdeburg, and other North German cities.)[20]

In these as in all his later travels Pettigrew made an effort to learn as much about as many things as possible, but two things held the greatest interest for him: the art museums and the historic battlefields. The latter he went over carefully and described in great detail, not knowing that he would participate some day in carnage greater than any those fields had seen.[21]

Leaving the Rhine, he passed through Heidelberg, Stuttgart, Ulm, Nürnberg, Augsburg, Munich, Salzburg, and then he traveled on to Vienna. The Austrians reminded him "most forcibly of our Southern people, open & hospitable . . . quite the reverse of the North Germans who are much more like the Yankees."[22] Clearly the experience of for-

eign nations was causing the young southerner to reflect on the degree
to which his own country was two nations.

One fine afternoon in the late fall of 1850 Pettigrew went on board
a Danube steamer in Vienna. That night, after a day of breathtaking
vistas of vast plains, the steamer reached Pressburg on the border of
Hungary. For the first time since he had left America, Pettigrew began
to feel a sense of great excitement as if he were entering a land gen-
uinely new and strange and yet somehow congenial:

> In Hungary . . . I could scarcely tear myself away from the friends
> I had made. . . . In Pest, I was quite the center of a circle of all sorts
> of people, gentlemen and peasants, who contemplated embark-
> ing for Arkansas . . . where a colony of their countrymen under
> a Colonel is already established. The appearance of the people at
> Pest is totally unlike that of the other nations of Europe. One sees
> at once that he is out of Europe as it were, or at all events out of
> the center of the Caucasian influence. . . . Indeed if the Indians
> still lived to any extent in the southern states and the Negroes
> were free, we should resemble Hungary very much; the Hungari-
> ans, being but the ruling nation, which conquered the others and
> kept them under a certain species of subjection. . . . The Hungari-
> ans have a feeling composed of hate and contempt, intermingled,
> for the Germans, and look down upon the other nations of Hun-
> gary with emotions, not much different from our own towards our
> Negroes, were they all suddenly liberated.[23]

He found still other similarities between Hungary and America, the
eastern and western frontiers of European civilization:

> In Hungary the common people are yet but half civilized and were
> it not for their suffering, not by any means calculated to enlist
> sympathy or love; but the order of Nobles, who are as much su-
> perior to the subordinates as we to our slaves, have all the virtues
> and the qualities of a superior order of beings. The situation of
> Hungary previous to the revolution, was very much like ours.[24]

There were other nations of Europe the young southerner was yet to
see where he would find himself even more at home.

After his autumn travels of 1850, Pettigrew returned to the university for his second term of study. In 1851, determining to avoid the previous year's attack of ague and fever, he took leave of Berlin for good in early March ahead of the first sign of spring and began eighteen months of travel.[25] At twenty-two, an appropriate age for adventures, Pettigrew was beginning the most pleasant period of his life, which in retrospect would seem to him idyllic. It was these months also which molded into final form the man he was to be.

The adventure began on the route to Prague when Pettigrew crossed the Carpathian crest on the border of Saxony and Bohemia, at night and in a furious snowfall:

> I sat on the outside of a sleigh, with the driver & assistant drivers in front, the horses floundering in the deep mountain snow, the people talking the Bohemian, a language entirely unknown to me, and the whole forest deadly still: at every house we stopped pistols hung up within reach of the bed, whether against wolves or men I could not say. In going down the hills, the assistant drivers would jump out and catch hold of the rope on each side of the sleigh to prevent its capsizing; add to this, the dim, ghostly light which the moon . . . spreads over the face of nature, and the scene will be quite romantic: if a pack of wolves had only attacked us and eaten up all, but myself the adventure would have been perfect, and I should have regarded it as the happiest moment of my life.

That was only a foretaste of delights ahead:

> In proportion as we approached Italy, [he remembered only a few days after the fact] my feeling of satisfaction arose; I felt as I used to do on leaving the Yankee land on the way to the South. At almost every railway station, one could perceive an increase in the beauty of the women, in the sociability of the men, and in the smiling genial aspect of the country.[26]

And when he crossed the mountain pass above Trieste into Italy, sensed the mild Adriatic climate, and saw the sharp contrast of colors in the sky, land, and water below such as he had not found in northern Europe, Pettigrew could not but think of The Lake and perhaps of Charleston: "I was once more *home*, for the first time since leaving home." So strong was this impression that even later, sitting at the mouth of the Grand Canal in Venice with pen in hand, he could scarcely realize that he was in a foreign country.[27]

Venice was followed by Padua, Ferrara, Bologna, Florence, Pisa, Rome, Mantua, Milan, and Verona. In Rome Pettigrew spent six weeks seeing the sights, with a decided preference for the classical over the medieval attractions. Following no inclination but his own, he drank in Italy avidly, moving on whenever, to wherever, and by whatever means of conveyance he chose, mingling with all classes of people and savoring every aspect of the country—the food, the wine, the atmosphere of the taverns and hotels, the beaches, the theaters, the art galleries, the natural sites, the relics of antiquity.[28] In his impulsive, effusive, episodic diary, which he was now keeping in French and Italian, the foremost attraction of Italy was evidenced by recurring panegyrics (translated):

> March 22 (at Ferrara): "The women are quite beautiful."[29]
> March 23: "Now the dark ladies begin to be beautiful, my angels!"
> (This entry is adorned with drawings designed to illustrate the superior beauty of the Italian female face to that of the English and German.)[30]
> March 26 (on the stagecoach to Florence): "Oh Lord, what heaven! Those beautiful girls."[31]
> April 8 (on the road to Rome): "Beautiful girls everywhere. How I suffered that day!! Temptation!!"[32]
> July 19 (in Italian Switzerland): "Adventure with the young ladies of whom I kissed the prettiest, aged fourteen, for a farthing. Alas what a difference between this one and the one from Naples."[33]
> July 27: "I spent the night at Realp where my beautiful Italian lady blushed while receiving me. Oh my Lord! Why did You create Italian women for tormenting us?"[34]

Despite this, Pettigrew's approach to Italy was not entirely sensual. To J. L. Petigru and other friends at home he penned eloquent but not injudicious essays on the burden of the Austrian yoke, to which he found the Italians, prince and peasant, unanimously opposed. Apart from its political condition, words could hardly convey his sense of continuing enchantment with Italy. "It surpasses any land I have ever beheld. With the people I am more pleased than even the country; so

much politeness, genius, and genuine good feeling, when one pene-
trates beneath the surface. Passionate as a tinderbox combustible; but
what of that? so are we."[35]

Twentieth-century observers are so used to thinking of the South
as the bastion of American Anglo-Saxon Protestant nativism that it is
difficult to achieve an adequate appreciation of the ethnic openness of
antebellum southerners, as demonstrated by Pettigrew's attraction to
what in his time were referred to as "the Latin races." The Creole
(and the Irishman and the Jew) often found a more hospitable reception in the South in antebellum days than in the North, where the
basically New England culture promoted Anglo-Saxonism (something
Pettigrew was later to condemn eloquently in print) and where the
only non-Anglo-Saxon immigrant who was completely at home was
the German Protestant.

A southern gentleman, secure in his social position, was (despite the
special case of the Negro) rather more inclined to approach people as
individuals and to judge them by their personal qualities rather than
by the negative group stereotypes (the drunken Irishman, lazy Italian, stiletto-wielding Spaniard, bowie knife-wielding southerner) that
tended to characterize the English and northern way of looking at
nonpuritan peoples. It was part of the southern gentlemanly code to
be honorable and polite to all. (One of William Faulkner's surviving
Mississippi aristocrats was to comment that there were two things no
gentleman ever made reference to: a person's race and his religion.)

This characteristic arose partly from the southern culture's having
cohered around personal and traditional (rather than impersonal and
institutional) factors of social life: family, manners, personal honor,
personal leadership, personal loyalty. The cement that held Pettigrew's
society together—classes, races, and regions—was intangible and personal. For the adult white male there were fewer legal and institutional
restraints imposed and life was freer and more spontaneous than in
the urbanized Anglo-Saxon societies. In this respect the South differed
from the North relatively, not absolutely. Still it was natural that the
southerner's tendency away from the cash nexus, the work ethos, the
puritan moral posture, and the collective social goals of northern and
English society should render him relatively more susceptible than the
northerner to an attraction to peoples such as the Italian and Span-

ish, whose values exhibited the same inclination to personalism and traditionalism over materialism and progress.

As was customary with English-speaking observers, however, Pettigrew made an exception of the Neapolitans, whom he visited by steamer from Leghorn, in his general praise of the Italians. The Neapolitans provided him with a new piece of information: "that the meanest nation on the face of the earth can inhabit one of the most beautiful countries." Pettigrew believed that most English and American travel writers, who typically tended to look down on the Latin races, had libeled Italy by mistaking Naples for the whole. To him the inhabitants of the rest of Italy were a distinct race from the Neapolitans, to be compared in neither body nor mind. The Austrian tyranny, so odious in the rest of Italy, would be a blessing to the south, exchanging a barbarous despotism for an enlightened one.[36]

In mid-June 1851, the traveler went to Munich to meet the Bostonian Frances J. Child. They set out afoot for Switzerland and ultimately Sardinia and Milan. The weather was pleasant, although there was still snow in the Alpine passes. Child and Pettigrew were now off the fashionable track of tourists in a wild Rhone valley country which had few amenities for travelers and a reputedly violent population. This policy of travel off the beaten path Pettigrew found rewarding, and he pursued it whenever he was able thereafter. Within two weeks he was an accomplished walker, once making fifty miles in a day. "Compliments from everywhere on my legs and my Italian," he wrote. (In the 1850s when Pettigrew vacationed at the Virginia springs, he amazed the dandies with his feats of distance and endurance walking up and down mountains and from spa to spa.) He traveled part of the way with an Italian family and formed an ever higher opinion than before of that "gifted race."[37]

At the end of the summer of 1851, after five months in Italy and Switzerland, Pettigrew departed for what he referred to in his diary as "la capital del Mundo." During his remaining year in Europe, Paris was Pettigrew's home base. He made several trips to the French provinces, spent four months in Spain, visited the Low Countries, Alsace-Lorraine, and the spas of the south of Germany, and made a whirlwind tour of England, Scotland, and Ireland. After each of these trips he returned to Paris.[38] He was delighted with France, but he left much scantier evidence in his letters and diary (now kept in Spanish) of his activities and impressions than he had earlier. Perhaps this was because he was now a seasoned traveler and did not feel obliged to keep records as detailed as he had previously. Possibly also it was because the adventures of a young man in Paris are not the kind one writes home about, particularly not to one's sisters and one's pious brother William.

We will never know for sure. Continental sexual mores were strong stuff for a young man out of puritanical America. On his first week in Berlin Pettigrew had taken note of the embraces allowed by the tavern girls, yet he also noticed that this was conventional and governed by limits. European women were much more free and easy than American ones up to a point, yet they also possessed the ability to stop matters at whatever point they wished.[39] It is impossible to determine exactly what Pettigrew's relationships were with the women who are mentioned frequently in his diary. It would be dangerous to take his Victorian verbal reticence at face value, yet it might be equally misleading to ascribe automatically to a nineteenth-century American student the same moral abandon we would suspect in a twentieth-century one. Pettigrew welcomed all sorts of adventures, but his taste was for adventures of his own choosing, not those that were well worn by others.

Certainly the opposite sex was much on his mind, as is quite evident in his diaries and quite understandable at his age. From the rosy-cheeked Liverpudlians of his first day in Europe to the divine Andalusians over whom he would later expend much ink, his mind, at least, was engaged with the fairer portion of the European part of creation. "I must confess, . . ." he confided to the diary, "that my enjoyment in a strange city depends much upon the beauty of the women."[40]

Tangible evidence on the nature of his relationships with women is rare. "The pleasant times in Old Spain often come back to my memory," an American friend once reminisced to Pettigrew, "and I sometimes think of that kiss you got at Poitiers to the cost of one franc extra to me. Do you still taste it?" Shortly before he left for America in the fall of 1852 Pettigrew made a hurried, out-of-his-way trip to Strasbourg, which he had already visited. Undoubtedly this was to see the lady who, after his return to America, sent him her daguerreotype. The picture was sent under the name of Madeleine Gerber: "not my friend's real one as you may imagine," Pettigrew explained to the American whom he asked to rescue it from the Parisian dead-letter office for him.[41] Neither the letter from his "fair correspondent" of Strasbourg telling him of the mailing of her portrait nor any other record of the lady is preserved among Pettigrew's papers.

Pettigrew's reaction to French society exhibited both his shrewd-ness and the gulf that divided the republican gentry of America from the aristocracy of Europe. The French political spectrum, according to Pettigrew's taxonomy, was composed of Bourbonists, Orléanists, Bona-partists, Republicans, and Terrorists. He dismissed the monarchical parties as stupid and reactionary:

> The Republican party is the strongest, but not in a majority. It is a matter of astonishment to us that there should be a Terrorist party at all: but we can form no conception of these European govern-ments before studying them. The whole system is arranged upon the principle that "those who have, shall be given; and from those who have not, shall be taken even that which they have." The taxes of Paris, for instance, are almost entirely upon provisions. . . . the workman . . . pays just as large a tax to the state, as the millionaire. Add that some 26,000,000 of persons in France cannot read; and it ceases to be surprising that some of them are led away. Yet all the monarchical governments pursue the same track exactly. . . . Universal suffrage is a bad thing here, undoubtedly, but it will be better than the present state of affairs.[42]

In France as in Germany, firsthand observation of the twin European evils of "mob law" and "martial law" confirmed Pettigrew's preference for the golden mean of American republicanism.

The high point of Pettigrew's several sojourns in Paris was the French army's semiannual Presentation of the Eagles. The spectacle of the mustering of eighty thousand armed men affected Pettigrew greatly. Every branch of the service was represented in full dress and arms. Foreign officers, including Turks and Arab chieftains in flowing white robes, were present for the review along with 150,000 specta-tors. The ceremonies were conducted on a platform 150 feet high with a gilded dome, accompanied by a high mass, 1,500 musicians, and a magnificent spring day. Pettigrew's only disappointment was that Louis Napoleon did not use the occasion to declare himself emperor as had been expected.[43]

Pettigrew would witness this event, however, on a later stay in Paris, in the spring of 1852. At the end of his first three months' stay in France, Pettigrew decided to go to Spain, although there was reason to be hesitant about the reception to be expected there by an American, whose countrymen had recently been filibustering in the Spanish colony of Cuba. He left Paris for the south of France on 1 December 1851.[44]

Chapter 6

Alas! Romantic Spain

Alas! Romantic Spain, I shall never see thee again. By the bye I have not a portion of heart remaining as large as a pea. The whole is left in Andalusia; the earthly Paradise.—James Johnston Pettigrew to Ann Pettigrew, 10 June 1852

Upon crossing the French border, Pettigrew took a seat on a light, fleet, high, crazy-looking Spanish stagecoach drawn by eight mules. A few days later, at an obscure village on the Castilian plains seventy miles from Madrid, he stepped down from the coach, leaving his baggage. Besides the clothes on his back Pettigrew had his passport, a handkerchief, a pocketknife, ten dollars, and all the symptoms of cholera. He walked out of the village a way, picked out a ridge with a good view, spread his cloak on the ground, and sat down to await death.[1] His position

> afforded an uninterrupted prospect toward the snow-covered ranges that bound the horizon to the north and north-west. Scarcely a tree or a shrub was in sight to break the continuity of waste. Long trains of laden mules would wind along the dusty road with the well armed arriero trolling lustily some old ballad . . . and from time to time a soldier belonging to the Guardia Civil would hurry past; otherwise no living thing disturbed the quiet of the solitude. . . . There were no green valleys, no warbling songsters, no gentle zephyrs, yet the scene had a strange fascination. And now this very loneliness, this grandeur of isolation, throwing the burthen of life upon the individual, and at the same time developing within him the qualities which enable him to bear its weight,

seemed to me indispensable to the idea of Castilian chivalry, with its freedom from dependence upon bodily enjoyments.[2]

A few hours later, deciding that the symptoms he had taken for the onset of deadly cholera were merely a chill and indigestion, Pettigrew walked back to the village, sat down on a bench in the square, and spent the afternoon chatting with the old peasants there, shifting his position only with the shifting of the shade.[3] He remembered later:

> The hardy life of the peasant in these lofty regions may be imagined when I state that a fire was lighted in the village once a week for the purpose of cooking bread. . . . about sunset, those who had gone out into the fields to labor commenced returning, and a finer looking race of men I never beheld. Of the medium height, sinewy in their persons, of grave and stately demeanor, these ragged peasants threw their thread-bare cloaks over their shoulders and walked into this collection of mud hovels with an air of dignified, courteous self-respect which many a sovereign would give half his kingdom to possess.[4]

There were many facets to the love affair which grew up between the young southern romantic Pettigrew and the most intransigently anti-modern nation of western Europe. These will be surveyed below when we discuss at length Johnston Pettigrew's mature worldview. This story of his first encounter with Spain, as he told it eight years after the fact, provides a necessary background for our understanding. During his first visit, Pettigrew felt only a sense of enchantment. His own full consciousness of the meaning would not come until later with the reflection and study that went into the book he published on the eve of the Civil War in celebration of the beauties and virtues of Spain and the Spaniards.

Most writers who have dealt with southern romanticism have emphasized the gilded elements—the pageantry, eloquence, and chivalry (or the tinsel, bluster, and violence, depending on the writer's sympathies). Less attention has been paid to the other side of the South's medieval revival, the ascetic one, particularly since the passing of the Confederate generation.[5] This has resulted partly from a tendency to read back into the Old South characteristics of its decadent phase in the Gilded Age rather than to grasp the society as it was in its prime, and partly from the modern tendency to reject the chivalric virtues as antidemocratic if not fraudulent.

James Johnston Pettigrew was a romantic. As Italy represented to him the sensual, self-indulgent, and bright-hued side of the romantic inheritance, "the unbought grace of life" of Edmund Burke's evocation of the medieval legacy, so Spain came to represent the austere, demanding, testing, self-sacrificing reverse of the coin of chivalry, Burke's "cheap defense of nations, the nurse of manly sentiment and heroic enterprise."[6] To the subtle intelligence and complex sensibility of James Johnston Pettigrew, the other side of chivalry, the martial, self-testing side, made a far stronger appeal than the self-indulgent and splendorous. Pettigrew had rejected the privileges of the German and French aristocracy as unjust and unearned. To the republican gentleman of America, aristocracy was not a technique of class rule but an ethic of personal integrity and civic service. Johnston Pettigrew's later life would prove a testament to this ethic.

To the American clay of Pettigrew's personality Spain added a glaze that brings out by exaggeration some features of the southern mold in which the clay was formed. Pettigrew was an unusual man with unusual opportunities to play the role of knightly ascetic. The particular opportunity that Spain gave him was to recognize and articulate what he was, for if his was not the most typically southern version of the romantic, it was not an untypical one. How else explain Francis Marion, or the Alamo, or Stonewall Jackson, or the North Carolina yeomen of Pettigrew's Brigade who slept tentless and uncomplaining on the ground in February and went just as uncomplaining up the Pennsylvania slope to death? The well-founded legend of Confederate valor?

Pettigrew's arrival in Madrid a few days after his sojourn in the Castilian village was a pleasant surprise to Daniel Moreau Barringer, the American minister to Spain. Barringer was a North Carolinian, a Whig, a man of scholarly interests and attainments, and a lover of all things Spanish. Quite naturally he took a liking to Johnston Pettigrew, whom he had met once before at the Virginia springs. Pettigrew's appearance in Madrid was particularly lucky since Barringer was about to lose his secretary of legation. The secretary, a cold Vermonter named Horatio G. Perry, whom Barringer did not much like, had informed the minister he was thinking of resigning and going home. Pettigrew was a godsend in this eventuality. The young man was perfectly fitted for the post: he was congenial to the minister, he was a North Carolinian, he had sufficient polish and manners, he was intelligent and shrewd, he spoke Spanish, and he would save Barringer the necessity of having an unknown quantity sent from home.[7]

Shortly after Pettigrew's arrival in Madrid in December 1851, Barringer offered him the post, which would begin the next April when Perry was to resign and last until March 1853, when the Fillmore administration expired. Meanwhile Pettigrew could travel and learn more of the country. The idea appealed to the young man greatly. The post was an honorable one and one which he would have attained on his own rather than by family influence. He would learn much and meet important people, both while in the post and later as a result of having held it. "It would give me a certain 'eclat' to commence life with," Pettigrew reflected, "the more important for me as I shall otherwise be weighed down by Mr. Petigru's reputation."[8]

Yet such was the strength of family considerations to the antebellum southerner that Pettigrew did not feel able to accept without first asking the advice of William S. Pettigrew, James C. Johnston, and James L. Petigru. There were many reasons for hesitation. He would have to spend money above his salary. His family might feel that he would prolong his stay abroad to a point that would damage him. Barringer might entertain political ambitions when he returned to North Carolina; would the family be obliged to support him?[9]

The strongest motive for hesitation was Pettigrew's pride. In part this was the Cincinnatian code of the early Republic. A patriot did not seek office; the office came to him. To solicit office was to demean individual honor and undermine republican morals. The image of Ebenezer Pettigrew, the simple country gentleman whose reputation was too valuable to be soiled in the political scramble, hovered in his sons' minds all their lives and held them back from the contest for the honors that could have been theirs. Pettigrew's name would have to go before the Senate for confirmation. That would be perfunctory but to some he might appear as a supplicant for public spoils. Who knew what mud might adhere to the family name as a result?

In January, Perry definitely decided to resign. A true thrifty Yankee, he tried to sell Pettigrew his ceremonial uniform. But Pettigrew waited until 6 March, after he had received encouragement from home, to write Barringer his acceptance from Granada. Prospects of glory were short-lived. Just before Pettigrew was to take office, the chilly Vermonter suddenly developed a very warm alliance with a Spanish lady who was older and neither rich nor pretty but with whom he shared a passion for writing poetry. To the surprise and against the advice of the entire American community in Spain, they ran away to Gibraltar and got married. Perry now wanted to retain his post and remain in the country. To this effect both Perry and the former Señorita Carolina Coronada wrote imploringly to Pettigrew. There was only one thing for a gentleman to do. He immediately replied, withdrawing all claim to the office. "Mr. Pettigrew has acted most nobly and will receive my deep and eternal gratitude," Perry told Barringer.[10]

The minister asked Pettigrew to stay on as attaché for a while, because he was certain the lady's family would make it too hot for Perry and he would leave the country after a few months. Pettigrew declined. Barringer then asked Pettigrew if he would accept the post of secretary of legation if it came open at any time before he left Europe. Again Pettigrew politely but firmly declined. Still, they parted friends, as is evident from Barringer's entrusting Pettigrew with the mission of calling on several congressmen on his behalf when Pettigrew returned to America. Barringer wished the congressmen to force the Fillmore administration, with whom he had differed, to publish his correspondence on the Cuban question in the interest of his own reputation. This Pettigrew accomplished, and in future years Barringer's mansion at Raleigh was a social and intellectual haven for him.[11]

A year's service in the legation might have altered the course of Pettigrew's life to some degree. Certainly he would have been thrown into public affairs sooner than he was. Madrid was at the time an important post in American diplomacy because the possible annexation of Cuba was one of the leading questions of American foreign affairs. A year's service as secretary of legation would have made him a better prospect for a diplomatic appointment which he contemplated seeking later on in the Buchanan administration. The cost of Pettigrew's chivalric gesture of relinquishing the post, a decision over which he did not hesitate for an instant, can be suggested by the fact that to be the American minister to Spain was always the height of his political ambition.[12] He was living up to his own concept of chivalry.

It was an exciting time to be an American in Spain, apart from the normal attractions of the country. The American-based, abortive

Cuban rebellion of Narciso López had taken place only a few months before. Even though President Fillmore and Barringer were both officially and actually opposed to the annexation of Cuba to the United States, it was a period of strained relations with Spain. Barringer, through poise and tact, a good command of Spanish, and the social popularity of his beautiful wife, the former Miss Elizabeth Wethered of Baltimore, was able to smooth over the Spanish court and foreign office despite the American filibusters and agitation for annexation. Pettigrew learned that it was only the Barringers' reputation which prevented the mobbing of the American ministry after the Cuban invasion. As a good Whig from the older South, Pettigrew quite concurred with Barringer on the Cuban question, believing "that the Spaniards were perfectly justifiable in their indignation" and could have "quite legitimately returned violence for violence." [13]

Despite his opposition to the annexation, Barringer was engaged in delicate negotiations looking toward the release of the Americans imprisoned in the wake of the López fiasco. This was one reason he needed a good assistant. One of the Americans for whom Barringer secured a release from hard labor at Ceuta was the colorful John Sidney Thrasher. Thrasher was a native of Maine but more southern in sentiment than any southerner. From childhood he had lived in Havana where his family ran a commercial newspaper. He had not been among the López filibusterers, but he had been imprisoned because his journalistic agitation had given obvious aid and comfort to the rebels. Upon Thrasher's release on a promise never again to set foot in a Spanish colony, he and Pettigrew became fast friends, and it was Thrasher who paid for Pettigrew's kiss at Poitiers. Thrasher would later achieve some note as a journalist and author. The burning passion of his life was to make Cuba one of the United States and thus save the fair island from "Africanization." Thrasher later almost persuaded Pettigrew to settle in Cuba, and in 1854, compelled by obligations of friendship, Pettigrew loaned Thrasher two hundred fifty dollars "to keep away the wolves while he engaged in a great undertaking, not pecuniarily profitable but of great value to the country," perhaps the planned Quitman filibuster of that year.[14]

Pettigrew left Madrid on 3 January 1852 and returned on May 20. In the interval he traveled and visited at his leisure as he had done in Italy, going to Seville, Cordova, Gibraltar, Málaga, Granada, Barcelona, Cádiz, Valencia, and surrounding countryside. Castile evoked Pettigrew's admiration but not his love. Madrid, he felt, was an urban eruption on the country, not really Spanish at all.[15]

It was in the former Moorish kingdoms of the south that Spain really grabbed Pettigrew's heart. Andalusia and Valencia were to him paradise. The arid scenery appealed to his asceticism, yet the climate, warm but dry, agreed with him more than any he had ever lived in, and he waxed fat after being sick in bed for two weeks in Madrid. The people enchanted him even more than had the Italians. He found conversation with Spaniards of any class always instructive and stimulating. They retained a freshness and individuality to their thoughts, a tragic earthiness to their worldview that was absent in more "advanced" countries where mass education had enabled everyone to parrot the newspapers. And the Andalusian women, Pettigrew said, would tempt one to turn Mohammedan.[16]

All the qualities of life he valued as a southerner he found in pure form in Andalusia: "Elsewhere in Europe there was little to compensate for the moss-draped oaks, the sweet-smelling magnolias, the flowering vines of my own home: for the sensitive honor running at times into extremes, which is yet the main spring to the character of a gentleman: for the enthusiasm, sincerity, and gentle nature of our own beautiful women." [17]

In the special diary he kept in Spain, in Spanish and in a separate volume from the one in which he recorded the rest of his European travels, Pettigrew stored up sights and impressions, conclusions and anecdotes. Yet there was little to indicate the mature understanding of the country which would later go into his book, *Notes on Spain*. That insight would come after much reading and reflection and a second visit.

At Gibraltar he spent several days trying to reach Tangiers but was not able to arrange passage. Thus the ambition stirring in his mind to write a history of the Spanish Arabs had to fuel itself on Arab history and literature and the Moorish survivals in Spain, since he was denied a firsthand look at the Arab world.[18]

At the end of four months in Spain, Pettigrew left Madrid for Paris on 8 April 1852, visiting the Biscayne Bay provinces of Spain and the south of France on his way. For six weeks after his return to Paris he was sick with fever and ague under a doctor's care and lost all the weight he had gained in Andalusia. This was certainly the low point of his stay abroad, "there being no situation better capable of recalling relatives and friends than that of an American sick in Europe." He was ready to go home, well aware that anything he saw after Spain would be an anticlimax.[19]

He knew, however, that his mentors, James C. Johnston and James L. Petigru, would consider his European sojourn incomplete if he did not tour the British Isles. Pettigrew did not relish this. Everywhere he had gone in Europe he had encountered Englishmen — snobbish, supercilious, narrow, conceited Englishmen. He developed an abiding dislike for them, regarding them as the polar opposites of the Spanish, super-Yankees in their aggressiveness and hypocrisy.[20]

In search of recuperation, Pettigrew left France for the Rhine and the Moselle in late May, visiting Metz, Mannheim, Saarbrücken, Wiesbaden, Karlsruhe, Freiburg, Strasbourg, Frankfurt, Heidelberg, Baden, Nancy, Trier, and Coblenz. In July he passed on to the Low Countries, seeing Haarlem, The Hague, Rotterdam, Brussels, the field of Waterloo, and Ostend. The Low Countries were interesting to Pettigrew but elicited no panegyrics.[21]

From Ostend he sailed to Dover and spent eighteen days in a grudging and whirlwind tour of the British Isles. London he found as disagreeable as expected. The same things bothered him in London that oppressed him in the large northern cities of America, except in greater degree: the harried crowds, the atmosphere laden with the coal dust and grime of industrialism, and the incredible extremes of wealth and poverty — an upper class more arrogant and snobbish and a lower class more degraded than any Pettigrew had encountered on the Continent. England was ruled by a class with all the bourgeois flaws and none of the aristocratic virtues, he felt.[22]

The horrid slums, strewn with gin-soaked, comatose women and children, repulsed Pettigrew more than anything he had seen in Europe: "There is more vice in London than any other city in the world: Paris, Lisbon, Naples, and New York together, would make but a small show beside the giant city. . . . The evidences of wealth in England are amazing; it could doubtless buy out France and the United States together. At the same time all the poverty and filth of the two latter countries would hardly equal what one sees in every large manufacturing town. Now it is the fine season, what must it be in Winter?"[23]

Pettigrew's reactions to the various European nationalities resemble those of another young southerner who traveled sixty years before. Thomas Jefferson, too, felt an affinity with the French and their manners and regarded the British lower class as the most depressed in Europe.[24] Pettigrew also reflected the reaction to the evidences of the industrial revolution of the tradition-minded country gentleman anywhere in Western civilization who had not adjusted his interests and thinking to the realities of industrial profits. His reaction also exhibits at least one pillar of the antebellum southerner's genuine faith that his society was superior to the progressive urban societies that attacked it, a faith by no means a mere defensive rationalization.

Pettigrew delighted that the British often mistook him, with his slender frame and southern aura and bearing, for a Spaniard or Frenchman. This impression enabled him to overhear himself discussed by persons who assumed he could not comprehend English, much to his amusement. Several times condescending Englishmen complimented him on the fluency of his English.[25]

From London he passed rapidly on to York, Durham, Edinburgh, the Highlands, and Glasgow, and thence to Belfast and through northern Ireland to Dublin. He visited only the most famous sights and recorded few of his impressions. He spent August in France, returning to Strasbourg. On 31 August 1852, Pettigrew sailed from Le Havre and two weeks later disembarked at New York.[26]

He had already shipped ahead boxes of books and paintings. For these and all his other expenses in Europe Pettigrew had spent more than six thousand dollars. As far as can be determined, he was not aware until after his return to America that James C. Johnston had reimbursed William Pettigrew for this sum so that his legacy, instead of dwindling, had increased in his absence.[27]

While in Europe Pettigrew had been a fellow student or at one time or another a traveling companion of half a dozen young Americans who later achieved some repute as artists or scholars. Among the American students mentioned in his diary and letters are Francis James Child, Alexander Wheelock Thayer, Basil Lanneau Gildersleeve, the classicist, and David Ramsay, grandson of the historian of the same name. Pettigrew met Hiram Powers in Italy and the "Hart" frequently mentioned in his diary may have been one of the American artists, James or Joel Hart, both of whom were then in Europe. Perhaps he had made some impression upon his fellow student-tourists. A North Carolinian traveling in Egypt in 1850 encountered two Englishmen who had recently been students in Germany. The southerner mentioned that an old Chapel Hill classmate, a man of great abilities, was in Germany also. "You must refer to Mr. Pettigrew," one Englishman replied immediately. "We all know of his remarkable abilities."[28]

Pettigrew had been abroad for two years and eight months. He left when he was twenty-one and returned at twenty-four. He had experienced a great part of the Old World in a way far more intimate and perceptive than was conventional. He had mingled with the nobility and notable personalities of several nations as well as with the ordinary people. Pettigrew had learned in Europe to savor life to the fullest and live each day as an open adventure. He had been alone, sick, and friendless in a foreign land, and being thrown back on his own resources and finding them sound, he had learned self-reliance, patient suffering, and psychological stability when confronted by danger and loneliness, qualities which would stand him in good stead in war.

Particularly after the trip to Spain, the maturity of Pettigrew's letters increased and his diary became more reserved and concise, with fewer adolescent reveries. Contrary to his brother's fears, Pettigrew did not return home too puffed up and corrupted for the workaday American republic. Undoubtedly his quixotic strain was enhanced, but that would never stand in the way of his doing his duty to family or country:

> I have never felt more sensibly the debt of gratitude which I owe to our Father, [Johnston wrote his brother from Paris] who by denying himself procured to his children the[se] enjoyments. . . . Indeed I have learned to appreciate Pa first here, where a brawling Politician or a thriving Merchant is never equal to the gentlemanly, patriotic agriculturist. . . . [If] after my return you and Brother Charles spend a year, there [Italy and France], I will take charge of the plantation as well as I can and inform you through telegraph, if I find things going to ruin under my administration.[29]

Pettigrew had learned more than gratitude and humility. "It is a consolation to know," he wrote Barringer several years later, "that experience of foreign parts, brings, not only new tastes but new ideas, a fund of the latter for contemplation renders the owner independent, to a great extent, of mere locality."[30]

Encountered at an impressionable age, Italy and Spain were charmingly different from Pettigrew's own Anglo-Saxon society, and yet at the same time congenial in that they diverged from Anglo-Saxon society in exactly the same direction that his own South diverged from the norm of the Anglo-Saxon world. For the rest of his life the encounter percolated within and beneath Pettigrew's consciousness and reacted in varied and subtle ways on his personality, both the part that was sophisticated and individual and the part that was paradigmatically southern. The maturing of his youthful impressions would bring him back, seven years later, to Italy and Spain, not as a student or tourist but as a patriot to Italy and interpreter of Spain.

Chapter 7

Kin

The plantation of the lower South, like the plantation of Virginia, unfruitful as it was in art and literature and philanthropy, was yet the source of more cordiality and kindliness in all the ordinary relations of men and women, of more generous impulses, of a more constant protest against commercialism, of more distinction of manner and charm of personality, than any other way of life practised by Americans before the Civil War.—William Garrott Brown, The Lower South in American History

Quite a party of Petigrus made a grand northern tour in the fall of 1852. They included James Louis Petigru's brother, Captain Thomas Petigru of the United States Navy, with his wife, daughter, and niece Caroline North, and Johnston Pettigrew's brother Charles and sister Mary from North Carolina. At Boston Captain Petigru was accosted in the parlor of his hotel by a slender, foreign-looking young man who introduced himself as "Mister Smith of Richmond." The captain sat chatting politely for half an hour trying to recollect where he had met the gentleman before. When Charles Pettigrew and the ladies entered, the captain introduced "Mister Smith." Charles Pettigrew bowed casually, took another look, and exclaimed, "Johnston!" Thus with a practical joke Johnston, a few days after his arrival in the United States, reintroduced himself into the bosom of the family he had not seen in thirty-two months.[1]

"It really was he," Carie North wrote, "so altered it would have been impossible to recognize him. His fierce yellow mustache, whiskers and short cut hair make a great change in his appearance, especially since he pays attention to dress and all the etceteras formerly too much neglected. One thing remains the same, the railroad speed at which he speaks." She reported, "Were you surprised that none of us knew him? Could you see how changed he is you would not be. He is sterner than formerly & (truth might as well be told) scarcely as amiable."[2]

Shortly after, the returned prodigal visited with James C. Johnston and James L. Petigru at the Virginia springs. Mr. Johnston found his namesake not at all spoiled by Europe but pleasingly plain and unaffected in his manners and very kind and attentive while the older man was laid up with a riding injury. Both Mr. Johnston and Petigru offered to do all they could to set Johnston forward in life, but they found him as independently minded as ever. When Johnston visited at The Lake, William Pettigrew, who always reacted exactly as Ebenezer Pettigrew would have done, was pleasantly surprised to find that his brother's allegiance had not been won away from his native land.[3]

The year following Johnston Pettigrew's return to the United States was a time of doubt and tribulation. He was required to decide what he would do with his life and where he would do it. Such a decision, important and often irrevocable, is painful to every thoughtful man. It was doubly so to Johnston Pettigrew. A man of great talents feels impelled to seek fame. It is not only a matter of ambition for glory in the usual sense but of an impulse of nature toward self-realization: talents know no rest until they have found fulfillment. At the same time great talents do not automatically bring great success or even find their own outlet. The genius must first put his shoulder to the wheel of the workaday world and wait, along with the average man, for luck and experience to open opportunities for the full play of his abilities.

Whether by his travels or simply by maturity, Pettigrew's ambitions had taken on a more manageable and realistic cast than his youthful dreams of glory. He had acquired, in Trescot's words, "an earnestness of purpose, which . . . taught him to substitute, for the desire of great distinction, the honorable effort for great achievement." As Pettigrew wrote his brother, "Personal ambition has faded away or rather has paled along side of another. I have felt for some time back, that the laudable, but selfish desire of advancement, for the pleasure it brings one's self, was getting very weak, and it necessary that the object should be more general, either the family or some grand idea or the world at large."[4] The telescoping of his ambitions did not make the choice immediately before him any easier, nor, perhaps, did Pettigrew ever entirely relinquish his dreams of glory.

It was characteristic of the society in which he lived that Pettigrew contemplated the idea of fame as bound up with a family rather than an individual destiny. In his mind the greatest penalty of lack of success would be in the failure to advance the family name. With a kind of desperation, Pettigrew feared that when the name was not advancing it was losing ground. On the other hand, he felt that no matter what his individual achievements he would truly succeed only to the extent that he carried the family with him. Thus he was disappointed that his two brothers were without any kind of ambition except to continue their quiet lives as planters. He frequently urged the brothers to cultivate their talents and wield their influence, for he daily saw men less able and honorable than they rising to high places in the world. The brothers were not contributing their share to what should be a mutually supporting struggle to keep the family reputation from the downhill slide that had begun with Ebenezer Pettigrew's death.[5]

When Pettigrew contemplated his prospects at Charleston they seemed dubious. His fortune was just sufficient to put him in competition but not sufficient to place him in the front rank. In the Low Country of South Carolina more than anywhere else, he found, possession of established wealth and family name aided the rise to eminence. "Thus every step upward would be made by force of labour and exertion and very unsure ones at that," he reflected. As Trescot pointed out, Pettigrew "was a stranger in a society . . . leavened by the spirit of family connection and local prejudice; one in which nearly all the leading interests of its social and industrial life were represented at the bar by young men . . . in whose fortunes the community was personally concerned; and the city was scarcely large enough for that sort of professional success which is entirely independent of personal connection."[6]

Like his ambiguous wealth, the sponsorship of James Louis Petigru was a mixed blessing, at the same time thrusting him toward the sun and casting a shadow over him. People were likely to regard him as a poor relation taken in by Petigru's goodness, he feared:

> The matter stands thus: of Mr. Petigru's practice and reputation [it] is not necessary to speak. . . . The question is could I succeed to them. Within his own family, there would be no opposition (except Mrs. P.) of course. Dan [J. L. Petigru's son] is utterly

worthless and degraded. The rest of the family, whatever be their abilities, have no aspirations; but without there would be much opposition of course: the world has been accustomed for a long while to regard Mr. Petigru, as necessarily compelled to die intestate, as it were, with regard to reputation, and there would be great unwillingness to admit the claims of a youngster.[7]

Pettigrew doubted not only the willingness of Charleston to accept him but also his own capacity to succeed as a lawyer. Intellectually he could excel, but he was conscious that his unconventional personality was not the sort to inspire men to entrust great business affairs to him. Thus his ambition would be constantly driving him to seek first place at the bar and his own limitations would prevent the realization. Then there was the recurring question of his health. Pettigrew had hardly arrived in North America before he was down with one of the illnesses that prostrated him intermittently for the rest of his life.[8] Health would require prudence, putting a restraint on too much close application. And for half of each year Charleston was directly in the path of raging fever epidemics.

As Pettigrew saw it, there were three courses of action open to him. Most of 1853 was spent in a painful wrestle among them. The first, conceived in Spain, was to abandon the law altogether and seek another kind of fame. This he broached to brother William:

For 15 months or more I have revolved in my brain an idea, which as yet I will honestly confess, that I had not the courage to utter. It consists in no less a matter, than leaving America for ten years at least, in pursuit of an object upon which I would concentrate my whole energies. You know that until the last 30 years the Spanish Arabs were little known. Two historians alone have thrown any true light upon their career; both Spaniards one of whom is still surviving; the subject is one of the noblest in the history of the world, and as yet scarcely touched upon by Conde Gyargoes [*sic*], Washington Irving, etc. The plan I proposed would be somehow thus: to spend five years in Andalusia and Madrid, Morocco, Algiers and the Kingdom of Fez in collecting the requisite information, and the next five years might be spent in composing a History that might place me where scores of . . . [?] years, spent at

the law would never do. You have the plan thus before you in un-
varnished phrase. It appears strange and romantic, as it undoubtedly is, but in no way chimerical. I have often considered it well
and dispassionately, and it seems to me reasonable. . . . this much
may be said in favor of Spain, viz., that poverty is not a damning
crime there as it too often is in America. . . . As for the practicality of the plan, Wm. [Hickling] Prescott and [George] Ticknor
are fair examples. And the advantages, resulting directly and indirectly would be very great; and not the least among them would
be the uninterrupted good health, upon which I might count.[9]

Pettigrew did not follow the course thus outlined, but he never completely abandoned the project. He learned Arabic and Hebrew, he collected notes and read everything he could find in preparation for the
task. The book on Spain he later published contained only a sugges-
tion of the book he wanted to write on the Moorish era, but from the
fragment it can be said that if Pettigrew had been able to complete his
project, there is no reason why he should not have achieved significant
rank among American historians.[10]

The second alternative was to stay with the law but try another location. John Sidney Thrasher, the enthusiast of Cuban annexation, had
tried unsuccessfully to enlist Pettigrew in that cause. He urged at least
a visit to the island, which he was sure would convert Pettigrew to his
view. Not long after Pettigrew returned to Charleston, he "fell inno-
cently under Mrs. Petigru's disapprobation, and she has consequently
declared war on me." Directly as a result of this, less than four months
after his return from Europe and without announcing his intentions to
anyone, Pettigrew sailed for Havana to look over the prospects there.
At the last moment he persuaded Joseph Blythe Allston, a young relative of Petigru and one of his best friends in Charleston, to go with
him. The sudden, unannounced departure led the family to fear that
the young men had joined some filibuster. Actually Pettigrew had no
such intention. He had been careful to secure a testament of character from the most notable official he knew, Secretary of the Navy
William A. Graham of North Carolina, and from the French consul at
Charleston.[11]

He spent more than two weeks on the island, visiting Havana and
some plantations in the interior and mingling in what he found to be

a hospitable society despite the raging of a terrible smallpox epidemic. Pettigrew's thought of locating in Cuba was another search for elusive glory. He was quixotic in impulse, but his strain of common sense and dignity was too strong to allow him to risk his life in a grimy filibuster with southwestern desperadoes. But, he thought, suppose one settled down in Havana, acquired a good income (which would be aided by his command of foreign languages and his European law training), lived pleasantly in a mild climate and agreeable Latin culture, and waited for a rebellion that had a chance of success or for a consummation of the American passion for annexation? There was no telling what posts of danger, glory, honor, and profit might appear then for an American resident familiar with Cuba.[12]

The island stood always on the brink of a precipice. Pettigrew found hatred between the Spaniards and the native whites far stronger than expected, "and the former would not hesitate to give the country up to the Africans in case they should not be able to retain easy possession. This renders any property in Cuba exceedingly unsafe." The possibilities of American annexation seemed more and more remote as Pettigrew studied the question.[13]

Another possible location was New Orleans. James C. Johnston was convinced that this was the American city most fitting to be the scene of the greatness he was sure Pettigrew would achieve. From Havana Pettigrew sailed to New Orleans, and he had a fine time there. Society was delightful. The leading lawyers of the city, including Judah P. Benjamin, received him with hospitality. Chief Justice George Eustis invited him to the most elegant dinner he had ever attended. Lincoln Lionel Levy, a former Chapel Hill friend who was then practicing law in the city, however, warned Pettigrew that it would take him years in New Orleans to build up the name that he would start with in Charleston under J. L. Petigru's sponsorship.[14]

Mr. Johnston, nevertheless, continued to favor New Orleans, gave "every inducement . . . and almost asked it as a personal favor." James Louis Petigru urged Charleston and thought New Orleans out of the question. His second recommendation was economically reviving North Carolina. Pettigrew had been struck on his return from Europe by what seemed to be a new bustle, expansiveness, and prosperity in the backward Old North State and had noticed too that two of the duller of his university classmates were already in the legislature. But Uncle John

Bryan declared that North Carolina was overcrowded with lawyers and pointed out that one of his own sons had gone to Baltimore.[15]

Pettigrew had "never been so knocked about by conflicting advice. . . . As usual when one gives himself a great deal of trouble in thoroughly considering a matter, I fear I shall make the worst choice of the three." He even briefly contemplated St. Louis or California as a way out. Both James C. Johnston and J. L. Petigru were looking for a place appropriate for a great man, Pettigrew realized. "Both these gentlemen go upon the mistaken supposition, that I am . . . which, however, I am not booby enough to believe myself," he wrote. "As it is I intend to toss up a half-dollar and follow the result. I have often done so in undecided moments. I have rarely had occasion to regret it."[16]

Meanwhile Pettigrew had been industriously working at the law under Petigru. Perhaps the success of his first appearance in the local civil court improved his opinion of his prospects at Charleston. The judge, Christopher G. Memminger, subsequently Confederate Secretary of Treasury, complimented him on his presentation, and his opponent told him that his speech had "electrified the courthouse." Petigru, when appealed to for advice about the Moorish history project, had cogitated upon it for two weeks and then given his opinion against it. In a long talk he frankly admitted that he wanted the young man in Charleston for partly selfish reasons. But he also believed that Johnston's debut in court augured legal success and that the death of Calhoun was changing the politics of the state and offering more opportunities for ambitious and able young men. The story was told that when Calhoun's body lay in state in Charleston in 1850 someone lamented to Petigru, "Where is the man to take his place?" To this Petigru immediately replied, "Johnston Pettigrew has a higher *morale* than Mr. Calhoun had, and a greater intellect."[17]

Possibly also some of Pettigrew's hesitancy about Charleston was overcome by the cordiality with which he was received into society. All the extended Petigru connection, which included Allstons, Porchers, Carsons, Lesesnes, Norths, and Kings, seem to have accepted him immediately and unreservedly, obviating his fears that he would be regarded as J. L. Petigru's poor relation and placing him on a social footing as good as any in the city.

Either because of these encouragements or the toss of the coin, Pettigrew finally decided (with "much disgust") to try his luck at Charleston.

On 1 January 1854 he was published in the press as the third member of the firm of Petigru and King. Petigru offered the young man one-eighth of the firm's annual profits, or about two thousand dollars. This Pettigrew declined, arguing that he was not worth it, and he accepted a five-hundred-dollar clerk's salary instead. He did not wish to add to the financial burdens of Petigru, who already supported a widowed sister's family and a ne'er-do-well son. Also, "strange as it may seem, I always feel more energy and am more industrious when working for honour or the love of the thing, than for money." [18]

From the formation of the partnership until the secession of South Carolina in December 1860, Pettigrew was a practicing attorney in Charleston. He was able in the preparation and the presentation of his cases, and he carried his weight in the firm. Johnston "is already beginning to bring to people's minds the old saying that the scholar often excels his master," J. L. Petigru wrote six weeks after the partnership commenced. Pettigrew was most successful in civil cases in higher courts where his well-researched, closely reasoned arguments, without bombast or tricks, appealed to the judges. After his first appearance in the state appeals court the judges informed Petigru's brother-in-law, Henry Deas Lesesne, who was to follow Johnston on the same side, that it was not necessary to hear him as Pettigrew had already covered the case conclusively. One of them commented that "he had never heard such a speech before from a young man in his life." [19]

Being taken into Petigru's firm propelled the young man at once into important cases for which he would otherwise have waited years. He practiced frequently in the higher state courts in Columbia, and in 1855 he was admitted to practice in the United States Circuit Court after examination by Supreme Court Justice James M. Wayne. Still, he was stuck with the cases the senior did not want to handle and once complained that "I keep my hand in defending rogues and robbers, which Mr. Petigru declines." On the other hand Petigru once laughingly remarked that "our friend Johnston is a genius, but I fear he will never make an advocate. No one can detect the legal points of a case quicker than he, but he must have equity, justice, law and morality all on his side before he will take a case." [20]

Previously his contacts with the ruling class of the state had been largely social and confined to the extensive Petigru family and friends, and to ladies and younger men. The important law cases gave him a chance to meet and be met by the older, graver, more powerful men. Frequently Petigru was in Washington or Philadelphia for cases or at his upcountry plantation, and during these absences Johnston dealt with important persons on large matters, apparently to Petigru's complete satisfaction.[21]

The law office, a stone, two-story Greek temple built in 1848, was located on St. Michael's Alley just around the corner from the church. J. L. Petigru had a large office on the upper floor, and Johnston used an adjoining room. The other partner, Henry C. King, Petigru's son-in-law, who seldom appeared in court and who supervised the internal business of the office, occupied the lower floor with the clerks and students. Petigru had bought the property across the street and constructed a garden there.[22]

Although Johnston Pettigrew's intellectual ability allowed him to be a successful lawyer, those who knew him well between 1854 and 1860 sensed that he was not an earnest one. His profession never engaged his deepest attention or enthusiasm and was never able to absorb all his intellectual energy. He was a lawyer only because he felt impelled to put his ability to some practical use and because law was the path to distinction in America. Without devoting his full energies to the profession, his capacity for quick perception, concentrated study, and clear expression allowed him to maintain a good reputation as a lawyer. He sometimes wondered what would happen if Petigru were to die or, as was often suggested, were to be made chief justice of the state. In that case, he wrote, "the business will devolve upon Henry & myself. Can we retain it? Quien sabe?"[23] He was never required to find out.

Between 1854 and 1860 Johnston Pettigrew, member of the bar of Charleston, legislator and militia officer, eligible bachelor and bon vivant, chivalric gentleman and eccentric genius, became known as one of the more notable younger men of South Carolina. Having made his decision at the beginning of 1854 to stay in Charleston, Pettigrew deliberately determined to throw himself into the life of the city and advance fame, fortune, and pleasure however he could, with the object, he said half-jokingly, of being attorney general of the state by 1856.[24]

He was not attorney general by his deadline, but a great deal had happened to him within two years. Besides being a member in good standing of the St. Cecilia Society, the Charleston Club, and the Jockey Club, he had, as he said in an 1856 progress report to James C. Johnston, "attained quite an elevated rank among the 'fast' men . . . have got the credit of [managing] a magnificent Fancy Ball . . . take part in political meetings and wire-pullings," had been elected to the legislature, had almost been involved in several duels, and had been laughed at for enthusiastically "dying of love to several divinities."[25]

South Carolina, so different from the modest neighboring commonwealth in which he had grown up that he had once described it as "to many purposes a foreign country from North Carolina," accepted Pettigrew and he accepted it. James C. Johnston found this distasteful. He suspected that his namesake's residence at Charleston was neither physically nor morally beneficial. "I fear he has fallen into the exclusive [*illegible word*] manners that make the South Carolinians disagreeable companions to all but their own countrymen," Mr. Johnston (who was probably the richest man in North Carolina) told William Pettigrew.[26]

Pettigrew had originally agreed with Mr. Johnston that South Carolinians were "conceited, consequential & aristocratic." His distaste seems to have dissipated after a few years' residence. Certainly he was accepted by the South Carolinians. When Pettigrew was down with the yellow fever in Charleston in 1858, a relative reported that "he has made friends everywhere he has been," and that many people at Columbia were asking about him.[27]

His South Carolina relatives, in all their extended branches, adopted him and he in turn made them his own. The South Carolina family, Petigru's daughters and their husbands, his sisters and brother and their spouses and children, gave the orphaned and restless man the only real family and home he had known. His sister Mary from North Carolina found on visiting Charleston that "it is quite marvellous to me that he is so much of a family man. The family here seem to like him extremely. He goes about with them and takes an interest in every matter that concerns them. At the same time he maintains a proper independence without regard to fear or favor." Nor did she think that South Carolina had adversely affected his character, but found him "the same as when he was a boy. . . . without exception the most accommodating and considerate young gentleman I ever knew."[28]

One of J. L. Petigru's sisters, Adele, had married Robert F. W. Allston, who was elected governor in 1856. Johnston Pettigrew was a welcome and frequent guest at Chicora Wood, Allston's magnificent rice plantation in the Georgetown District and at the nearby Allston seashore home on Pawley's Island. Among Pettigrew's close friends were Ben Allston, the governor's son, and Joseph Blythe Allston, his nephew. The two young Allstons both married sisters of Caroline North, who in turn married Pettigrew's brother Charles, thus lacing the family ties over double. Another Petigru brother-in-law was Henry Deas Lesesne. Lesesne took a particular liking to Pettigrew, looked after him during the great yellow fever epidemic of 1858, and took charge of Pettigrew's personal business affairs when the younger man went to war.[29]

Pettigrew was always available as an escort for the women of the family, whether for a ball or for a trip to New York. All of them seem to have been fond of him except Jane Postell (Mrs. J. L.) Petigru. He was able to persuade one of Governor Allston's daughters to become a conscientious student when no one else in the family could. A close relationship developed between Pettigrew and J. L. Petigru's daughter Caroline Carson, eight years older than he and widowed in 1856. The other ladies of the family regarded her as a bad influence on Johnston, probably because she was ultrafashionable, cynical, and satirical.[30]

Mrs. Carson went north during the Civil War and ended life in 1893 as an expatriate in Europe. Pettigrew was not particularly close to the other Petigru daughter, Susan King (wife of Henry C. King), who was near his own age and a published novelist. Yet she wrote of him: "He was so true, so reliable, so thorough. It took us years to know each other; & we began with no sympathies, but all that was honest, & unsparing of double-dealing, in our mutual natures brought us together. I would not have selected him as my most agreeable acquaintance for a dinner-table, or a morning visit, but if I needed a friend, or wished an honourable, straightforward counselor, it was he, that I would have chosen."[31]

Louise Porcher, J. L. Petigru's sister, spoke with pleasure of having Pettigrew as a house guest: "His simple habits & most unpretending tastes gives [*sic*] neither trouble or expense. . . . He is a most uncommon young man," she wrote, ". . . a mind more pure and noble in all its aspirations never existed." Pettigrew's integrity, unpretentious reserve, and ascetic simplicity won him friends wherever he went. "Indeed he is a very nice fellow," said his sister Mary who saw him rarely enough to have some detachment. "I can not help being proud of him. . . . He is extremely agreeable and gentlemanly, kind and polite. . . . His notions about improving yourself all the time in every thing are very correct because while engaged you are happiest and then every one respects you besides."[32]

Many a youth has vowed never to marry and succumbed to wedlock before the vibrations of his vow died away. Johnston early took the vow and not in vain. The one woman who could have changed his mind was his beautiful distant cousin Caroline North whom he regarded as "as near perfection as any mortal I have ever met" and who thought of him as "clever and noble." In 1853, to his astonishment, Carie became engaged to his plodding older brother Charles, who was ten years her senior. This occurred despite the belief of their sister Mary Pettigrew that Carie would marry Johnston and the fact that Carie had referred to Charles six months before the engagement as a tiresome, prosy old fellow. The courtship had slowly unfolded while Johnston was abroad. Charles and Caroline were wed in April 1853. On the surface at least Johnston Pettigrew never betrayed any discontent with this arrangement. He remained on apparently comfortable and friendly terms with Carie and took delight in the several Pettigrew heirs that graced the union.[33]

Pettigrew's unwed state was naturally viewed as a challenge by the whole female connection, who believed, probably correctly, that a good wife was all that was needed to straighten out his quixotic temperament and put him on the road to successful accommodation with the conventional world. "He might make a great man if well married," said one lady relative. "I feel very sorry for Johnston," Carie wrote after her own marriage. "I have never seen any one who more requires a judicious friend who would influence his vagaries into some reason. He ought to be married." "Poor fellow!" Pettigrew's sister once commented. "He is his own to act as inclination or whim prompt him."[34]

The most likely candidate to remedy Pettigrew's unfortunate state was Mary Singleton McDuffie, orphaned daughter of the statesman George McDuffie. Miss McDuffie had inherited Cherry Hill, adjacent to Badwell, the Petigru-North plantation in the Abbeville District. Pettigrew was a frequent visitor to Cherry Hill and often paid attentions to Miss McDuffie in Charleston. It was frequently suggested by his female relatives that Johnston could easily have the lady if he wished, but he refused to pursue the matter onto serious ground.[35] In 1858 Miss

McDuffie did very well by marrying Wade Hampton III, a widower twelve years her senior. Her plantation, Cherry Hill, was purchased by Charles and Caroline Pettigrew.

One of James Louis Petigru's sisters wrote another concerning Johnston Pettigrew: "I always thought ambition the ruling motive of his life. . . . ambition will dictate his choice if he should ever marry, but his heart occupies so diminished a portion of his individuality that I do not think his wife will be an enviable woman, but I like him notwithstanding." She found Johnston an original and stimulating conversationalist except that he was extremely laconic about himself.[36]

Law practice and social life by no means absorbed all of Pettigrew's mental energy. That which was left over was expended in intellectual, political, and military interests and enthusiasms. He acquired a considerable reputation in the city for eccentric genius. An acquaintance remembered his deep and concentrated studies in what others considered arcane areas of knowledge but which his restless mind seemed to be driven to master.[37]

Pettigrew studied Arabic and Hebrew and continued his research into the history of the Spanish Moors. He subscribed to German scholarly periodicals and bought scientific, literary, theological, and philosophical books from Europe. He installed a pianoforte in his lodgings and took music lessons. He maintained his interest in mathematics and made himself, by study, the equal of a professional soldier in the mastery of the various phases of engineering. He astonished fellow lawyers by solving rapidly any mathematical puzzle they could devise, and he pleased James Louis Petigru by correctly setting the gnomon on the sundial Petigru had erected at his upcountry plantation.[38]

Even in the midst of his first year as a law partner he undertook to edit the foreign news of the daily *Charleston Standard* and anonymously penned editorials which the proprietor, Leonidas W. Spratt, told him attracted considerable statewide attention. On at least one occasion when Spratt was out of town Pettigrew managed the entire paper.[39]

Along with his other activities Pettigrew performed several literary devoirs to his family. After extensive perusal of his grandfather's papers, he wrote, on request, a sketch of the life of Bishop Charles Pettigrew which was included in a work of North Carolina Revolutionary history published in 1858. Pettigrew insisted on anonymity, so the author,

Griffith J. McRee, included the sketch as an appendix to his work and ascribed it to "a friend whose modesty forbids further allusion."[40]

This piece of historical writing was done with a proper detached spirit. The sketch was not fulsome but was reasonably critical. For instance, he commented that James Pettigrew, the Irish immigrant to America, "seems to have fallen out bitterly with his people" and that Charles Pettigrew's literary attainments "though considerable for the time, were probably not very deep."[41] Johnston thought too highly of his family name to embarrass it by claiming credit that was not due. At the same time he felt that he could not with seemliness give Charles Pettigrew praise where it was deserved if he were known as the author.

A little later he was asked by William Buell Sprague, a New York author, to write a sketch of Bishop Charles for inclusion in the Episcopalian volume of his *Annals of the American Pulpit*. This Pettigrew did, again insisting on anonymity. Sprague felt he could not claim credit for Pettigrew's literary composition, so when Pettigrew refused to yield anonymity, Sprague was obliged to rewrite the sketch even though he admitted his own composition was inferior to Pettigrew's.[42]

Another literary devoir was the writing, after considerable research, of a lengthy defense of the Spanish ministry of his friend Barringer, that was published in the *Charleston Standard*. Pettigrew's reputation as a scholar spread and became public property. He was asked by veterans to write a history of the Palmetto Regiment in the Mexican War. He was invited to give a speech before his old college society and to lecture at an upcountry lyceum. In 1859 he was appointed a member of the Board of Visitors at South Carolina College, no small honor.[43]

Pettigrew became friend and companion to a number of Charlestonians with intellectual interests. The theologian James Warley Miles opened his library to Pettigrew, and they studied Arabic together. William Henry Trescot, who became United States assistant secretary of state and had some fame as a scholar, recalled "many hours and days of pleasant intercourse when over our cigars we used to speculate on the life that probably lay before us and which we failed utterly to anticipate."[44]

Pettigrew subscribed to the Charleston Art Association. In 1857 he was the main speaker at a dinner in honor of the aged Charleston painter Charles Fraser. He was invited to a small dinner party to meet

William Makepeace Thackeray when that luminary visited Charleston, and he was in charge of the arrangements for a public lecture by the poet Paul Hamilton Hayne. Of a slightly different order of culture was his playing host to a Cuban danseuse, a friend of John Sidney Thrasher.[45]

Another form of diversion from his profession was travel. Pettigrew made occasional trips to the northern metropolises, to the spas in the Virginia mountains, or to the homes of relatives in various parts of the Carolinas. On one occasion he accompanied James C. Johnston on a tour in the grand manner. With a carriage, five horses, and two slaves, they traveled to the springs, made a tour of the copper and coal mines of western Virginia, and returned by way of a lengthy, leisurely swing through the North Carolina upcountry.[46]

In his first few years at Charleston Pettigrew lodged at 33 Broad Street with a friend and fellow lawyer, Benjamin Rutledge, and Rutledge's mother. After Rutledge's marriage Pettigrew rented a house on St. Michael's Alley near his office and furnished it to his taste. He continued to live there until 1859 when he purchased a fine house at 59 Tradd Street. Much of his time was spent at the Petigru mansion at Broad and Friend (now Legaré) streets or at Mrs. Carson's on King Street. When he became Governor Allston's military aide, Pettigrew acquired a horse, and for health and relaxation he rode into the country when he could.[47]

The mutual love and respect between James Johnston Pettigrew and James Louis Petigru deepened over the years as the old Federalist grew sadder over the shortcomings of his immediate family, over the fading of his literary ambitions, and over what he considered the political lunacy of his fellow South Carolinians.

Pettigrew was once called upon to answer a request for biographical information on the older man. His answer indicates his opinion of Petigru and perhaps also tells something about himself. He regarded Petigru as unquestionably a great man. The pillars of this greatness were, according to Johnston, the mental capacity to cut through to the heart of matters; mental, moral, and physical courage, as indicated by Petigru's long residence in the midst of political opponents without lapsing into misanthropy; lack of control over himself in small matters but complete mastery of himself on great occasions (lesser men were the opposite, according to Pettigrew, firm in small things and weak in great crises); an acquaintance with the law and literature of the Old World immeasurably greater than that of most American lawyers; and a charitable heart.[48]

Even as Pettigrew played an increasingly active role in the sectional clash which the older man decried, their personal ties bound them tighter. Pettigrew paused in the midst of military duties in the summer of 1861 to refute publicly and at length an editorial by Robert Barnwell Rhett, Jr., calling James Louis Petigru a "monarchist" for his antisecession views. "I value the latter incident as it proves that you understand me; which is one of the tests of a kindred mind," Petigru wrote. During the war the older man signed his letters to Pettigrew "your parental friend" or "thy loving friend." In 1858 when Pettigrew was sick with the yellow fever, Petigru told his niece, if "I hear bad news of poor Johnstone [*sic*], I shall feel as if there was nothing to do but to lay down and die." [49]

Another evidence of Johnston's complete identification with the South Carolina family was his continued refusal to add to James Louis Petigru's financial burdens by taking more than a small salary from the law firm. His sense of honor led him to prefer less than he was due, and he declined a percentage of the firm's profits. In 1856 Petigru made him the present of a house and lot to satisfy the freehold requirement for being a candidate for the state legislature.[50]

The annual interest on the sum owed Pettigrew by his brother William under their father's will was sizable. Of this Johnston usually drew only as much as he needed or as he felt William could conveniently pay. The interest, with occasional proceeds from New Bern property and lands in Tennessee that had been left by his grandmother and aunt and from William's annual hire of his slave, allowed Pettigrew to live comfortably as long as he remained a bachelor and did not undertake to seek a high political office. In 1858 he was still due over twelve thousand dollars of the fifteen-thousand-dollar legacy, although William had been paying approximately one thousand dollars per year, chiefly in interest.[51]

That same year the oldest Pettigrew brother, Charles, who had always been held up to Johnston as a model of practicality and good sense, got into severe financial straits by the default of a businessman for whom he had signed notes. Charles's property, including Bonarva, was at the mercy of his creditors any time they chose to press. While they were not eager to do so, they might at any time be forced into it by exigencies of their own.[52]

Neither Johnston nor William hesitated for an instant over their duty to help their brother and to keep the family property intact. Luckily both were bachelors. Johnston began economizing with a vengeance, reducing his standard of living and his hopes for the future, which suddenly looked bleak. He felt that he had almost reached a plateau in his climb to fame. He had achieved some notice during his term in the legislature, and he was thinking of making a race for the Charleston congressional seat that was coming open with the retirement of William Aiken. Now all his hard-earned reputation seemed to be slipping back into the abyss of anonymity, for he could no longer count on sufficient income to cut a respectable figure in society. The demon of family ambition, which drove him on, convinced him that there was no standing still. One either climbed ahead or slipped back.[53]

James C. Johnston, who was seventy-six in 1858, decided to help out the sons of his departed friend Ebenezer Pettigrew in their distress. Johnston's share of his beneficence was a gift of fifty thousand dollars. Twelve thousand was paid through William to release William finally and completely from his debt to Johnston. Along with the gift came advice: "I wish you to make a permanent investment and I hope [this] will make you a sufficient establishment to sustain your position and if you should wish at any time to get married will with the income from your profession enable you to support a family decently. I hope you will confine your expenditures to the interest and never make yourself responsible for others on their debts."[54]

The extent of Mr. Johnston's affection for his namesake is indicated by his making it possible for Pettigrew to do two things of which the old aristocrat highly disapproved—to become a candidate for Congress and to get married. Serving in Congress Mr. Johnston regarded as degrading to any gentleman and damaging to true distinction. As for women: "The less a man has to do with them the better particularly the old tabbies[;] the young kittens are amusing enough sometimes but they sometimes scratch a man before he knows it." "Such favors in themselves and as a mark of friendship are so astonishing and overwhelming, as to admit of few words," Pettigrew wrote of Mr. Johnston's gift. "One's gratitude must be shown in the future rather than the present. . . . after this suppose I was to turn out badly!"[55]

The Pettigrews were by no means the only recipients of the wealthy old bachelor's largess. Mr. Johnston was noted for his charities. He supported several relatives, and when he died he left the Hayes plantation to his manager. Probably Mr. Johnston's gift to Johnston Pettigrew was in part intended to help the struggling Charles indirectly. One of Johnston's first acts with his newfound fortune was to purchase a twelve-thousand-dollar note of Charles's from Wade Hampton III. Later he loaned Charles twenty thousand dollars. The rest of his fortune Johnston, after contemplating Arkansas cotton lands, put into the bonds of several railroads and of the city of Charleston and into a fine house at 59 Tradd Street.[56]

In 1859 when he went, he thought, to war in Europe, Pettigrew left a will in the keeping of Henry Deas Lesesne. When this was opened on Pettigrew's death in 1863 it was found that he had left his entire fortune, sixty-four thousand dollars at prewar values, to William Pettigrew. Clearly he intended this for the use of the entire family, but nothing could be given to Charles directly for fear of his creditors. William was to look after the two sisters as his judgment dictated. Pettigrew also made a discretionary, nonbinding request that his executor, William, repay to James Cathcart Johnston his thirty-eight thousand dollar gift. This Mr. Johnston declined to accept.[57]

Chapter 8

Of Death and Fate

Death on the battlefield is doubtless very pleasant, but next to that is certainly life in Andalusia. —*James Johnston Pettigrew*, Notes on Spain

Along with his resolution to make Charleston the scene of his labor and ambition, Pettigrew determined in 1854 to face his first summer in the Low Country since childhood. He had the feeling that before he could be fully accepted as a Charlestonian rather than a visiting adventurer he must get acclimated by weathering out a sickly season in the city. The recurring fever epidemics which struck in the summer or early fall were most dangerous to newcomers. If one survived his first attack he was considered "seasoned," with a degree of immunity from future danger. Pettigrew felt he must make firm his identification with the city if he were to seek professional, social, and political advancement with a good face. Also, he was tired of the threat of illness hanging over his life, and he had reached a state in which he was ready to risk death in order to remove the threat once and for all.[1]

The interaction of a weak constitution and a romantic temperament had induced an attitude of fatalism. The resulting conduct struck some as courageous, others as foolhardy. By exercise and effort Pettigrew had filled out his slender frame. Mr. Johnston found in 1853 at the springs that Pettigrew "is very muscular and active and ascends the highest mountains on foot. . . . His muscles are firm & hard and he seems capable of going through any fatigue of body or mind." This strength and endurance were products of mind over nature, although Pettigrew remained highly susceptible to disabling illness. His brother noticed shortly after Johnston's return from Europe that he was in delicate health. "He said several times while sick here [The Lake], that he had no constitution," William wrote. "I felt much for him, while the ague was on him, to see his difficult respiration, resulting probably from an enlarged spleen."[2] (The symptoms suggest malaria.)

The year that Pettigrew decided to test himself against the yellow fever proved to be the worst epidemic year in Charleston since 1817. An estimated 627 people died in the city, scarcely a family in any class of society going unscathed.[3] In the early part of the summer Pettigrew was temporarily blinded by an eye affliction. He was forced against his will to go to the upcountry and then to the Virginia springs to recuperate. He was so depressed by this spell of disability that he returned to Charleston in August at the height of the epidemic.

"For one or two reasons, positively wishing to get the fever and be rid of this mortal coil and for most reasons feeling quite indifferent," Pettigrew decided on a settled policy of tempting fate. He was already weakened and susceptible. On top of that, the train carrying him from North Carolina to Charleston wrecked and he was forced to spend a night in the cars in the middle of the Pee Dee Swamp. When he reached Charleston he took no precautions at all for his health. A friend who was just leaving town as he arrived told him he would not give him a quarter of a dollar for his life for coming back when he did. "I had rather die at once than be fearful as some people are. . . . I am determined not to let myself be troubled by insurmountable obstacles," Pettigrew said.[4]

He came down with a variety of the fever and was very ill for two days. What he caught was not the deadly yellow fever, although the milder variety may have given him some immunity to the more dangerous form. Pettigrew believed that if he were susceptible to the yellow fever he would have caught it then, and he was indifferent to the danger thereafter. He was inclined to think that his very recklessness in facing down Fate had saved him a great deal of unnecessary anxiety. A hurricane struck in September, disrupting the city still in the midst of the epidemic. Pettigrew reported that he went about for several days in water thigh-deep and took no precautions except his customary temperance. The result was that, he said, "I throve: the devil either despises me or else thinks he can get me at any time, so does not hurry himself."[5]

Throughout the epidemic he went afoot wherever he pleased, although it was common belief that "changing the air" made one particularly certain to catch the fever. It was during this epidemic that Pettigrew became a member of the Harvard Association, a charitable society of well-to-do young men whose object was to relieve the suffering of the poor white residents of the city, many of them recent Irish immigrants. He was one of the few members who was active and not just contributing. Each day he walked up to the lower-class quarter and made the rounds of his assigned area, performing services for the sick and distributing food. Despite the exposure entailed, the only ill effect he suffered was a bad rash. "It is a miracle that he does not get fever. . . . I hope Heaven intends for him an instrument by which good is to be done," reflected one of J. L. Petigru's sisters when Pettigrew was risking his life on these rounds.[6]

"I have seen more people dying than I ever expect to do again," Pettigrew wrote at the end of the catastrophe of 1854, "and never desire to see another such epidemic in Charleston." He was a poor prophet. In 1855 he remained in the city throughout the entire sickly season managing business in J. L. Petigru's absence. It proved a mild year, as did 1857. The fever struck in 1856 but with less than half the severity of 1854. But 1858 saw the worst epidemic in contemporary memory. The fever, a new and deadly type, did not spare seasoned natives. Pettigrew was considered especially vulnerable since he had never had the yellow fever. Still he lived with his usual indifference and made his customary charitable rounds for the Harvard Association.[7]

Joseph Blythe Allston, Pettigrew's distant kinsman and close friend, came down with the disease and was pronounced by the physicians as certain to die. Although not well himself, Pettigrew nursed Allston night and day and was generally credited with saving Allston's life at the risk of his own. "In nursing Joe through his illness he runs the risk of his life — for all who nurse in this fever, if not acclimated, is [sic] sure to take it," reported a relative of the young men from the stricken city. "Oh! what a valuable life is Johnston's to risk as he has done this last month! . . . If he takes yellow fever I see no *human* prospect of his recovery — I am sure Dr. Giddings thinks so too from what he said to me . . . he thinks his friends ought to have put him into the lunatic asylum when he persisted in coming back at this time."[8]

Allston lived to become a Confederate soldier and an Episcopal priest and survived into the twentieth century. The epidemic seemed to have passed when in November it broke out again suddenly and Johnston came down deathly ill. He received the careful nursing of Allston, of Henry Deas Lesesne, and of a number of other friends. His relatives were certain that the young man was lost, but somehow the fifth-day crisis of the disease passed and he lived.[9]

Pettigrew continued to be bothered with physical afflictions, a severe facial neuralgia being only one. In September 1860, only two months before he went on active military duty in Charleston harbor, he succumbed to a particularly painful illness known as "break-bone fever." He was left debilitated and susceptible to relapse.[10] Through sheer will-power he refused to let this hamper his military activities during the Fort Sumter crisis.

A man with Pettigrew's indifference to fatal illness was not likely to be hesitant about submitting himself to the ritualized risk of the dueling field when honor seemed to require it. And, perhaps, with Pettigrew, there was not only the requirement of honor but the desire to make himself felt as a man of force in a society where he was a stranger. On half a dozen or more occasions Pettigrew was involved in the preliminaries of affairs of honor which, had they developed further, could have been lethal. These affairs were about equally divided between those that were social and those that were political in their origins.

In 1856 Pettigrew demanded and received apologies from the entire board of editors of the *Charleston Courier* after a misunderstanding about a costume ball he was managing. Pettigrew had given the paper a list of the guests' disguises with the understanding it would be published after the ball. When the news was published prematurely, Pettigrew aggressively pursued a demand for full apology and considered the matter important enough to keep a detailed memorandum. This was not the only episode of its kind.[11]

Another near miss grew out of his participation as a second in a celebrated and fatal political duel, the Magrath-Taber affair, which is discussed below. Two other occasions involved attacks on his South Carolina relatives, whose reputation he undertook to defend on his own. Once he contemplated issuing a challenge to a politician who had attacked Governor Allston in a manner he considered personal and excessive, but the duel never came off.[12]

Another occasion concerned J. L. Petigru's kindly brother, Captain Thomas Petigru. In 1855 Captain Petigru, who had entered the Navy as a boy midshipman in 1814 and who had held such responsible positions as the superintendency of the Washington Navy Yard, was cashiered from the service by a naval board. The *Charleston Mercury* published a scathing attack on the officers who had besmirched the captain's reputation. Commander John DeCamp, a member of the board, replied with a pamphlet which reiterated damaging accusations against the captain and attacked bitterly the author of the *Mercury* article.[13]

Johnston considered the responsibility for vindicating the family honor his, since Captain Petigru was in no position to issue a challenge. The day after seeing the pamphlet he sent a note to DeCamp at the Brooklyn Navy Yard, identifying himself as a relative of Petigru. The author of the *Mercury* piece was only a slight acquaintance of Pettigrew's, but, Pettigrew said,

> he is a gentleman . . . and I cannot consent that he should be put to the slightest inconvenience in consequence of his generous conduct. Whatever obligations or responsibilities, he may have incurred will, I hope, be transferred to myself. Endorsing fully his statements, I shall be most happy to give satisfaction either by sustaining the accusation upon its merits, or by referring the question to the decision of the Tribunal, appealed to by gentlemen.
>
> For obvious reasons, it is scarcely in my power to take the initiative, but any invitation will be promptly responded to by my friend, Mr. Rutledge. [Benjamin Rutledge's card enclosed.][14]

The naval officer refused to meet at the Gentleman's Tribunal, on the grounds that "I do not see the wisdom of entangling myself in an endless quarrel with your family toward whom I entertain no hostile feelings."[15]

The southern recourse to the time-honored Western tradition of the duel, which seemed barbarous to many when it had gone out of style elsewhere, was a natural expression of regard for a man's personal reputation, the loss of which could lead not only to intangible but practical vexations. "There can be no doubt that duelling is a relic of barbarism, and should be abolished," Pettigrew said once in print, "but so should the causes which furnish occasion for it, or else enlightened public opinion should afford some satisfaction for the insults which now drive gentlemen to this antiquated and absurd remedy."[16] Dueling was absurd, but as long as one's sense of reputation and responsibility was so intensely personal and necessary there must be a means to satisfy offense.

Ever-present reminders of mortality in the form of sickness and violence gave a constant undertone of melancholy and controlled desperation to southern society. While this undertone appears morbid from the standpoint of a modern practical and technically oriented society, there is nothing extraordinary about it. Violence and sickness were always the lot of mankind. What is of real interest is the behavioral and spiritual means that southerners adopted to deal with these aspects of life and how those means increasingly set them apart from the modernizing North.

The incident between Pettigrew and DeCamp illustrates in microcosm, exactly as did the Charles Sumner–Preston Brooks affair the next year, a growing chasm between southern and northern psychology. The southerner could only regard it as contemptible to hide a personal act behind an official position. A northern society that was increasingly urban and impersonal, where the ethics of American aristocracy were being replaced by middle-class respectability, and where public and private morality were increasingly separate played by a different set of rules. To the North, Brooks was the barbarian for first initiating physical violence. To the South, Sumner was the barbarian for not being willing to take responsibility for his words.

Captain Petigru died in 1857 before the final hearings were held on his appeal for vindication of the charges against him. His widow presented Johnston Pettigrew with the captain's matched set of pistols.[17]

Danger had always exercised a fascination over Pettigrew. While still a youth he had often expressed a wish to experience a storm at sea, a desire which was gratified on his first trip to Charleston. Fatalism induced by frequent illness and by the inclination constantly to put his own nerve and endurance to the test undoubtedly dictated Pettigrew's attraction to things military. No doubt his self-commanded indifference to death was a virtue in a soldier, yet it was also excessive in a way. When Pettigrew was mistakenly reported killed in action in 1862, Susan Petigru King's reaction was: "I have heard nothing [of the details]. . . . yet I feel assured that he has exposed himself unnecessarily

& . . . might still have been spared to us, if his prudence had equalled his courage. . . . From the beginning I have felt (& many others did the same) that Johnston's first battle would be his last." [18]

The truth was that danger, sacrifice, and glory seemed to Pettigrew to give his life meaning. They were his means of meeting positively the constant reminders of vulnerable mortality with which he lived. Law practice, political office, society, study—nothing seemed to allay his restlessness or give him a sense of purpose until he immersed himself in war. After his return from Europe, he was always complaining of a sense of restlessness and emptiness except when some enthusiasm temporarily relieved his pessimism.

"The romance of my life has been plucked up by the roots some time since," he wrote once. "I live for nothing that I am aware of. . . . I believe I should turn my head toward getting rich: one must have some object in view; that would be better than nothing; this floating along is rather unsatisfactory: I always feel disposed to fly off at a tangent." The desire to advance his family name, at which he felt he had had little success, "is almost the only duty I feel in the world & certainly the only gratification," he reflected on another occasion.[19]

Pettigrew needed a cause greater than himself to absorb his mental energy and moral enthusiasm, to express his drive toward excellence, and to fulfill his talents and his sense of purpose. As his friend Trescot put it after his death,

> He was essentially an earnest man. From his early youth whatever he did was done with an intense purpose. As his experience widened and his mind matured, the purpose was changed, but the intensity was constant. Those who knew him best will, I think, agree with me that this earnestness was every year concentrating upon a higher purpose and proposing to itself a loftier aim, that the restlessness of his early ambition was subsiding, the effort of his intellect growing steadier, and that it needed only this final consecration to an unselfish cause to perfect the nobleness of his character.

At the same time

> His learning, his accomplishments, his talents, were all under the control of his moral sense. He was a man who desired to be, and

not to seem. His ambition was large, but it was an ambition to do what was worthy to be done. . . . and, although as strong men will desire, he desired the vantage-ground of place and power — the standpoint where from to use the lever of his intellect, yet his life was instinct with a consciousness that a great end can never be compassed by low means.[20]

Possibly Pettigrew's being partook strongly of what would be described by a psychoanalyst as the death wish. It may indeed have been one of the unrecognized accomplishments of the chivalric heritage to turn the death wish inward or direct it into ritualized, socially controlled, and often socially useful channels, the fading away of which has led to the increased irrational destructiveness of man in the twentieth century. Both consciously and instinctively Pettigrew set out to mold himself into a living example of the positive virtues of the inheritance of chivalry. Temperament and situation permitted him to live out the tendencies of southern society in a relatively pure form. With a genius that could find no satisfactory outlet, no wife and children to bring his life into a more mundane perspective, and the hovering threat of physical illness and the evident approach of a time of national crisis, Pettigrew selected from his cultural inheritance, in a way both individualistic and archetypal, a pattern of behavior for coping with life — the model of the simple, honorable, brave, self-abnegating knight, the model of which the Castilian was the most exquisite refinement.

Once when friends contemplated a trip to Havana, Pettigrew warned them that they would not be able to endure the spartan, comfortless, Spanish-style hotels, "although they suit me well enough." Among all the famous works of art he viewed in Europe, a picture of Charles V at the Battle of Mühlberg, in the Prado at Madrid, moved Pettigrew most. As he described in his book, *Notes on Spain:* "Every movement, every position, every feature betrays the warrior Emperor struggling against physical disease and exhaustion — the triumph of unconquerable will over the weakness of the body."[21] Pettigrew was describing himself.

A southerner's imperative of honor inevitably manifested itself collectively — that is, politically — making politics as much a matter of honor as of practical interest-brokering. Since American politics were structured by a republicanism that was constitutional and federal, the state was the focus of collective allegiance. The same impulses that drove Pettigrew to the code duello were responsible for the fact that South Carolina participated only to a limited degree in the national party politics in the 1850s.

There were two tendencies in the state after the death of John Calhoun. One group, loosely headed by Robert Barnwell Rhett and the *Charleston Mercury*, was composed of "immediatists" whose goal was secession. This party was convinced that the North would grow increasingly hostile and that the sooner a break was made the better. All its political acts were in effect agitations toward that end. The other, or "cooperationalist" party, loosely headed by James Lawrence Orr, was quite as firm in its allegiance to state rights and slavery but differed sharply on strategy. It desired for South Carolina to remain within the Union, at least until the wisdom of secession had become clear to enough other states. It disapproved of provocative acts against the North and was willing to cooperate with and give all possible encouragement to nonhostile northern politicians in the national Democratic party. It was rising in strength at just the time Johnston Pettigrew entered political life.

As a native of North Carolina, as a relative of James Louis Petigru whose differences with the radical party dated back to Nullification days, and because of his own well-considered views, Pettigrew unsurprisingly identified himself with the second party. There was no party in South Carolina that represented the views of his North Carolina relatives, who were conservative Clay Whigs. But Pettigrew had always been more Jacksonian and less nationalistic than they. "You all thought me deeply tinged with Locofocoism," he wrote his brother in 1848. "It is true that I am not an uncompromising Whig upon the Bank, tariff or currency." Pettigrew supported Buchanan and the national Democrats in 1856 while his old-fashioned North Carolina relatives voted for Fillmore and the American party.[22]

Pettigrew's first, typically North Carolinian reaction toward the South Carolina radical party was expressed in a letter to his brother during the sectional crisis of 1850:

> Of all the incapable, impolitic and onesided men in creation, the set of Carolinians who have been modelled by Mr. Calhoun are certainly the most inefficient and untrustworthy; and although the fanatics of the North and the real danger to our property drive us

to the brink of dissolution, yet the thought that these mouthing fellows will probably have a hand in the new Government, causes me instinctively to draw back a step and ponder. . . . unless the South has better advisers than Rhett &c it will be necessary to keep on terms with the Yankees as long as possible.[23]

The cooperationist party reached the peak of its influence in 1856. Pettigrew was one of a group of mostly younger men who organized in Charleston that year to cooperate with the national Democrats in their effort to head off the ominous new Republican party. In May, with many distinguished citizens, Pettigrew attended the state Democratic convention in Columbia, convened to select delegates for the national convention. He sat on the resolutions committee, which resolved to support the national nominee, whoever he might be, and expressed gratitude to those northern Democrats who had supported southern rights. His correspondence indicates that he became intimate with a number of important political figures and was engaged in behind-the-scenes maneuvering related to the drawing up of the slate of delegates to the national convention.[24]

Pettigrew's next political activity was to arrange a "ratification" meeting at Charleston to demonstrate support for the Democratic presidential and vice-presidential nominees. Pettigrew managed the preparations for this affair, which went off a few days after he received the telegraphed word from the South Carolina delegates at Cincinnati of the nomination of Buchanan and Breckinridge.[25] All this was chiefly for publicity. The state legislature still chose the presidential electors in South Carolina, and the only possible alternatives were to support Buchanan or, if the radicals controlled, to withhold the electoral votes from Buchanan in order to help the Republican Fremont's election and thus precipitate secession.

Meanwhile Pettigrew was himself a candidate for the state House of Representatives and was elected in October 1856, his name being rather low on the list of eighteen winning House candidates in the two city parishes of St. Michaels and St. Philips. The election was a general triumph for the conciliatory party, especially since the radicals had an efficient political machine in the lower-class areas of the city. It was also considered something of a personal triumph for Pettigrew, whose friends had canvassed vigorously.[26] The Charleston delegation included such notables as Christopher G. Memminger, the banker Joseph Johnson, the historian Edward McCrady, Jr., and Speaker James Simons.

In the South Carolina view, the General Assembly of which Pettigrew became a member remained more truly a deliberative body than any other legislature in America. It was a body in which men of substance and talent met to debate public business in an honorable manner rather than to "log roll" or to promote a party. South Carolina came closer than any American state to being a unified polity in which the franchised citizens spoke with one voice and where divisions occurred on principle rather than according to special interests or factionalism for its own sake.[27]

In 1856 the legislature met on 3–4 November to elect the governor and presidential electors. It reconvened for its main session on 24 November and adjourned before Christmas. The House of Representatives of which Pettigrew was a member contained, besides the Charleston delegation, such notable figures as Wade Hampton III, Benjamin F. Perry, and Samuel McGowan. Pettigrew was appointed chairman of the committee to arrange the inauguration of the newly elected governor: his relative R. F. W. Allston. He was also appointed to the Judiciary Committee.[28]

The Charleston delegation had long been seeking reform of the state judicial system, which had not been altered since the eighteenth century, by the establishment of a separate high court of appeals. The function of such a court was still being exercised by a panel of circuit judges. Charleston, a commercial community, was interested in expediting the wheels of justice and securing swift and clear decisions. It was in support of a bill to this end that Pettigrew made his maiden speech to the House, following a line of veteran speakers. His speech, which was printed in full by the *Charleston Courier*, was couched in just the proper tone of modesty for a freshman member. Pettigrew took an elevated and long-range approach to the question, touching all bases — historical, philosophical, and practical — and alluding to French, English, and American Revolutionary history.[29]

"It was an argument made after close investigation, showing great research, elegant in diction, giving the highest evidence of a finished scholar, one which would have been an honor to an older head than his," the *Courier* reported. "For more than three-quarters of an hour did Mr. Pettigrew keep the ear of the House, not so much by his eloquence as by the great force of his arguments."[30]

If his friends and the newspapers sympathetic to his party are to be believed, Pettigrew attracted considerable notice from this speech. "You would be amused if you could see what a distinguished personage you have become," wrote a friend from Charleston. "Your movements excite public interest." The *Charleston Standard* equated Pettigrew's talents to those of the late Hugh Swinton Legaré, which was a high compliment. B. F. Perry's upcountry paper reported that the speech placed Pettigrew among the first debaters of the House. The measure for which Pettigrew spoke was defeated in the House by seventy-three to thirty-seven. Except for Charleston, the South Carolinians were quite content with their hallowed and economical judicial arrangements, particularly since the rural bar feared that a new court would require them to travel to Columbia.[31]

Pettigrew performed his legislative duties conscientiously. A group of Charleston mechanics enlisted him in behalf of a lien law. He made some researches into the best form of such a law and dealt with other routine matters with like thoroughness. He described his office as "really hard work for those who attended to their duties. I was generally occupied from 10 A.M. to 10 P.M."[32]

In his second annual session, which met in November and December 1857, Pettigrew acted as a sort of floor leader for Governor Allston, being one of the committee of three appointed by the House to receive the governor's messages and making all the motions from the floor to refer the various parts of the message to committees. At this time he was also the governor's military aide. Besides strictly military duties, he performed sundry small official and political tasks for the chief executive, such as advising on appointments and representing him in dealing with an artist whom the state was paying for a statue. Allston offered Pettigrew a place as delegate to the Southern Convention held in Montgomery, Alabama, in 1858, but Pettigrew declined.[33]

At the federal level, Buchanan's triumph in 1856 put the South Carolina Democratic regulars in a good position for patronage. Pettigrew contemplated seeking appointment as secretary of legation at Madrid. He went so far as to secure letters of recommendation from prominent South Carolinians to the president. Perhaps William S. Pettigrew and

James C. Johnston dissuaded him from carrying through the idea with the argument that "one year of residence in America is worth half a dozen in a foreign land if distinction is one's object."[34] Or possibly Pettigrew, for reasons of his own, changed his mind.

It was partly his new interest in politics and partly friendship that embroiled Pettigrew indirectly in one of the most celebrated and controversial Charleston duels of the 1850s.[35] In September 1856 the *Charleston Mercury*, chief organ of the immediatists, published an article strongly attacking, in what was considered by some an excessive and personal manner, some official acts of Judge Andrew Gordon Magrath, one of the conciliatory Democrats, then a candidate for the United States House of Representatives. Magrath was at the time in Aiken at his wife's deathbed. His brother Edward called on Pettigrew and asked him to act as his second and carry a challenge to William R. Taber, Jr., one of the editors of the *Mercury*. Pettigrew agreed, but after Edward Magrath departed he began reflecting that it was unseemly for him as a candidate for the legislature to participate in the affair, especially since he had recently acted as second to another antagonist of Taber.

James Conner (a Charleston lawyer who subsequently became United States district attorney, Confederate brigadier, and attorney general of South Carolina) was at this time Pettigrew's close friend. Troubled by his reflections on his role in the impending duel, Pettigrew called at Conner's lodgings late the same night for advice, proposing that the only solution was to withdraw his candidacy for the legislature. Conner objected to this and said that he would get Pettigrew honorably re-leased from his obligation. Conner went to Edward Magrath, explained the situation, and agreed to act as Magrath's second himself, although he was inexperienced in the requirements of the office.

The next day Taber was accompanied to the field by his principal second, Colonel John Cunningham, who was a political enemy of James Louis Petigru since Nullification days, by two other seconds, and by Alfred Rhett, brother of Edmund Rhett who had written the offensive articles. Edmund and Alfred were the sons of Robert Barnwell Rhett. Magrath was accompanied by Conner, two other gentlemen, and Pettigrew. Pettigrew went because of Conner's last-minute plea that he had not been able to find anyone else with sufficient experience to coach him in his duties as second. Doctor John Bellinger stood by.

Two shots were exchanged without effect, much to the surprise of

Magrath's party, since Taber was a veteran duelist. Pettigrew stood behind Magrath expecting to catch him when he fell. What happened after this was subject to controversy in the Charleston press for the next three months and attracted attention beyond the city.[36] There were enough ambiguities to cloud the reputations of all concerned.

Dr. Bellinger, a neutral, attempted to arrange a settlement after the second shot. Taber expressed willingness to declare that he had not intended to malign Judge Magrath's private character. This proposal was near acceptance when Conner, after consultation with Pettigrew and the other seconds, insisted further that Taber express his regrets for whatever in the articles *was* personal. This Cunningham declined on Taber's behalf.

On the third shot Taber was mortally wounded. The conduct of the third shot was considered highly improper by the friends of both antagonists. Alfred Rhett stood at Taber's side and, just before the firing, shouted loudly. According to Magrath's party he had a pistol held at his side and made a threatening remark to Magrath. By his own account he had no pistol and had spoken a warning to Cunningham, Taber's principal second, to be on guard.

Taber was a popular young man, and Pettigrew had borne him no ill will. He had roomed with Taber shortly before at the Virginia springs. Taber had published the article defending Captain Thomas Petigru the previous year.[37] The young editor's death was considered by many a great tragedy and was construed in some quarters as an attack on the freedom of the press to comment on public officials. Public meetings were held passing resolutions to that effect. The Taber party implied that Conner and his advisers had caused the death by preventing a settlement after the second shot. On the other hand, supporters of Magrath felt that his seconds had not acted firmly enough in his interest at the time of Alfred Rhett's impropriety, some even claiming, on the example of Andrew Jackson, that Conner should have shot Rhett down before allowing the third shot to proceed.

Almost everyone concerned felt obligated to justify his own conduct and the papers were full of "cards" justifying at length the behavior of particular individuals in the affair. Colonel Cunningham, in a "card" published in December in reply to Dr. Bellinger, spoke of a deliberate plot to kill or humiliate Taber. Of the failure of settlement after the second shot, he wrote: "It is universally admitted that Mr. Conner only acted under advisement. . . . Then tell the world, sir, who it was, who warped their judgment and fatally directed their counsels."

Both Conner and Pettigrew then sent notes to Cunningham demanding clarification and apology. Cunningham refused to clarify, on the grounds that he could not allow himself to be required to explain his opinions to anyone, but he did publish the statement that "I have not imputed, nor intended to impute to you, dishonorable motives." This apology was accepted by Pettigrew and Conner, perhaps at the vigorous urging of James Louis Petigru, who did not want to deepen the tragedy by other encounters. In this he possibly teamed up with the elder Rhett, who was a political enemy but a personal friend. Petigru reportedly threatened the editor of the *Courier* with a libel suit if he agitated the matter any further.[38]

This public controversy unfolded during the time Pettigrew was a candidate for and was serving in the legislature. Excitement eventually faded, and Cunningham and Pettigrew seem to have been reconciled in 1857. The next year, however, Pettigrew again contemplated sending a challenge to Cunningham because of an attack he had made on Governor Allston. Apparently this affair did not come off.[39]

Despite James Cathcart Johnston's gift of fifty thousand dollars, Pettigrew decided not to seek the House seat which William Aiken gave up in 1858. Instead he was a candidate for reelection to the General Assembly. It was a strange election, occurring in the midst of the worst epidemic in over forty years when many of the more well-to-do citizens were out of the city. The cooperationist party had passed the peak of its strength with the apparent relentlessness of northern hostility. The radical party in the city was unusually well-financed by a banker so that its machine was more than usually effective. Pettigrew did not canvass but spent the time preceding the election nursing Joseph Blythe Allston back from death's door. The radicals seem to have been especially out for Pettigrew because of his report against the renewal of the slave trade. Legislative elections in Charleston were also influenced by the supporters of various men who hoped to be elected United States senator by the new legislature. At any rate Pettigrew was twenty-seventh in a list of twenty-nine candidates for eighteen House seats from the two city parishes.[40]

His defeat reflected a general debacle of his party that felled more venerable candidates than Pettigrew. James Simons, speaker of the

House in the previous session, was barely reelected. As James Louis Petigru put it, "My friend Johnston has by this time digested the affront the best way he can. If misery loves company, there is plenty of that." Comparing the names of the winners with the losers made the old Federalist shake his head over the failings of democracy and reflect "that there is great advantage in deciding by lot."[41]

This effectively concluded Pettigrew's brief political career. He contemplated being a candidate for the legislature again in 1860 but decided against it. He did continue to collaborate with the Orr party, participating in the local and state conventions and the local canvass in 1860 and keeping Representative William Porcher Miles in Washington satirically informed of the Charleston political situation.[42] But after 1858 Pettigrew was more interested in the art of war than in the arts of statecraft.

Chapter 9

Of North and South

Rejecting that delusive folly which seeks an apology in the conduct or sympathy of others, we should act according to our internal convictions—the only source of true moral strength. —James Johnston Pettigrew, Report of the Minority . . . As Relates to . . . the Slave Trade

Undoubtedly the most noteworthy part of Pettigrew's brief legislative career was that related to combatting the agitation in favor of reopening the foreign slave trade. Reopening had been supported in the early 1850s by the Charleston *Mercury* and *Standard*, by certain papers in the Gulf South, and by some delegates to southern commercial conventions, but the question died away until 1856, when the outgoing South Carolina governor, James H. Adams, raised it again in his message to the legislature by recommending that the state seek the removal of all restrictions from the trade.

The question was largely academic since reopening the trade fell in the constitutional sphere of foreign commerce and would require an act of Congress which would receive minimal support even in the South. The issue was raised by the secessionist party as a means to exacerbate the differences between sections (which it accomplished since northern antislavery elements found this a handy example of southern depravity) and for reasons of ideological consistency. The main points of Adams's argument were that an increased supply of cheap labor would lower the price of southern cotton in world competition with the products of coolie labor in Egypt and India, that multiplying the chance for ownership would be beneficial to the nonslaveholding whites, and that legal and diplomatic branding of the slave trade as piracy was an insult to the South which had to be refuted.[1]

In the 1856 House session the governor's message was referred to a committee ordered to report at the 1857 session. Most of the committee members were in favor of the governor's position. By the behind-the-scenes maneuvering of James L. Orr, it was arranged during the 1857 session for one of the members to resign so that Pettigrew could be appointed in his place and write a minority report opposing reopening. Orr thought that the radical party was raising the question for the sake of agitation, and he wanted, as he told Pettigrew, to force them to defend actively their "monstrous recommendation" for reopening, knowing that the clearer the question became the more public opinion in the state would react against the immediatists.[2]

Pettigrew set to work to prepare a report. His main resources were found in the library of the College of Charleston: the colonial statutes of South Carolina, Bryan Edwards's history of the West Indies, and current statistics on trade and agricultural production. He was not dissuaded from his task by a sly hint from his former associate Leonidas W. Spratt, editor of the *Charleston Standard*, who was the leading spokesman for reopening, that it would be of value to his political future to support removal of restrictions from the trade.[3]

The minority report which Pettigrew wrote and he alone signed was in one sense a mere tour de force on an academic question, but in another sense it was a timely state paper, at the same time realistic and ethical. It is difficult to imagine a more persuasive argument against the slave trade directed at a southern audience.[4]

Pettigrew began with a disquisition that established the proper viewpoint from which the question should be seen. If he were a philanthropist with the welfare of Africa as his main concern, contrasting the condition of the African in Africa and the African in America, he might very well favor reopening the foreign slave trade. As a legislator of South Carolina, however, he could have only one concern, the long-range best interests of the people of the state.[5]

Southerners quite rightly resented the "diseased philanthropy" of outsiders ignorant of southern life:

> A great many worthy persons are honestly disposed to make issues with the North from a spirit of pure combativeness, without regard to the ostensible cause. The undersigned does not boast an entire exemption from this failing, and is hence disposed to view it with leniency in others. There can be no greater mistake in politics than this; combativeness is a capital quality in action; but in

counsel most useless and injurious. In taking a false position, we voluntarily move down from our stronghold and offer the enemy an advantage. . . . The subject is too important to justify us in assuming any ground not fortified by both justice and expediency. . . . it is highly desirable that we should continue to be right [as in previous encounters with the North].[6]

Here Pettigrew not only drove home his point about the slave trade issue but aptly characterized the thrust of all the radical party's agitation, which was to urge the South rashly out of its secure, conservative ground to give battle where the right was by no means certain.

Southerners should not be guided by the temptation to taunt the enemy but by their own convictions—"the only source of true moral strength." Indeed, Pettigrew reflected, by reopening the slave trade southerners would betray their own best moral instincts and transform their settled and paternalistic system of slavery into an imitation of the vices of their worst enemies—the British. The latter, he said, hypocritically attacked slavery while conducting the coolie trade, which combined the worst evils of slavery without its southern mitigations with the worst evils of capitalistic exploitation. "Far from furnishing an example, the conduct of these abolitionists should arouse in us only those feelings which are inspired by the union of a systematic cruelty with hollow hypocrisy," he said.[7]

Having thus set the stage on which the whole question should be viewed by the southern public, Pettigrew proceeded to demolish the arguments in favor of the proposal. The branding of the slave trade in treaties and laws as piracy was not an insult to southern slavery. Piracy was private warfare, a *malum prohibitum*, once legal and now prohibited, not a *malum in se*, a thing illegal by its nature. Washington and the other great southerners of the early republic had opposed the trade without feeling themselves branded as pirates for buying and owning slaves. Southern slaveholders were not pirates since they had not made slaves out of free men. It was ridiculous to agitate the question on this theoretical ground since reopening of the trade could not win the support of ten percent of the people even in South Carolina and could only divide and weaken the South, while the object of the reopening was supposedly to strengthen and unite the South.[8]

As for the alleged need of more slaves to increase production and bring down the price of southern cotton in world competition, Pettigrew pointed out that cheap laborers were not the same thing as cheap, efficient labor. Newly imported "barbarian" laborers would be far less efficient than native slaves but would cost just as much to support. Moreover, "slovenly barbarians" would corrupt and make less productive the industrious native-born Negroes. Further, an increase in the supply of slaves would inevitably cause a fall in their value, taking money out of every owner's pocket.[9]

All this was designed to secure a *cheaper* price for cotton that, even if it were achieved, would only hurt the South for the benefit of its enemies:

> Thus, after years of toil, spent in convincing the world of the propriety of the Slave Trade, or, in trampling their prejudices under foot—after revolutionizing and remodelling, with infinite risk, one of our most important social institutions; after filling our fair land with hideous barbarians, we find the barren result of our labors to be an increase in the profits of our bitterest foes, whose only sympathy with us is through the pocket. Oh! most lame and impotent conclusion! . . . So much for the argument of cheap cotton.[10]

The notion that South Carolina's prosperity had been hurt by the movement of population to the West he regarded as false. True, hundreds of thousands of Carolinians were now contributing their talents to new commonwealths, but when Pettigrew surveyed the state he saw prosperity and bustle everywhere. Moreover, demand for two of the state's three main crops, rice and Sea Island cotton, was not much affected by competition. For the third crop, upland cotton, a new supply of slaves could only increase the comparative advantage of the West over South Carolina, since the advantage was based on fresh lands and not on labor. Additionally, Pettigrew did not think that Asian and Egyptian cotton would ever compete in quality with American.[11]

Pettigrew also branded as false the argument that cheaper slaves would allow the poor white man to become an owner. Since the poor white man's chief wealth was his labor, the cheapening of labor would cheapen his chief asset. Slaveholders and nonslaveholders alike would be harmed by reopening the traffic. Pettigrew chided the proponents for descending to the level of abolitionist demaguery in asserting that the opposition to reopening the trade came from aristocratic owners who wanted to monopolize the advantages of slavery for themselves.[12]

Having thus confronted his opponents' arguments, Pettigrew went on to paint a picture of the social damage to be expected from the importation of a horde of uncivilized Africans into the midst of southern society. In making his point Pettigrew employed the conventional American-European concept of the native black African — a lesser breed without the Law, to whom cruelty, theft, violence, and falsehood were virtues, and disorder, rapine, and inhumanity were the customary mode of life. Such laborers would require brute force to control, and the good relations previously existing between master and slave would be destroyed. Masters would be brutalized, and civil life would be soured by constant unease. Here Pettigrew drew upon the history of the West Indies and of colonial South Carolina itself, itemizing the brutal measures of slave control ensconced in the law of the colony which he felt his readers had forgotten ever existed because they had been so long out of use. These brutal measures, Pettigrew said, existed not because the South Carolinians' ancestors were a brutal people, but because in spite of themselves they had been driven to strong measures by the necessity to control the barbarian horde.[13]

Then Pettigrew reviewed the history of South Carolina's own opposition to the slave trade, pointing out how the colonial assembly had frequently protested, restricted, and taxed British slave importations and endeavored to promote white immigration. He suggested that the opposition of South Carolina to federal power to suppress the trade in the Philadelphia convention of 1787 was just that — an opposition to federal power and not an endorsement of the trade. He pointed out that South Carolinians did not engage in the trade themselves but left it to New Englanders whom they held in contempt. He wrote: "It is apparent from this sketch, that the injurious tendency of the importation of barbarism, is not an idea originating with Yankee abolitionists, and forced upon the reluctant South as a stigma; it was recognized in Carolina as far back as 1714. . . . There was no hint of abolition, no distrust of slavery, but these sterling citizens had sufficient wisdom to perceive a vast difference between a system of civilized, and a system of barbarian slavery."[14]

In thus setting forth explicitly his negative view of the importation of more slaves into the South, Pettigrew implicitly described his positive view of southern slavery as it then existed. Actually his portrait of the potential and past evils of slavery veered dangerously toward the critiques of abolitionists (except that the abolitionists offered the southerner no satisfactory alternative to the evils they decried). But Pettigrew was taking his stand for slavery as he found it and believed it to be—characterized by peaceful, industrious, and virtuous slaves and honorable planters motivated by self-interest, custom, community sentiment, and moral training toward paternalism. Slavery was now less burdensome for both master and slave than it had ever been. A half a century of civilizing effort and intercourse would be destroyed by the reopening of the foreign trade. All the progress of the past half-century would be washed away. Not only would this be against the owners' economic and civic interest, but (and it was clear this was a moral consideration Pettigrew was invoking in his fellow southerners) it would worsen the lot of the native slave by bringing harsher treatment and causing him to retrogress from the civilizational progress he had made. This was something southern slaveholders, if they were true to their own best moral convictions, could not do to the loyal, native-born slaves who were under their protection. The absence of the slave trade, Pettigrew suggested, was the reason that the blacks had increased in the South while suffering a high mortality elsewhere. This multiplication was both the result of and the proof of kind treatment in the South, which in turn was possible because of the closing of the trade.[15]

Amelioration in slavery had been the partial result of a number of factors, Pettigrew felt: the general progress of the Western world away from physical cruelty, liberty for the white man since the Revolution which made him free from "that petty tyranny, so universally characteristic of those who have themselves a master," but chiefly the civilizing of the Negro population.[16] The slaves were not restrained from revolt by an ignorance of their strength but from an intelligent perception of their weakness and, here was the important point, by the blacks' own internalization of the concept of order. Pettigrew remarked at length upon the great power of the concept of law to create social peace:

> The Americans afford an illustration of this principle. Perhaps no nation on the globe is more high tempered, restless, excitable and violent in resistance to illegitimate authority, than the

inhabitants of these Southern States; yet, none submit with more cheerfulness and alacrity to the commands of the law, however disagreeable. The American General at the head of a conquering army in Mexico, with a prostrate nation at his feet, was ordered to lay down his command and appear before a court martial; he unhesitatingly obeyed the mandate; Mexicans were unable to comprehend such conduct; an American would have been incapable of comprehending any other; the one had been educated to law, the other to anarchy. Our slaves have been subjected to the same influences as ourselves; they obey, without question, the law of their position; and as a remarkable consequence, there has not been a commotion in the slave population of this, the most decidedly slave state in the Union, since the suppression of the Trade, with the single exception of 1822, which was entirely owing to emissaries from the West Indies; and was, moreover, much exaggerated in the reports of the time. Nor is it probable that another will ever take place. A partial outbreak they, of course, will not make; and the same knowledge which would fit them for a general insurrection, will most effectually deter them, by showing its utter futility. With the introduction of savages, a new night would descend; the very ignorance by which they would be incapacitated for a grand scheme, would urge them to outrages, individual and concerted, of a minor character, for which an unknown tongue would afford convenient means of concealment. Thefts, murders, plantation riots, would be the order of the day, until the old West India system was introduced, to which we would soon be driven.

Such would be the natural effect of the realization of this project, upon slaves, slaveholders, and the community at large.[17]

At the 1857 legislative session, the majority of the committee filed a report which supported Governor Adams's arguments and bolstered them with statistical tables. The majority recommended resolutions asking the state's senators and representatives to seek abrogation of all parts of treaties and repeal of all laws regulating or prohibiting the slave trade or declaring it piracy. The House, after hearing the majority and minority reports, laid the question on the table without debate. The Senate postponed consideration indefinitely.[18] There the slave trade question rested officially.

Pettigrew had one hundred copies of his report printed and mailed them to friends and prominent persons across the South. Requests for copies poured in at such a rate that he had to have one thousand more printed. In the second printing he appended a brief note replying to some of the published criticisms of his report, particularly to the charge that he was a wealthy aristocrat who wanted to monopolize the benefits of slave labor for his own class. *De Bow's Review* of New Orleans, which favored the reopening, carried Pettigrew's report in full as the ablest argument on the other side.[19]

The minority report attracted wide attention and discussion. The *Columbia Carolinian* characterized it as "eminently correct in tone, sentiment, and conclusions. Wise and conservative in character, it probably reflects the sentiment of the State in general." The *Winnsboro Register* found it "not only the ablest paper we have read on this subject but the ablest . . . made for years on any subject to our Legislature." The *Carolina Spartan* found the report "creditable to mature statesmanship and destined to conclude the argument." The *St. Louis Herald* quoted and praised Pettigrew at length.[20]

Beyond the South the *New York Times* discussed Pettigrew's argument and called the author a "subtle thinker" and a "well-grounded political economist." Horace Greeley's *New York Tribune* paused in the midst of an antisouthern diatribe to comment that "the author of this minority report . . . is a great deal more than a match for the majority."[21]

Orr wrote Pettigrew from Washington that the report was "perfectly conclusive." It had defeated Adams's "nefarious proposition" and had made Pettigrew an enviable reputation within and without the state, Orr felt. Complimentary letters came in from Wade Hampton III and United States Representative William W. Boyce. From beyond the state, friendly messages were received from President Swain of the University of North Carolina, Pettigrew's friend Daniel M. Barringer, Thomas C. Reynolds, later the Confederate governor of Missouri, Roger A. Pryor of Virginia, and from friends, relatives, slight acquaintances, and strangers all over the South. Matthew Fontaine Maury felt "as proud of it as though I had helped to make it. . . . We greatly need men who can write such papers." William Pettigrew found the report talked of in Mobile and New Orleans when he visited the Lower South in January 1858. Caroline North Pettigrew wrote her congratulations and reported that when she read the report aloud to a small planter of the Bonarva neighborhood in North Carolina, he "gave a humph of approval at every pause."[22] Pettigrew's report was used for ammunition in arguments all over the South in legislative halls, conventions, courthouses, and crossroads taverns.

In a critical note the *Charleston Mercury* put its editorial finger on the major flaw of Pettigrew's argument from the point of view of southern policy: "It relates only to South Carolina and does not consider the slave trade question as it effects the South as a whole." This was true enough, as Pettigrew admitted in the note appended to the second printing, for he had calculated only the disadvantages to South Carolina from the reopening of the foreign slave trade, not the possible advantages to new southwestern states and the southern position as a whole.[23]

The slave trade question continued to be agitated at some of the southern commercial conventions of the late 1850s, but by 1859 the issue had been dropped, probably by tacit agreement among the secession leaders that it was too divisive. Pettigrew's arguments doubtless helped put the issue to rest. The Confederate States Constitution of 1861, forbidding unequivocally the foreign slave trade, vindicated Pettigrew's representation of the preponderance of southern opinion.

Pettigrew was one of the fairly large class of young southerners who benefited from the profits of the plantation economy without having to be involved directly in the management of a slave labor force. In his own name he owned one slave who remained permanently with his brother William in North Carolina. Since he regarded this man as a special legacy from his father, he took some interest in what he considered his moral well-being, inquired after him in his letters, and brought him a present from Europe. At the time he was serving as Governor Allston's military aide, Pettigrew hired a slave as body servant. In 1859 after Pettigrew sailed to Europe for the second time, this man, Nat, asked James Louis Petigru to write his master "that he was already counting the days till he should see him again." "Nat, is that sincere, or does it come from the teeth outwards," asked Petigru, who was known as a protector of mistreated slaves and free Negroes. "Sir," Nat replied, "it comes from my heart."[24]

Nat and his wife were left in charge of Pettigrew's Tradd Street house during the Civil War with the occasional superintendence of James Louis Petigru. For a time at Charleston Pettigrew also had with him one of his brother William's slaves, Jack. Jack sailed on a schooner from North Carolina to Charleston and stayed with Pettigrew for some months while the Charleston physicians attempted to cure a disabling hand infection that doctors in North Carolina and Baltimore had failed to cure.[25]

The black man to whom Pettigrew was closest was his brother Charles's slave Peter who accompanied him as body servant during the Civil War, to Pettigrew's entire satisfaction. It was probably Peter who, nine years after Pettigrew's death, called several times at the office of a North Carolina newspaper editor to view a picture of Pettigrew which the editor had.[26]

In his personal life, Pettigrew was only marginally concerned with the day-to-day workings of the plantation system. Yet because of the power of the extended family, he thought automatically of himself as a member of the planter class and spoke without reflection of northern threats to "our property."[27] In this he was typical of thousands of southerners, particularly the offspring of the planter class, who were psychologically though not physically a part of that class.

The Negro slavery system was a given of Johnston Pettigrew's world. Even to expect him not to defend it is to put matters in an unhistorical light. Pettigrew was capable to a degree of analyzing the past, present, and potential evils of slavery, but as a practical matter he could envision no bearable alternative, economic or social.[28] Did the educated New Englander question the Industrial Revolution? Yes, in just exactly the same way that Pettigrew questioned slavery. He could reflect on the evil consequences of it but could find no way as a practical matter to give up its benefits. In his mind to disturb slavery as it was or to increase and unsettle it by new importations were alike intolerable threats to the social order.

A curious private postscript to the slave trade controversy indicates the degree to which Pettigrew's celebrated report was no more than political tactics on the surface of southern life and perhaps the degree to which he was ensnared in the necessities of a system that could not be touched. During a visit to Washington in 1859, the same trip on which he saw a dramatization of *Uncle Tom's Cabin* in Philadelphia, Pettigrew encountered a naval officer who had seen much service on the coast of Africa. "To judge by his account," Pettigrew wrote, "you would think that this traffic, which we are accustomed to regard as the most horrible, was on the contrary a beneficent institution of the deity, and that the 'Middle Passage,' far from being a succession of cruelties, suffering and death, was one scene of cheerfulness and festivity. How essentially different are the opposing views of every matter and how absolutely necessary to hear both sides." [29]

When he had first gone to Charleston in 1849 Pettigrew had been struck by the military aspect and efficiency of the armed city watch, the like of which he had not encountered before. He was inclined to approve of this since the slaves in the city "are in a majority and are liable in a seaport town to be much corrupted." To James C. Johnston, to whom he described Charleston's patrol, this was just another example of South Carolina foolishness: Mr. Johnston pictured the slave-watch "attacking a bunch of poor negroes about like Don Quixote after a flock of sheep." At his plantations in the Roanoke River valley of North Carolina, Mr. Johnston pointed out, there were two hundred Negroes to each white man, and he did not even bother to lock his door at night. "It would be better to show the negroes that we are not afraid of them and show the abolitionists that the negroes are attached to their masters." The Charleston foolishness was "perfectly characteristic of a city whose inhabitants are all Knight Errants." [30]

Pettigrew at first had been inclined to agree with Mr. Johnston that the South Carolinians were distastefully "conceited, consequential, and aristocratic." He had found that they wasted their time in "slavery meetings, disunion speeches, and subjects of like unprofitable nature." In 1849 the South Carolinians had reminded him of "our ancestors in the days of religious oppression, whose zeal and firmness rose in proportion to the power and bigotry of their persecutors." [31] Pettigrew's increasing accommodation with South Carolina after his return from Europe was on the one hand a personal adjustment and on the other a perfect microcosm of the South drawing together and putting aside its internal differences under outside pressure.

In 1848 before he had thought of going to Charleston, Pettigrew went to New York to see an artist about a portrait of his late father. He called on the painter who had been recommended and introduced himself. "I knew you were a Southerner," the artist told him. "I can always tell them." "It is a great pleasure to me," Pettigrew reflected, "that I have never yet been taken for a Yankee or a Locofoco." [32]

When he visited Washington before his departure for Europe, just after he had been complaining of the sectional feeling he had found in South Carolina, Pettigrew observed Congress in session on the Wilmot Proviso. The Wilmot question, for Pettigrew as for many moderate southerners, put things in an entirely new light. The new illumination was heightened when he visited Boston before sailing and found that there the question occupied much more public attention than in the South. "Anti-slavery sermons, anti-slavery lectures and anti-slavery fairs are advertised every day." He found it surprising and incomprehensible that the Bostonians should be so exercised. On another trip to Boston five years later, the same phenomena of northern preoccupation with southern society again surprised him. "Our mutual acquaintances at Boston," he wrote J. C. Johnston, "persons connected with the College and innocent as babes unborn, of all political knowledge, yet rave about the Nebraska Bill, without even having read it over."[33]

After the controversies of 1850 Pettigrew accepted it calmly as a fact of life and death that the Union would eventually dissolve. The only questions were when, whether the North or the South would secede, and the nature of the war that would ensue.[34]

While in Berlin in 1850 he expected war to break out in America and was prepared to return and do his part. It was not that he was anxious for this result or would do anything to promote it himself. On the contrary, he later associated with the conciliatory political faction in South Carolina and worked for Buchanan, whose election he correctly believed would give the Union another four-year lease on life. But the perspective acquired by his sojourn in Europe intensified Pettigrew's identity as a southerner. From Europe it became more forcefully apparent that America was made up of two uncongenial nations. In Europe Pettigrew's subtle and perceptive mind sensed the movement of history carrying along the Yankee, the Englishman, and the German toward centralization and reform and thus threatening extinction for the older culture of the South. Indeed it was this perception that underlay Pettigrew's affection for the Italians and Spanish, who represented to him a countervailing tendency toward more traditional values. In 1851, speaking of Italy and France (before he had been to Spain), Pettigrew wrote: "These two countries have raised my enthusiasm to the utmost; because they . . . present more that is worthy of admiration, but also because they resemble us exceedingly. . . . Our Yankee friends resemble the English and North Germans more."[35]

The American community in Berlin, overrepresenting the two extremes of Boston and Charleston, was more sharply divided than the home country. "As for the abominable Yankees," Pettigrew wrote from Berlin in the midst of a criticism of South Carolina radicals, "I believe them with a few exceptions to be the most despicable of the human race, and my contact with them abroad has convinced me." The conversation of New Englanders with Europeans, he found, "consists mostly of bragging about the United States and abusing a certain portion of it in order to hide if possible their own defects." One American in particular kept urging a German scholar at Berlin to write a pamphlet against slavery, despite the German's insistence that he was not familiar with American conditions and had heard only one side of the question. The only American newspaper obtainable in Berlin was the *New York Tribune*, "filled with dirty abuse of the South." Because of all this, Pettigrew requested his brother to send him books and pamphlets from America giving another view to pass on to his German friends.[36]

As early as 1851, at the age of twenty-two, Pettigrew had written:

The political aspect of our unfortunate Country gives also the greatest concern. Precipices around us on all sides, and amid the universal decline of principle among the younger politicians, it is difficult to say whether there be more danger in resistance or submission. In a few years the great *National* men, such as Mr. Clay, Webster &c, will have died and the best we can hope for is that their places will be filled by Fillmore &c, who . . . having gained a certain position, see that a dissolution, with its possible consequences, is not a trifling subject. In South Carolina . . . many a glance was cast toward England . . . but all this is a sad deception, and in the event of dissolution we must be prepared to trust to our own strength alone.[37]

In 1859 Pettigrew visited Philadelphia, where he moved in the best society among Gambles and Biddles who were his distant relatives. He found his northern kin polite but lacking in warmth. "How great a difference between them and my Southern relatives of the same degree! I found it impossible to squeeze out 'cousin.' "[38]

On this same trip to Philadelphia Pettigrew went to see a performance of *Uncle Tom's Cabin*.

We expected to see great outbursts of feeling and to have our sensibilities very much shocked by the exhibition, but not a word of it. The moral effect of the exhibition on the audience (except the negro gallery) was positively nothing. Even when Uncle Tom comes in to be killed, the mirth of the auditors could not be restrained when one of his jailors said to the other "Git out of the way, nigger." . . . the dramatising takes the edge entirely off the novel. Of course it is perfectly absurd to hear a man declaiming on the stage about the equality of the negro, with the white man, and to see at the same time his coloured brethren stowed away in a dark little gallery in the North Eastern corner of the House.[39]

By 1860 Pettigrew was hoping that men would begin to look beyond their noses "and rise to the position of regarding the Southern States as a Nation among Nations." Like thousands of other originally antisecession southerners he accepted Lincoln's election as proof that northern hostility was permanent. "You know I am no fire-eater, but . . . the continuance of the present form of the Constitution under a settled anti-slavery rule, is a consummation to be avoided by all means short of destruction," he wrote his brother in the fall.[40]

Old men like James Louis Petigru and James Cathcart Johnson, whose sensibilities had been formed in the Era of Good Feelings, thought of the United States as a network of virtuous, national-minded, republican gentlemen like themselves. They looked at their southern neighbors turning increasingly to a romantic sectionalism and reacted negatively. In a way their reaction was shortsighted because they noted only the changes around them in the South and not the changes in the North that were in part a cause of the southern changes. They did not take account of the fact that gentlemen like themselves, with whom they had once collaborated in holding the Union together, no longer ruled in the North, or that the Union to which they clung as the legacy of the Founders no longer meant to the northern leaders what it meant to them but had been transformed in meaning by industrialization and reform.

Petigru regarded the South Carolina radicalism to which he was opposed as the product of too much democracy, as the result of foolish notions of majority rule carried to extremes. "That the Majority are wicked is a truth that passed long since into a proverb," Petigru wrote during the secession crisis. Profoundly conservative, he realized that the South was most likely to lose what it valued by being too aggressive in its own defense, by provoking a war that would allow the stronger outside force to stamp out its civilization with a ruthlessness that could never be justified in peace. This was stated most vividly by Petigru's personal friend and political opposite number, Robert Barnwell Rhett, the radical, who said: "Mr. Petigru was essentially a conservative — conservative in all his views of society, government and religion. . . . He feared change, for change in governments too often, he knew, produced lawlessness in power . . . [and] broke off those habits of submission and support to government, which often constitute its strongest elements of stability." Like thousands of the best men of the South, Rhett continued, Petigru could not bring himself to believe in the hatred and hostility of the North for the South, which seemed so much against both the North's duty and its interest, until the hostility was unequivocally revealed in war.[41]

Unlike their elders, the political ideas of Johnston Pettigrew's generation were formed in a different context, one in which outside attack rather than the necessity of union was the salient feature. Johnston Pettigrew in person exemplifies what the South underwent between the Mexican War and secession — the smoothing over of internal contradictions, the knitting together of a unity to combat the outside threat, and an increasingly aggressive elaboration of those features that were peculiarly southern. Pettigrew's conscious political life overlapped the era of heightened sectionalism exactly.

Although exaggerated by the South's own version of the culturewide romanticism of the 1850s, the southern qualities which Pettigrew personified so well were not creations of a new sectionalism but were as old as America itself. The emphasis on military values can be clearly seen in the officer corps of the Revolution, although it had taken on an even more militant cast with the exuberant expansionism of the Jacksonian era. (Unlike Johnston Pettigrew, James Cathcart Johnston was not troubled in sleep by dreams of empire.) The emphasis on aristocratic virtues, decentralization, and the agrarian way of life that included Negro slavery were implicit in the Jeffersonian philosophy of the South from its beginnings in eighteenth-century Virginia.

One generation of southerners had made a Revolution. The next generation, that of Ebenezer Pettigrew and James Cathcart Johnston, had inherited postwar chaos, had been preoccupied with material building, and had no philosophy except unionism—the cautious, visceral impulse toward stability. The men of Johnston Pettigrew's generation, with the freedom won by their grandfathers and the leisure and position inherited from their fathers, were ready to preserve, elaborate, consolidate, and extend the civilization that had grown up in the southern three-quarters of the settled United States.

James Louis Petigru's grandson described many years after the Civil War the South Carolinians among whom he grew up:

> Broad-minded men liked them, even if they did not approve of them, and timid men, who hesitated to form convictions or to express them, feared these self-centered masters who asserted their beliefs with boldness and absolute conviction that they were right. Their strength of conviction on political questions came partly from the fact that the chief political issues of their day were questions which affected each one of them in his home and family life. Thus they took the lead naturally in the movement to destroy a nation which, it was plain, was making up its mind to destroy them.[42]

The decision of the South Carolinians to strike for independence was, in their own minds, a product of the same spirit which led the American colonists to resist the placing of a small tax on their commerce by the British Parliament. The strenuous insistence on abstract legal rights and the martial sense of individual and collective honor, which guided the planters as a class in 1861, was to them the Revolutionary spirit, preserved and handed down intact, not a distant myth but a living memory. Slavery provided the occasion, but a long history of political education in the necessity for bold insistence on the self-government of communities and in suspicion of outside authorities provided the impulse and direction.

Secession was not motivated immediately by fear of the slaves, for which there was less reason, as Pettigrew argued, than at any previous time. More directly the fear was of the power and instability of the North, the reactions of which seemed increasingly less familiar and predictable. That was the lesson of the John Brown affair. "We are at the mercy of any little band of filibusters," Pettigrew wrote his brother William after the Brown raid. His usually mild and moderate brother agreed.[43]

The challenge was not imaginary but concrete, direct, and personal. The instinctive response of the southerner to a challenger was to hurl the challenge back in his teeth. Southerners suffered from an excess of self-confidence, not an excess of self-doubt. They had always been masters in their own households, and they would continue to be so as long as it was in their power.

"It is a matter of perfect indifference, whether foreigners approve or disapprove of our internal arrangements," Pettigrew wrote once in reference to the favorable reception given in Charleston to an English writer who had approved slavery, "and their presuming to give an opinion upon the matter at all, strikes me as the highest impertinence. For this reason the conduct of Mr. [Robert] Toombs, in condescending to argue the question before the Boston people filled me with disgust. If the Boston people are capable of hearing the question discussed before them, it seems to me that they are capable of deciding it after the discussion is heard."[44]

There had originally been a considerable overlap of cultural and political tendencies between the South and the North, at least the non–New England North. Just as old ways of thinking were being swallowed up by a new ethos in the North, they grew in strength and salience in the South. Southerners of Pettigrew's generation faced the choice of seeing the values of their civilization wither away or of making a gamble for political independence which could guarantee their survival into the foreseeable future. Being the kind of men they were, it was inevitable that they would put aside even the most persistent doubts and choose a bold and uncertain gamble for independence over a timid and certain path to extinction.

Chapter 10

Of Arms and Men

It was on the night of the 4th of July, 1859, that I crossed Mount Cenis, on the way to Turin. Though the precise date was a matter of accident, its associations were in happy unison with the object of the journey and the sentiments which prompted me. It was my birthday; but far more, it was the day that ushered into life my native land—a day ever memorable in the history of the world—not so much because it had added another to the family of nations, as because it had announced, amid the crack of rifles and the groans of expiring patriots, the great principle, that every people has an inalienable right of self-government, without responsibility to aught on earth, save such as may be imposed by a due respect for the opinions of mankind. Once more this great battle was to be fought, no longer in the wilds of the American forest, but on land renowned through all ages, and rendered sacred by recollections of intellect, art and religion. Now, as then, a tyrant empire had, with vain boastings, poured her legions upon a devoted land; now, as then, the oppressed few, forgetting their dissensions, had risen to burst their chains asunder; and now, too, as then, a great nation, the generous French, were rushing with disciplined battalions to aid struggling, expiring humanity. It was certainly humiliating that so large a portion of Europe should have remained unsympathizing spectators of the contest. On the part of an American, acquiescence in such neutrality would have been treason against nature. Inspired by these sentiments, I was hurrying with what speed I might to offer my services to the Sardinian Government, and to ask the privilege of serving as a volunteer in her armies—perhaps a foolish errand, if measured by the ideas of this unromantic century. No emotion of my life was ever so pure, so free from every shade of conscientious doubt or selfish consideration. At the distance of four thousand miles, we were happily ignorant of the underhand intrigues, if any there were, which so frequently disgust one in the turmoil of politics. I saw but the spectacle of an injured people struggling, as America had done, to throw off the yoke of a foreign and, comparatively, barbarous oppressor, and as we passed battalion after battalion of brave French, slowly ascending the mountain, I felt toward them all the fervor of youth, fired by the grateful traditions of eighty years ago. —James Johnston Pettigrew, opening passage of Notes on Spain

Fatalism, the appeal of military glory, a conviction of the inevitability of a civil war, and a consciousness of his own latent powers of leadership led Pettigrew deliberately to prepare himself for a role in the coming crisis in America.

> Bad times seem to be approaching [Pettigrew told his brother William in 1856] and it is time for everyone to look out to windward. I am doing, that, as well as I can, but there is no telling where the storm is coming from. For that reason, I am preparing myself to assume a position, if there be necessity, for in such an event, those who depend upon the negative power and qualification, so acceptable in peace, will be in a forlorn state indeed. Throughout the land there [seems to be] . . . less of vigorous, independent character than ever before in the history of the Country, and a firm, active character is of more importance in such a crisis, than any other gift.[1]

Pettigrew was in part inspired by his own newly discovered abilities. That year he was invited to join the Washington Light Infantry, a Charleston militia company which traced its traditions back to Colonel William Washington's command in the American Revolution. In the spring of 1856, the company combined maneuvers and patriotic observance by marching two hundred fifty miles to the upcountry to erect a monument at the site of the battle of Cowpens. This ten-day, twenty-five-mile-a-day excursion, made with full arms and equipment, taught Pettigrew a great deal about marching, camping in the open, and himself:

> With the exception of the Captain, one of the Lieutenants, & myself, every person at one time or another, was compelled to take refuge in the waggons [*sic*] to cure blistered feet. Each day's march improved me, and the knapsack at last became only a good balance-weight. For some reason or other, it had been thought,

that I would break down, and the fact of holding out through rain and sun, and being a strict disciplinarian, earned me quite a reputation, so that they say I have mistaken my profession. About the latter part I cannot say: the *profession* of a soldier has always appeared to me tiresome and odious in the highest degree, but I am sure I could do something in time of *war*, on account of my powers of endurance, and physical elasticity, which Napoleon says is the first requisite of a warrior.[2]

This military exercise also taught him a great deal about human nature:

Many persons, whom I had thought well of before, proved quite deficient in stamina, when tried, and unreliable, and one fact was conclusively shown[,] that the quality of a soldier depends more upon his elevated tone, than any of us had suspected; not that birth had any thing to do with the matter, but the requisite, was that species of qualification called character, which may be found in one rank of society as well as another. It was also surprising to see how quickly the men found out each other's true value, and how soon mere popularity gave way before the more valuable recommendation of knowledge and capacity.[3]

When R. F. W. Allston was inaugurated as governor in December 1856, he appointed Pettigrew the senior of his ten aides-de-camp with the rank of lieutenant colonel of the militia. That Pettigrew took his duties quite seriously is indicated by the fact that he thenceforward kept a horse and a servant, paid out several hundred dollars for a uniform, sword, and equestrian trappings, and purchased a quantity of military books which he studied assiduously.[4]

His chief duty was to arrange the governor's itinerary for the annual muster and review of the militia in each district of South Carolina, accompanying or preceding the chief executive on his tour of inspection. This duty consumed the entire summers of both 1857 and 1858. It took Pettigrew, by rail or horseback, into every part of the state, introduced him officially and socially to the gentry everywhere, and acquainted him with the people and resources of every region. Besides reviewing the entire assembled militia—infantry, cavalry, and artillery—of each district, Pettigrew kept a rigorous social schedule and was required to make public speeches, bettering his predecessors by making an oration to the German settlers at Walhalla in their native tongue.[5] Although the form was doubtless of little importance to him, Pettigrew acquired the right to be addressed throughout the state as "Colonel Pettigrew." When Allston's term as governor expired, however, Pettigrew returned to the ranks of the Washington Light Infantry.

Pettigrew had continued to keep a close watch on affairs in Europe. In 1859, when war broke out between the Austrians and the French and Sardinians, which would result in the liberation of part of northern Italy from the Hapsburg empire, Pettigrew decided to join the struggle. Probably he had long been hoping for such an opportunity—to repay Italy for the priceless gifts it had given him and to acquire experience that would be of value in the coming struggle in America.

He hastened to Washington to secure letters of recommendation and then continued to New York from which he sailed on 8 June. He arrived in Liverpool on 18 June and was in Paris three days later. In France he presented his letters of recommendation (to the authorities from Matthew F. Maury and John Y. Mason, and to Marshal Murat from a Charlestonian who knew him) and attempted unsuccessfully to enter the French service. After more than a week in Paris, he moved on to Italy. Pettigrew had brought with him a complete military outfit— two pistols, spyglass, compass, boots, sash, bugle, and a uniform costing two hundred dollars.[6]

Pettigrew had known all along he was racing against time, for the campaign promised to be short and decisive. "If the Austrians are easily beaten my chances are nothing," he told Henry Deas Lesesne before his departure. "If the reverse takes place, the volunteer stock will rise." [7]

On 4 July, both American Independence Day and his thirty-first birthday, he crossed into Italy, a trip that he later described romantically in the opening passage of his book. The next day he reached Turin, the capital of Sardinia. The day after that he sent a note to Count Cavour, the prime minister, requesting an opportunity to serve in the Sardinian forces. He stressed that he was not an opportunistic adventurer and that he wanted neither a salary nor a command, but that he wished to be of use as a volunteer aide to some general officer in the advance. The following day an armistice was signed in the field as a result of the battle of Solferino. Cavour left to join the army, promising to speak to the king about Pettigrew's application. On 13 July, Pettigrew was summoned by Count Bardesono, Cavour's private secretary, who told him that in view of the armistice and the evident intention of the French to carry the war for Italian liberation no further, nothing else could be done. Should war break out again before Pettigrew left Europe, Bardesono promised, his application would be reconsidered. Pettigrew's brother later wrote that he was to be given a colonel's commission, but there is no direct evidence of this. "I have lost a glorious opportunity of distinguishing myself & seeing the world in its grandest phase," Pettigrew lamented.[8]

His desire for military education did not go entirely unrequited, however. He had observed troop movements in Italy firsthand, and he spent some time intermittently in Paris, "the metropolis of war," studying the French army. Several contemporaries of Pettigrew made much of his military studies at Paris and the knowledge he acquired there. There is little specific evidence detailing what he did, but apparently he mingled with French officers and learned something about organization, discipline, morale, tactics, and logistics. That he received lessons of value is evident from the authority with which he discussed details of the Italian war in his book and by some of his ideas and actions during the Civil War. He also learned much in Spain of military interest when he visited there.[9]

Pettigrew prolonged his stay in Europe in hope that the inconclusive Italian war would break out again. This seemed highly likely according to Pettigrew's shrewd analysis of the motives of the various powers involved, both governments and publics, and what the war revealed about future conflict. He correctly predicted that the situation at the end of 1859 was unstable and that Italy would liberate itself eventually with Sardinia as leader. The war did not break out again before Pettigrew returned home in the fall of 1859. In 1860 he considered going over once more if he could get an advance guarantee of a commission from the Sardinian minister in Washington.[10] Events in America overruled this mission, however.

Leaving Turin, Pettigrew did some further traveling in Italy, examining rice plantations to pick up what information he could for South Carolina. Thereafter he was intermittently in France, but the greater part of his four months in Europe in 1859 he spent reacquainting himself with Spain.

During this second trip he began forming the idea of Spain which he would later put into a book. Pettigrew's account of his entry into the country through a Pyrenean pass encapsulates this idea:

> Suddenly turning, I saw above me the Port de Benasque — a simple split in the rocky wall, just wide enough for a loaded mule to pass, and not more than ten feet in length. We ascended a stair-case of zig-zags, some fifteen feet each, entered the pass, and beheld one of the grandest views in the world. It was Spain! noble, romantic Spain! Adieu pretty landscapes! meandering brooks and verdant prairies! luxurious couches and artistic meals! Adieu to the circean enticements of Europe! Adieu to a civilization which reduces men to machines, which sacrifices half that is stalwart and individual in humanity to the false glitter of centralization, and to the luxurious enjoyments of a manufacturing, money age! Welcome *dura tellus Iberia!* Welcome to your sunny plains, your naked mountains, your hardy sons and your beautiful daughters! your honored cities, sacred by the memorials of a dozen rival civilizations, and your fields watered by the chivalric blood of as many contending races! [11]

He spent a month in Andalusia going over old sights and new ones: "Andalusia is the only part of the world that gives me an idea of what Paradise must be. . . . of Andalusia a very respectable Heaven might be made with a few alterations. To the fertility and warmth of our own country, it adds an entire exemption from Malaria and its attendant ills." [12] Andalusia was the South, without yellow fever and malaria, without slavery and the Negro, without any encroachments of Yankee puritanism and materialism — paradise indeed!

He also saw much of other parts of the Spanish kingdom, although he was unable to find out what had become of Horatio Perry and his Spanish bride. In Toledo Pettigrew purchased a pair of poniards made from steel cast before his very eyes. "I have no doubt they will prove equal to any emergency," he commented. "I only hope there will be no necessity for trying them." [13]

Of his departure from Spain, he later wrote: "To say that I regretted the necessity of leaving Spain would be superfluous. Seven times had the orange bloomed since I first set foot upon her soil, yet it now seemed to me as of yesterday. Enjoyment, far beyond the most sanguine expectations, had fallen to my lot. The romantic dreams of youth seemed to be half fulfilled, and no subsequent events of life, however untoward, could deprive me of those pleasing recollections."[14]

In October Pettigrew returned to the United States full of inspirations, military and literary. "I am sincerely rejoiced to know that you are going home—for to say the truth I should not have been surprised to have heard of you in Morocco—fighting on one side or the other," wrote a friend.[15]

The most admirable units of the French army Pettigrew observed were the variously named organizations of light infantry, groups of select men armed with light, modern, and accurate rifles (rather than the standard infantry musket), of superior morale and agility, and used as skirmishers and for other duty requiring daring and individuality beyond that of the common soldier. Pettigrew observed such troops in action in Italy:

> One portion of the French army—the light corps, such as Zouaves and Chasseurs à pied—is beyond criticism. They seem to unite every requisite of a soldier. As skirmishers, in the advance or retreat, they are naturally without superiors. Yet it is in line with the bayonette, that their principal glory has been acquired. Easily subsisted, always cheerful, having the courage of desperadoes without their lawlessness. . . . At the battle of Palestro . . . they were seen one moment thrusting the Austrians over the bridge, and the next extending the butts of their rifles down to save them from drowning.[16]

The idea of leading such a unit appealed to Pettigrew greatly. He did not give up the thought until the Civil War was well under way and it was apparent that there would be no units designated separately as light troops but that every Confederate infantryman would be called upon to perform such duties. It was natural that Pettigrew would introduce what he had learned in France—the special drill, the special designation, and the special élan of the light troops—to the militia of Charleston and that he would become celebrated for this.[17] The ideal of the Zouave appealed to many Americans, and volunteer units on both sides entered service at the beginning of the Civil War thinking of themselves as light troops.

Pettigrew was elected lieutenant of the Washington Light Infantry after his return, and he made it the crack company among many in the city. People turned out to watch the company run through its French drills on the Battery, and it became the model that other companies in the city strove to emulate. Pettigrew's zeal and expertise went far toward preparing the local men for the war they were to inaugurate. According to Trescot, "He not only perfected their discipline and organization, but he fostered and developed in his command the conviction that their discipline and organization had a purpose beyond parade display, and that all its dignity sprang from the great duty for which it was preparation, and the hour of that duty was fast approaching." [18]

The seriousness that Pettigrew helped inspire is indicated by the advertisement for members of a Zouave company founded shortly after his return to Charleston and for which he acted as instructor. The company would accept any young man over seventeen of "moral character and gentlemanly deportment." Any member frequenting a place of drinking, gambling, or ill-fame would be expelled. Dues of five dollars per year supported a clubhouse and gymnasium, and the members were expected to do regular gymnastic exercises as well as drill. The uniform was modeled after the French "Chasseurs D'Vincennes" — blue jacket, scarlet pantaloons, and jaunty little scarlet hat.[19]

Pettigrew's interest in things military and preparation for the coming effort at southern independence was by no means untypical of his generation, but a South-wide phenomenon. Young men all over the South (in addition to those who were professional soldiers) were drilling and studying the art and science of war. Even before John Brown's raid, Turner Ashby and his mounted volunteers were perfecting their horsemanship and organization in the Valley of Virginia. Young William E. Baldwin pored over military literature at his book shop in Columbus, Mississippi, and spent all his spare time drilling the "Columbus Rifles." Cullen A. Battle's volunteer company at Eufaula, Alabama, considered itself combat fit enough to offer its immediate services to the governor of Virginia during the John Brown raid. The kinsmen John Hunt Morgan, Basil Wilson Duke, and Joseph Orville Shelby galloped the roads of the Bluegrass with the "Lexington Rifles." These were only a few young men who were near Pettigrew's age and, like him, had no formal military education but who were to become general officers under the Confederacy.[20]

The Harpers Ferry business raised to new heights interest in military affairs. Pettigrew wrote his brother from Charleston:

Unfortunately the Militia and Patrol system are dying out everywhere. The want of the commonest military knowledge, on the part of the militia of Virginia was truly lamentable, even farcical, and it looks as if a thousand organized men led with skill, could have marched from one end of the state to the other. I doubt whether things in the Old North State are much better. There is rather more of that sort of thing here, yet there is a continual disposition to break it down, and then we would be at the mercy of any little band of filibusters.[21]

The increasing frequency and earnestness of military drill was only one indication of Pettigrew's interest in preparing for the coming conflict, which appeared in sharper focus after the John Brown raid.[22] Pettigrew's travels and activities as the governor's chief military aide had given him a broad view of the state's military situation. A special commission appointed by the legislature to recommend changes in the militia law filed conflicting majority and minority reports in 1859. The minority report, by Edward McCrady, Jr., stressed reliance on elite volunteer units in an emergency. There was also considerable discussion of the state's military posture in newspapers and pamphlets.

Dissatisfied with all this discussion, Pettigrew wrote his own recommendations for the state militia which were published anonymously in March 1860 at Charleston in *Russell's Magazine*. This essay, "The Militia System of South Carolina," was written with Pettigrew's usual combination of humor and earnestness. As always, taking the long view and putting matters in philosophical and historical perspective, he first discussed the role of the military in society, which he defined as the protection of the property of the society against the greed and ruthlessness of the exterior enemy. Then he discussed the necessity that a free republican society depend upon an armed citizenry or militia rather than a standing force. Having set this background, he proceeded to discuss the specific military virtues, defects, requirements, and problems of South Carolina.[23]

Implied in his discussion, although not explicitly stated, were three types of potential threats that the militia of South Carolina should be prepared to meet. The first of the three threats was slave uprising. It was clear that this was the least important of Pettigrew's worries, although he pointed out that it would be both unsafe and dishonorable for South Carolina to rely on the small federal standing army in such a case.[24]

The second threat was that of a foreign, presumably European, army's descent upon the coast. From his travels and study Pettigrew was far more aware than most Americans that America was a factor in world politics. The entire American coast was vulnerable to attack by a foreign fleet at any time, and in such a case it would be unrealistic to rely on a small, widely dispersed regular army for safety.[25]

The third threat was a raid similar to that led by John Brown, a military offensive launched from northern soil with the objective of conquering the white inhabitants of the South. This quite naturally loomed largest in Pettigrew's mind. What he had to say about this would apply equally by a slight extension of the imagination to war with an attacking United States government under Republican control. The outlines of the future were vague. It was by no means self-evident to even a farsighted observer like Pettigrew that the coming Civil War would be a clearly defined battle between the southern states and the northern states, with the North controlling the federal government. The future was more uncertain and complicated. The one thing that was clear, from the John Brown raid and the Republican response to it, was that the South would be wise to rely on itself for physical safety, since the federal government could at any time fall into hostile hands.[26]

Luckily, all three major threats to South Carolina were to be prepared for in the same way—by having at least part of the militia well trained and mobile enough to concentrate at any threatened point in the state in a relatively brief time. A strong force in the right place at the right time could prevent much bloodshed and mischief, Pettigrew pointed out, citing the maxim that "one sabre drawn frequently keeps nine others in their scabbards." The militia or at least some part of it must be fast enough to muster and concentrate at a threatened point and proficient enough to offer a deterrent to a would-be attacker. Here Pettigrew elaborated weaknesses of the state that worked against military success and that indeed were the same weaknesses which ultimately undid the Confederate cause: hundreds of miles of coastline which could be assaulted at many points, population dispersed over wide distances, lack of transportation, and the inappropriateness of what transportation there was for military concentration.[27]

Before setting forth his remedies Pettigrew put to work his satirical talents to expose what he considered the existing unreadiness of the militia due to the laziness and lack of realism of its members, giving a comical account of the debacle to be expected if a disciplined British force were to land in South Carolina:

> The military would be marched to meet them. Here comes the column, arrayed in glittering habits, sonorous metal blowing martial sounds; many a brave heart beats high with noble anticipations. They pass by amid the plaudits of their fellow-citizens, while waving handkerchiefs attest the interest of the fair. But what throng is this, whose ebony hue contrasts darkly with the preceding glories? Behold the servants who go to cook, to brush the arms, black the boots, and perform the labours of their warrior-masters. Behind them follow trains of baggage, stretching far into the distance. They meet the enemy, the sharp crack of the skirmisher's rifle, the booming of cannon, the heavy tread of advancing columns succeed each other. The enemy wavers; a gallant charge of cavalry disperses his retreating multitudes, and covers the ground with fragments of humanity. The recall is sounded. Afric's sons have, in the meantime, prepared a collation. The battle recommences upon unresisting venison and wild turkey. The roar of small-arms is succeeded by the popping of champagne-corks, and *batteries de cuisine* take the place of batteries of cannon. Toasts are offered and speeches delivered. The road back is strewed with flowers. Heroic bachelors marry blooming heiresses, and are returned to the next Legislature, where they vote a statue to their victorious general.
>
> Such is the idea of the military inculcated by the Militia system. Now, let us see what it is in reality. The first day's march goes off well enough, though a bed upon the damp ground is not comfortable. The next day, the knapsacks become intolerable; the more impatient pitch theirs off into the swamp. . . . That night an attack is made upon the camp; half the sentinels are asleep, great disorder ensues, but the enemy are repulsed. Half of our killed are shot by their own comrades. A general bad humour ensues. Next day an abattis is found across the road. Cutting it away is rather

more difficult work than whittling pine-chips. The negroes are ordered to advance and perform this manual labour. A few balls fall among them, and they incontinently take to the woods. Upon the approach of danger, their countrymen in the rear [the cooks] follow the good example, and are no more seen until peace is declared. The army is now as it should have been at first — dependent upon itself alone. After much trouble, and loss of life, the obstacle is cleared away. That day those of the messes who know how to cook, eat; the officers cannot instruct the rest. So, on the army goes, hungry, disappointed and mad, anxious to meet the enemy upon any terms, and ready to jump into the lion's mouth, forgetful that his teeth have been considerably sharpened by skill and science.[28]

The failings of the militia Pettigrew attributed chiefly to the officers' lack of real interest in their duties. Once he had observed some children playing soldier. After much argument the boy with the longest paper plume was selected as the general. The criteria by which the citizen soldiers elected their militia officers were as relevant to true military ability, Pettigrew implied, as the length of the plume. The recent debacle of a brave and disciplined British army in the Crimea was the result of stupid and incompetent officers who had bought their commissions and were not equal to their duties: "Under such circumstances, the courage and gallantry of the Cid would be of no avail," he pointed out. "In the Militia system, it is not to be expected, that the officers should be equal, in all respects, to the emergencies of a campaign; but they should at least be required to know the rudiments of their duty." [29]

The most important recommendations Pettigrew had to make for militia improvement involved the training of officers. He had no thought of changing the system of election of officers by the men. This was natural to a republican form of government in his mind. Once elected, however, officers should be under compulsion to make themselves equal to their duties and not treat their position simply as a political or social honor. Pettigrew proposed that three months after election every company, field, and staff officer be subjected to a rigorous examination by a board of officers of equal or greater rank. Governors, he also implied, would have to be more vigorous than they had been in the past in seeing that the generals performed their duties and in bringing them to task if they failed.[30]

The existing system of requiring (at least nominally) militia service from all male citizens from eighteen to forty-five Pettigrew also accepted as natural. The trouble was that the system was not taken seriously. Its requirement of periodic drill was not enforced. His European experience no doubt reenforced his preference for universal service.

> Now it must be self-evident, that every Militia system should have for one object to practically undeceive both officers and men as to the real nature of service; to instruct them, by example, that it involves privations and hardships; that its pleasures should consist in excellence of drill rather than in carousing around the festive board; in a word, that it is a serious preparation, and not an idle amusement. To this effect the laws should be rigid, and rigidly enforced, whatever grumbling may be occasioned thereby. Eternal vigilance is the price of liberty, and those who cannot make this slight sacrifice are unworthy of the blessing. The security of the commonwealth is not to be endangered, that a few idlers may squirt tobacco-juice over the pavement.[31]

The young men of South Carolina were lazy and unused to fatigue. "The government has no right to prescribe to individuals how much exercise they should take; but certainly the great duties of the citizen must not be neglected because the benches of the jury-box may be without cushions, or the rifle and canteen inconvenient, to carry on an August day," Pettigrew wrote.[32] As remedy, Pettigrew proposed a series of practical steps to make training more regular for men between eighteen and twenty-eight, to make certain that training acquainted every able-bodied man with the rudiments of soldiering, and to make sure that no one escaped service as some had. In regard to this last, he proposed requiring every man to present to the tax collector annually a certificate that he had faithfully discharged his militia duties that year or else be subjected to a stiff tax. Only the disabled would be excused. All other loopholes would be plugged. Those who were out of the state for college would be required to make up the years they missed by serving beyond twenty-eight. Persons who resided out of the state but owned property in it would be taxed in lieu of service.

A well-trained force of men from eighteen to twenty-eight, relatively free from encumbrances of family and property, would be relied upon for fast assembly and action in time of emergency. Older men would be organized into two classes according to age. They would drill less frequently but would still be available as a reserve if needed. Older men who were fit and willing could remain enrolled in the eighteen-to-twenty-eight class. Pettigrew even suggested the desirability of tying the franchise to the faithful performance of militia duty, although this would require a change in the state constitution.[33]

Pettigrew disapproved of elite companies such as he himself belonged to, that is, units of men more active in military enthusiasm than the average citizen militiaman. He doubted that these companies promoted true military efficiency, and he feared that the pomp and esprit of these units seduced the state into a false sense of confidence about its preparedness. Also, such units tended to become social organizations, since many good men were excluded by the expense of uniforms and dues.[34]

Such exclusive militia units, admitting only the rich, were undemocratic: "It is a matter of vital importance to a republic, that the separation of the upper from the lower ranks of society, such as exists at the North, should be prevented; and no means is so efficacious for this purpose as the duty of Militia service. When thus forced into contact, education and character will always have their influence; if separated, the practical government of the country is given into the hands of those who are least capable of exercising it."[35] This was a prophetic observation on Pettigrew's part, for a democracy of the masculine fellowship of war, in which ability was more important than social position, held the southern gentry and yeomanry together during the long, bloody struggle of the Confederacy for independence.

Pettigrew also attacked the prevalent American myth, handed down from the Revolution and the War of 1812, that an American, a frontiersman, was naturally superior to the European professional soldier. This was a delusion, Pettigrew told South Carolina: "The Zouaves and Chasseurs d'Orléans are as good rangers as the best backwood's-man, and know a good deal more about the art of taking care of themselves in a tight place, besides being much better armed." Even the English could make a fair show at this. His solution was a rigorous training of the militia in the skirmish drill, which encouraged both teamwork and initiative.[36]

Pettigrew made other, detailed suggestions about weapons, training, and finance of the militia. He concluded: "It may be said that this system is too stringent. It certainly is in earnest, and nothing but an earnest system will be of any avail to the purpose. If the State be not really in earnest, it is better to abolish the military part of the duty at once, and confine ourselves to suppers."[37]

Very little of what Pettigrew suggested was adopted. In the crisis that was then less than a year away, South Carolina depended chiefly upon volunteers from the militia backed up by the reserve of the universal militia, and it also depended upon spontaneous morale rather than the regulated organization and discipline which Pettigrew advocated. After Fort Sumter, the military problems and policies of the state were swallowed up in the larger problems and policies of the Confederate States government. At any rate, Pettigrew made himself the kind of officer he hoped would become common in the militia. He became a master of the mysteries of fortification and artillery. His fluency in French and German gave him an opportunity few Americans had to keep abreast of European refinements in war.[38]

Pettigrew mingled and became friends with the small group of regular United States Army officers in the garrison at Charleston. This in itself demonstrates the strange mixture of expectations, viewpoints, and allegiances with which Americans approached the crisis of 1861. The officers at Charleston worked enthusiastically with Pettigrew in improving his military knowledge and the efficiency of the local militia. Pettigrew's closest associate in the garrison was Lieutenant John Gibbon. Gibbon was a native of Pennsylvania, although he had been raised in North Carolina. He remained with the federal government during the Civil War and rose to major general. Yet in February and March 1860, he was collaborating enthusiastically with Pettigrew in improving the state defenses. Americans were not certain a sectional conflict was coming, and they were even more uncertain of the form it would take.

When Gibbon visited Georgia, he sent Pettigrew a review of a new artillery manual, urging him to have it published in Charleston for the edification of the local militia officers. Gibbon expressed his delight with the activity and efficiency he found among the militia at Savannah, Augusta, and Columbus. In turn, Pettigrew wrote a review of a military work by Gibbon for *Russell's Magazine*, although the magazine folded before it was published. When Gibbon was transferred to Utah Territory in March 1860, he wrote Pettigrew, "I heartily second your wishes for the perfecting of the higher military branches in Charleston, and could not wish for a more pleasant position than that of assisting you in any branch of the service. I think however that you would find the officers now stationed at Fort Moultrie both ready and willing to give you every assistance in their power." [39]

During the summer of 1860 Pettigrew was in contact with northern arms manufacturers. "By sending your order to the Secretary of the Maynard Arms Co. you will be sure to receive a perfect article [rifle]," one northern agent wrote. "I hope that there will never be occasion for any ungracious use of fire arms by the people of our country," he added as an afterthought. [40]

As late as November 1860, the month before secession, Pettigrew was keeping up his northern contacts. Caroline Petigru Carson was living in New York City. Pettigrew asked Mrs. Carson to request of Captain George Washington Cullum, a regular army officer who had recently been stationed in Charleston, his plan for the best defense of the city. Cullum wryly commented that Pettigrew certainly had the first quality of a soldier—boldness—and requested that if Charleston were attacked, Pettigrew use his spyglass in order to make sure his shots missed Cullum. Cullum, subsequently a general in the federal forces, sent along the plan requested.

"I won't put up any sous for the success of this [independence] movement," Mrs. Carson wrote in delivering Cullum's message. "The idea of being delivered into the hands of Keitt[,] Conner and Cunningham is horrible and grotesque. For you who have the alternative of Andalusia or Heaven it may do very well, but for us who have not the free choice of residence, it is not all the same thing." Mrs. Carson sent along the estimated prices for New York purchase of field glasses, compasses, micrometer telescopes for determining distances, and military whistles, as requested. [41]

In April 1860, Pettigrew had given voice to a general uneasiness and vague fear of impending catastrophe which seemed to loom over America. He had told his friend Daniel M. Barringer: "Bad times are ahead in this Country. It is not simply a dissolution of the Union, that is comparatively a small matter, but I see all through the extreme sections, at least, a rottenness of political principle, a cowardly terror, which are the sure precursors of despotism in some shape or other. It is humiliating to think, that after 80 years of freedom, men of high position are to be found declaiming against the American Revolution and the principles upon which it was successfully fought." [42]

A painful but vague feeling of uneasiness, a sense of the breaking up of old forms, was in the air. In September there were alarms and rumors of a possible slave uprising timed for the coming elections. Caroline North Pettigrew, at Cherry Hill in the South Carolina upcountry with her children while her husband was in North Carolina, was upset by the rumors but was unable to convince any of the neighborhood white men of any necessity for alertness. Most of them did not even own arms, she found. Her husband Charles Pettigrew laughed off the idea of an outbreak among the slaves: "I really see no reason to apprehend any difficulty among the negroes; it is mainly resulting from the panic on the part of the whites. I think there is a profound agitation in the south, a feeling as if something was going to happen, if not that which each one thinks then something else." [43]

Southern opinion in general was still behind that of South Carolina, but the gap was closing fast. Pettigrew's cousin at New Bern, North Carolina, wrote for a copy of the rules of the Washington Light Infantry. William S. Pettigrew, who until the John Brown raid was the most moderate and cautious of Whigs, was thereafter on fire with secession sentiment. William told Johnston that he need no longer cross the water to find a war to fight in, for "our Yankee enemies manifest an ardent desire to test our spirit." In South Carolina itself, Rhett and the old radical leaders were in the background, and the men formerly regarded as unionists were talking of secession. [44]

In strange contrast to southern alarm was the incredibly innocent, business-as-usual attitude of the North. Pettigrew's old friend Francis J. Child wrote him a chatty, friendly letter from Harvard in November 1860. Designed to bridge the gap between the sections, it only exhibited how far apart they were. Child had voted for Lincoln. He viewed the election in conventional political terms. He was pleased that a respectable, nativist, businessman's party had ousted the Democrats whom he thought of as disreputable, lower-class, and foreign. He had no understanding of the seriousness with which the South viewed Lincoln's election.[45] The South, which harked to the eighteenth century in its political instincts, listened to what the Republicans said and believed what it heard. The North did not take its politicians at face value and could not grasp that any one else did. The South was behind the times, not sophisticated enough to understand the new system by which Lincoln's statements were made for their calculated effect on strategic segments of the electorate rather than as serious statements of intent. These different frames of reference prevented any realistic attempt at compromise. The South was ruled by lions, the North by foxes.

Whatever other men's attitudes might be, however vaguely or casually they might prepare for the future, the citizens who watched Pettigrew and his company drilling three times weekly on the Battery as the November elections drew near could be sure that they, at least, were in earnest.[46]

Pettigrew believed that the war to come would be a desperate one, as the very term "civil war" implied, an all-consuming, last-ditch affair. He knew that successful wars of national independence required courage, energy, skill, and sacrifice far beyond his fellow citizens' daydreams of easy victory. In his book, *Notes on Spain and the Spaniards*, which he wrote in the spring of 1860, among the many little-known historical characters he introduced was an eighteenth-century Basque general named Zumalacarregui:

> This remarkable man is little known in America, and as he supported an unsuccessful cause, his reputation in Europe is waning, but there were few greater born in the eighteenth century. A larger field or more romantic times only were requisite to make him a hero in the history of the world. An officer of the army at the death of Ferdinand, he espoused the cause of Don Carlos and was its main support. Taking his station in the Basque provinces and gathering up a handful of peasants, he cast cannon, armed his troops from the spoils of his enemies, and subjected every army that approached to ignominious defeat. . . . But the hand of resistless fate was interposed to arrest his progress, and when he was preparing to march upon Madrid a stray ball at the siege of Bilbao relieved them from the unconquerable foe. Had he been disposed, like most leaders of civil war, to accept a compromise,

he would have received dukedoms and countships without number; yet the chieftain who wielded, one may almost say the destiny of his country, left scarcely enough to inter him. This is the stuff of which true heroes are made. The high road from Vitoria to Ernani, near San Sebastian, passes through a country every foot of which was contested, not once only but frequently. One of Zumalacarregui's greatest victories was just here about his birthplace, by which he foiled the well laid plans of four times his number, led by the best of the Christianist generals, to envelop him in a trap. . . . The surprising resistance made by the Basques in their mountain fastnesses against the united opposition of Spain, France and England, finds its only parallel in the exploits of [Francis] Marion among the swamps of our own country. Between the two heroes there was a striking resemblance of character. Both were upon the highest tone of honor. Chivalrous, unselfish, indifferent to the charms of wealth or luxury, they moved with a single purpose of patriotism. Appearing upon the theatre of action in the midst of prostration and despondency they restored confidence, created armies, and with naked, starving soldiers gained victories over troops who enjoyed every advantage that money could procure. Whether Marion would have displayed also the talents of a General is not known, as his force was always small. Zumalacarregui was more fortunate in opportunity, but both will fill an enviable place in history, and in their deeds will offer fit subjects for the Muse of succeeding generations.[47]

In such a character Johnston Pettigrew found a model.

Chapter 11

The Devil Unchained at Last

Well, the Devil is unchained at last, you have been talking fire a long time, now you must face it. —Johnston Pettigrew to the fire-eaters, November 1860

On 18 November 1860 Pettigrew was summoned from Charleston to Columbia by Governor William Henry Gist. It was known that the Republicans had won the presidential election in the electoral college. A convention of the people of the state was to assemble before Christmas, and there was little doubt but that it would sever the ties of South Carolina with the Union of the states. Opinion in South Carolina, once sharply divided over secession, was now nearly unanimous. Pettigrew shared the conviction that continuing the Union with the federal government in hostile hands was not tolerable. Whether he or South Carolina expected permanent independence or whether they thought that decisive action would bring eventually a satisfactory arrangement within the Union is not clear.[1] Once they had determined to act, action itself carried them forward irrevocably.

The immediate problem before the governor was military. The state in effect had to form an army overnight, and, out of the ersatz materials at hand, create a military force sufficient to defend Charleston and the coast from an attack by sea. Probably at the governor's request, Pettigrew drew up a "Memoir on the Armament of South Carolina" much more elaborately detailed than his earlier essay on the militia system. He discussed the potential military problems of the state, how to organize infantry, artillery, cavalry, rifles, ordnance, commissary, engineers, staff, and medical corps, the possible uses of blacks, exactly the arms needed by each branch—what kind, how many, and why, and the cost and the steps for procuring them. He particularly stressed the need for immediate action in procuring arms and for organization of military administration and supply—the state's greatest lack, for it had lots of pluck and enthusiasm. Officers must be prepared for the mundane logistical duties of war as well as for its dangers and glories, he stressed. His paper was predicated upon the conditions to be expected "if the course of events is developed and South Carolina becomes either a nation by herself or a party in a great Southern Confederacy." [2]

The spectacle of South Carolina preparing to fight the United States was not as irrational as it seemed to some later observers. History was replete with examples of small but determined and unified peoples maintaining their freedom from much larger nations by better organization and greater élan—the American Revolution, not a distant myth but a living memory, being one of the most obvious. South Carolinians thought of war as short, decisive, and limited campaigns like that in Mexico or the recent Italian encounters. Few on either side conceived that the ensuing Civil War would be one of nearly total mobilization for the South. Besides, South Carolina well knew that the rest of the South and some of the North, however the people might feel about secession, would not countenance military coercion of a state by the federal government and that therefore any attack must be made from the sea. Secession was a risk but not a preposterous one.

The problem of defense from sea attack was complicated by the only representation of federal military power in the state—the small but strategically situated garrison occupying the fortresses in the harbor of the state's largest city and chief port, Charleston.

In December, Gist was succeeded as governor by Francis W. Pickens, who immediately appointed Pettigrew the first of his military aides. From his summoning by Gist until the firing on Fort Sumter, Pettigrew sat in most of the important councils of the high officials of the state. [3]

Meanwhile, at the end of November, Pettigrew became colonel of the First Regiment of Rifles of South Carolina, newly formed out of the best volunteer companies at Charleston and armed with the best available weapons. Pettigrew was evidently elected colonel of the regiment by a unanimous vote of the men, since he had stated that he would decline to serve unless so elected. The First Regiment of Rifles and the First Regiment of Artillery under Colonel Wilmot Gibbes De Saussure were the nucleus of the army of volunteers on which South Carolina would rely to fight, if necessary, the forces of the United States. [4]

The reasons for Gist's and Pickens's confidence in Pettigrew are evident. They needed a military adviser who was calm and judicious in counsel; who could move quickly, efficiently, and in deadly earnest when action was called for; who had some competence in artillery, engineering, and logistics; who could keep a confidence; and who could lead enthusiastic but unruly volunteers. The resigned officers of the United States Army had not yet come in to offer their services to the state. Pettigrew had been preparing himself for just such a role: the self-mastered man who steps from the sidelines in the great crisis to take control when all about is confusion. The importance and prominence which he assumed in South Carolina in November and December 1860 was indicated to observers of such niceties by the fact that Pettigrew was seated beside Mrs. Pickens at dinner.[5]

Pickens was to write later: "You will recollect you were the first man I telegraphed the evening after I was inaugurated to come to me at Columbia on important business. You recollect . . . the orders given as to Charleston, in taking the forts, and in all other military matters you were my constant and most confidential Councillor, and . . . for sincerity, accurate knowledge, disinterested patriotism and bravery I have never met with any man upon whom I could more surely rely."[6]

Pettigrew's interview with Pickens occurred on 18 December. The ordinance of secession was passed on 20 December. That day in Charleston, Pettigrew encountered Robert F. W. Allston's daughter Elizabeth stranded in a sea of mud while she was trying to reach a boat in which she was to sail to Georgetown. "Without a word of warning," she remembered long after, "Cousin Johnston picked me up in his arms and carried me all the way to the boat. . . . I never saw Cousin Johnston again."[7]

The First Regiment of Rifles was now drilling daily and keeping surveillance of the federal garrison. The regiment, which Pettigrew would command for the next four months, was made up of his old company, the Washington Light Infantry, and the German Riflemen, Carolina Light Infantry, Moultrie Guards, Palmetto Light Infantry, Zouaves, and Meagher Guards. Later the Beauregard Light Infantry and the Charleston Light Infantry were added. The soldiers were by no means all members of the gentry. Among them were many workingmen and artisans, as well as a number of Irish and Germans, groups which made up a sizable percentage of the white population of Charleston. Later, volunteers arrived from Baltimore, Norfolk, and Wilmington. John L. Branch was the lieutenant colonel. Ellison Capers, later Confederate general and Episcopal bishop of South Carolina, was major. Theodore Gaillard Barker, prominent in postbellum politics, was adjutant. Among the company officers were James Conner, Edward McCrady, Jr., and Charles Henry Simonton, who was later of some note as a legal scholar.[8]

On 20 December Pettigrew's command assembled for its first regimental parade. During the exercise the ordinance of secession was received and read aloud by Pettigrew.

On the night of 26/27 December, Major Robert Anderson, commanding the federal forces in Charleston harbor, withdrew his small force from unfinished Fort Moultrie to Fort Sumter, the most defensible of the various posts scattered about the harbor, spiking the guns and burning the gun carriages at Moultrie. This surprise move greatly alarmed the public in South Carolina. It was the first federal act that could be interpreted as overtly hostile in intent, and it seemed to the South Carolinians an act of bad faith, violating their understanding of a tacit agreement with Washington to maintain the status quo until a political settlement could be worked out by the delegates the state had sent there. Indeed, it was this act and not the firing on Sumter that South Carolinians regarded as the commencement of hostilities.[9]

Anderson had been alarmed by the military bustle in the city and the patrol boats passing up and down the harbor. He feared he might be attacked in Moultrie, an indefensible position. Actually the state had no intention of attacking his garrison at the time, and the patrol boats were designed chiefly to keep overzealous citizens from precipitating an incident. The fear that unauthorized attackers would set off an unwanted altercation was Pettigrew's greatest concern.[10]

Pettigrew and Capers were dispatched to see Anderson early on the morning after the removal to Sumter. Arriving at the fort's landing, Pettigrew sent in his card, and the two were courteously ushered in to meet Anderson and his assembled officers in his private quarters. Pettigrew conveyed the governor's astonishment at Anderson's move. By an understanding between Washington and South Carolina, he said, the state was to respect federal property, and the federal posts were to remain in an unchanged condition. The settlement of the status of the forts was to be political, not military. South Carolina had lived up to her part of the bargain, and the governor insisted that the federal forces live up to their part by returning to their original position.

Anderson replied that he was a southern man by both birth and feelings, that he knew nothing of the agreement with Washington and had received no orders of any kind from there, that he was commander of all the forts in the harbor and did not consider that he had changed the status quo by transferring his men from one to another, that he had information that he might be attacked and as a soldier he felt it his duty to remove from the indefensible position at Moultrie, and that he had acted entirely on his own responsibility in order to avoid bloodshed and had considered the step well before acting. He declined the request to return to his original position. Pettigrew and Capers went away with their mission unfulfilled, but they were convinced of Anderson's lack of aggressive intent. "I cannot express myself too favorably as to the impression made upon me by the soldierly, courteous, even kindly bearing of Maj. Anderson," Pettigrew wrote in his report to the governor.[11]

That afternoon, Pickens told Pettigrew he wished him to take two hundred especially chosen men to Castle Pinckney, another of the posts in the harbor, and take possession of the work. This might be dangerous since there were an unknown number of soldiers still in the post and it was thought that the approaches were mined. Pettigrew was off before the words were out of his mouth, Pickens later recalled.[12]

Pettigrew carried in his pocket the following official order: "Sir: You are ordered to take possession of Castle Pinckney. You are to act with the greatest discretion and prudence, and to let it be known that you take possession in the name of the Governor of South Carolina, and in consequence of the extraordinary orders executed last night in relation to Fort Moultrie and with a view at present to prevent further destruction of public property, and as a measure of safety also."[13]

Men from the First Regiment of Artillery had already taken over the vacant Fort Moultrie works. Pettigrew assembled three companies from the First Regiment of Rifles on the Citadel green at 4:00 P.M. on 27 December. They double-timed to the water and, fully armed and equipped with scaling ladders, boarded the steamer *Nina* and sailed to Castle Pinckney. According to the perhaps embellished account of a New York reporter, Pettigrew banged three times at the locked gate and demanded the surrender of the fort. Receiving no answer he scaled the wall and found inside Lieutenant Richard K. Meade, a sergeant, and some workmen. Meade was leaning against the wall chewing tobacco and at first refused to acknowledge Pettigrew's presence. Meanwhile, some of Pettigrew's men had scaled the wall and opened the gate, letting in the entire force. Finally, after once turning his back and walking away, Meade asked by what authority this entry was made. Pettigrew replied that he was acting on the authority of the governor of South Carolina, that he was now in command of the post, and that he would give receipt for the public property there.

Meade refused the receipt on the ground that he could not recognize the authority that gave it, and he asked if he were under arrest. Pettigrew replied no, but that if he left he would not be allowed to return. Meade and the others then were permitted to remove themselves to Fort Sumter. Meanwhile, a guard was mounted and the flag of the *Nina*, a white star on a red ground, was hoisted. The public property seized included a full powder magazine, a nearly full complement of guns, and a month's provisions.[14]

Until mid-January Pettigrew remained in Castle Pinckney with some of his troops, awaiting developments at Sumter. Among his men was seventy-six-year-old Alfred Huger, a former Unionist, a close friend of James Louis Petigru, and long the postmaster of Charleston, who insisted on being admitted to serve with his grandson. Difficulties arose when a fifteen-year-old soldier of the Meagher Guards accidentally shot a member of the Carolina Light Infantry. Pettigrew slept between the two companies to prevent a fight.[15]

In mid-January Pettigrew was sent to Fort Morris where most of his regiment already was. He took command of all the troops, artillery, and fortifications on Morris Island, which was directly south of Fort Sumter and the closest point to it among the forts ringing the harbor. Pettigrew's command post was 1,260 yards from the guns of Sumter.[16]

From the time of the removal of Anderson to Fort Sumter in December until the assumption of official responsibility for the situation at Charleston by the newly formed Confederate States government on 1 March, prodigious work was done by the makeshift South Carolina army in preparing fortifications and setting up batteries on Sullivan's and Morris islands. This work was under the general supervision of a former United States Army officer, Roswell S. Ripley, and a former U.S. seaman, Clement H. Stevens (both later generals and both, incidently, adopted South Carolinians of northern birth). Pettigrew was in immediate charge of the work on Morris Island. Starting nearly from scratch and with ersatz materials such as railroad iron and cotton bales, he progressed so well that the Cummings Point batteries were able to turn back the *Star of the West* on 9 January. At the same time Pettigrew was responsible for the training and governing of bodies of volunteers "unused to service, impatient of restraints, and ignorant of the first requirements of camp life." Pettigrew's zeal and efficiency were given a share of the credit for the rapid progress of the defenses and the bringing of officers and men into good discipline.[17]

He was not away from his command for more than three hours until late February. Having occasion to deny other men leave, he would not take leave himself. Establishing a policy he followed for the rest of his career, he considered it a commander's duty to live on the same fare as his men. He refused to eat the delicacies sent out to him by his relatives in the city but distributed them among the regiment. Tents were too few and those on hand were unsatisfactory, although there were plenty of blankets and lots of straw. Also, some of the new rifles proved defective. The men on Morris Island remained in high spirits and full of fight despite all this and despite high winds, rain, and unusually high tides. The Washington Light Infantry presented Pettigrew, its former lieutenant, with an inscribed sword. This was followed by a collation, and then by a hard day's labor in constructing a battery.[18]

The slapdash nature of the military situation is revealed by a note sent to Pettigrew by Ripley (a graduate of West Point and a veteran of the Mexican War), to whom he had appealed for tactical advice in case the federals landed on Morris Island.

> Should the enemy attempt to land, I can see but one way to win. That is to annoy him by cannonade & musketry until he jumps out of his boats, & then rush down on him for a free fight. You put your pluck against his discipline & that very often sires a kill. If you wait to look out & let him have a chance to form & get over his confusion he might make good his ground for some time. . . . If he is received with a promiscuous row, which in future history will be called a charge, he will be very likely to be thrashed from the beginning.[19]

Pettigrew worried that his rifles were of inferior quality, that the battery ammunition was inadequate, that the signal system between his post and the city would not be equal to an emergency. He was concerned about inefficiency and waste and lack of energy in the newly organized state commissary, quartermaster, and medical departments, and about the lack of clearcut chains of command, which undermined discipline. The Citadel cadets serving on Morris Island refused to obey any but their own officers. Pettigrew was quite willing to whip them into line but felt he lacked authority to do so. In short, he felt that very few of his colleagues, in the midst of the armed standoff in Charleston harbor which might at any moment develop into war, were undertaking their duties with sufficient energy and earnestness.[20]

He kept up a steady flow of pithy letters to his superiors Richard G. M. Dunovant, the state army general under whose nominal command he was, and David F. Jamison, newly appointed secretary of war of South Carolina, suggesting measures to correct various unsatisfactory situations or to expedite work, or bringing to their attention contingencies they had apparently not noticed. These letters Pettigrew wrote were very different from most of the correspondence of the officials and officers at Charleston during the Sumter crisis, which was, in general, courtly and vague. Pettigrew's letters by contrast were crisp and razor-sharp, with zeal boiling below a calm surface. Formally, the letters were couched in terms respectful to superiors, but ironic rebuke hovered just below the surface, as he quietly but pointedly brought home the superiors' vagueness in orders, lack of system, or failure to take account of all relevant factors.[21]

Pettigrew's deadly earnestness was unusual at a time when many people on both sides conceived of war, if there was to be one, as an easy and colorful affair. Ellison Capers, major of the Regiment of Rifles, was an able officer who served throughout the Civil War and rose to brigadier general. His background was formally much more military than Pettigrew's, as he was a graduate of the Citadel and a teacher in a military high school. Yet he regarded his martial activities at Charleston as a duty, not a pleasure, and clearly would rather have been at home with his young wife and child.[22] But there was no place Pettigrew would rather have been. The war was his realization.

Still, strangely, the zeal with which Pettigrew immersed himself in his pressing tasks did not at all preclude his customary ironic detachment, the hallmark of a good mind able to rise above its immediate circumstances. From Castle Pinckney, in easy sight of Sumter, he casually wrote a North Carolina friend in January:

> For the last month and a half I have been very much occupied by other affairs than my own. . . . The Politicians and Newspaper agitators have certainly brought things to a pretty pass. . . . I am not disposed to throw up my hat and rejoice over the downfall of the great American Confederacy. Nor can any one else do so who has felt the flag wave over him in foreign countries. Our State government was for a while a perfect picture of imbecility and confusion. It is in a better way now and I hope the whole South will join us shortly, for I have no desire to live under the Independent Republic of South Carolina.[23]

It is clear that after Anderson's surprise removal to Fort Sumter Pettigrew was operating under a war psychology, since he regarded the armed federals as the enemy. He did not blame Anderson, who was a decent fellow doing his duty. But he felt betrayed by the bad faith of the Washington authorities. He blamed himself for having advised Pickens against the seizure of Sumter earlier before it had been ready for resistance. He had advocated postponing hasty action in hope of a political rather than a military solution. This erroneous advice put him under obligation to be foremost in the assault that might now be necessary to reduce Sumter, he felt. Indeed, right up to the bombardment and surrender of Sumter in April, the First Regiment of Rifles was slated for the honor of leading an assault if one were to be made.[24]

Pettigrew especially resented the pits and mines that had been prepared at the Sumter landings by Captain John Gray Foster, although quite naturally that was the sort of ungentlemanly thing to be expected from the New Englander and Republican among Anderson's officers. "The consequence will be that we shall lose a great deal of life [in storming of the fort] and that the garrison will richly deserve and perhaps receive the penalties demanded by the usages of war against those who by a useless resistance cause the shedding of blood," Pettigrew commented.[25]

On 18 February, the same day that Jefferson Davis was inaugurated at Montgomery, the Regiment of Rifles was relieved from duty on Morris Island by newly enlisted six-month volunteers of the Confederate States Army under Colonel (later General) Maxcy Gregg.[26] Pettigrew had been on constant duty since 27 December.

"Johnston is not at all the worse for his turn of duty and he has earned a good deal of reputation," James Louis Petigru reported. A local musician dedicated a composition called "The Rifle Regiment Quickstep" to Pettigrew and his men. The governor hinted that Pettigrew might have any post he wanted in the permanent state military establishment then being organized. Carie's sister heard him spoken of about the city often as "the man on whom public confidence seems most to rest." "You seem to be in the state in which the [*illegible*] warns when he says, 'Woe to you when all men speak well of you,' " Louise Petigru Porcher told him.[27]

During its brief leave after relief from Fort Morris, the Regiment of Rifles was honored by the city. Forming at Military Hall on 25 February, the regiment marched "in brilliant parade" down Meeting Street to Institute Hall where, with much ceremony, it was presented with a flag of white-ribbed, gilt-fringed Parisian silk with the coat of arms of the state, on a pole resembling a gold spear. James Tupper, a prominent citizen, presented the flag on behalf of its "fair donor."

Pettigrew, "his countenance expressive of deep feeling and emotion," according to a reporter, made a graceful talk addressed to the crowd and the fair donor. He spoke of the honored associations of patriotism and liberty surrounding the old flag of the Union which he recommended be put away with due respect. He remarked upon the moral beauty of the donor and the physical beauty of the flag itself. He reminded the crowd that the future was uncertain and that valiant deeds were far more needed than loud professions. Then he turned to address the regiment. He praised its recent services. He praised the individual good character of the men upon which good soldiership was based. He singled out the foreign-born soldiers for particular praise for their loyalty to an adopted land. He warned of hardship, danger, and death to come and recommended consecration to the flag as symbol of all that was worth fighting for. The ceremonies were concluded with a speech by Governor Pickens in praise of Pettigrew's courage and dispatch and his services to the state in the crisis, accompanied by cheers. Then the regiment marched away to boats to return to duty, this time on James Island.[28]

"Your cousin Johnston," James Louis Petigru wrote his grandson, ". . . is no longer a pale inmate of the obscure building in St. Michael's Alley, where he used to pore over dusty books in a foreign tongue; but bestrides a gallant steed, with gay trappings, long spurs and bright shoulder knots." In a more serious tone Petigru told his sister, "I saw him [Pettigrew] in full feather for the first time, issuing from the Institute Hall with the flag. I felt proud of his soldierly bearing." But he feared that if an assault were made "we may as well be prepared to hear that his sun has set. He is just in the vein to 'seek the bubble reputation,' where he is more apt to find his grave than ever to tell the story."[29]

On 1 March the Confederate States government formally assumed the war powers of South Carolina, and on 3 March General P. G. T. Beauregard arrived to take charge of the situation in Charleston harbor. Shortly thereafter, Pettigrew and most of his regiment were transferred from James to Sullivan's Island, where Pettigrew remained on duty until the bombardment and surrender of Fort Sumter in April. Sullivan's Island was the place most likely to be attacked if the federals attempted to land troops at Charleston from the sea or attempted to enter the harbor by a route other than the main channel. Pettigrew had much to do on Sullivan's Island, being in charge of troops and batteries spread miles apart and of boats guarding the creeks by which federal vessels might seek entry into the harbor.[30]

On 5 March Captain James Conner rode up to the headquarters of the Regiment of Rifles at Secessionville on Sullivan's Island with the latest newspapers.

"War or no war?" asked Major Capers.

"War to the knife!" replied Conner, throwing down the first telegraphed accounts of Lincoln's inaugural address, forever crushing the hope that the federal troops would be peacefully withdrawn from Charleston. It was evident that independence would not be secured without a struggle from a government that was wealthy, powerful, and already convicted, in the South Carolina view, of lack of candor. Major Capers consoled himself with thoughts of the successful repulse of the first British attackers eighty-five years before.[31]

Duty was still agreeing with Pettigrew, despite the impending possibility of his leading an attack landing on Sumter. A relative visiting

J. J. Pettigrew's European Diary
Drawings to illustrate the superiority of the Italian female face
to the German. (Pettigrew Family Papers, Southern Historical
Collection, University of North Carolina)

Two Southern Unionists
James Cathcart Johnston of Hayes plantation near Edenton,
North Carolina, family friend and benefactor of the Pettigrews.
(North Carolina Department of Archives and History)

James Louis Petigru at the time of Fort Sumter. "That the Majority are wicked is a truth that passed long since into a proverb." (South Caroliniana Library, University of South Carolina)

James L. Petigru's Law Office
The building in St. Michael's Alley, Charleston, from which James Johnston
Pettigrew practiced law from 1852 to 1860. (Photograph by Carl Julien from
the Gibbes Museum of Art / Carolina Art Association)

Jane Caroline ("Carie") North Pettigrew
J. J. Pettigrew's sister-in-law and friend and James L. Petigru's niece.
(Portrait by Thomas Sully. Courtesy of Mrs. John H. Daniels)

Harry Burgwyn
Henry King Burgwyn, Jr., colonel of the Twenty-sixth North Carolina
Regiment, Pettigrew's Brigade, who was killed on the first day at
Gettysburg at age twenty-one. (Archie K. Davis)

Pettigrew's Brigade at Gettysburg
"In the midst of all our trials it is a consolation to reflect, that our reputation, next to Greece, will be the most heroic of nations." (Mural at the Institute of Government, University of North Carolina)

Brigadier General James Johnston Pettigrew, C.S.A.
"For none who fought so briefly in the Army of Northern Virginia was there
more praise while living or more laments when dead," wrote Douglas
Southall Freeman. (Posthumous portrait by William Garl Brown,
from a wartime likeness. Pettigrew Family Papers,
Southern Historical Collection, University of North Carolina)

him on Sullivan's Island found him looking fit, with a good appetite, and full of activity and zeal.[32]

James Louis Petigru clung to the hope that the federals would compromise, that Anderson would be withdrawn, and that there would be no occasion for bloodshed. Despite his opposition to secession and his skepticism over the new southern Confederacy, Petigru was far from being a coercive Unionist. He regarded Lincoln as a low schemer who was using Anderson as a scapegoat, and he could not believe that the North would really invade the South. Indicative of Lincoln's misunderstanding of the meaning of southern unionism was the call paid on Petigru by Lincoln's informal emissaries at Charleston, Ward Hill Lamon and Stephen Augustus Hurlbut, who expected to receive surreptitious assistance from local Unionists. Petigru repulsed the callers with the statement that there was no longer any unionism in the state to appeal to.[33]

Still, Petigru hoped that his young protégé at least would not join the Confederate army after the settlement at Charleston, believing there would be peace soon. "A soldier in peacetime is a very unimportant personage," he told Johnston. "Spain is worth more than a Regiment under the Confederacy and a good retainer in my opinion better than either." Petigru's daughter, Caroline Carson, now in New York, also believed there would be no war. The field glasses she sent Pettigrew she thought would be used only to watch Anderson's exit.[34]

Back home in North Carolina people were still divided. James Cathcart Johnston had written Pettigrew in January bitterly attacking the South Carolina secessionists as "deranged or drunk." Pettigrew had heard no more from him. William Pettigrew, on the other hand, had caught secession fever. Breaking his lifelong rule to avoid politics, he was a candidate for the state convention to be called in North Carolina and was stumping Washington and Tyrrell counties vigorously.[35]

On 12 April, the Confederate States opened fire, and, after an artillery bombardment that caused no significant casualties on either side, Anderson surrendered. Despite their conspicuous role in the beginning of the Fort Sumter crisis, Pettigrew and the First Regiment of Rifles had no part in the climax except to stand at their post on Sullivan's Island in case a federal fleet outside the harbor attempted to relieve the fort by a land or naval assault, an attack which never materialized.[36]

Pettigrew, with his usual detachment, did not share in the public pleasure at what seemed to be the easy victory at Charleston. The tepid conclusion of his three and a half months of active service involved a considerable personal deflation. He had started the campaign as the hero of a small but proud state defying all comers. With the formation of the Confederacy; with the appearance on the scene of a Confederate army commanded by military professionals, graduates of West Point and veterans of Mexico receiving their orders from Montgomery; and with volunteers flocking in from all over the South, multiplying the number of men and regiments, Pettigrew and the Regiment of Rifles had gradually dwindled in importance. He became a secondary officer doing secondary duty.

On the other hand, he had gained experience of value, commanded perhaps one thousand men, won public acclaim in South Carolina, and had by his zeal and efficiency stored up credit with several high-ranking officers and influential politicians. General Beauregard spoke warmly of Pettigrew's services.[37]

Chapter 12

All Quiet Along the Potomac

In the lull after the surrender of Fort Sumter, Pettigrew, with the approval of Governor Pickens and General Beauregard and the active aid of Theodore Gaillard Barker, set out to organize what he hoped would be an elite regiment for service in Virginia. This regiment was to be made up of select volunteer companies, consisting of men of sober character who were to reach "the highest point of efficiency and discipline" and be trained in European light infantry tactics before taking the field. It was hoped they would be equipped by the state with the best available rifles before joining the service of the Confederate States.[1]

Offers of service poured in, and Pettigrew had his choice of the most eager companies. The regimental organization was nearly complete, with ten companies selected and Pettigrew and the other officers agreed upon, when a hitch developed. In early May, Barker went to Montgomery to see about acceptance of the regiment by the Confederate States. By the latest legislation, the president of the Confederacy was allowed to accept into service companies of volunteers electing their own officers. These companies were to be formed into regiments at the discretion of the Confederate States, however, and the regimental officers could be appointed rather than elected. The president declined to accept a regiment already formed with its officers already elected. He also preferred, as was allowed under the latest law, volunteers enlisted for the duration rather than for twelve months.[2]

Probably the administration had no objection to Pettigrew and his regiment as such but did not want to set a precedent to which other applicants might point. Privately, several members of Congress told Barker that if the companies of the Rifle Regiment offered their services, they would probably be kept together and Pettigrew appointed colonel. Pettigrew and his men refused to accept this compromise. Pettigrew went to Montgomery where he was depressed by the general lack of energy he found in the War Department and by his failure to secure any understanding about his regiment. Davis was probably right, for he was thinking of the requirement of system and policy for a protracted struggle. Yet South Carolinian pride, in both officers and men of the regiment, balked at compromise.[3]

Pettigrew, despite his capacity for the long view, partook of the South Carolina provinciality. He was aware of the need for energetic and serious efforts—he deplored the incompetence and lack of energy he found at Montgomery, and his letters to North Carolina were full of stirring and specific calls to action. He was quite willing to fight and die for southern independence. At the same time, he could perceive no necessity to yield anything in principle to a central government in the great struggle ahead. He was, in fact, ready to accuse the Montgomery government of "undermining the principles for which the Revolution was inaugurated" and to believe that the proviso for enlisting men to serve for the duration at the will of the president was designed to foster a dictatorship. He told his brother that the soldiers from North Carolina should be required to give an oath of first allegiance to the state before they left its borders.[4]

Pettigrew clearly understood that the states individually were defenseless and that the way to victory was concentration of all resources for a decisive strike at the North. Thus—and this was a typical Confederate flaw—he was willing to sacrifice life and property for independence but was reluctant to yield one jot or tittle of the personal liberty and state rights which he valued in order to secure them. This, in his mind, would be throwing away what he was fighting for. And, while he knew that military skill and energy were demanded, he preferred the courage and zeal of patriotic volunteers to professional soldiers hidebound by routine and tradition.[5] His distaste for West Pointers was reenforced by firsthand observation and was also quite a typical Confederate reaction in 1861. The southerner's often stiff-necked, short-sighted, and provincial insistence on his principles, as has frequently been pointed out, undermined his own cause. At the same time, these qualities made him the kind of man he was and therefore, paradoxically, sustained the Confederate cause.

In understanding this phenomena we are here, as at so many other places, misled by historians' penchant for treating the South of the late antebellum period as if it sprang full blown into life with the Wilmot Proviso and refusing to link it to the older America. Analogies to the southerner's insistence on the finest technicalities of personal liberty and state rights, even in the midst of a revolutionary gamble, can be found in the Revolutionary and Jeffersonian eras and in the Polk administration's much-criticized conduct of the Mexican War. Fear of the central authority and preference for the patriotic citizen-soldier over the standing army were among the oldest of American democratic instincts. This is only one of many examples of how southerners were still acting out the part of eighteenth-century Americans with directly inherited and still-living principles that in the North had been forgotten.

The Rifle Regiment was disbanded, and the companies went separately into other regiments then forming. The Washington Light Infantry became part of the Hampton Legion. Governor Pickens had already offered Pettigrew the post of adjutant general, or, in effect, chief of staff, of South Carolina. But this position would keep him in South Carolina and in administrative duties. His eyes were now on Virginia and his hopes still on leading troops in combat. In April Pettigrew offered his services to the governor of North Carolina.[6]

Pettigrew's state of mind, his apprehension for the cause, and his as-ever shrewd analysis of the situation were indicated by a letter on 25 May to his brother William, who was now a member of the state convention in North Carolina:

If General Scott is ready, we certainly are not. *Between us* I will give you a little plain information. The Secretary of War [Leroy P. Walker] is utterly unfit for his place. The two months which he should have spent in establishing powder mills and manufactories for arms, in importing weapons, sulphur, nitre, medicine &c &c he wasted utterly and now they cannot be procured. Gen. [Walter] Gwynn in Norfolk I like very well, but he is entirely incompetent and drinks like a fish. Almost all the South Carolina officers know very little about the business of war, and our troops (except the artillery) are only half drilled; and of the science of the thing are utterly ignorant. I expect the same is true of other States. The best officers of the old Army are with us, Johnston, Lee, Beauregard,

Bragg, Mordecai, &c &c, so that the General office will be well filled, but they can do little, without good Brigadiers Colonels &c &c, and no pains have been taken to instruct them. Our troops are first rate material. The enemy must and will make a desperate effort when they commence, so that we should exert ourselves to the utmost during the short time that remains, as everything in Missouri & Kentucky depends upon the first success. It is absolutely necessary therefore to throw the party hacks overboard. Otherwise nothing can be our fate, but defeat and destruction.

I am very far from being free of apprehension, for I know what is required in an army, particularly when we act on the defensive, but if the Executive department of the government is well managed, we have everything to hope. That however can only be attained by the Conventions and the people of the different States, requiring that none but competent men should be placed in position.[7]

He urged William to push vigorous military measures, giving specific suggestions about the organization North Carolina should undertake, particularly stressing the need for reliable and energetic men in the ordnance, quartermaster, and commissary services and the need to hold them to strict account for weapons and supplies. "In these times a week is a year, as we will learn to our cost. . . . Above all act with *energy. Time* is the article most to be valued in war." Pettigrew also saw a chance for family glory. He urged William to step forward and take a leading role in the convention, believing this could lead to his election as one of the North Carolina delegates to the Confederate Congress. To the first part of Johnston's urging, William responded enthusiastically, taking an active part in the military affairs committee of the convention.[8]

Johnston had acquired some note for his services at Charleston. William heard him discussed in connection with high military posts in North Carolina — some suggesting his appointment as member, with very prominent citizens, of a state board of war, or appointment as major general commanding the state forces. He could have any post he wanted if he would only come to Raleigh and electioneer a little, William told Johnston. This Johnston absolutely declined to do. "Pray do not *ask* anything for me," he wrote. "I have not made a personal request since the war commenced and do not wish to do so," because in the present crisis every man should do his duty, not seek office as a favor. "I have a sort of military reputation somehow but I cannot shut my eyes to the fact that it is owing rather to the deficiencies of others than any merits of my own."[9]

Besides, he was not interested in the board of war and did not want the generalship unless he could be guaranteed opportunity to lead troops in combat after duties of organization were over. Pettigrew still had his eye on Virginia where the big battles were to be fought. He would not budge from his decision to refuse to seek office despite William's persuasive urging that such would not be spoils-seeking since the dangers of the office sought outweighed the profit, like Lafayette asking a general's commission. Johnston "seems very quiescent," wrote a lady relative at Charleston. "He is exceedingly tenacious, and will not move a peg toward asking for anything, but if he were appointed would soon show himself capable & prompt. So I think and so do many others think."[10]

Pettigrew's disgust with Montgomery deepened in June when it was agreed, after all, to accept the Regiment of Rifles. But the regiment had already been disbanded and most of the companies had left for Virginia in other units. During the quiet period of late May and June, Pettigrew spent his time getting his book on Spain through the press and visiting quietly with James Louis Petigru, the crisis drawing them closer together than ever.[11]

July arrived and still Pettigrew had received no word from North Carolina, not even an acknowledgment to the letter he wrote in April offering his services. This was undoubtedly because Governor John W. Ellis was overwhelmed by applications and suffering from a terminal illness. Wade Hampton offered to get Pettigrew appointed major in the Hampton Legion, but he declined. He was elected in June as captain of the Washington Artillery Volunteers, a company of the Legion. This he declined also. Pettigrew finally determined to go to Virginia as a private in the Legion in his old company, the Washington Light Infantry, commanded by his friend James Conner. Conner reluctantly accepted this arrangement, telling Pettigrew: "Plenty of men can make privates. Few are as capable as yourself of being in command." "Johnston has something of the Roman and this step is more in accordance with antiquity than modern times," commented James Louis Petigru on his protégé's decision to serve in the ranks.[12]

Meanwhile, Pettigrew's brother, his uncle John Herritage Bryan, and other friends had been active on his behalf in North Carolina. On 11 July Pettigrew, in camp with the Hampton Legion near Richmond, received a telegram notifying him that he had been elected colonel by a vote of the Twenty-second North Carolina Regiment then organizing at Raleigh. Unofficially he was told that his election had been nearly unanimous, that the regiment was almost ready to depart for Virginia, and that it "is composed of Western men. They are a stout athletic set & look as if they would fight." [13]

Pettigrew left immediately for Raleigh, thus missing a chance for action—the first battle of Manassas in which the Legion took a distinguished part on 21 July. At about the same time Governor Pickens offered him his choice of a brigadier general's post that had just become vacant in the South Carolina state forces or a colonel's commission in a South Carolina Confederate regiment then organizing. He declined both and hastened to Raleigh. He regarded North Carolina as his first allegiance and had all along hoped for the chance to serve with a North Carolina unit.[14]

When he joined his regiment Pettigrew had just turned thirty-three years old. He was about five feet nine inches tall and had a high forehead, piercing hazel eyes, a prominent nose and pointed chin, brown hair and beard, and a complexion that was fair but usually sunburnt.[15]

Walter Clark, later a justice of the state supreme court and noted North Carolina public figure, was a fifteen-year-old drill instructor, fresh from Hillsborough Military Academy and assigned to the Twenty-second, when Pettigrew arrived. Clark observed the new colonel daily for the next few months. He remembered Pettigrew as "slendor [*sic*] of build, swarthy of complexion, dark hair and moustache, with dark eyes the most brilliant and piercing. He was quick in perception and in decision. . . . His habit was to pace restlessly up and down in front of his tent with a cigar in his mouth which was never lighted." [16]

Postwar encomiums to dead Confederate heroes were so abundant as to suggest caution in taking them at face value. The general thrust of Clark's description of Pettigrew's personality and the attitude of the soldiers toward him, however, was so often repeated with the same emphasis by different observers that there must have been a degree of truth to it: "As gentle and modest as a woman, there was an undoubted capacity to command, which obtained for Pettigrew instant

obedience, but a kindness and bearing which won affection and chivalry and courtesy which marked him every inch a gentleman."[17] The
terms of praise used by nineteenth-century southerners seem to us in-
flated and fulsome, but although southerners sometimes omitted the
unpleasant, they did try to describe accurately elusive and distinctive
qualities of personality that were for them an important part of reality.

A lieutenant of the Twenty-second recalled Pettigrew's "modest and
thoughtful bearing for which he was distinguished" and the respect
returned by the men. "How we all loved him! A noble, gallant soldier and gentleman," remembered another soldier who served a year
as Pettigrew's headquarters clerk. This man, Samuel Finley Harper,
served for three years under other officers, none of whom he spoke in
his memoirs with the same enthusiasm as he did for Pettigrew.[18]

The Twenty-second was made up of ten volunteer companies raised
in several piedmont and mountain counties of the state. It had already
been busy drilling at Camp Carolina three miles from Raleigh. The
men's first acquaintance with the harsher realities of war was the sight
of Yankee prisoners from Manassas on railroad cars, some of the regiment being detailed for guard duty. The men of the regiment ranged
in age from mid-teens to late twenties. Most were farmers or the sons
of farmers who listed themselves as laborers or mechanics. A few were
clerks or professional men.[19]

At Raleigh Pettigrew went to dinner at the mansion of his old friend
from Spain, Daniel M. Barringer, where he impressed the company by
his shrewd knowledge and predictions about military developments.
Pettigrew was for "*sharp, quick & thorough* work—which discarded all
Fabian policies, and which he thought would have carried us through
Washington to the centre of the North & brought an early and favorable peace," Barringer recalled. Making a quick visit to Charleston,
Pettigrew told his relatives that Virginia was in more danger of being
overrun than was generally supposed and that southerners could expect
to be outnumbered at every point. He was in general optimistic for the
cause, however, relying on southern morale.[20]

For eleven months Pettigrew and the men of the Twenty-second,
numbering something under one thousand in the beginning, were one.
In late July the regiment ceremoniously received a stand of colors and
on 1 August was armed and equipped by the state. In early August
the Twenty-second traveled by rail to Richmond, marched through

the center of the city between cheering crowds and blaring bands, and went into camp nearby for two weeks. Then the regiment took the train for Brooke Station, a point on the Richmond and Fredericksburg Railroad only a few miles from the Potomac, an armed frontier. The regiment now belonged to the Department of Fredericksburg, Confederate States Army.[21]

On 28 August Pettigrew received orders to take his regiment to Evansport on the Potomac and there assist engineer officers in constructing batteries. Besides his regiment, he was to have under his immediate command an artillery unit, five unattached infantry companies, and two troops of cavalry. The artillery company was made up of young Marylanders who had crossed the federal lines.[22]

Pettigrew was ordered to avoid attracting the attention of the federals across the river while constructing gun emplacements. He took great pains to conceal his activities, doing most of the work at night, only to learn later that his mission had been reported in the Washington newspapers even before he had received his orders. He was also discouraged by the poor showing of his men on the two-day march to Evansport, which he attributed to the illnesses of his lieutenant colonel and major.[23]

Throughout the fall of 1861 and the winter of 1861–1862, Pettigrew and his men remained in the Evansport vicinity, constructing and manning river batteries and their associated defense works. They were part of the eastern segment of a long, thin line which guarded the frontiers of Virginia from the Appalachians to Chesapeake Bay. Their mission was to watch the enemy in and across the Potomac and to blockade the river to prevent the passage of ships upstream to Washington. The blockade was effective, although an occasional boat slipped past at night. Indeed the Confederates took pride that, despite the proclaimed federal blockade of southern ports, Washington was the only city in North America at the time actually blockaded by water.[24]

Pettigrew was energetic in the construction of the batteries, work for which his antebellum military studies had well prepared him. He evidently received considerable credit for his skill there. The commander of the Fredericksburg department was Major General Theophilus Hunter Holmes, a North Carolinian whose thirty-five years in the United States Army had not completely prejudiced him in favor of West Point. Holmes quickly developed a respect for Pettigrew's ability.

To Pettigrew's surprise the commander suggested that Pettigrew try to secure a commission as colonel in the regular Confederate States Army (in place of his volunteer, Provisional Army commission). Such a commission would make him the ranking officer in the department after the commander instead of the colonel of lowest seniority.[25]

Accordingly, Pettigrew asked several North Carolina and South Carolina members of Congress to see what could be done, but it appeared to be impossible for anyone who was not a West Pointer to receive a regular's commission. In an interview President Davis told William Porcher Miles, now representing Charleston in the Confederate Congress, that he had respect for what he had heard of Pettigrew's ability but he could not comply. He pointed out that Pettigrew would have to give up his elective post as colonel of a volunteer regiment and be subject to assignment anywhere if he became a regular army officer.[26]

Pettigrew was acquiring a valuable reputation. A soldier of the Hampton Legion stationed some miles away wrote home that he had heard that Pettigrew "stands very high among officers." Although his superiors were pleased with him, Pettigrew, as usual, was dissatisfied with his situation. He fretted over the slowness of work on the batteries, over waste and irregularity in the supply of needed equipment, and over confusion of authority—while he was in command of the post and most of the men at Evansport, he had to deal with engineer and supply officers without knowing whether he or they were senior and cope with visiting generals or their aides who were always popping in and giving orders. "I am willing to obey any body in the world, but it is out of the question to obey two or three," he told Holmes. Once he asked to be relieved, and another time he requested transfer to the main army at Manassas where he thought he was more likely to see action. Both requests were refused.[27]

Measles struck in October, an epidemic common in army camps where thousands of rural youths never previously exposed were gathered together. Several dozen died in the Twenty-second. Pettigrew believed that his strenuous efforts in sanitation and in forcing the careless and high-spirited youths to take care of themselves (to eat carefully and not to leave the hospital too soon after an attack) had held the number of deaths down, for a neighboring regiment lost seventy men.[28]

A North Carolina newspaper reporter visited the camp of the

Twenty-second and wrote of Pettigrew: "He is emphatically a military genius, and if the yankee balls spare his life, his star will shine brilliantly. . . . If you and he live, [the readers were told] you will desire some day to know all you can learn of him. . . . Colonel Pettigrew and staff are strict disciplinarians, but not in that despotic, tyrannical, and brutish way, that is so much complained of . . . [in West Pointers.]" [29]

Except for the measles epidemic the men were in good health at Evansport, and except for bouts of boredom they were in good spirits. Food and clothes were adequate, and fairly good tents were available for winter quarters. Life during that snowy, rainy winter was mostly a fatiguing routine of digging and guard duty. Occasionally shells were exchanged with federal batteries across the river, where troops could be heard moving about, or with federal gunboats attempting to pass. There were few casualties from these encounters, since the river was two miles wide at Evansport. [30]

Infrequently, an alarm relieved the boredom of the post. Once the enemy were reported raiding out of their base at Alexandria upstream. Pettigrew's infantry was ordered out. They started within half an hour, each man carrying only arms, a loaf of hard bread, blanket, and canteen. They marched nine miles upriver only to discover that the reports of the advancing enemy were a false alarm and to march back in the dark. Despite the futile eighteen-mile march, Pettigrew was glad of the diversion which he thought improved the health and spirits of the men. "What we need is mental and moral stimulus," he wrote. On another occasion two boatloads of Yankees from a ship in the river landed at night, burned a boat on the Confederate side, and retreated without being discovered until the last moment. Pettigrew was certain that this easy victory would not have happened if his regiment had been on duty. [31]

By November the force in Evansport vicinity had grown to seven regiments plus auxiliary troops, and Pettigrew had been placed under the immediate command of Brigadier General Samuel Gibbs French, a West Pointer, a courtly and sardonic New Jerseyan who had gone with the South. Pettigrew got along famously with French, as he did with Holmes, for both men recognized in him a subordinate who would perform his duties with skill and energy and who could be self-reliant and enterprising when called for without being disloyal to his commander. [32]

Pettigrew hired a slave as body servant, but the man proved sickly.

As a replacement, his brother Charles sent from North Carolina his slave Peter who "can take care of horses, make clothes, & is a first-rate nurse," but who needed to leave home just now because he was in disfavor both with his wife and his master for having made one of the house girls pregnant. Peter stayed with Pettigrew thereafter, and he was proclaimed a superb servant. Peter was a thrifty manager and was able to accumulate a sizable sum by work in addition to his regular duties. Pettigrew also employed a cook named Jim.[33]

Two prominent Charleston politicians presented Pettigrew with a sword. He purchased a horse from a transferred general. While he was at Evansport an old classmate sent him a pair of socks and a comforter made by the classmate's wife, and he also received a "small token of regard from a Mother whose 'Darling Boy' is entrusted to his care."[34]

On Christmas 1861 the streets of the regimental camp of the Twenty-second were decorated with evergreen branches. A shooting contest was held, and the prize was a pig donated by the colonel. After the contest the colonel was serenaded with Christmas carols, to which he replied with a brief speech.[35]

Despite Pettigrew's able performance of his duties, his mind, as usual, ranged far beyond his immediate situation. He drew up a plan to reorganize his regiment after a French model, correcting defects which he felt Confederate organization had taken over directly from the regular United States Army. The plan received approval from his immediate superiors, but the Richmond authorities turned down the idea since they could find no legal authorization.[36]

Pettigrew, unlike most of his colleagues, had the proper mentality for a revolutionary. He was well aware that the war of southern independence must be earnestly, even desperately prosecuted if it were to be successful. After the fall of the outer coast of North Carolina to the federals, Pettigrew furnished his brother William with detailed instructions on how to take care of himself in the field. He added:

> I take it for granted that the enemy will attempt to ravage the country and that consequently every man must become a soldier. . . . If you are in command of the militia, train them to a few, very simple maneuvers. Battles are not won by maneuvers. Their use is to accustom men to obey the voice of the officer, to act together, and to harden the body, for after all a battle gets down to that. I

do not think you will surrender under any circumstances. Inculcate the same feeling in your men. This is not an ordinary war. It is a war of peoples not of soldiers. If necessary turn swamp fox. We have been receiving bad news for a month past, and will perhaps receive more but it amounts to nothing so far as the ultimate success of the war is concerned.[37]

Concerning troops who had surrendered on Roanoke Island, he wrote: "They may be excusable, but I have no pity for a soldier in this war who surrenders."[38]

Affairs in eastern North Carolina did not develop into quite the desperate guerrilla war that Johnston envisaged. The services of a Francis Marion or a Zumalacarregui, though perhaps needed, were not requested. William was near the upper age limit of conscription and debilitated from an attack of measles he had succumbed to while in Raleigh as a member of the secession convention. He did not rush immediately into the field as Johnston had expected, although late in the war he did see action when the senior reserves were called out to help defend Fort Fisher. But Pettigrew's sister Mary was doing her part as one of the chief nurses at the First North Carolina Hospital at Petersburg, Virginia.[39]

The Twenty-second had enlisted for one year, and its twelve months would expire in the middle of the expected summer campaign. An intensive drive was opened in February to secure reenlistment for the duration of the war, an effort which proved largely successful. Most of Pettigrew's regiment signed up, and he sent officers to North Carolina to recruit new men to fill the vacancies.[40] Later the recruitment problem was eased by the passage of the Confederate States conscription law.

At the end of February, to his surprise, Pettigrew received notice that he had been commissioned brigadier general in the Provisional Army of the Confederate States. Pettigrew's sense of honor and public ethics asserted itself immediately. He sent the following note to General Samuel Cooper, adjutant general of the army:

I acknowledge with much gratitude the honor conferred upon me by my promotion to the rank of Brigadier General, but after mature deliberation I am of the opinion that, I can serve the Confederacy much more efficiently and profitably in my present position, for reasons which it is not necessary to specify. It is but proper to add, that I am not conscious of having earned so flattering a position.

I beg leave therefore most respectfully to decline the commission of Brigadier General.[41]

The reasons that Pettigrew felt unnecessary to specify may be surmised: he was needed with the Twenty-second, which was at the moment undergoing reenlistment; he did not want to be transferred to a new command and lose credit for the training he had given his regiment, which he was sure would distinguish itself in its first battle; and most important, on principle he believed that no one should be commissioned general who had never led troops in combat. Also, the command suggested for him in northeastern North Carolina was, he believed, offered under the mistaken impression that he was familiar with the topography of the area, and it would take him from the main theater.[42]

"He declined for reasons that are not likely to injure the service by becoming popular," J. L. Petigru commented on Johnston's decision. "It will be no disadvantage to him, perhaps, at some future day, that he was not anxious to jump at any future chance of promotion." Mary Boykin Chesnut, however, who heard rumor of the incident in Richmond, remarked, "He was too high and mighty. . . . Modest merit just now is at a premium."[43]

Pettigrew was summoned to Richmond to state to President Davis in person his reasons for refusing the command. The most direct testimony to this interview is secondhand, that written down two years later by James Conner to whom Pettigrew must have related it: Pettigrew declared that he had never handled troops in action, and his conviction was firm that no man should be a brigadier who had not. Davis replied with a smile that the responsibility for the appointment was his and that he was entirely satisfied with Pettigrew's qualifications. Pettigrew again politely and firmly declined. The President remarked with some amusement that he wished the whole country could overhear their conversation. He had been submerged with applications for commissions, and this was the first time anyone had turned one down on the grounds that he had not demonstrated his ability to discharge the duties.[44]

Pettigrew left Richmond still a colonel, and when he rode back into the camp of the Twenty-second, where report of the interview had preceded him, he was cheered. It was General Holmes who had, unknown to Pettigrew, recommended him for promotion. When Pettigrew returned to the Potomac, Holmes continued to urge his acceptance.[45]

Meanwhile, the spring campaign was developing with several massive federal threats, the most important of which proved to be McClellan's amphibious landing on the Peninsula in an attempt to reach Richmond from the east rather than the north. On 8 March 1862, as part of the general Confederate fallback and concentration, the batteries at Evansport were destroyed, and General French's command withdrew south to the Rappahannock defense life, camping for some weeks in the woods near Fredericksburg.[46]

It was evident that the troops of the Fredericksburg department would be in action before long, and it was expedient to form the regiments into brigades. Holmes called a council of war and, seconded by other officers, told Pettigrew that it was absolutely his duty to accept promotion. Persuaded by this pressure and by the consideration that the brigade he would now command would include the Twenty-second, Pettigrew reluctantly accepted, and on 22 March his commission as brigadier general was returned by the War Department.[47]

"Johnston has disappointed them that didn't think he would ever do anything like anybody else. For he has actually allowed himself to be persuaded out of his refusal of promotion," was J. L. Petigru's comment. Petigru approved his loved protégé's decision because "a man is bound when he engages in a cause to do his best for it, and those who have the control ought to be supposed best judges of the way in which he can be most useful." A few days later, however, James Conner, whose election to succeed him as colonel of the Twenty-second Pettigrew had arranged, found the new general chafing at having given up his own ideas of what was proper. To Conner Pettigrew remarked that a man's own convictions are the surest guide and he ought not to listen to anything else.[48]

Holmes was shortly thereafter assigned to command in North Carolina. He officially requested that Pettigrew join him, because "he is from North Carolina, and I need his strength to discipline new recruits rapidly." But action was imminent in Virginia and the request was turned down. Later that year, when Holmes was made a lieutenant general and given command of all Confederate forces west of the Mississippi, he asked the War Department to send him a general who could be trusted with the command of a corps of his widely dispersed forces. He suggested that Pettigrew, promoted to major general, would be just such an officer. This transfer, too, failed to materialize.[49]

The promotion to brigadier general was a considerable honor and a signal testimony of the good impression Pettigrew had made on serious-minded officers. Many men younger than Pettigrew and with no more antebellum military experience eventually became general officers in the Confederate army—almost all of them later on in the war and after many casualties in the ranks of high command. In the winter of 1862, when Pettigrew was first offered promotion, almost all generals were veterans of the United States Army or politicians of considerable influence. Of the twenty-two brigade commanders other than Pettigrew who went into action on the Peninsula in 1862, all but a few were older than Pettigrew. Eleven were former regular army officers, and three others were graduates of Virginia Military Institute. Six had been prominent politicians of the rank of governor or member of Congress. Of the remaining two, one was Wade Hampton, ten years Pettigrew's senior and a veteran of First Manassas, and the other, Joseph B. Kershaw, though not a professional, had been a volunteer officer in the Mexican War.[50] In other words, Pettigrew's promotion was patently the result of merit so conspicuous that it transcended lack of experience and political influence.

Chapter 13

Fleeting Glory

The brigade of which Johnston Pettigrew took command near Fredericksburg about 18 March 1862 consisted of, besides his own Twenty-second North Carolina, the Thirty-fifth Georgia, the Forty-seventh Virginia, an Arkansas battalion of three hundred men, an unattached company of Maryland infantry, and a small battery manned by the young gunners from Baltimore. For his adjutant, Pettigrew summoned from Charleston the able and congenial Louis Gourdin Young, a veteran of the First Regiment of Rifles and Charleston harbor, who was anxious to get into the fight despite his family's opposition.[1]

Soon the brigade was in motion to the Virginia peninsula where the greatest enemy threat was to be met. Union general George B. McClellan had landed a huge and superbly equipped army and, with effective naval control of the lower York and James rivers, was intent on marching up to Richmond. Unknown to McClellan, his force was far greater than anything the Confederates could put between him and the capital. For several weeks in April and May, Pettigrew's brigade was a part of the Confederate army which slowly fell back toward Richmond, deceiving the enemy as to its weakness. The brigade did a great deal of marching and digging and saw and heard the enemy more than once, but it did not get into action, although at the skirmish of Barhamville (or West Point) on 7 May it waited under arms in the reserve to supplement the forces repulsing a federal attack if needed.[2]

The Confederate force before Richmond had only recently been brought together under General Joseph E. Johnston, and the organization of large units of command was vague. Pettigrew's was one of five brigades loosely drawn together in a division under Brigadier General William Henry Chase Whiting, a division which was part of a "wing" commanded by Major General Gustavus Woodson Smith.[3] Both Holmes and French had been transferred to other duties.

By the end of May, the federals were in sight of Richmond church spires. They were not to come so close again until 1865. It was determined to yield no further but to counterattack, hoping to smash a part of the invading army cut off from the rest by the rising Chickahominy Creek. The assault was launched on 31 May. The action which developed, known officially as the battle of Seven Pines or Fair Oaks Station, took place in a morass of swampy creek bottoms and tangled woods out of sight of the commanders in charge. The fight was so haphazard and uncoordinated on both sides that it has been referred to by the leading student of the war in Virginia as "the Battle of Strange Errors."[4] The grinding carnage which ensued made First Manassas seem like a picnic.

The mission of Whiting's division was to support the main attack. From early morning until late afternoon Pettigrew's brigade waited at a crossroads, hearing the battle ahead but in the dense woods and smoke seeing nothing. Late in the afternoon the division moved forward at the double-quick through the mud, overran a thin line of enemy skirmishers, passed over what had recently been a federal camp, and in a few minutes charged directly into the heavy fire of enemy infantry and artillery posted in and around a wooded ravine near the Fair Oaks railroad station.

The attack temporarily halted in the face of a withering fire from three sides, but not before the troops had moved up to the enemy position. "Very seldom, if ever, did any troops in their first battle go so close up to a covered line under so strong a fire and remain within such short distance so long a time," General Smith reported later.

As the attack halted Pettigrew conferred with Whiting and with Wade Hampton, who was commanding one of the other of the three leading brigades. They did not know the strength of the enemy in position before them, and they determined to attempt to capture the batteries if possible and keep pushing forward.[5]

Several times the Confederates charged but could not reach the enemy in the ravine. The federals would neither come forward from their protected position nor retreat. The Confederates could not take the position but would not be driven off, after each bloody charge falling back slightly to cover and continuing to fire. All was chaos; the woods were so thick that Pettigrew could see only a small part of his command. Dispatching aides to rally the other regiments, Pettigrew personally led the Twenty-second into the zone of fire in front of the federal position in another fruitless charge.

Within a few minutes, as he was trying to get as close as possible to get a view of the federal position, Pettigrew was shot through the throat, a rifle ball (it was later determined) grazing his windpipe, severing an artery, and tearing bone and muscle in the right shoulder. Some soldiers helped him dismount, but he was so feeble from rapid loss of blood that he lay down immediately where he was. Lieutenant Colonel Gustavus A. Bull of his Georgia regiment stopped Pettigrew's bleeding, probably saving his life. They were in the zone of fire and Bull himself was shot down while tending to Pettigrew. A young officer with Bull left in search of help. The Confederates were falling back to cover out of the zone of fire before the federal position.

A passing captain detailed four men to carry Pettigrew out. Pettigrew asked how the action was going and the captain replied: Against us. Pettigrew then ordered the officer to look for his aides and tell them to bring up support. He ordered the four men to rejoin their company. "I refused to allow myself to be taken to the rear after being wounded," Pettigrew reported later, "because from the amount of bleeding I thought the wound to be fatal; it was useless to take men from the field, under any circumstances for that purpose."

It was now getting dark, and the Confederates withdrew from the exposed position and formed further back. Pettigrew passed out. A retreating officer saw him insensible, his eyes fixed, decided that he was dead, and so reported.[6]

The federals counterattacked across the ground where Pettigrew had been struck. At some point in this action, while lying on the field, he was shot again, in the left arm, and was bayonetted in the leg, the latter a type of atrocity that seems to have been rare in the Civil War, but about which Pettigrew made little fuss.[7]

All night Pettigrew lay on the field among the dead and wounded, unable to move very far and intermittently unconscious. Some of his men and some friends from the Hampton Legion formed a party to search for his body but were not allowed to proceed beyond the Confederate picket lines. The place where Pettigrew lay was now within the federal lines. Early in the morning of 1 June he was picked up by a group of soldiers from the Twentieth Massachusetts Regiment. Lieutenant Colonel Bull was also captured and later died of his wounds.[8]

Pettigrew was taken to a residence, now a field hospital, a short distance behind the battle lines and locked in a smokehouse. "He looked as if he expected us to execute him," recalled the federal doctor who opened the door of the dark smokehouse some hours later. What was going through Pettigrew's mind may be easily imagined: the effects of weakness and pain; shame at having been taken prisoner; and his memories of the Austrian captives he had seen going to the rear in Italy in 1859 who had seemed to him scarcely human.[9]

Upon examination Pettigrew's neck wound, despite considerable bleeding, proved to be not dangerous. The shot, however, in passing through his body severed muscles and nerves, and Pettigrew never again recovered full use of his right arm. The leg wound too was serious, and full use of that limb was regained very slowly. The wound in the left arm was minor. After these wounds were tended to, Pettigrew was marched, under guard and limping, to another house-hospital further to the rear.[10]

Meanwhile, his own side had concluded that Pettigrew was dead, and the news was officially telegraphed to his family. No one was surprised. "Johnston Pettigrew was rash, I suspect," someone told Mary Boykin Chesnut. "They called him eccentric and crack-brained because he was so much in earnest," Mrs. Chesnut recorded respectfully. "He did not waste time haranguing about Kentucky resolutions, States Rights, Cotton is King! That fatuous style left the talkers looking like imbeciles when the time for action came, and the time for talk was over."[11]

President Davis, who had been on the field throughout the action, rode into the brigade camp one or two days after the battle of Seven Pines and inquired of the officers the details of Pettigrew's death. Pettigrew's aide, Lieutenant Young, and his servant, Peter, had been disconsolate since the general's death. Peter was pointed out to the president. Davis rode over to Peter, expressed his sympathy, assured him that everything possible would be done to recover the body, and then, it was reported, turning his head weeping, touched his hat to Peter and rode off.[12]

From the smokehouse Pettigrew was taken to the house of Dr. William F. Gaines behind the federal lines, where he remained for ten days. He was kept there under guard but in comfortable circumstances, socializing with the doctor and with Yankee officers who paid a number of calls during which politics and war were barred from the conversation. The war was still conducted with some notions of chivalry at this early point. Pettigrew refused to give any information about the Confederate forces and to his captors presented a good-humored but unshakable confidence in the victory of his side. He was allowed to keep his watch and personal papers.[13]

Pettigrew had three concerns. One was his shame at being captured. He feared that his capture would be construed as a surrender. He was able to get a note sent over under a flag of truce to General Whiting explaining his situation: "As I was in a state of insensibility, I was picked up by the first party which came along, which proved to be the enemy. I hope you know, General, that I never would have surrendered, under any circumstances, to save my own life, or anybody else's, and if Generals Smith or Johnston are under a different impression, I hope you will make a statement of the facts in the case."[14] Pettigrew need not have worried that his reputation would be damaged. There had been enough witnesses to prevent that.

His comrades and family did not know that he was alive until they read it in a captured New York newspaper on 4 June. Dead generals, although Pettigrew was not the first, were still a novel phenomenon at this stage in the war, and Pettigrew, when he returned to the Confederacy, had the strange experience of reading his own splendid obituaries.[15]

Wounded and captured generals were even rarer than dead ones. When William Pettigrew arrived in the camp of the brigade to take care of the general's affairs, he found that his brother "seems to have acquired the highest admiration & affection of every one that I have seen." President Davis in person told William of his gratification at the news the general was still alive, and Whiting told him that Pettigrew had charged into a terrible fire "with the utmost bravery and coolness." In his official report, General Smith said, "The chivalric and accomplished Pettigrew went forward into action with the high, hopeful, and enthusiastic courage which so strongly marks his character as an officer."[16] Still, Pettigrew had missed his chance again. At Fort Sumter he had been shunted aside at the last moment. He had been summoned to North Carolina just in time to miss the victory at First Manassas. Now he was shot down and captured on the first day of his first battle and separated from the command into which he had put so much effort.

Thus the second of Pettigrew's three concerns was his hope to get exchanged and return to duty as soon as possible. In his note to Whiting he said that he would gladly be reduced in rank to facilitate his exchange. Since he would not be physically fit for active service for some time, he was perfectly willing to become a junior officer of artillery at Charleston.[17]

Pettigrew's third worry was the future of his brigade. The brigade had distinguished itself in the Seven Pines battle, having 341 casualties among slightly more than two thousand men taken into action. A few days after Pettigrew's capture, the brigade was turned over to the command of Brigadier General William Dorsey Pender, a young North Carolinian and West Pointer, and in the terrible Seven Days battles which followed in late June and early July just outside Richmond it saw much action. Subsequently, the brigade was broken up and the Twenty-second went into a new, all–North Carolina brigade which served with the Virginia army until Appomattox.[18]

From Dr. Gaines's, Pettigrew was sent to Fortress Monroe on the tip of the Virginia peninsula. He arrived on 12 June without any accompanying orders governing his disposal. Since there were no hospital facilities at Monroe, the commander immediately put him on a steamer bound for Baltimore. Meanwhile, one of the Pettigrew family factorage firms behind the federal lines in Norfolk had arranged for Pettigrew to draw money on their associates in New York if he needed cash while a prisoner.[19]

Pettigrew spent six days at Baltimore. In the city were his old law tutor James Mason Campbell, his father's longtime friend and mercantile agent John Williams, and his cousin William Shepard Bryan who was almost a brother, not to mention numerous sympathizers personally unknown to him. Pettigrew was allowed to lodge at Guy's Monument House hotel while he underwent medical treatment, having given his word not to escape. He received the attention of his friends and relatives and was showered with food, wine, and flowers by local admirers.[20]

Meanwhile, Pettigrew and Colonel (later General) Roger W. Hanson, a Kentuckian captured at Fort Donelson who had also ended up as a prisoner in Baltimore, had become a public issue. A part of the northern press and public was aroused at the notion that fiendish rebel officers were living at ease and receiving courtesies from the citizens of Baltimore.[21] The North was now making up its mind whether it would fight the war under the code of chivalry as the South and General McClellan were attempting to do or respond to the urgings of fanatical Republicans for total war.

Most of the army officers Pettigrew encountered held the first view. Pettigrew found them to be gentlemen "provided," as he told a Charleston lady after he returned to the Confederacy, "you make the allowance for them which you must for all Yankees, [that] they will lie." General John E. Wool, the federal commander at Baltimore, was of the older school of northerners. When he received an order to send Pettigrew to Fort Delaware he attempted to delay, reporting that he was determining whether the prisoner was medically fit to travel. That dour zealot, Secretary of War Edwin M. Stanton, however, won out, ordering Wool to send Pettigrew immediately to Fort Delaware.[22] No chivalry for him.

About 20 June, Pettigrew reached Fort Delaware, a fortress prison in the middle of the Delaware River. His removal from Baltimore was considered an act of cruelty by his friends and family since he did not have the use of his arm and could barely walk. Only in Baltimore could he secure the medical skill that might save the use of his arm. At Delaware he was still able to receive mail and presents, however, including reading matter, wine, and a cap and slippers from friends in Baltimore. He also received offers of personal assistance from a number of Pennsylvanians and New Yorkers, some of whom were old acquaintances and others who were sympathetic to his cause or his confinement. His imprisonment was further alleviated by the fact that his jailer, a Captain Gibson, was an acquaintance of one of his own prewar northern acquaintances. Thus he was as comfortable as could be expected, but Pettigrew was worried about the paralysis of his arm. He requested permission to go to Baltimore for galvanic battery treatments, promising to turn himself in whenever requested, but he was refused.[23]

Pettigrew spent about six weeks at Fort Delaware. Meanwhile, after long negotiations, a general exchange of prisoners had been worked out, and in early August Pettigrew was passed over the lines to the Confederacy in exchange for a federal brigadier. He was still weak and partly incapacitated, but he reported for duty at Richmond immediately. James Louis Petigru, shaking his head over Pettigrew's insistence on an early return to service despite his paralyzed right arm and stiff leg, commented: "There's no hopes [*sic*] for genius."[24]

"The Yankees say that it is very hard to kill the North Carolinians entirely," Pettigrew told one of his former soldiers who congratulated him on his return, "and it does seem so, though they wound a great many of us. Those of us, who had the bad luck to fall into their hands are now more anxious than ever to have another trial." To Barringer, who offered him his mansion at Raleigh for recuperation, Pettigrew reported, "It would give you pain and at the same time pride to see Baltimore [Barringer's wife's home]. . . . How nobly they bear up under it [occupation]. As for the ladies, I think they are angels one and all."[25]

From Richmond, Pettigrew went to Petersburg. James Conner was there at the home of some relatives, recuperating from a wound received in the Seven Days' battles. Each day he invited Pettigrew to the home for lunch, and the ladies entered into a conspiracy to make the recalcitrant general eat and rest properly. "There was always a good deal of diplomatism required to make him take care of himself," Conner recalled, "although no man was more careful for others."[26]

William Henry Trescot wrote jokingly about Pettigrew's return from the dead: "What right have you to come back and eat the fatted calf and drink the old madeira that society gives to living heroes and at the same time feed on the ambrosia of flattery that is given to the dead, only because they can't enjoy it. . . . But jesting apart I am rejoiced that I may see you again and that the poor Arabs in Spain may yet have justice done them. . . . And now . . . you must prepare for lectures on rashness."[27]

At Richmond Pettigrew was disappointed to find that he was not to rejoin his old brigade but was to have a new command in a backwater away from the glorious fields of the war. He ordered a new uniform from his Charleston tailor, told his brother to send Peter and his horses up from North Carolina, had Louis G. Young assigned once more as his adjutant, and prepared to do his duty.[28]

Chapter 14

An Interlude with Bandits

The men of the brigade of which Pettigrew formally took command at Petersburg on 18 August 1862 were scattered across the Low Country of Virginia and North Carolina from the James River to the Cape Fear. They were assigned temporarily to various other generals and were not concentrated in one place under Pettigrew's command for several months. These men had been recently engaged in surveillance and containment of the federals who had taken the coast in 1861 and who occupied a string of fortified towns on the lower tidal rivers from Suffolk, Virginia, southward to New Bern, North Carolina. The brigade continued this duty under Pettigrew's command until the spring of 1863.[1]

In that desultory backwater of the war there was little glory to be won, and there were few roads and much fever and chronic shortages of weapons, ammunition, and tools. The men were there because the federal garrisons, which were relatively quiet but large compared to what the Confederates could put in front of them, must be watched in case the federals should attempt some major offensive; because the Confederate government was politically obligated to try to defend its scattered civilian population despite the military desirability of concentration of forces; and because the country within and around the federal lines was rich in corn and hogs that had to be denied the enemy and added to Confederate larders if possible.[2]

Pettigrew almost immediately importuned the Confederate authorities for transfer to a more active post in northern Virginia, suggesting that many officers would gladly trade his quieter post with him. He even asked to give up his general's commission and serve as a volunteer aide to General Lee. Pettigrew worried about missing the big action and probably preferred the risk of combat in Virginia to the risk of fever in the Low Country. "If the accidents of the service keep General Pettigrew from a more active field, he is certainly too much of a soldier to complain," the secretary of war replied. Transfer was refused even though Lee requested Pettigrew's services.[3] So Pettigrew chafed in southeastern Virginia while others fought at Antietam.

If the theater was not to his liking, the command was a good one, not as seasoned in great battles as some, but composed of good men. The brigade had been that of General James Green Martin who was now assigned to other duty in western North Carolina. General Martin took with him from the brigade the Seventeenth North Carolina Regiment, which was commanded by his brother.[4]

Of the regiments remaining, the Eleventh was the best. It was made up largely of veterans of the First North Carolina or "Bethel" Regiment, the earliest volunteers from all parts of the state, who had reorganized as the Eleventh when their first six months' enlistment had expired. The colonel of the Eleventh was Collett Leventhorpe, a veteran British army officer who was a North Carolinian by marriage. The Eleventh was well drilled and had taken part in some small battles in eastern North Carolina since its reorganization.[5]

The Forty-fourth North Carolina Regiment, under Colonel Thomas Singletary, had also seen service in eastern North Carolina, where its first colonel had been killed in a skirmish. It was made up of both eastern and piedmont men, and among its officers was Robert Bingham, son of Pettigrew's teacher. The Forty-seventh North Carolina, led by Colonel George H. Faribault, was made up mostly of eastern North Carolina men and had done considerable marching and skirmishing in North Carolina and southeastern Virginia, although it had been in no major battle. The Fifty-second, under Colonel James K. Marshall, made up of companies from all parts of the state, had had a career similar to that of the Forty-seventh.[6]

In exchange for the Seventeenth, Pettigrew was fortuitously assigned, from General Robert Ransom's brigade, the Twenty-sixth, perhaps the best regiment of North Carolinians in the field. Made up of early volunteers reenlisted for the duration, the Twenty-sixth had been in the battle of New Bern in March 1862 and had received a real baptism of fire in the Seven Days at Richmond. Zebulon Baird Vance had been its colonel until he was elected governor. The Twenty-sixth was now commanded by twenty-year-old Henry King Burgwyn, Jr., one of the youngest colonels in the army and a modest and single-minded soldier much like Pettigrew himself. The two men hit it off beautifully.[7]

The strength of the brigade fluctuated considerably. The returns for October 1862, near the peak, gave an official strength of 5,256 men, of whom 4,417 were present for duty, but in March 1863 only 3,582 men were present for duty. The brigade was officially part of a military department encompassing southeastern Virginia and eastern North Carolina, with headquarters at Petersburg. The department commander was General G. W. Smith, second to whom was Pettigrew's friend, General French.[8]

During the last months of 1862 several of the regiments continued to take part in scattered skirmishes under other commanders, operations designed to bring in the fall harvest of corn and hogs from behind the federal forts. With part of his command, Pettigrew engaged in similar work along the Blackwater River in Virginia, watching the enemy in Suffolk, countering their occasional foraging raids, and annoying them as much as possible. During much of this time, even those men under his direct command were widely dispersed, guarding bridges and fords or bringing in the garnered crop.[9]

As usual Pettigrew was both efficient and pessimistic. "With proper energy the enemy might be rolled out of Suffolk and North Carolina, and yet I am certain it will not be done," he wrote. He presented his superiors with a plan for taking Suffolk. They complimented it but turned it down on the ground that it would require more experienced troops than were available. Pettigrew's energy did not diminish, however. Here (and the next year in North Carolina) he proved himself adept, despite a lack of cavalry, at sending out scouts, questioning citizens and deserters from behind the federal lines, piecing together information to discern the enemy's movements and intentions, and learning the unmapped terrain. The sheriff of Prince George County, Virginia, found that Pettigrew knew the topography of the county better than he.[10]

In September, Pettigrew had an important part in a demonstration against Suffolk. This failed to dislodge the federals, although valuable provisions were gathered. On this expedition Pettigrew's men spent a week marching about, repairing a railroad, and sleeping on the ground in the rain without tents. "We have just returned [to Petersburg] from a rather badly conceived expedition. . . . The Yankees outnumbered us, but they were green and we were green and I think we could have caught them," Pettigrew told his brother at the end of this campaign. "Instead of striking like the lightning of the tropics, we spent a whole week in rolling up our little thunder cloud, right before their faces, so that any fool would have raised his umbrella," he reported with some disgust.[11]

That fall on the Blackwater, Pettigrew's men got a good deal of seasoning in hard marching and digging fortifications. Although there was no real battle because the enemy always withdrew into Suffolk after slight contact, the brigade gained steadiness by encountering federal infantry and the shelling of gunboats.[12]

Pettigrew put together a good staff. Louis Gourdin Young and Pettigrew's young kinsman from New Bern, William Biddle (Willie) Shepard, were his aides. Captain Nicholas Collin Hughes was adjutant general of the brigade; Major George Pettigrew Collins, a neighbor of the Pettigrews at The Lake, was chief quartermaster; Major William J. Baker was chief commissary; Captain W. W. McCreery was inspector general; and Captain Walter H. Robertson was chief of ordnance.[13]

These staff officers were mostly young, although Pettigrew, so he told his brother, would not object to mature men if he could find them. Pettigrew wished all his staff officers to be gentlemen "both interior and exterior." He looked for good health, education, congeniality, and intelligence. He would tolerate no man who was selfish, conceited, or mentally slow.[14] In short, he wanted a staff that would make a good appearance and inspire respect from the brigade and from other officers, that was equal in energy and ability to its work, and whose efficiency and fellowship were unmarred by personality flaws. Pettigrew wanted to do his duty, but he wanted to do it in style.

Pettigrew was a good commander, firm but fair. He applied discipline as training, just to the extent that it was necessary for the soldiers' own good, and eschewed rigor for its own sake. As a settled policy he lived on the same fare as the privates. From the mother of a private for whom he had allowed leave to procure a new set of clothes from home Pettigrew received a thankful note: "I know in your official capacity you must have trouble enough in attending to the interest of our distressed country, yet, from all I have learned, there is largeness of mind, sufficient in General Pettigrew, to admit a petition from one individual without scorn." [15]

John Cheves Haskell, an artillery officer who served with Pettigrew in North Carolina in the spring of 1863, recalled: "He was a singularly charming man, whose men were devoted to him and felt the most implicit confidence in him. I had never previously met him, but soon fell under the influence of his charm and was devoted to him ever after." Haskell also found Louis Young and most of the field officers of the brigade to be unusually young, dashing, bright, and respected men. [16]

Pettigrew was just getting into the prime of life. The eccentricities and diffidence of his youth dropped away as he found fulfillment in a sphere of action that absorbed his mental energies and satisfied his moral longings. His Seven Pines wounds still made physical activity uncomfortable, but his perennial illnesses had ceased to appear. During the epidemics at Evansport he had been about the only man in his command who had not been sick. [17]

Pettigrew was aware that keeping busy was the clue to a soldier's contentment. Leonidas Lafayette Polk, a young North Carolina planter and sergeant major of the Twenty-sixth, who many years later would be a prominent national leader of the Populist party, wrote his wife from Camp French near Petersburg in October, "I am busy from light until breakfast, as soon as I can eat, I have to go out on Battalion drill, & drill very hard for two hours. This dose is repeated in the evening & then Dress Parade. Besides I have a good deal of writing to do & recite lessons in tactics." [18]

Pettigrew applied some of his observations in France to problems of logistics. With his commissary officer, Major Baker, he conducted an experiment in baking bread on a large scale as a substitute for the men baking their own over campfires. For his interest in camp cookery he was commended by President Davis, who wrote: "The views and actions of Genl. J. J. Pettigrew are approved, and it is gratifying to know that so much of zeal and intelligence has been directed to the important matter of proper cooking in camp." Pettigrew also let the medical officers know that they would have to meet certain standards of performance. [19]

North Carolina was much alarmed and demoralized by the federal occupation and depredations in the east and was besieging the Confederate government for relief. Governor Vance and the members of Congress from North Carolina asked in September that the state be made a separate military department and that Pettigrew be placed in command as "an officer who, besides his high qualifications for the office, is identified with the interests of the state and possesses the full confidence of the people." Richmond declined on the grounds that it was desirable to keep eastern North Carolina and Virginia south of the James in the same department, and that Pettigrew could not be assigned command of operations in North Carolina without removing four senior officers. Vance told Pettigrew, "When at Richmond I asked the President to make N.C. a Dpt. in itself, & put you in command of it, but he suggested those unhappy difficulties of rank & precedence for which your West Point gentlemen are so famous." [20]

In November and early December 1862 Pettigrew with part of his brigade moved into North Carolina, engaging in the same type of operation as on the Blackwater: watching the federals and bringing out the fall harvest. It was a swampy country with bad roads. Supplies, tools, ammunition, maps, and transport were inadequate, and there was little cavalry to hold up a screen before the enemy and watch him. Much of the time was spent behind the fortified federal posts. The soldiers found the people mostly loyal to the Confederate cause but demoralized and depressed, for they were constantly subject to foraging raids in which the federals carried off corn, hogs, and slaves and vandalized dwellings.[21] The ensuing hardships to a rural people were considerable.

In December Pettigrew's old nemesis at Charleston, John Gray Foster, now a general in command of the federal forces in eastern North Carolina, marched out of his base at New Bern on the lower Neuse River with 10,000 infantry, 640 cavalry, and 40 guns, and headed up-country toward Kinston and Goldsboro and toward the Wilmington and Weldon Railroad, the great north-south trunk that was the main artery of supply for Lee's army. Only two thousand Confederates were in his front. General Smith was immediately dispatched from Petersburg with Pettigrew's and French's brigades.[22]

The men stumbled out of railroad cars at Goldsboro in the night of December 16/17. The next day Pettigrew, with part of his brigade, formed line of battle in a railroad cut and watched the Yankees advance in a mile-long line in good order to within five hundred yards of his position. Colonel Burgwyn, who had once been tutored by the federal commander, reportedly stood on the railroad and exclaimed softly, "Ah, my mother!" as the enemy advanced. Just as the men were bracing themselves for the attack, dusk began to fall and the Yankees withdrew. Orders had been to wait until the Yankees were within twenty paces, then give them a volley and charge.[23]

The Fifty-second Regiment, temporarily attached to another brigade across the river, had eight killed and seventy-nine wounded when drunken General Nathan G. Evans sent them on an unsupported charge on a battery. The Forty-fourth was also heavily engaged on the same part of the field.[24]

After burning one bridge, losing 591 men, and paroling a few prisoners taken, Foster withdrew to New Bern. Pettigrew's brigade was assigned to watch him safely back to his base. During this December shadowing expedition the men slept on the ground without tents.[25]

This debacle, the battle of Goldsboro, showing up the weakness of Smith's command in North Carolina and the ease with which the vital Wilmington and Weldon Railroad could be cut, awakened Richmond. A Department of North Carolina was created. Major General Daniel Harvey Hill, a North Carolinian, a veteran of the great Virginia battles, a kinsman of "Stonewall Jackson," and a man of great energy and dedication although of decided eccentricities of character, took command.[26]

All of Pettigrew's brigade was finally brought together in January 1863 and encamped in winter quarters at Magnolia in Duplin County. The soldiers expressed happiness at being under Pettigrew's command after their sojourn under other generals, and the Forty-second North Carolina, having been temporarily under Pettigrew, protested being taken from him.[27]

During the winter of 1863, from its winter quarters at Magnolia, the brigade operated at times along the railroad as far north as Petersburg—with much opportunity for drills, inspections, marching, and construction of field works. Pettigrew subjected the officers of the brigade to a candid appraisal and then to a rigorous program of study and examination. He found them on the whole adequate to their immediate duties but not very zealous in improving their military knowledge and overly casual about camp police. During this period Pettigrew was temporarily in command of French's division, three brigades with over 8,500 men present for duty.[28]

The esprit and fitness of the rank and file was excellent despite the absence of tents. This lack was compensated by an adequate supply of food, clothing, and blankets. The soldiers were incorrigibly individualistic, and in the midst of drill they would openly carry on a democratic dialogue in evaluation of the correctness of the officers' orders. "As for hardship," wrote a member of the Forty-fourth, "they have some hardship — that is what other folks call hardship — but hardship means an unusual exposure — to us being without tents is no hardship as we are used to it — not having had a tent now for some nearly two months, since Dec. 14." Pettigrew's camp was in a beautiful setting — an old field thickly set with second-growth pines.[29]

That winter the men spent much time drilling, sometimes marched out to meet alarms, and sometimes loaded trains and performed other similar work. Snowball fights and baseball occupied leisure hours. Many of the soldiers had the feeling after the victory at Fredericksburg that the war was over and southern independence established, so there was considerable tendency toward absence without leave. Such absences resulted as much from a desire to get home during a quiet period than from an intention to evade service, but they still constituted a serious military problem. On 26 January, the Twenty-sixth Regiment was drawn up in a hollow square for the execution of a deserter, an occasion of "a solemnity I have not felt since I have been in service," L. L. Polk wrote his wife. At the last moment the condemned man was reprieved and later died with bravery at Gettysburg. The point was made, however.[30]

The standard of hardiness, steadfastness, and physical courage among these men must be rated high. No one who reads the letters of Pettigrew's soldiers can believe that the tradition of Confederate valor is only myth. The solid core of truth to the tradition can only be disputed by the most cynical and shortsighted of debunkers. Many of the officers and men of Pettigrew's brigade were, like the commander himself, of mature age and substantial property. Yet they were physically and morally ready for battle. They went to meet the foe and risk their lives repeatedly, not with the impersonal terror of modern warfare but with an intensely personal sense of mission. Their courage arose in part from the fact that they were physically hearty men used to meeting life aggressively, in part because they had a very personal civic ethic, in part because they truly believed their fate was in God's hands. And in part it was because they had actually seen the enemy's heel upon their home soil, for in eastern North Carolina there was ample opportunity to view the depredations of a conquering foe.

Pettigrew's friend General French, who was a northerner by birth and raising, wrote of the federal activities in eastern North Carolina in 1862 and 1863: "The pianos and furniture shipped from there decorate to-day many a Northern home. At Hamilton most of the dwellings had been entered, mirrors broken, furniture smashed, doors torn from their hinges, and especially were the feather beds emptied in the streets, spokes of carriage wheels broken, and cows shot in the fields by the roadside, etc. It was a pitiful sight to see the women and children in their destitute condition. . . . The main object of small expeditions was to steal private property." [31] The reaction of southerners, to whom the concept of honor was still a reality, was a powerful desire to meet the foe and make him pay for his crimes.

Much of Pettigrew's attention, both on the Blackwater River and in eastern North Carolina, from August 1862 to May 1863 had to be directed to the ethically and legally gray area within and around the federal enclaves. Governor Vance entrusted Pettigrew with selection of the commander of a partisan battalion he had organized to operate behind the federal lines. Pettigrew selected Major John N. Whitford and collaborated closely with his guerrilla band. He was vexed by certain citizens who hung around his outposts, gathered information, and carried it back to the enemy. He had no legal authority to stop them. Pettigrew urged Vance, with whom he had developed a close relationship, to secure a law from the legislature allowing such people to be detained without punishment until they could do no harm. He could not understand the legislature's refusal to make this provision. He told Vance he could easily understand jealousy of the Confederate authorities but could not understand the unwillingness to give the power to suspend habeas corpus temporarily to the governor of the state. The men in the field, he reported, were highly dissatisfied with the legislature, which had done nothing to rally the people: "It is not that we object to this or that particular measure . . . but it is because they give us no word of encouragement, nor manifest any of that enthusiastic detestation (or hatred) of the enemy for his outrages, which animates us, who witness them."[32]

Pettigrew was particularly incensed at the federal proposals to arm blacks, many of them recent slaves who had run away or been abducted to the federal lines. "Bad times are coming here, for the Yankees have selected this state and Louisiana for the practical experiment of arming the negroes in the midst of the white population. From all appearances the 'black flag' is now imminent." He urged that the legislature set up courts to try officers found leading such troops.[33] His outrage arose from the fact that the federals were now conducting a definite policy of disrupting the slavery system where they could reach it, thus striking both at the war effort and social system of the South. On their "foraging" raids from garrison towns they took away as many slaves as possible to be used for their own labor and potentially as soldiers.

After the fall of Roanoke Island and the Outer Banks in early 1862, William Shepard Pettigrew had burned his standing crops and moved his plantation operations and slaves to rented land upcountry in Chatham County, for his home at The Lake was in easy reach of raiding parties landed from Albemarle Sound. Charles Lockhart Pettigrew was more obstinate. He sent part of his slaves upcountry but insisted on remaining at Bonarva despite the fact that two thousand federals raided the nearby town of Columbia, destroyed a number of private homes, and carried off some slaves. Charles lasted through most of 1862, but in the fall the enemy raided Bonarva. Some of his slaves escaped. Others stayed with him and accompanied him to the upcountry.[34]

Pettigrew had not heard from James Cathcart Johnston for eighteen months—since the bitter letter he had received in Charleston just after secession. After his return from captivity he wrote and received a note in return from Mr. Johnston's nephew saying that the old gentleman was glad to hear from him but had been ill and had not left his yard in months. Pettigrew urged Mr. Johnston to take his slaves upcountry. The Yankees would soon be at Hayes "and he thus lose half his property, for they will take the negroes by force." William Pettigrew, on his brother's plea, paid a visit to recommend the same action. The old gentleman would not listen. He was in an untenable and pathetic position, a man without a country. Unable to sympathize with his neigh-

bors in breaking up the Union, he found to his sorrow in December
that the federal soldiers who visited Edenton were not restorers of the
old Union he had loved but the marauding vanguard of a new regime.[35]

Thereafter the old gentleman (who would die with the Confederacy
in the spring of 1865) dwelled entirely in the past. One of his preoccu-
pations was recalling the lost old virtues exemplified by his departed
friend Ebenezer Pettigrew: "That high moral courage he possessed in
a higher degree than any man I ever knew which enabled him to stand
firm erect & deeply rooted like the gnarled & rugged oak while the . . .
fire flies flash of *modern chivalry* were seen around him but treated with
contempt or merited scorn."[36]

The other aged remnant of Federalism, James Louis Petigru, was
also in the twilight of life. With his health going, sorrow upon sorrow
piled on the old man's head. At about the same time he received the
false news of Johnston Pettigrew's death, he received the true news of
the mortal wounding of his son-in-law, Henry C. King, at the battle
of Secessionville, South Carolina. Shortly after, his own son, Dan,
died, although not in the war.[37] The deaths and maimings among his
nephews and sons of friends are too numerous to detail. On top of this,
his grandson, James Petigru Carson, who had been left in his keeping when his mother went north, was seventeen, almost of age for the
service.

The old gentleman spent his time in an activity as remote from the
war as he could find—tucked away in Johnston Pettigrew's house on
Tradd Street codifying the civil statutes of South Carolina. Never were
he and Johnston closer, despite their political disagreement. Petigru
was quick to point out the path of personal duty even when he disapproved the cause. When Johnston contemplated resigning in disgust at
not being given his original brigade on his return from prison, Petigru
counseled: "It seems to me that you would do very wrong to resign: not
only because you would thereby quit the post to which the constituted
authorities have assigned you; but because you would thereby give a
reasonable ground to accuse you of fickleness." Resignation under such
circumstances would not be of comparable moral stature to Johnston's
original refusal of promotion, Petigru hinted, and signed his letter
"Your parental friend."[38]

Petigru's health declined steadily in the winter of 1862–1863. Johnston requested transfer to Charleston, hoping to be near the old gentle-

man and also, because a major attack was always imminent there, hoping to see more action than in North Carolina. He drew on his credit with General Beauregard, then in command at Charleston, to request his assignment there. Beauregard would be glad to "borrow" him "for the coming Battle," but had no command for him.[39]

James Louis Petigru died in March 1863, not knowing that he preceded his beloved protégé to the grave by only a few months. In a gesture of chivalry, he was laid to rest with highest honor by the city, state, and country whose loyal opposition he had long been. Petigru had achieved in his last months a sad and resigned detachment. In one of his last letters to Johnston he took a dispassionate, long-range view of the war that foreshadowed the mood of the reveries of old Confederates of about 1900 who recall the justness of their youthful cause and at the same time are content with the triumph of nationalism, recognizing that the war was a necessary travail for a new birth that could not be foreseen by either side. After the news of James Louis Petigru's death, Pettigrew felt a chapter in his life had closed. Charleston seemed to him a blank and the prospect of returning to it, should the war ever end, unappealing.[40]

Pettigrew was completely absorbed in the war. He kept urging his brother William, who was old enough for the Senior Reserves, to get into the service. William should be a cavalry officer, Johnston recommended: "Arrange your private affairs, buy the books on tactics, and outpost duty, read all the descriptions of battles and skirmishes carefully, and digest them, awaken the confidence, courage, and enterprise of your men and you cannot fail to be a good officer." But William did not have Johnston's love of things military, and Johnston did not have William's land and slaves to watch over.[41]

To James Petigru Carson, who was just under conscription age and hesitated to enlist because of his mother's and grandfather's disapproval, Pettigrew wrote unequivocally his opinion of the right course to be taken, while at the same time trying to preserve the boy's respect for his grandfather: "My advice to you unhesitatingly, is first, to do your whole duty to your country. . . . Men of advanced age, who have seen the working of human affairs, the roguery & selfishness of men, the want of patriotism, in a word, the 'humbuggery' of the thing, are excusable for apathy. But such is not the case with youth. Avoid being wise above your years. Who knows, but that the wise experience of maturity is as great folly, as the thoughless enthusiasm of inexperience."[42] A very Latin attitude!

Pettigrew's state of mind can be seen in his letters, which, particularly after his return from prison, are brief, pointed, and hurried, as if written under pressure of some dreadful and unnameable deadline. Concerning a young acquaintance who solicited a "safe place on his staff," Pettigrew advised, "I assure you, that, the most unsafe place in the Brigade is about me. I would advise Johnny to give up all idea of a snug, safe berth. . . . By all means let him get rid of this idea of a safe place, which he will regret in after time. The post of danger is certainly the post of honor."[43]

The spring of 1863 promised as much action as even Pettigrew could desire. The brigade came out of winter quarters in February and went on a demonstration in force with artillery and wagons into Martin, Tyrrell, and Washington counties, Pettigrew's home country, with purpose to attack and harass the enemy at every opportunity, bring out supplies, and bolster civilian morale.[44]

While this operation was under way, the new commander of the Department of North Carolina, General D. H. Hill, announced that he intended to reduce the Yankee conquest to plots of six feet by two. Hill was under orders to make a general advance against the federals in eastern North Carolina in order to prevent them striking again at the railroad and to tie down as many troops as possible which else might be shifted to attacks on Virginia or Charleston.[45] This new aggressiveness of Confederate policy provided Pettigrew with his first opportunity for independent command in battle.

Hill concentrated at Goldsboro and set up a three-pronged attack to strike directly at Foster's main force in New Bern sixty miles to the east. Pettigrew was to take his brigade and Haskell's battalion of artillery and attack the federals by surprise on the fortified north bank of the Neuse River across from the city of New Bern. Everything depended upon Pettigrew's "skill, prudence, and good management," Hill told him. Hill himself would take Junius Daniel's brigade and attack on the south, or city, side of the river. Beverly H. Robertson's brigade of cavalry, recently from Virginia, was to attack by a third route.[46]

Pettigrew departed on 9 March, and pushed on at night across the swamps with pontoon bridges. He arrived with his men exhausted and hungry and several hours ahead of their supply wagons. Pettigrew still had some things to learn about the complexities of war. The brigade lay within a few miles of the federal post for twenty-eight hours without being detected and got into position early in the morning of 14 March. At daylight Pettigrew began to shell Fort Anderson, as the federal work on the north bank was known, with his light field artillery. The fort was on the river and surrounded by swamps. It could be reached only by a causeway a quarter of a mile long and wide enough for a small wagon. Pettigrew hesitated to send his infantry into this trap, calculating that fifty casualties would be a minimum, although the Twenty-sixth stood by ready to rush the causeway. Pettigrew gave the fort a shelling and then sent Young in under a flag of truce to demand surrender.

Colonel Hiram Anderson of the Ninety-second New York, occupying Fort Anderson, asked for an hour's ceasefire to consult Foster across the river about surrender. This Pettigrew granted, against the advice of Young and Haskell. It soon became apparent that Anderson was simply stalling for time. Pettigrew opened fire again, but a heavily armed and armored gunboat came steaming up the river and began shelling the Confederates from the safety of a position two miles downstream. General Whiting, Confederate commander at Wilmington, had been requested to send up a long-range Whitworth gun for the expedition, but he had failed to do so. Haskell had four guns, twenty-pounder Parrotts, of sufficient range to trade shots with the gunboat. One of these guns exploded at the first shot, killing several of the crew. The axle broke on another. When the remaining two were fired, the shells burst a few feet beyond the muzzles. Meanwhile the brigade had twenty-three killed and wounded from the fire of the gunboat.

Pettigrew knew he could take Fort Anderson, but he did not see how he could hold it or what good it would do to take it. He gave the order to withdraw. The Twenty-sixth, eager to storm the causeway, pulled out with some disappointment. Pettigrew drew off a short distance and lay in line of battle till nightfall. There was considerable danger of being cut off. He communicated with Hill, who ordered him to return to Goldsboro.[47]

Pettigrew had failed in his first independent battle. Yet his failure had been mostly due to circumstances beyond his control. Hill did not blame Pettigrew. In fact, he told him: "Nothing has been further from my thoughts than censure. I have no doubt that you have done the best in every instance, saving demanding a surrender, which was a mistake, nothing more." In his official report, Hill said, "Had the Whitworth been sent, the gunboats would have been beaten off and New Berne [*sic*] would have been at Pettigrew's mercy." Hill and Daniel had had some success in their part of the attack, driving the federals back to their inner defenses, but they had withdrawn when Pettigrew failed. Hill was a stern but just judge, and he had many others to blame than Pettigrew: General Robertson, who completely failed to carry out his part of the attack; General Richard Brooke Garnett, who failed to arrive in time with his brigade to take part; General Whiting, who failed to send the two Whitworth guns as promised; and the government at Richmond, which had failed to give him clear authority over Whiting and had sent defective ammunition for Haskell's guns. Regarding the failure to be given authority over Whiting, the blunt and peppery Hill said in his official report, "I will not submit to the swindle." About the defective ammunition, he told Pettigrew, "There is treachery in the Ordnance Dept." [48]

Referring to Pettigrew's blunder of demanding surrender, Haskell recalled: "It seemed hard to realize that a man of Pettigrew's force and of the coolest, personal bravery could have made so grave a mistake, but he was a very tender-hearted, sensitive man, who shrank from danger and suffering to others, of which he seemed careless for himself." [49] That was part of the story, yet at Gettysburg, where the stakes were higher, Pettigrew would show himself ruthlessly efficient in pushing soldiers into the bloody breach. But, as J. L. Petigru had once commented about his legal arguments, Pettigrew had to be convinced that he was right. He could take Fort Anderson, but to what point? As long as the gunboats had free range of the river it could not be held. Nor did the capture of a small garrison of second-rate troops seem to justify the Confederate casualties demanded by an attack.

There was, besides, considerable ambiguity in the objectives of the operation. The federals had more men in New Bern than Hill had for the attack, and only by an unusual stroke of good fortune could Hill hope to drive them out. The mission, in the mind of Richmond, was conceived chiefly to harass the enemy, divert federal troops from Charleston and Virginia, and bolster morale in North Carolina by a show of activity. Pettigrew probably did not choose to get men killed for such vague objectives. In his report, he said that he did not wish to sacrifice men for temporary possession of a breastwork and capture of a few hundred conscripts, however brilliant such a victory might appear. In addition, there was a general understanding that casualties were to be held to a minimum to save troops for the spring campaign in Virginia. Thus Pettigrew had fulfilled his mission as well as could be expected, and he was subjected to no disapproval.[50]

Pettigrew candidly began his official report of the battle of New Bern with the statement that the expedition entrusted to him had failed. He stated frankly his blunder in demanding surrender, blamed the artillery failures for the debacle of the operation, and praised his men for marching 127 miles in seven days without an uninterrupted night's sleep and often without fires, for wrestling twenty pieces of artillery across swampland, much of which had to be bridged as they went, without straggling or even sickness, and for undergoing a severe shelling without wavering.[51]

There was ample opportunity left for Pettigrew to redeem any reputation he might have lost at New Bern, for Hill intended to give Foster no rest. On 30 March, with reenforcements from Virginia, Hill laid siege to the town of Washington on the Pamlico River, where the federal force was smaller than that in New Bern, and for two weeks cut off the garrison from support by land or water.[52]

On 9 April Foster sent out from New Bern a relief column under a political general, Francis Barretto Spinola, that was to march overland to Washington. Pettigrew with part of his brigade, a force numbering less than half that of the federals, and in a position selected by himself, met this column at Blount's Creek in Beaufort County and sent it retreating precipitously back to New Bern, felling trees and burning bridges behind it to discourage pursuit. This affair completely redeemed his reputation. "We whipped the Yankees every time we could get at them," Pettigrew reported, pleased.[53]

On 15 April, several boats managed to get through to Washington with reenforcements. Hill's orders to save troops for Virginia forbade a costly attempt to take the city, so at the end of two weeks' siege he withdrew, much to the disgust of the Confederate rank and file who felt they had never properly come to grips with the enemy.[54]

Hill's growing dissatisfaction with Richmond, which he felt had tricked him into an inferior command, had begun to exacerbate his already considerable eccentricity. During the siege of Washington, both officers and men had become dissatisfied with his seeming desire for risk for its own sake. Affairs came to a head when, during the withdrawal from Washington, Hill flew into a rage about a cannon that had been left behind, though spiked. He held Pettigrew's and Daniel's brigades in line exposed to the fire of federal gunboats while he made arrangements for an ox team to go back for the cannon.

Pettigrew and Daniel were much annoyed at this useless exposure of their men and with Haskell went to Hill to protest. Pettigrew was designated as spokesman. Hill heard him quietly and then said in a mild voice, "General Pettigrew, if you do not like to stay under fire, turn your command [over] to Colonel Leventhorpe." Pettigrew recoiled speechless and walked off. Daniel and Haskell remonstrated with Hill over the insult, but Hill only repeated it in the same mild manner.[55]

This uncomfortable situation was soon resolved, for in Virginia the main federal army had crossed the Rappahannock once more and the Chancellorsville campaign was under way. On 1 and 2 May Pettigrew's and Daniel's brigades boarded trains at Kinston bound for Petersburg. The two brigades had for some months been the subject of a quadrangular discussion between Davis, Lee, Vance, and Hill, the conclusion of which was their being ordered to Virginia in exchange for two veteran brigades that were to be sent to North Carolina.[56]

A large federal cavalry raid on Richmond was developing. Arriving at Richmond on 3 May, part of Pettigrew's brigade was left in the city defenses. With the rest he proceeded under orders to Hanover Junction, the vital rail center north of Richmond, where he was to command his and all other troops in the area in anticipation of a federal strike at the railroad bridges. For a time the command was dispersed in company-sized lots over a wide area, guarding the junction and railroad bridges over the North and South Anna rivers.[57]

Although for the moment a part of the Department of Richmond under Major General Arnold Elzey, Pettigrew was within operating distance of General Lee and the legendary Army of Northern Virginia, at that very time fighting the great battle of Chancellorsville not far to the north. Veteran officers of that army who remembered Pettigrew from the Peninsula the previous year were pleased at the prospect of his return.[58]

After two weeks of guarding Hanover Junction against Stoneman's raid, Pettigrew received on 19 May orders from General Lee to be prepared to move with great promptness. On 1 June Pettigrew was officially incorporated into the Army of Northern Virginia. His brigade was one of four in the new division of Major General Henry Heth, a part of the newly formed Third Corps under Lieutenant General Ambrose Powell Hill. Moreover, Pettigrew, having the earliest brigadier's commission in the division, would command it if anything happened to Heth.[59]

By 8 June the brigade was in the trenches at Fredericksburg on the Rappahannock, a part of Lee's extreme right placed to divert the enemy while the left of the army moved toward the valley, the short route to Pennsylvania. Pettigrew was in great anxiety that he would be left behind and miss the great campaign, but on 14 June, Heth's division came out of the trenches and marched west. Pettigrew was in command of the Eleventh, Twenty-sixth, Forty-seventh, and Fifty-second regiments. The Forty-fourth had been left behind at Hanover Junction where it distinguished itself by beating off a much larger federal force in a desperate fight.[60]

As the Gettysburg campaign commenced, Pettigrew totally identified with his revolutionary cause. His absorption into patriotism and the military virtues was nearly complete, and the prospect ahead promised all the opportunity for danger, glory, and sacrifice that even an admirer of Zumalacarregui could hope.

From Hanover Junction, Pettigrew had written Governor Vance an urgent letter which well displays his state of mind:

Hanover Junction, May 22, 1863.
To His Excellency Z. B. Vance:
Dear Sir: Inclosed you will find a couple of letters sent by people at home to induce soldiers to desert. . . . General Lee telegraphs me that men from our State are deserting every day, carrying off guns and ammunition. I fear the thing has gone to such an extent that requires the axe to be laid to the root of the tree. . . . I can attribute these desertions to but one cause, the unfortunate state of public opinion at home, produced, I am convinced, by a small but very active portion of the community. We have watched closely for some months the course of certain newspapers, and of a majority of the Legislature. I regret to say that I have not seen from either a single word calculated to aid us in our efforts to save the community from subjection to the worst of all tyrannies. They

utter nothing but declamations calculated and intended to make us dissatisfied, not only with the Confederate Government, but the Confederate cause; to impress us with the hopelessness of the struggle, and thus to unnerve us preparatory to submission. That the majority of the people have no sympathy with these papers I am convinced since my campaigns in the enemy's lines near Washington and New Berne. Those people, with a few vile exceptions, are true, and did everything to encourage us to bear with the privations entailed upon us by the hard necessity of the times. Since my arrival among the troops of this army, I am equally convinced that when the war is over, and our true soldiers return to their homes, there will be a bitter day of reckoning with the enemies behind us. But that is not sufficient for the present. A certain class of soldiers is influenced by this condition of public opinion. They are told, as you see by the letters, that they can desert with impunity: that the militia officers will not do their duty; that they can band together and defy the officers of the law, while their comrades are fighting the enemy. . . .

The result of all this upon our regiments is demoralizing to an extent you can scarcely conceive. The torrent of North Carolina blood shed in the battles of last summer washed out the stain left upon the State by the defeats of Roanoke and New Berne, and I found her on my return highest among the high. I regret to say that the suspicion cast upon her by the misconduct of a few unworthy sons has undone everything. I sympathize with every party in its efforts to arrest the first step of our Government toward despotic power, and even abuse of the Confederate Government I consider a matter of comparative indifference, though it had as well be left out, but I have no manner of sympathy with those who overlook their country in their opposition to a government or a party. I would rather see the whole State desolated as Virginia is than dishonored by a feeble effort to look back on its escape from the Yankee Sodom. I write this to you because you are the only person in the State having sufficient influence, as I think, to reform matters. It is absolutely necessary to bring the public opinion again to the condition of patiently and manfully meeting those trials which every people struggling for independence must meet;

and so far as the army is concerned, the best way to accomplish this is to convince them that a man who meanly deserts them in the face of the enemy will be met at home with scorn and speedily returned to deserved punishment. . . . The great majority of my brigade would shoot a deserter as quick as they would a snake, but our place is here and not in the rear. . . . If a strong arm is required I doubt not that General Hill will furnish the men, as we have nearly as many troops in North Carolina as the Yankees have, since the discharge of their two-years' men. I assure you we need every man with his colors, if a peace is to be conquered this summer.

Very respectfully, your obedient servant,

J. Johnston Pettigrew,
Brigadier General.[61]

To Mrs. North, J. L. Petigru's sister and Carie's mother, he wrote at the same time concerning his sorrow at Petigru's death, apologizing for his lack of frequent communication with the family, pleading for news from home, and urging her to write down family recollections while they could still be gathered. "In the midst of all our trials it is a consolation to reflect, that our reputation, next to Greece, will be the most heroic of nations," he added.[62]

As the Pennsylvania campaign commenced, the rapport and mutual respect among Pettigrew, his officers, and men were as complete as could be hoped for in an imperfect world. Lieutenant Colonel John Randolph Lane of the Twenty-sixth North Carolina Regiment, a miller by trade who had little formal education, recalled that the men were of good stock—not aristocrats but "the great middle class that owned small farms in central and western North Carolina." Many were without formal schooling, but most were quick of mind. "They would endure no domineering, they would suffer no driving," but officers who set an example of courage they would follow willingly. "At this time the men had come to understand and to trust the officers, the officers the men," Lane remembered.[63] In the trials ahead neither would disappoint the other.

On 20 June Pettigrew's brigade crossed the Blue Ridge and turned north. On 25 June they waded the Potomac at Williamsport, Maryland, and camped that night beyond Hagerstown. The next day they crossed Antietam Creek and marched into Pennsylvania. On Sunday, 28 June, they halted at Fayetteville, and religious services were held.[64]

Lee had given strict orders against depredations against civilians. Despite a feeling that reprisals were due, Pettigrew was very energetic in enforcing this chivalric rule among his own men and those of other commands. Once his officers rode out of their way to pay a farmer for some beehives that had been taken. Pennsylvanians worked unmolested in their fields as the army columns marched by.[65]

On the march Pettigrew remarked to Captain Hughes that life was only to be desired for what could be accomplished in it and death only to be dreaded for what had been done amiss. For himself, Pettigrew said, he was ready to die at any time, at that very moment, if he could do so with honor and usefulness. He meant it.[66]

Chapter 15

Falling Waters

For none who fought so briefly in the Army of Northern Virginia was there more praise while living or more laments when dead. — Douglas Southall Freeman of James Johnston Pettigrew

The Army of Northern Virginia moved by several roads into Pennsylvania in the summer of 1863 at the peak of its strength and confidence. It was Johnston Pettigrew who made the first, unexpected contact with a significant force of the enemy.

On 29 June Heth's division was at Cashtown. The army badly needed shoes, and Pettigrew was ordered to take his brigade the next day to Gettysburg, a town eight miles southeast, and capture the large supply of footwear reportedly there. With hardly time to dry out from the night's rain, the brigade started at 6:30 A.M. on 30 June on a hard march down the Chambersburg turnpike to Gettysburg.[1]

On the outskirts of the town Pettigrew encountered a strong picket line of federal cavalry. Then he distinctly heard the drums of marching infantry beyond the town. Since he had no cavalry to feel out the force in front, since his superiors were ignorant that the enemy was in the area, and since he had orders not to bring on an engagement, Pettigrew decided to return to Cashtown and report. Federal cavalry followed at a distance but made no attack.[2]

While Pettigrew was giving his report to Heth, General A. P. Hill, the corps commander, rode up. Hill doubted Pettigrew's report of enemy infantry in Gettysburg. He had recent word from Lee's scouts that the main body of federals was still in Middleburg. Pettigrew called in Louis Young, whom Hill knew from the Seven Days, to supplement his testimony, but he failed to convince either Hill or Heth that there was a large force of infantry around Gettysburg. Heth asked for and received permission to return next day with the whole division and see to the business of the shoes.[3]

That night the pickets of the Twenty-sixth North Carolina halted some ladies who wanted to get to their homes in Cashtown. Since his orders strictly forbade permitting anyone beyond the picket line, Lieutenant Colonel Lane courteously advanced his line several hundred yards to encompass the ladies' homes. Meanwhile Pettigrew briefed Brigadier General James Jay Archer, who would lead next morning, on the Gettysburg terrain and on where the federals could be expected. Archer, too, was skeptical.[4] Reports to the contrary were too definite. Perhaps also the veterans of a dozen great battles considered Pettigrew green and too easily alarmed.

The next day, 1 July, the head of Heth's division crossed the Marsh Creek bridge northwest of Gettysburg and encountered cavalry and then artillery fire, to the surprise of everyone but Pettigrew. A considerable force of federals was strongly posted west of the town, and, it was soon discovered, they were not Pennsylvania militiamen but the First and Eleventh corps of the Army of the Potomac, as good as any federal troops in the business.[5]

Heth, with Lee's permission to attack, put Archer's and Joseph Robert Davis's brigades in line on either side of the turnpike and sent them forward, while holding Pettigrew's brigade in reserve for the moment. The Confederates pushed ahead for a time and captured several batteries and many prisoners, but they were finally halted and badly shot up by the federals rushing in on the other side of the battlefield. Archer was cut off and captured with part of his command. Davis, after suffering a front and flank barrage of artillery, withdrew with heavy losses, only three officers above captain in his brigade still on their feet. Meanwhile two divisions of Ewell's Second Corps had arrived and could be heard on Heth's left engaging the federals.[6]

During Archer's and Davis's action, Pettigrew's brigade lay in the rear in line of battle, subject to the harassing fire of sharpshooters. Details were sent back for water and marksmen sent to the front to deal with the snipers. Pettigrew rode his gray horse up and down the line, a perfect target for the sharpshooters, with great coolness and was cheered. The men had full opportunity to view the position they were to charge later.[7]

Heth re-formed. About 2 P.M. the division was ordered forward, Pettigrew's three thousand men in the center with Brockenbrough's small brigade and what was left of the brigades of Archer and Davis on the flanks. In front, across the creek known as Willoughby Run, were three lines of enemy infantry on the slopes of McPherson's Ridge, posted in a wheat field and woods and anchored by artillery. Directly in front of Pettigrew, perhaps three hundred yards away, was the black-hatted Iron Brigade, the best men the Army of the Potomac had to offer.[8]

Pettigrew's brigade crossed the creek under artillery fire in perfect order and went up the ridge, halted, and fired into the thin first line of federals, who gave a ragged volley and fell back into the second line. Halfway up the hill Pettigrew's men smashed into the fire of the second line. After some minutes of volleying into each other's faces twenty to forty yards apart and then fighting hand to hand, the second line fell back. The line of Pettigrew's dead was as straight as if on dress parade at the point where they encountered the second line. Taking and giving incredible casualties, Pettigrew's men drove the last line off the summit of the ridge and back across the next hill, Seminary Ridge. The Fifty-second had overlapped the enemy while the Twenty-sixth and Eleventh bore the brunt of the attack in front. On Seminary Ridge the brigade halted while a fresh division came up and drove the federals on through the town. The whole action had taken less than half an hour, perhaps no more than twenty minutes.[9]

The charge of Pettigrew's brigade on the first day at Gettysburg was as heroic and bloody if not as decisive as the more famous action on the third day. The exact and complete casualties of the first day (distinct from the whole campaign) will never be known. Heth estimated 2,700 dead and wounded in the division in the first day. The Twenty-sixth reportedly had 588 dead and wounded out of slightly more than 800 men. This loss, 71.7 percent, has been judged the greatest of any single regiment on either side in a single day in the war. The losses of the federals had been almost as great. The Eleventh North Carolina had over 200 dead and wounded out of 550, it was estimated. These reports of wounded included only the disabled, not those who had been grazed but were still on their feet. Colonel Burgwyn was dead at twenty-one, shot through both lungs. Colonel Leventhorpe and Lieutenant Colonel Lane were badly wounded. Fourteen men had been shot down carrying the colors of the Twenty-sixth, including Captain McCreery of Pettigrew's staff, who was dead. Hughes of the staff was mortally wounded and Robertson disabled for life.[10]

The brigade had done all that could be asked and it was not their fault if dusk began to fall and Hill and Ewell hesitated and failed to render certain the mastery of the Gettysburg terrain by pushing on to take Cemetery Ridge and the Round Tops on the other side of town.

On Seminary Ridge, Pettigrew's brigade stacked arms in the yard of the seminary. Captain Cureton of the Twenty-sixth chatted with the scared girls in the basement of the school and assured them that southern soldiers did not make war on women. After a short time the exhausted survivors were ordered back to the woods from which they had charged that afternoon. Wounded from both sides lay all about waiting to be tended, and the men spent part of the night carrying water to them between snatches of sleep.[11]

A rifle ball had grazed General Heth in the head, and he was unconscious. Pettigrew assumed command of a badly battered division. Archer's brigade, Tennessee and Alabama regiments, was veteran but badly shot up. The survivors were led by Colonel (later General) Birkett Davenport Fry of the Thirteenth Alabama. Brockenbrough's Virginia brigade was smaller than average, had a history of poor leadership and morale, and was also under a new commander, Colonel Robert Mayo. The brigade commanded by Davis, the president's nephew, was made up of Mississippians except for one North Carolina regiment. Davis's brigade was as new to the Army of Northern Virginia as Pettigrew's and even less experienced. Most of Davis's field officers had been felled in the day's action, and several regiments were under captains. The division had been created only a few weeks before and as a unit had only the esprit which the individual brigades brought to it. Pettigrew's own brigade, to which Colonel Marshall of the Fifty-second now succeeded, had also lost many officers, only one regiment having the same commander as in the morning. There was little time to take exact reckoning of the losses, and the extent of damage to the division was evidently not known to the high command, else it would not have been selected for the attack of 3 July.[12]

On the morning of 2 July Pettigrew ordered military duties resumed in Heth's division. Reports were written, rolls called, and the dead buried. Pettigrew went around to the hospitals and rousted out all the men who could walk. He armed the cooks and other special duty men and put them in the ranks. He ordered the band of the Twenty-sixth, one of the best in the army, made up of Moravian musicians from Salem, to play. The trumpets and trombones sounded all day, and by afternoon the gloomy survivors of Pettigrew's brigade could raise a cheer.[13]

In camp they waited most of the second day of Gettysburg while inconclusive fighting was carried on by others. At 4:00 P.M. the division marched a mile toward the army's right and got into position opposite the federal works on Cemetery Ridge, adjoining the left of Longstreet's First Corps, and behind the massed artillery of their own corps.[14]

Lee had decided that it was necessary to dislodge the federals. This was to be done by attacking their center, Cemetery Ridge, which was heavily fortified but topographically the weakest part of their position. Elements of the First and Third corps were to take part. Details, as was customary, were left to the corps commanders. Pickett's division of three Virginia brigades, fresh to the battlefield and not engaged previously, was to assault the stone wall, supported by two brigades from Anderson's division. Heth's division under Pettigrew was to charge Pickett's left, supported by two brigades from Pender's division. The two brigades of Pender's were supposed to move up in echelon (i.e., in staggered formation) to cover the left of Heth's division, which would be exposed to fire from the flank as well as from the front.[15]

The usually competent and reliable General James Longstreet was opposed to the assault and failed to organize it on as large a scale as Lee had intended. He failed to take into account the reduced ranks and missing officers in Heth's division. Almost any other division was in better shape for the task than Heth's. Longstreet failed to coordinate with Hill, whose troops were also involved, so that the brigades of Pender, which were to support Pettigrew, were not given specific instructions. On the next day's battle they came up behind and to the right of Pettigrew's men instead of in echelon on the left. Pettigrew received no orders about the arrangement of his own division. Brockenbrough's and Davis's, the weakest brigades, were on the left, the toughest spot, and remained there.[16] How much of this confusion was known to Pettigrew cannot be determined. Nor did he know, probably, that his friend John Gibbon was on the spot he was to attack, commanding a division of the federal Second Corps.

All morning on 3 July Heth's division lay in the woods behind the massed Confederate batteries. After conference with Lee, Longstreet, and Hill, Pettigrew went about giving careful orders for the assault, for it would be a tricky business to keep good order when the division moved out of the woods, through the Confederate guns, and into the valley before Cemetery Ridge.[17]

The artillery bombardment, which it was hoped would soften the federal position, began at noon. The greatest cannonade in the history of warfare, it continued for two hours. A number of men were hit by the answering federal shells as they lay in the woods. The sound was tremendous, literally an earthquake, one soldier remembered. On the right Pickett's chaplains could be heard conducting services. Pettigrew's men sorely missed their own who were at the hospitals.[18]

About 2:00 P.M. the Confederate guns ceased. The day was clear and warm, and as the black smoke began to lift Cemetery Ridge could be clearly seen a mile away across the Emmitsburg Road, bristling with cannon and regimental flags. Heth's division was getting on its feet and to attention. It advanced several hundred yards and halted in front of the Confederate guns.[19]

Far over on the right, the Confederate artillery commander had told Longstreet that if the charge was to be made it must be made now, and Longstreet had reluctantly, wordlessly given Pickett the order to go ahead.

Slender, graceful, full-bearded, piercing eyes bright, left hand on the reins, in gray uniform and soft gray hat, Pettigrew rode on his gray horse down the line of his own brigade to Colonel Marshall.

"Now Colonel, for the Honor of the Good Old North State, Forward!"[20]

Heth's and Pickett's divisions moved out, Heth's on a front of four brigades in one line with Pender's men coming up behind, Pickett's on a front of two brigades with his third in a second line. Colonel Fry, commanding Archer's brigade on Pettigrew's right, knew his business and had made arrangements for Pickett's left brigade to dress on his line, which would be the center of the attack. After some momentary confusion which seemed to far-off observers as wavering in Heth's division, the lines straightened and went forward. The bandages in Heth's division from the wounds of the day before last were conspicuous to General Lee from his vantage point.[21]

Pettigrew rode up close behind his line. His division would have several hundred yards further to go than Pickett's, for the stone wall angled away on his part of the front. Fourteen thousand men in dirty butternut, a third of them Pettigrew's, started up the slope toward the enemy.

The batteries in front were as yet quiet, but those on the left were already tearing holes in the butternut ranks. The men spread out, closed up the gaps, and trotted ahead. On the left Brockenbrough's and Davis's brigades were taking the heaviest fire, front and flank, and were slowed by a series of fences.

Where were Pender's men who were supposed to be in echelon on his left to protect his weak flank? Pettigrew sent Young to the commander urging him to come up faster and changed the front of Davis's men, causing another halt.

The line moved on up the ridge. Now they were taking grape, canister, and musketry from the front as well as shot and shell. The senses of smell and hearing were choked off by the barrage. On the right, Pettigrew's own brigade and Archer's were merging with Pickett's men. Things still looked good. These men had performed miracles as great before. Colonel Fry, who was down with a shot through the leg, told the men who tried to carry him off: "Go on! it cannot last five minutes more!" Then the colonel heard Pettigrew behind him shouting for an aide to rally the left.

Brockenbrough and part of Davis's men had broken. They were beginning to fall back or to lie down among the dead, uncovering the other brigades to their right to the terrible flank fire. Pettigrew's horse was hit. He dismounted and sent it back with a wounded man. Grapeshot smashed the fingers of his right hand, but Pettigrew stayed with his line.

Still Pickett and his own brigade and Archer's and some of Davis's went on. At a quarter of a mile, less for Pickett's men, they halted and gave a volley and went on. Pettigrew could see the stone wall clearly. Some of Pickett's men passed over the angle and were inside. His own were thirty to forty feet away.

The fire on the left was kept up. Some of Pettigrew's men rallied in the lee of the wall, as did Armistead of Pickett's inside the angle, to hold on until the support came up. But the support was already fading back, shot to pieces before they reached as far as the men they were to assist. The men who had rallied by the wall to hang on were captured as the federals swarmed out. The survivors began to fade back in small, sullen, broken parties. The prolonged cheers from the federal lines taught them their failure.[22]

Magnificent, but not much like Zumalacarregui.

Pettigrew made his way afoot back down the slope and was one of the last men to leave the field. Captain Cureton of the Twenty-sixth saw him and, holding Pettigrew's wounded arm, helped him up the hill to the Confederate artillery line from which the charge had begun. Pettigrew set to work immediately to rally the remnants. General Lee had ridden up as the men were streaming back. Pettigrew told the commander that he was responsible for his brigade but not for the division (referring to the breaking of Brockenbrough's and Davis's men). Lee leaned from the saddle, grasped Pettigrew's left hand and said, "General Pettigrew, it is all my fault." [23]

By dusk Pettigrew had a substantial skirmish line established to meet the expected counterattack on the now unsupported Confederate artillery. That night and most of the next day, 4 July, the men lay with the artillery waiting for the counterattack that never came. There was occasional musketry fire on the picket line. If the charge had succeeded the enemy would be suing for peace, Pettigrew told the survivors. His men heard from enemy pickets the news of the surrender of Vicksburg. It was Pettigrew's thirty-fifth birthday. A little before dark the division was pulled back and began the first leg of the long march back to Virginia.[24]

Pettigrew's disclaimer to General Lee of responsibility for the morale of troops who had been under his command less than forty-eight hours was well considered. Even as the army returned to Virginia the traveling correspondents of the Richmond newspapers filled the press of the South with accounts of the charge of Pickett, a Richmond boy, and his gallant Virginians, that had failed, they said, because Pettigrew and the North Carolinians had failed to support it. Thus began the romantic and superficial account of the climactic action of the most famous battle in history, the account of the heroism of the dashing, golden-maned Pickett and his brave Virginians, which would be repeated by popularizers and partisans over the world until "Pickett's Charge" became a household phrase.[25]

At his bravest moment, Pettigrew's name was overshadowed and even tarnished.

From the day they read the first newspaper accounts and for a half century thereafter, Tar Heel veterans chafed at the popular version of the charge of "Pickett and his Virginians." The speeches they delivered and the pamphlets and articles they published in refutation of the implications of the story would fill a shelf in the small library that would be required to hold all the printed matter on Gettysburg. Pettigrew himself died with his report unwritten.

Despite the valiant efforts of the Tar Heels to stem the tide, the false legend rolled on. It was even said abroad, an embroidery invented to explain the failure of the brave Virginians, that had the cowardly North Carolinians not been told they faced only Pennsylvania militia they would not have charged at all. Thus was offered an egregious example of how history can be obliterated by fancy, for on the first day Pettigrew's brigade had charged and driven the best brigade of the Army of the Potomac.[26] It was not until long after half a century passed that the myths were excised from the popular histories.

The name Pickett's Charge, first given by the Richmond press, was a misnomer. Pickett commanded approximately one-third of the men engaged, at most a few hundred more than Pettigrew. Pettigrew commanded a front of four brigades, Pickett a front of two. The name probably should be "Longstreet's Assault" since Longstreet was in command of the operation. Pettigrew went up to the stone wall and was wounded. Pickett, according to best testimony, stopped at a house at least six hundred yards from the stone wall (although as a division commander he could not be faulted for this). Pettigrew's men had been badly mauled the first day. Pickett's were not engaged until the third day, although they had had a hard march.[27]

In part, the reputation of Pettigrew and of the North Carolinians was damaged by loose thinking: the assertion that Pettigrew and the North Carolinians faltered in the charge confused the identity of Heth's division temporarily commanded by Pettigrew with Pettigrew's brigade of North Carolinians. It was Davis's and Brockenbrough's brigades which broke, the last Virginians. "Tell a man in this army that North Carolinians failed to go where Virginians went and he would think you a fool," wrote Major John Thomas Jones of the Twenty-sixth North Carolina shortly after the return to Virginia. Well he knew, for he crossed the Potomac in command of what was left of Pettigrew's magnificent brigade. He was the highest ranking officer still on his feet in the brigade, and he had been wounded twice.[28]

Every other colonel, lieutenant colonel, and major in the North Carolina brigade was dead or badly wounded except for one who had been captured a few yards from the stone wall. The Twenty-sixth North Carolina had gone into the first day of Gettysburg with more than 800 men and came out with 216. After the third day's action there were eighty men present for duty, a good-sized company.[29]

The casualties tell the story. The total killed and wounded reported for Pettigrew's brigade in the entire Gettysburg campaign was 1,105; this figure, which does not include the lightly wounded or the missing, most of whom were dead or wounded and captured, was 208 more than the next highest brigade in the army and nearly twice as many as the heaviest hit brigade of Pickett's division. The casualties in Heth's division were officially reported as 2,310. Those in Pickett's division, which was smaller, were reported as 1,366. Pettigrew's brigade had numbered 3,000 on 1 July. On 4 July it mustered 835 men present for duty. In the charge of the "gallant Virginians," about 700 North Carolinians were killed and wounded, about 400 Virginians.[30]

It is also misleading to speak of Pettigrew as the support of Pickett. "At the very moment that Pickett's claims to have had, and did have a portion of the enemy's works, and was looking to the rear for Pettigrew's troops," wrote one North Carolina survivor, "those troops *were on the line with him*, battling as hard and breasting as bravely that storm of death," and had as much right to look back to Pickett for his support as Pickett for theirs. That Armistead and some of his men had crossed the stone wall and held the angle for some minutes indicated to some that the North Carolinians had failed. But the men of Heth's division who came up near the wall had traveled a longer distance under greater fire. A captain and several men of the Fifty-fifth North Carolina, the lone North Carolina regiment of Davis's brigade, were killed a few feet from the stone wall, and, although outside it, were further forward of their starting point than Pickett's men; thus the middle part of the Tar Heel boast was filled out: "First at Bethel, farthest to the front at Gettysburg and Chickamauga, last at Appomattox."[31]

One discouraged Tar Heel veteran, who entitled his polemic *Pickett or Pettigrew?*, pointed out that no Virginia regiment was among the top twenty-seven Confederate regiments in casualties for the war. He concluded that the Richmond press had so exaggerated the accomplishments and sacrifice of the Virginians and ignored the bleeding of other states that the Virginians had actually come to believe their own propaganda.[32]

All this was in the future. On the night of 4 July Pettigrew's men left their position and marched all night through mud and rain until they reached South Mountain in Maryland. Heth had returned to duty, but Pettigrew commanded what was left of his own and Archer's brigades. His hand, in splints and in a sling, was very painful. The survivors were battered but by no means vanquished. They were still perfectly confident of their ability to turn and defeat the enemy if he pressed too close.[33]

For the next ten days they moved in slow stages toward the Potomac, marching hard, often in rain and always in mud, sleeping in the open in wet clothes with insufficient food and a short supply of ammunition, several times turning to dig in and meet the federals. Pettigrew was everywhere, talking to the men, restoring morale, and very energetic in covering the rear. On the outside he was as calm and determined as he had been on the march north, whatever may have been inside his far-ranging mind.[34]

On 7 July they passed through Hagerstown and camped for two days on the other side. Here Pettigrew dashed off a note to Governor Vance, in a tone as exultant as a victor, telling him that his old regiment, the Twenty-sixth, had covered itself with glory. On the afternoon of 10 July he formed line of battle near Hagerstown and fought off federal cavalry. Then they marched well into the night and camped. On 11 July they marched a few more miles and dug trenches where they lay all night and from which they repulsed cavalry the next day. At twilight on 13 July they moved out again, marching all night and into the morning of the 14th through thigh-deep mud. About 9:00 A.M. they halted on a hill overlooking the Potomac, where troops that had preceded them had thrown up entrenchments. About two miles away, at Falling Waters, Confederate wagons and artillery were crossing on pontoon bridges into Virginia.[35]

Most of the army was over the river except for the cavalry and the trains now passing. Heth was in command of the rearguard, his own and Pender's divisions, and Pettigrew was again in charge of Heth's division. The men stacked arms. Some sat about the trenches. Others lay down on the ground and were asleep in a few minutes. Pettigrew posted a picket line.

Heth rode up and found Pettigrew standing in a garden near a barn. Heth began to give instructions about the crossing. To Pettigrew, Heth seemed too casual about the safety of the small force still left north of the Potomac. Pettigrew was particularly worried that there was no artillery with which to make a stand if the enemy crashed into the rear in force. Heth had seen a screen of Confederate horsemen behind him as he had approached Falling Waters, and he believed that they were still there. Unknown to him they had run into two federal cavalry divisions and had gone upstream to cross at Williamsport.

Suddenly a troop of forty or fifty cavalry came out of a nearby wood and rode at a gallop straight at the group of officers in the garden. Someone gave the order to fire. Heth quickly countermanded this. He believed they were certainly Confederate. Almost all the southern cavalry wore captured federal coats, and the Union guidon they carried was no doubt a captured banner waved in exultation. Heth was about to give the cavalrymen a dressing down. Some of the Confederate infantry grabbed up rifles and fired, against orders. Now the cavalrymen dashed into the middle of the Confederates, revolvers flashing and sabers slashing. Pettigrew attempted to mount with one hand, for his right was still in bandages. His horse shied and he fell.

There was a melee all about. The Confederates were reaching for their rifles, many of which were unloaded or too wet to fire. The outnumbered cavalrymen were knocked from their saddles with clubbed rifles, tree limbs, fence posts, and farm tools.

Pettigrew saw a big trooper, a corporal, shoot several men with a revolver near the barn. Pulling his small pistol from his breast with his left hand, he advanced afoot on the man. His pistol was of short range. At eight feet Pettigrew pulled the trigger. A misfire!

The Yankee fired the Colt at his stomach and Pettigrew fell. Someone shot the trooper's horse. He jumped free and ran for the barn, firing as he went. Several Confederates ran after him, and he was finally brought down, dead, by a large stone crushed into his chest. In a few minutes it was over. All the troop of federal cavalry were dead or captured.[36]

"The funniest affair I have ever been in," wrote one veteran of this skirmish at Falling Waters. The federals, a squadron of the Sixth Michigan Cavalry riding ahead of the main force of pursuit, had believed they were rounding up a few stragglers not yet over the river. They had not known until too late that they were riding directly into the middle of two divisions of infantry. Possibly they were drunk.[37] Pettigrew had received his fifth and last wound in an insignificant skirmish.

The main body of federal cavalry, two divisions with artillery, now came up and attacked. The Confederates formed line of battle without artillery and held off the cavalry until the trains were over. Most of the men got across, although five hundred of the rearguard, of various brigades, were cut off and captured.[38]

Pettigrew in the meantime had been examined by a doctor and carried across the river and two miles further on to a house. The pistol ball had entered his abdomen on the left side just above the hip and passing downward had come out behind. He had lost a great deal of blood.[39]

The medical officers saw immediately that the wound was probably mortal. Mortification — peritonitis — would soon set in. By surgical procedures then known but not widely used, Pettigrew's life might easily have been saved. Without such procedures recovery from such a wound could be hoped for in one case in ten, and then only with total immobilization. The medical officers offered to leave Pettigrew at the house. Federal surgeons would certainly find him there before long. Deliberately, Pettigrew chose his old friend death, preferring to die than be captured again.[40]

The next day relays of four men carried him eighteen miles in a litter. As he jostled along the route, Pettigrew bantered with the men carrying him. "Don't be disheartened. Maybe I will fool the doctors yet," he said. General Lee rode part of the way beside him and expressed his regret at the wound. It was nothing that he had not reasonably expected when he entered the service, Pettigrew said, and he was perfectly willing to die for his country.[41]

That night he was placed in the home of the Boyd family at Bunker Hill, in what is now Berkeley County, West Virginia. The next day he seemed stronger for a time and was given some messages. He gave his horses to his aides, Louis Young and Willie Shepard — the gray he had ridden at Gettysburg and that had been slightly wounded to one, Zaida, the beautiful mare he had bought when he joined the militia at Charleston, to the other. He bore his pain calmly.[42]

In the afternoon an Episcopalian clergyman, the Reverend Joseph P. B. Wilmer, came in. He asked if Pettigrew were in the proper spirit to meet his maker. Pettigrew replied he believed he was. Would he take the sacraments, then? Pettigrew shook his head no. The clergyman feared some lingering trace of skepticism such as he had often found in men of high intelligence. "It is not from a want of faith or a want of disposition," Pettigrew said weakly, "but from a feeling of unworthiness. I fear to incur the guilt of presumption." The old humility, medieval in its intensity, asserted itself once more. Wilmer was called away, but promised to return as soon as he could. He had never seen a finer example of Christian resignation in death, he told the family later.[43]

As the afternoon faded into dusk the mortification began to make headway. The general was given morphine. During the night he hardly moved. At 6:25 a.m., 17 July, he stirred. "It is time to be going," he said faintly to Louis Young, and ceased to breathe.[44] It was not ordained that Pettigrew die an old man in bed.

"A daily association with him was a liberal education," wrote a friend. "Had he been spared to us what a power he would have been among us; what a help in time of need would have been his lofty intellect and loftier character." Another friend recalled "the rare modesty that characterized his life and actions and the generous self-denial and self-sacrifice, the tenacity of his friendship . . . the delight of his conversation when in the freedom of intimate acquaintance he disclosed his full thoughts. Gentle and soft as a woman in all the offices of friendship, yet true as steel to all his obligations and duties."[45]

Yet another friend said of Pettigrew: "More than all he loved liberty. . . . but he felt that to love liberty was an empty mockery, unless that love was exhibited in the sacrifice which its acquisition requires. With him to be free, was to be prepared for and to engage in the struggle it ever demands." "I considered Pettigrew the most promising young man of the South, and, as young as he was, I advocated him for the post of our Generalissimo," wrote Matthew Fontaine Maury a few years after the war.[46]

"His untimely death . . . added sensibly to the gloom then gathering finally around the Southern cause, for there were many who believed he was to be the good genius of that cause—he was the coming man who should yet guide us to victory," wrote a North Carolinian. "He had much, very much to live for. Had he survived the cruel war he went forth to subdue, the future lay before him refulgent with the richest promise," said a South Carolina friend. "What is Life," asked Mrs. North, ". . . that so much labour and culture should be bestowed upon a man of so much genius and capacity to come to this!! and thousands upon thousands of useless mortals left to fill their ignoble places. Questions arise which must be put down, for they cannot be answered without uttering discontents unlawful for a Christian." [47]

The actual achievements of Pettigrew's life failed to explain, said Trescot, "the strength and breadth of the impressions he made upon those among whom that life was passed. The influence was in himself. . . . He had that in his nature which made men love him. . . . He was a man who desired to be, and not to seem." [48]

"He was my beau ideal of what a gentleman and a soldier ought to be," said a young man who was with Pettigrew in his last months. "None had more deeply at heart than he the cause for which he shed his blood," wrote Colonel Leventhorpe. "He gave himself up to it wholly, with all his fine energies, extraordinary talents, and the courage of a heart literally ignorant of fear. . . . I tell you the truth when I say that I have never met with one who fitted more entirely my 'beau ideal' of the patriot, the soldier, the man of genius, and the accomplished gentleman." [49]

The body was taken to Raleigh where, on 24 July, it lay in state in the capitol, surrounded by wreaths, weaved by the fairest ladies, of flowers from the fairest gardens in the town. The afternoon business was suspended for funeral services in the capitol square, conducted by an Episcopal clergyman before a crowd of soldiers and civilians. Then Pettigrew was carried to the nearby burial plot of his uncle, James Biddle Shepard, where he would remain until November 1865 when the instructions left in his will written four years before when he had gone away to another war, that he be buried in the family ground at Bonarva, could be carried out. [50]

Chapter 16

The Mind and Heart of a Carolinian

Adieu to a civilization which reduces men to machines, which sacrifices half that is stalwart and individual in humanity to the false glitter of centralization, and to the luxurious enjoyments of a manufacturing, money age!—Johnston Pettigrew, Notes on Spain, *on entering Spain for the second time*

During the spring of 1860, as if impelled by a foreboding that he would not survive the coming war and a desire to leave something of himself to posterity, Johnston Pettigrew spent the moments left over from his law practice and militia activities in writing a book—"an offering" he described it, "in memoriam of the happiest days of my life." This work was completed in June 1860. Then he put the manuscript aside in a drawer.[1]

Exactly a year later, at the end of four months' active military service in Charleston harbor, in the brief period of quiet before he left to join the Hampton Legion in Virginia, Pettigrew took out the manuscript and had it printed at his own expense by Evans and Cogswell of Charleston, using his salary as colonel of the First Regiment of Rifles of South Carolina. The volume was entitled *Notes on Spain and the Spaniards in the Summer of 1859, with a Glance at Sardinia*. The author appeared only as "A Carolinian (J.J.P.)." Three hundred copies were printed. One hundred of them were bound into 437-page octavo volumes with "for private circulation only" on the title page and were given to friends and relatives.[2]

The book is at the same time a travelogue, an exploration of Spanish history and manners, and a defense of the Spanish against the prejudices of Anglo-Saxons. "Very clever and very like himself," a relative found Pettigrew's book. James Louis Petigru, no mean critic, told Pettigrew that his opinion of the book's merit increased with each reading.[3]

Except for presenting copies to friends and relatives, the author made no effort to distribute the book. There was probably no moment in the entire nineteenth century when a new literary work was less likely to be noticed than that between the fall of Fort Sumter and the battle of First Manassas. And a work the title of which indicated that it was a travel book on Spain (of all places) could never at any time have more than a very limited appeal to American readers. Though a few copies survived here and there, Pettigrew's work has scarcely been noticed since, except by a few local scholars in the two Carolinas.

The few who have looked at it have been impressed and have found a good deal more than they bargained for. There is nothing exactly like it in the literature of its time. This was the judgment of a South Carolina literary historian of the early twentieth century, Ludwig Lewisohn, who wrote, "Pettigrew's single book is as interesting a volume of its kind as one can well imagine." Lewisohn found Pettigrew destined to shine as a man of letters and regarded it as a flaw of the old regime that most of his energies were spent in other pursuits.[4]

Theodore B. Kingsbury, a North Carolina scholar who knew Pettigrew when both were students, declared in 1875 his belief, after reading *Notes on Spain and the Spaniards*, that Pettigrew "had a purer intellect and of broader range" than any man ever born within the borders of North Carolina. He doubted that Webster or Calhoun, had they died at the same age as Pettigrew, would have left as certain evidence of genius.[5]

"On every page is revealed the scholar, thinker and keen observer," Kingsbury wrote, "whilst we have frequent glimpses of a statesman and philosopher at home among the social and political systems of the Old World." He described the book, correctly, as "fresh, witty, vivacious, thoughtful, kindly. . . . Distinguished by a catholic and generous spirit quite uncommon among travellers. . . . Spaniards never before had such a genial, honorable, appreciative, magnanimous, sympathetic" observer among them: "The book has been rather a surprise to us. . . . There are occasional passages of a humorous turn that we were not prepared to meet with. It is, besides, more artistic, hearty and eloquent, than we anticipated. . . . Will compare most favorably in its main essentials, with the best [travel] works that have been written by men of the North, . . . whilst in elevation of sentiment, purity of tone, fairness of judgment—in raciness, strength, breadth and learning, it is altogether superior to them."[6]

A generation later, another North Carolina scholar, who collected excerpts for the early twentieth-century *Library of Southern Literature*, judged: "That the author had the temperament of the man of letters, and possessed literary ability and skill of a high order, will readily be seen by even a glance at his work. Large tolerance and intellectual flexibility are everywhere apparent, and one realizes here and there the touch of the master's hand and feels that nothing could be much finer than some of his descriptive passages. Deep poetic feeling and imagination, delicate humor, refined wit, a 'rare gift for the happy word,' are some of the author's ear-marks."[7]

William Henry Trescot, generally recognized as one of the best literary talents in antebellum South Carolina, said of *Notes on Spain:* "This book is admirably written. The country and the people whom he described had for him a romantic charm, and his enthusiastic sympathy with their history and character gives to his descriptions a warmth and truthfulness which a colder observation could never have imparted. His thorough knowledge of Spanish history and his familiarity with the language taught him both what to observe and how to observe."[8]

What these readers discovered is that *Notes on Spain* is not merely a travel account or a personal memoir. It is literature. The work has an individuality and clarity, a coherence, a sustained effect, a capacity to simulate both reflection and imagination, that mark it as a significant piece of writing. After his "brief glance at Sardinia," Pettigrew records a journey through Spain that is not only geographical. It is a historical, aesthetic, intellectual, and spiritual odyssey.

He rode into every nook and corner of the country, far off the beaten track. He mingled sympathetically with all classes—nobles, middle class, and peasants—urban and rural, men and women, young and old. The resulting experiences, impressions, and judgments were rendered with apparently effortless artistry. The total impact is difficult to categorize. The closest analogy that can be found in twentieth-century literature is probably Hilaire Belloc's *The Path to Rome*. Like Belloc in his minor classic, Pettigrew constructed, in the form of a travel account, a work from which a unique individuality and a strong philosophical position emerge, though Pettigrew's book was more an expository treatise and less a deliberately crafted work of art than Belloc's. (Both books, interestingly, were written in their author's early thirties.) Belloc's journey was a pilgrimage for the Church. Pettigrew went in quest of the South, though less consciously and explicitly.

The value of Pettigrew's account of Spain is enhanced by his knowledge of the Spanish and Arabic etymology of place names, which allowed him to unravel traditions back to their original knot of truth. The Spanish countryside was alive with history for him. He knew in depth its battles and battlefields and its history as told by the traditional chroniclers, both Christian and Islamic. He demonstrated a good critical sense in working grains of truth out of the old traditions. For instance, he revived the beautiful La Cava, an early medieval woman who had caused schism among the Iberian Christians. Modern historians had been overly hasty in discarding her story as a "monkish fabrication" on the ground that she did not appear in Christian chronicles until four hundred years after she was supposed to have lived. Pettigrew, by reference to Arabic writings, showed that La Cava was real, although her story differed in some details from the chronicles.[9] Evidently Pettigrew had laid well the foundations of the history of the Spanish Moors he hoped to write.

Except for historical and public figures, no character including the author is mentioned by name in *Notes on Spain*. To mention names, Pettigrew felt, would be bad manners to those who had shown him hospitality and would be pandering to cheap sensationalism like the typical gossipy travel work of the time.[10] Anonymity adds to the authority and literary effect.

In the course of his travels about Spain and examination of its people, sights, manners, and history, Pettigrew showed himself, among other things, to be a fine critic of painting and architecture, and his treatments of Spanish dancing and of the bullfight are as pertinent today as when written well over one hundred years ago.[11]

Notes on Spain and the Spaniards is suffused with a romantic worldview, but it is not trivial or sentimental. There is no forced or cheap romanticism such as was common in the era. Indeed, on the contrary, the style and tone are restrained and sometimes ironic. Although the style is rather informal, a certain reserve, such as marked Pettigrew the man as well as Pettigrew the author, saves it from too great casualness.

The style is perhaps best conveyed by some of the occasional, surprising, humorous passages noted by Kingsbury: "Consistently with the truth, it is difficult to praise the ancient town of Venasque, though the antiquarian may find among the houses and walls numerous relics of the olden time, when the Moors garrisoned it against the irruptions of Charlemagne and other less distinguished fillibusters." [12]

Pettigrew's description of renting a mule from villagers in the Pyrenees also conveys his humorous style: "In vain did they assure me that he had never had a bridle in his mouth, and that mules went much better with halters. I replied that I had consented to waive my dignity in mounting him at all, solely because I reflected that bishops, and even the patriarch of the Indies, rode such animals, and that an humble believer might safely follow their good example, but that it was utterly out of the question for an American grandee and colonel in the militia to use a halter." [13]

Consider three descriptive passages presented in the *Library of Southern Literature*, the first on the Seville Cathedral:

As the excellence of the Cathedral does not consist so much in the contemplation of particular parts as in the general effect of the whole, it should be visited at all hours of the day in order to appreciate it fully. A stranger, with a guide and a guide book, will detect, perhaps acknowledge, its manifold beauties; but really to feel it, he should saunter in alone, with a mind free from preoccupation and ready to imbibe its mysterious influences. I was never more profoundly impressed than one evening, about sunset, in the month of September. The vesper chaunt had just ended, and the last notes of the organ, faintly echoing their mellow cadence, were dying away in the vaulted roof. Priests and choristers hurried out, with doubtless very prosaic feelings — it was their daily occupation — and I was left almost alone, with here and there a pious devotee lingering before some favorite altar. The expiring rays of the sun streamed in through the western portal, but were lost in the vast recesses of the edifice; the whole eastern portion lay shrouded in gloom. A faint gleam of light, struggling through the painted windows of the dome, fell upon the lofty crucifix, and seemed to point to the life of purity beyond. At such a time, one cannot but feel that there is an ethereal spirit within, a spark of the Divine essence, which would fain cast off its prison house of mortality and flee to the Eternal existence that gave it birth. This edifice is one of the few creations of man that realizes expectation. Morning, noon or night, none can enter without acknowledging that he stands on holy ground. The accessories, the trembling swell of the organs, the sweet odor of incense, the beautiful works of art, which elsewhere distract the attention, here combine in universality of grandeur to establish that harmony of the soul so conducive to devotion; and if the excellence of architecture consist in the accomplishment of the rational purpose assigned, to this must the palm be awarded. Political economists may reason that such an expenditure in unproductive stone withdraws from the general circulation a sensible capital; the severe reformer may preach against the adoration of saints and images; the abstract philosopher may denounce the appeal to the senses, but their remonstrance will fall pointless upon the heart. There are occasions when humanity rises above the earthly rules of logic, and acknowledges obedience only to those hidden laws which govern the divine portion of our nature, and whose sequence is beyond the reach of human intellect.[14]

The second passage describes Spanish ladies:

Upon the delivery of your letter of introduction, a Spanish gentleman immediately presents you with his house, *Mi casa está á su disposicion* or *esta easa es suya*, without thereby intending to make you a conveyance, and give you the right to institute an action of ejectment, which would involve you in all the troubles of housekeeping, but merely to inform you that you are welcome in the evening, if you can find anyone in. Do not think, however, that he or the household are going to put themselves out in the slightest degree. Some families are at home on stated evenings, and it generally happens that you find them in; but if you do not, why you can pass on to another acquaintance, and there is no offence meant and none taken. Nothing can surpass the fairy aspect of a family evening party, viewed from the grating. The suspended lamps give just enough light to see the sparkling drops of the fountain, and to recognize the ladies, half hid among the flowers. With their beauty, so suited to a scene of the kind, they scarcely seem to be of this earth. You enter, are welcomed, pointed to a seat. If the ladies of the house be agreeable you are seldom the only guest. The time flies by, chocolate, sweetmeats, perhaps ices, perhaps pure water, help it along. The watchman cries the hour in your hearing. Heavens! can it be so late? You place yourself at the feet of your fair entertainers (*me pongo á los piés de vm. señorita*). They kiss your hand (*beso la mano á vm. cabellero*). You skip along the street as though supported on the airy pinions of the wind. You dream of black eyes and glossy hair, of guitars and delicate fingers, of fairies seated in opening rosebuds, waving their fans to you and enveloping your eyes with tiny lace veils.[15]

The third is on the Alhambra, a subject made familiar to American readers by Washington Irving:

I have not attempted to describe the Alhambra. That were presumption. Even the genial writings of our own celebrated countryman, whose name is a household word in the palace of Al Ahmar, seem tame and artificial beside the moonlit glories of the reality. Of most of the great triumphs of architecture it is easy to convey a reasonably distinct idea by the united labors of pen and pencil. But the genius of Moorish art, like the perfume of a rose, cannot be imprisoned in fetters. Its thousand columns, its endless figures, its inscriptions torturing the ingenuity, all combine to produce the indistinctness which is its characteristic. As a summer palace it seems to be perfect. Its spacious marble courts, its delicate columns, its bubbling fountains and curtained doors suggest, irresistibly, the idea of a refreshing coolness and blissful repose. The Alhambra, however, to be appreciated must be seen by moonlight. Then, seated alone in the hall of the Abencerrages, and looking forth upon the Fountain of the Lions, does it become re-peopled with the spirits of by-gone days. Boabdil and his queens, Zegris, Abencerrages, Gomeles, Gazules, Abenamars, crowd its audience halls, or saunter along its silvery corridors, while the warning spirit points ominously to the few sands yet remaining ere the Christian bugles shall sound at its gates. The Alhambra is seldom mentioned by Arabic historians in any unusual strains of commendation. Ibn Batutah does not even allude to it. We can thus form

some conception of the grandeur and beauty of the palaces of Az-
zahra and Azzahira upon the banks of the Guadalquivir, which fire
the imagination of their writers. Indeed the city of Granada was
built in the decadence of the Moorish Empire, when its territory
was restricted to the upper valley of the Genil and the sea coast of
Malaga and Almeria, and its treasury exhausted by war and trib-
ute, so that it boasts few edifices of note except the Alhambra itself.
The founder of the kingdom, Al Ahmar, was the same I have mentioned as aiding St. Ferdinand in the conquest of Seville, and this
was the last of the great Mohammedan cities of Spain. And yet the
ruins of the Alhambra, the least celebrated of the Moorish palaces,
is the gem and wonder of our age.[16]

To concentrate on Pettigrew's social philosophy is to neglect his literary art, but for our present purpose that social philosophy, elaborately
though indirectly developed against the background of his odyssey,
gives access to some of the reaches of his mind. Since he was a thoughtful member of the generation of southerners who came to maturity in
the late antebellum period, his mind illuminates at least some aspects
of the southern protonationality that was truncated by military defeat,
all the more so since he was exhibiting his ideas for himself and friends
and not for deliberate effect on public opinion.

Pettigrew was, of course, an unusual man with unusual opportunity
and capacity for self-expression. He cannot represent all the tendencies
of southern life, but he does represent some of them. That these were
idealized tendencies not fully realized in the quotidian world does not
make tham any less meaningful as signs. And that they may have co-
existed with other tendencies that were different or even contradictory
does not make them any less real. Such contradictions exist at all times
in every society. Nor does it really matter much whether Pettigrew was
correct or not in his judgments, since we are most interested in what
he believed and how he thought.

The single most remarkable characteristic of *Notes on Spain* to the
twentieth-century reader is Pettigrew's freedom from ethnocentricity,
or "Anglo-Saxonism" as he called it. Indeed, a hostility to Anglo-
Saxonism was part of the impulse that moved his pen:

Nothing was further from my intention on crossing the Pyrenees
than to become an author. . . . On my return, I was strongly im-

pressed with the erroneous ideas prevalent . . . upon this subject [Spain]; ideas transmitted to us generally by the oftentimes clever, but always partial writings of English travellers and historians. . . . The conception we still retain of the Spaniard . . . would represent him enveloped in a huge cloak, shaded by a still huger *sombrero*, and rejoicing in a half-drawn stiletto, his country devastated by the Inquisition, and the abode of ignorance, idleness and prejudice. Such I have not found it.[17]

Part of this was an aristocratic disdain for the stereotypes which took the place of thought and direct encounter for a shallow middle-class reading public. But Pettigrew's stance also in part rested on a sense of kinship between American southern and European Latin civilizations as compared with the societies of northern America and northern Europe. Spain's relative freedom from the utilitarian ethos which was the Englishman's and Yankee's pride was what most attracted him. The same feeling led him to defend the Italians against an impression that they were too unstable to be capable of self-government. He pointed out that the provisional governments of 1859 had established order and liberty where confusion and anarchy had been predicted by most of Europe.[18] The Anglo-Saxon stereotype of the lazy, violent, unstable Italian and Spaniard had its counterpart in the abolitionist stereotype of the lazy, violent, bowie knife–wielding southerner. Anglo-Saxon societies ascribed similar undesirable and threatening qualities to both.

The negative stereotype of the violent, lazy southerner, allegedly lacking in the virtues of self-control, order, industry, and thrift, was propagated by New Englanders and those under the influence of the New England culture from the earliest days of New England and the South as conscious, contrasting communities until long after the Civil War. The stereotype is still deeply implanted in American thought, and it was the central feature of abolitionist discourse, although in fact it predated the slavery controversy by decades. Pettigrew shows the other side of the coin, for one man's violence and laziness is another man's courage and spirituality. At a time when Protestant nativism was on the rise in the North, Pettigrew took pride in claiming kinship with the Latins and turning the stereotypes upside down. He was pleased that in Italy he was taken for a Spaniard and in Spain for an Italian.[19]

Like much of the southern gentry, Pettigrew found distasteful the

Know-Nothingism of the 1850s, while many if not all of the reformers who coalesced in antislavery and the Republican party were strongly nativist. In a series of articles written for the *Charleston Courier* in 1857 Pettigrew had attacked and satirized the anti-Catholicism and nativism of the American party. He evidently considered these tendencies as yet another example, like antisouthernism, of New England prejudice and intolerance. The advocates of prohibition, the "Maine law," a sister of nativism, he regarded as mad. "Though their object is a good one, the doctrines they preached up were such as would entirely break down every thing like personal liberty," he wrote.[20]

Pettigrew devoted the better part of a chapter of his book to attacking explicitly what he called Anglo-Saxonism, which he defined as an unjustified assumption of superiority by the English-speaking peoples, the criteria for superiority resting upon the "disposition . . . to place a money value upon everything." The ultimate sinner in Anglo-Saxonism, the ultimate bourgeois nation, was England, although there were disturbing signs of the growth of the phenomena in America. England's materialistic values and great extremes of wealth and poverty as well as its lack of the ameliorations and comforts which softened the lot of the lower classes in the more traditional, agrarian, and aristocratic countries of Europe had repelled Pettigrew on first encounter. To Pettigrew the Latin countries and the South were at the same time more democratic and more aristocratic. The English and northern ruling classes had the power of aristocracy without its virtues. Their democracy, he felt, consisted only in honoring money over birth.[21]

So powerful was Pettigrew's Anglophobia that he actually favored as a resolution of the tensions with Spain over Cuba that the United States make war on England to help Spain recover Gibraltar or Portugal, in exchange for which Spain would cede Cuba. This would secure an objective while spiting a natural enemy: "We should thus incur the mortal hatred of the 'mother country' which we have enjoyed for a century past, and, in all probability, will enjoy for a century to come. . . . On the other hand, we would have the satisfaction of acting a manly, dangerous part, and of generously aiding a noble nation." Besides, he added, "six months in camp on the Bay of Algeciras, within three days' horseback of the marvels of Andalusia, would not be the most disagreeable lot that could befall an American volunteer."[22]

The reaction of a North Carolina intellectual, Cornelia Phillips

Spencer, to Pettigrew's pro-Latin and anti-English sentiments when she wrote about his book in 1887 exhibited the extent to which divergent tendencies of the antebellum South had been reversed toward the Anglo-Saxonism of the prevailing national ethos by that time. Finding Pettigrew blind to the ignorance, superstition, and cruelty of Spain, she explained:

> His prejudices and predilections were all in favor of the dark-eyed, dark-haired sons of the South. Their history, their literature, their manners, their climate attracted him. France, Italy, Spain — his sympathies were with them and with singular perversion of his keen and thoughtful intellect he was disposed to believe that among these races lay the hopes of liberty and national progress for the masses of Europe. It is not a little provoking to note his . . . distrust of the great Protestant powers, and more especially of England, to deride and depreciate whom he omits no opportunity.[23]

The Spaniard's proud localism and provincialism was a point of kinship, Pettigrew discovered. The Spaniard was by nature if not by situation a good state rights man. Pettigrew included in his book a lengthy analysis of the evil effects of political centralization on the economy, liberty, culture, and society of the nations of Europe.[24] An encounter with a cultivated Castilian gentleman, who showed Pettigrew around his little village, stimulated a disquisition on the true roots of patriotism:

> Like all Spaniards, he was jealous of his locality, and dwelt upon its peculiar beauties and excellencies — an amiable failing which is always agreeable to me, for I have never found one worth knowing who did not think his native land, all things considered, the first in the world. Local attachments are pronounced, by the modern school of social philosophers, to be relics of barbarism, ignorance and prejudice, forgetting that prejudices are given us by the all-wise Diety, as well as reasoning faculties, and equally for some beneficent purpose. The time may come when prejudices will disappear, when one's country will have no greater claim upon him than China or Hindostan, and the sufferings of the Bushmen will arouse as lively a feeling of sympathy as those of his fellow-

citizens. But this millenium has not yet reached Spain. Patriotism, an attachment to, a preference for one's home, is still a virtue prolific of measureless good, and for its foundation rests upon enlightened prejudice. Of all nations, Spaniards have this sentiment most strongly developed. Every Spaniard believes that Spain, with all her faults, is, or can be made, the centre of the earth, and his own province the centre of Spain. Nor is this sincere conviction on their part distasteful to strangers, being founded upon a good opinion of their own country, not a depreciation of others, the contrary of which renders Englishmen so odious throughout the world. I should have a poor estimation of one who was above this *prejudice*, for it is the main spring to the exertions which they are making for the improvement and regeneration of their country.[25]

Again, he wrote: "The States rights principle is profoundly ingrained in the Spanish heart—far more than in the United States." Here he described the characteristics of the various historic provinces and commented that lack of unity created problems. "But, on the other hand, it saved the country in the great contest with Napoleon, who vainly thought Spain conquered with the capture of Madrid." Past ministries had gone too far toward centralism "and one of the good actions of the present Ministry has been to undo their work and to restore vigor to the extremities. Such is evidently the path of true statesmanship."[26]

So great was Pettigrew's distaste for what he regarded as the centralizing thrust of Anglo-Saxonism in society that he denied that America was an Anglo-Saxon country and advocated his own version of the melting pot. America's virtues came from its diversity, not its Englishness, he said.

The increase of steam and financial communication, and the little leaven of Anglo-Saxonism unfortunately left among us, has of late years caused many Americans to look up to England as the mother *country*, according to the phrase. Though, perhaps, not one in ten of those who use the expression so frequently has any great amount of the much prized fluid in his veins. The manner in which the homage is received beyond the water depends very much on the state of relations with France. As the one goes up, the other goes down.[27]

England always had been America's greatest natural enemy because "selfishness, an utter, unholy and inconceivable desire to sacrifice the happiness and prosperity of every other country to their own even most trifling advantage is their invariable rule of action," he believed.[28]

> There is no earthly reason why Spain and the United States of America should not be the best friends in the world. . . . Yet somehow all this seems to be over-looked, and politicians and newspapers speak as though we were natural enemies. The rise of this spirit seems to have been simultaneous with that of Anglo-Saxonism. . . . there has sprung up a class, proclaiming that we are only an offshoot of the Anglo-Saxons. [Here he reviewed the progress of America toward liberty and equality, in contrast with English class society, and the differences of America in blood, institutions, and social organization.] And yet we are told that we have done nothing, that this is the legitimate and inevitable fruit of Anglo-Saxonism which we have only developed. . . . the unfortunate effect, in the eyes of the world, is to abnegate our proud position as a new nation, receiving and assimilating the energetic spirits from every country in Europe, and moulding them all into gigantic proportions for the secondary one of a member of the Anglo-Saxon race, of which England is the head, and our respected selves the tail.[29]

Were not the sins of England the same as the sins of Yankeedom and what Yankeedom was becoming in contrast to a true American spirit? Did not the Yankee like the Englishman have a talent for cloaking self-interested aggressions in a mantle of self-righteous moralism and a penchant for intellectual fads like Anglo-Saxonism in preference to tradition and common sense? Economic aggression was the real clue: "England is a conglomeration of monopolies. The land is a monopoly of a few thousands; the Government of a few hundreds. The whole number of capitalists does not exceed a few millions. All below is a toiling, ignorant, vicious, discontented multitude, who know not one week where they will find bread for the next," Pettigrew wrote. America had not quite reached that state, but in 1855 Pettigrew had observed: "From what I see in the papers about the meetings of workmen in New York to discuss their rights and to see that poor people are not to be injured by their landlords and oppressors under plea of hard times, I suppose that" socialism is growing in that part of America as in Europe.[30]

For Pettigrew distaste for excessive concentration of wealth was more than a handy charge to hurl at enemies of the South. In his report on the slave trade he had written of the great Sea Island planters of South Carolina who allegedly feared foreign competition that: "Indeed, there are no evils to apprehend for this class of our population, except those which result from excessive wealth."[31] Pettigrew's impulse was Jeffersonian and antedated the slavery controversy.

Emerging between the lines of Pettigrew's view of Spain was a view of America. The America to which Pettigrew gave his allegiance was a version anchored in the South, a version which had predominated in the first half of the nineteenth century, a volatile but not completely unsuccessful combination of frontier individualism and eighteenth-century aristocratic values which was still evolving and seeking a mature apologia. He rejected the version of America which had been offered by New England and, in a partly Westernized form, was once again competing for predominance—the urban, industrious, manufacturing, orderly, communal, puritan, nativist ideal for American society that was at the time he wrote being summed up as "Free Soil, Free Labor, Free Men." For Pettigrew, his version of America was synonymous with what the founding fathers had meant by republicanism. Republicanism was natural to that version, unlikely under any other social ethos. What resulted was a defense of the South, but it was also a complete worldview developed with sincerity and sophistication.

Spaniards were not formally republicans because their traditions and their highly personal sense of loyalty to the monarchy forbade it. But like Americans they had the qualities necessary for successful republicanism: "the combination of national, local and personal pride which fits men for living in an organized community, with the advantages of self-government."[32] Spain and America were alike in that they both produced the kind of men who could sustain republicanism. Anglo-Saxonism, an expression of the other, bourgeois America, had not created republicanism but was a diseased offshoot of it. Free government rose not from Anglo-Saxon blood but from a certain spirit. In this respect Pettigrew was closer to the eighteenth-century American concept of republicanism than were some contemporary and later northern thinkers who had begun to reflect fashionable notions of Teutonism and corporate society.

In his discussion of Spain Pettigrew indicated what he regarded as the genuine basis of republicanism: personal independence, local pride, and a conservatism against the pretensions of would-be rulers whether reactionaries or reformers. The important thing was not the form of the government but the restraints. True republicans in Europe he defined as those who "believe that liberty consists in the absence of tyranny and unnecessary control, not in a mere change of masters; that power begets oppression, and that that government is best which governs the least—necessary to preserve the society for which it was established. . . . In Spain there is no question as to who shall be King. . . . But the question warmly contested, is *how* shall we be ruled?"[33]

To Pettigrew, the core of republicanism everywhere was the landed man. He decried a growing urban proletariat and the dimunition of Spanish virtues which it entailed. But the gentry too, were neglecting their old duties, he wrote, and surely the passage was suggestive for America:

> Then, the gentleman resided on his estate, and led his neighbors both in peace and war, setting before them for imitation his own light, feeble though it were. Now, he has abandoned the manly simplicity of this life for the luxury of cities, and his virtues and influence wilt beneath the baneful shade of idleness. . . . It seems to me that this is the growing evil of our civilization . . . the progress of this continually spreading cancer—the substitution of a few overgrown capitals, with a fermenting mass of discontented paupers, for the healthy vigorous, honest population of the country. . . . The welfare of the agricultural laborer imperatively demands the substitution of steam machinery on the plantation as well as in the manufactory. Yet this might end in establishing there, also, the regime of the capitalist, sympathizing with the proletariat only through wages grudgingly paid and thanklessly received.[34]

Not government or wealth but character made republicans, and character was a product of independence. This distinction could, at its worst, engender its own snobbery, exemplified when Pettigrew wrote, at the age of twenty-one, when one of his relatives was to marry the daughter of a tailor: "The fact of his having exercised a menial occupation is enough for me." Some of the Pettigrews had been very poor or drunkards, yet none had ever "condescended to buy and sell or engage in any business of life, which was not compatible with thorough and perfect independence. Though poor, they have always farmed their own soil and stepped upon their own inheritance . . . and they have never yet been caught measuring cloth behind a counter or frisking about a dining room with a napkin." [35]

This is the snobbery of a rich and retiring youth without experience of the world, not the considered opinion of a man, and Pettigrew outgrew it. Four years later he wrote a letter of introduction for the son of a Charleston tailor in which he said that both father and son "are as naturally-born gentlemen as one meets." [36] Still, the preference must go to the landed man, at the same time more democratic (a greater lover of liberty, a greater enemy of privilege not earned by merit) and more aristocratic (more honorable, patriotic, duty-conscious).

In one aspect Pettigrew and the class he represents were eighteenth-century American republicans seeking to defend the ideals and social organization of the early republic. The Englishman, the German, and the Yankee exemplified to Pettigrew the corrupting tendencies of the nineteenth century, movement from an ideal of virtuous liberty to a concept of the state as a fountain of material favors. This tendency also promoted the worst features of class power and dissipated the best features—duty and honor. The Spaniard and the southerner represented to Pettigrew an opposite tendency—preference for honor above money, service above privilege, patriotism above interest. The Castilian knight, the ideal of unselfish and complete consecration to service, was the ultimate expression of this ideal, and, as the ultimate, was available only to a most subtle and sophisticated spokesman for the South—Johnston Pettigrew.

There was as much in the knightly ideal that was republican as there was that was feudal. This extended across a wide range of life and manners where, according to Pettigrew, the southern and Spanish worldviews meshed.

Speaking of the purchase of peerages and army commissions in England, he wrote: "It would be thought an astonishing thing with us if the presidential electors were to inspect the pockets of the candidate rather than his head and heart; or if . . . General Taylor had sold out his commission — things perfectly consonant with Anglo-Saxon ideas." Among the American diplomatic personnel in Europe Pettigrew noted that "those of our ministers who have reflected most credit upon the nation were persons of very moderate means, living in the simplicity and integrity of true republicanism, and therefore depending for position entirely upon social and intellectual accomplishments, which, in our country, are not often united with large fortunes." [37]

The image held by southerners of Pettigrew's sort in the 1850s of the republican gentleman was something more than mythologizing to reassure a threatened ruling class. It was an essential element in the American tradition, held as sincerely by Pettigrew as by Jefferson and George Mason, as by James Fenimore Cooper and other Jacksonian thinkers. Nor did it disguise reality; rather it corresponded to reality as much as social conceptualizations ever do in any society. The country republican represented a golden mean between "a savorless communism and the despotism of capital," [38] to Pettigrew, who had written in the slave trade report:

> Absolutists dare not view with indifference a nation of republicans, who have . . . succeeded in counterposing the destructive element contained in every free government, and preserving the stability of their institutions through the conservative influence of slavery. We are a standing contradiction to their dogma of the incapacity of mankind for self-government, and a silent reproach upon the means necessary to maintain their power. The Democrats of Europe, the antipodes of American Republicans, hold us in still greater horror; theirs is the centralized absolutism of the many, changing its head day to day, and vibrating fitfully on the extremes of military empire and socialistic tyranny; to them the self-government of individuals, the corner-stone of our system, as distinguished from the mutual oppression of the masses, is a stumbling block and foolishness. [39]

Pettigrew included in this description of the American polity a defense of slavery, but it was not merely and only a defense of slavery but also a sincere defense of a conception of the American republic by one who deplored the "preponderance of a few" and "the utter insignificance of the mass" [40] that he found in most of Europe:

An aristocracy of any sort, whether of money, blood or intellect, is absurd in our age of the world. But considering the circumstances in which they are placed, the nobility in Spain . . . is about as good I suspect as in other countries. Persons endowed with an attribute or a distinction, which is respected, are apt to respect themselves, and to become worthy to a certain extent of the respect of others. . . . If mankind in their wisdom had agreed to revere long noses, long nosed people would probably be higher toned than before, and a family who had possessed this attribute for generations, would be a great family. This I take it is the only sensible foundation for the principle of hereditary honors. But the Latin nations have been weaned from the idea of an aristocracy, and consequently the difference between their aristocracy and their commonalty has ceased to be so great in appearance as that of some other nations still enveloped in the fog of mediaeval barbarism.[41]

Recent history was a conflict among autocrats, the mob, and true republicans. The two extremes, whether a king or a committee of safety, were expressions of the same idea: "that mankind are made for government." Republicans stood for the countervailing notion that "government is made for mankind." Spain was formally a monarchy, but, more than any other country except America, Pettigrew felt, it possessed the attributes of republicanism. The old Aragonese government had embodied the Calhounian principle of constitutionalism: "Aragon and the United States are the only countries in the world that have ever embodied the true conception of a free Government, viz: a machine which shall preserve order and protect the nation, while guarantying the rights of the minority against the power of the mere majority," he wrote.[42]

The Anglo-Saxon ingredient in the mix of Pettigrew's Cavalier worldview was nonetheless strong enough for him to find distasteful the Spanish nobility's aversion to trade. Perhaps remembering his industrious father, he commented that the pride of the Spainards "guards them from the commission of many a deed of low villainy. On the other hand, it frequently prevents a poor gentleman from engaging in honest industry." Yet those in the modern, commercial societies who made sport of Spanish pride daily committed similar sins by exercising social distinctions that had no basis in justice. "For my own part, I consider all honest occupations alike honorable, and cannot conceive why a capitalist is more respectable than a street ditcher, provided they be otherwise equal. . . . a laugh or a sneer at these old Castillians comes with a poor grace from us who are daily committing the same errors.[43]

To Pettigrew much of the apparent freedom of northern society resulted from mere rootlessness and indifference, something other than what the southerner conceived of as freedom. The capitalist and the laborer were theoretically equal since there were no inherited and formal distinctions between them, but in the southern view there was an actual inequality, unmitigated by the graces of admittedly unequal societies. Equality in the North, Pettigrew believed, was only an empty formality, lacking in that fraternity which comforts men and strengthens nations. In contrast, Pettigrew wrote, "If there be one trait in the Spanish character more strongly developed than another, it is self-esteem. . . . In comparison with this, all the accidents of birth, wealth and office are as nothing. A certain degree of respect is acknowledged and paid to some of these accidents, but it is a respect of form, and confined within very narrow limits. Hence comes the practical equality that reigns among all classes, manifested even in the jealous application of *Usted*."[44]

An American of non–New England culture, of the southern/western ethos, could admire the Spanish as independent, proud, and freedom-loving, while the Englishman or New Englander, partaker of a communal and goal-centered society, disliked them. Two antagonistic ideals of social community were at stake

However close Pettigrew's Spain was to Pettigrew's America, in some ways they were inevitably different. Once Spanish friends asked Pettigrew if there were beggars in America, as in Spain:

> I replied no; . . . that every honest, industrious man could at least gain a livelihood, and though there were many disagreeable things home, this alone would compensate for them all if one were reduced to a comparison with Europe. . . . A long train of freight cars was drawn up in the station, to avoid the trouble of going around which, I was about to pass between, but was stopped by the guard. This caused me to mention for their doubting admiration another precious privilege of the freeman in America, equally incompre-

hensible, viz: that of getting yourself killed, whenever you feel in the humor, without the hindrance of officious philanthropists in police uniform.[45]

Individual liberty was available in America to a degree not possible among the most republican of Europeans. But in America it was endangered by the centralizing spirit of Anglo-Saxonism. Bound up in Pettigrew's conception of liberty was equality of a particular kind. The practical liberty and equality so uniquely American were the social cement and context of the southern/western society. Speaking of his dealings with Spanish guides and their superiority to those of other nations, with whom "the connection is measured by money alone," Pettigrew wrote that "your Spanish servant is insensibly drawn towards you by a sort of sympathy, proceeding partly from the fact that he does not recognize any inferiority in his position, and discharges his duty to you rather because he is your guide, and you are under his guidance, than because he expects to be paid for his services. I have never parted from one without receiving a hearty shake of the hand, indicative of real good feeling, very different from the way of the world leave-taking of your cosmpolite."[46]

In other words, mutual respect transcended the money connection and the difference in social status on both sides. Pettigrew's reaction to Spanish manners tells us something significant about the dynamics of the Old South, at the same time intensely democratic and intensely aristocratic, and about the spirit that day-by-day bound the gentry and yeomanry and possibly at least some of the bondsmen together in the great contest by fire for southern independence. "A muleteer will . . . offer his meal to a passing acquaintance with all the air of a grandee, and beggars salute each other with regal majesty," Pettigrew wrote on another occasion of the Spanish spirit of equality, so different from the abstract Anglo-Saxon conception. He admired the aristocratic virtues of the Spanish plain people, an attitude which is surely related to the esprit of the yeomen he led in the war.[47]

Individualistic self-respect had national ramifications, for a nation of proud men was bound to be a proud nation. Among "the thousand traits of Spanish character that find a counterpart in the United States, or at least in the Southern portion of them," Pettigrew found "that sensitive, even thin-skinned national pride, which feels that the conduct of every individual reflects either for good or evil upon the general character, and regards the public as inseparable from the individual reputation of its members."[48]

In the Andalusian—patriotic and individualistic, tenacious of tradition, warlike and courteous, proud and honor-conscious beyond material considerations—Pettigrew felt he found the perfect counterpart for his ideal conception of the southerner. In contrast were the parvenus of the North and northern Europe, where the social cohesion provided by birth, rank, and intellect had given way to the single distinction of money, and an extravagant and tasteless consumption was the predominant characteristic of the leading classes, as was observable, Pettigrew asserted, in the parks of the northern cities on any Sunday.[49]

Spain had carried the virtues of chivalry to their greatest refinement while restricting the evils of the feudal system to the narrowest scope, Pettigrew believed. Spain had never had primogeniture and had never forbade the passage of lands and titles to women. In Spain, he wrote, "Any such government as that of England, where both parties unite in reserving the honors and emoluments of office for the younger relatives of their leaders, would not be tolerated a week." The Spanish gentry were more like the republican gentry of America as Pettigrew conceived them than any other European class. The Spanish nobles were on a greater basis of ease and familiarity with the lower classes and abided by the American republican maxim "that the post of honor is the private station."[50] Thus Pettigrew was able to reconcile American republicanism and medieval chivalry:

> There is one feature which distinguishes Spaniards from all other nations in Europe—the absence of that respect and adoration for the mere possession of wealth which is the moving spring of society elsewhere. Men are not ranked according to the length of their purses, and poverty is neither a sin nor a disgrace. The poorest beggar feels his full dignity as a man. [Here he showed how Spanish habits of daily life in housing, dress, and speech minimized evidences of wealth. Houses were for privacy, not for exhibition.] In England or Germany there is an unmistakeable difference between the higher and lower classes, not only in dress but in manner; this latter has as little existence in Spain as the former, all are gentlemen alike, and it is often impossible for a stranger to

judge of the exact social position of the parties even after a slight acquaintance.[51]

Pettigrew felt much more at ease in a society of this sort than in the urban society with its sharp class divisions and extremes of poverty and wealth, conspicuous consumption, and lack of a sense of community. Those who are familiar with descriptions of manners of the antebellum southern gentry by travelers will recognize here in Pettigrew's concept of the Spanish a common portrait of the southern planter, of whom an informal and unostentatious dignity, candor, and friendliness were often cited characteristics, even by hostile observers.[52]

Spain is "a nation where caballero and gentleman are still synonymous," Pettigrew wrote, that is, where the warrior and aristocrat were one and the same, where the aristocracy retained its original function as the nation's servants in war rather than its privileged in peace. The long struggle with the Moor on the frontier (another similarity with America) had created a kind of aristocratic tradition in which service and simplicity outweighed privilege and display. Here the ascetic elements of medieval chivalry, dignity and abstemiousness, reached their greatest realization. The Spaniard is courageous yet mild of manner. "A Spanish soldier will march all day on a cup of chocolate and a crust of bread," while "any modern Englishman . . . would drink enough at a sitting to send a company of Spaniards to the asylum." The Spaniard was (like Johnston Pettigrew) capable of great endurance and devoted to women on the intellectual more than the sensual plane.[53]

Pettigrew's analysis of the historical development of the institutions of chivalry in Spain displays much about his concept of aristocracy and his lack of ethnocentricity among white nations. It also indicates the orientation he would have brought to the history of the Moors he desired to write and his high estimate of the Moorish contribution to European civilization. From the immediate context of the Inquisition and the removal of the Moors from Spain, he wrote:

> It must, however, have been a mournful sight to witness the extinction of this gallant race, to which mediaeval Europe was indebted for so many ameliorating institutions—ameliorations she has not been eager to acknowledge. Most of what formed the romance of earlier days throughout the Continent is traceable to the Penin-

sula, where the rude, sturdy Teutonic and elegant, poetic Oriental were subjected to mutual influences. One of the most conclusive evidences of the utter rudeness and barbarism of Europe in the eighth, ninth and tenth centuries, the darkest of the dark ages, is the unanimity with which the feudal system was received. This was a great progress, a long step in advance, but how miserable must have been the condition of society which required such a remedy. It had no existence in Spain, because the Spanish civilization had never reached such a pitch of violence and anarchy as to require it. About that time the Beni Omeyah were at the acme of their glory, and the softening light of Cordova penetrated even to the farthest corners of the north-west. The Spaniard inherited from his Gothic ancestors fierce courage, valor, the sentiment of personal honor, the duel, the judgment of God, fidelity to his chieftain, and the other points which characterized the Teutonic civilization. The Oriental to a valor quite the equal of his rival, united other qualities which were considered no less necessary to the character of a warrior, viz: poetry, grace, elegant horsemanship, skill in weapons, gallantry, fidelity to plighted word, and mercy to the conquered. The result was a military fraternity between the warriors of the two nations, and a common military character to which the Teutonic element contributed the strength and the defects, the Oriental the virtues and elegancies. Hence sprang chivalry, which spread gradually over Europe, and contained the first germ of civilization. . . . Indeed, it is questionable whether the institution of chivalry as described in the romances had a veritable existence out of Spain. . . . They [the Moors] are justly entitled to the credit of having revolutionized war. Before their day, it was a brutal, bloody, ferocious means of destruction. Gentle mercy to the vanquished was as unknown to the Hebrews, Greeks, or Romans, as to the Franks or Anglo-Saxons. Hence arises the charm of romantic chivalry hanging around these Andalusian battle fields, which will be vainly sought elsewhere, for here alone was a distinction recognized between the armed foe, careering in the pride of equal strength, and the same foe dismounted and prostrate under the victor's feet. It is no wonder then that the gallant spirits of the rest of Europe should flock to Spain as the land of romantic adventure, and the proper theatre for the display of knightly prowess; . . . and

that Chaucer should consider the proudest recommendation of a
knight—

> In Gernade at the seige eke hadde he be
> Of Algesir.

Yet what historian has had the justice to trace chivalry to its true
source. Spaniards have never been given to book making, and,
verily, Esop's fable of the man and the lion is the experience of
all ages.[54]

The origins of chivalry led Pettigrew to the subject of a feminine
ideal. He included a lengthy panegyric on the beauty, charm, and sincerity of Andalusian women in *Notes on Spain*, but this was more than
a romantic effusion. His chapter on Spanish social life, covering the
manners, customs, domestic life, and private personality of the Spanish, was superb. He described and explained the Spanish feminine ideal
as well as praised it, making a shrewd historical examination of the
development of the Spanish attitude toward women.[55]

Pettigrew had once written that the women of New Orleans were the
most charming he had ever met because they exhibited "the grace and
elegance of Paris united to the warmth and sincerity of the Southern,"
essentially his picture of the Spanish woman condensed and simpli-
fied.[56] A relationship between Spain and the South is again apparent.

The sincerity and devotion of Spanish women, which Pettigrew contrasted favorably with the insincerity and manipulativeness of better-
educated and more worldly ladies of northern nations, formed a central
point of his social ideal. It had, as well, an obvious connection with the
kind of republicanism that drew nurture from classical sources rather
than nineteenth-century democracy. In a traditional and personalized
society, public and private morality were inseparable. The sanctity of
the home and the sanctity of the state were synonymous, and the sanctity of the home was a vital principle of political cohesion in the deepest
sense, just as the honesty of the merchant was not a strictly private
matter.

An interesting perspective in this regard is provided by Pettigrew's
reaction to a performance of *Camille* in Charleston, if it is remembered
that his was not a puritanical but a liberal and catholic mind. Signing
himself "An Admirer of Virtue," Pettigrew penned for the *Courier* a

satirical review of the play. To begin with, the bourgeois sentimentality of the bowdlerized version, cheapening true morality, offended Pettigrew's classical aesthetic sense. The heroine was transformed from a prostitute to a coquette, and lines were inserted to imply the possibility of marriage "where none was, nor could have been intended." He added: "In Paris, surrounded by the living exemplars, it was sufficiently uninteresting, but 'moralized' in America, it is beyond endurance."[57]

The main thrust of Pettigrew's reaction was related to his conception of the inseparability of private morality and public virtue, for Pettigrew's was the unconventional mentality of the satirist who can grasp the true importance of convention and thus the seriousness of its violation: "I venture to address you this communication . . . because I believe that a nation's greatness, finds its strongest safeguard in the unsullied purity of its women, who, Lucretia-like, prefer death to dishonor, and because I consider the performance of the 'Dame aux Camelias' before an audience of respectable people to be almost an offense against public decency." What Pettigrew exhibited was neither Victorian prudery nor race obsession but a classical ideal of virtue: "The legitimate object of serious drama, is to excite and elevate the better passions. The Athenians, those pure critics, if not virtuous men, are said to have even driven an actor from the stage for repeating verses, which shocked their ideas of public morality. Test the 'Dame aux Camelias' by this standard."[58]

Pettigrew's attitude toward religion as revealed in *Notes on Spain* and elsewhere is another indication of his liberal worldview, his divergence from the provincial Whig view of history and Protestant prejudices which characterized the predominant, Anglo-Saxon societies of his own time. His tolerance of an understanding of the Roman Catholic faith was evident in his description of a visit to a cathedral at Zaragoza:

> My attention was particularly attracted to a beggar in the depths of poverty and misery, if his outward man corresponded with his real circumstances. Dirty, shrivelled, and resting upon two crutches, he limped up to the grating in front of the altar and threw in, one by one, coppers to an amount that, by a reasonable calculation, might have supported him a whole week. It would be useless to question the sincerity of his belief. The rest of the worshippers, though not so demonstrative, were, doubtless, equally in earnest, as their countenance, plainly evinced.

I took my place among them on bended knees. True, I did not believe that the Virgin had descended upon the pillar, any more than a great many good Catholics. Yet, there was a certain pleasure in participating in the worship. Was it religion? was it poetry? was it sympathy with the by-standers? or was it mere revery? I cannot answer satisfactorily even to myself; but it was a pure, placid emotion, that I have often felt upon such occasions, and which, if not religion, is very nearly allied to it. Some Protestants regard such ceremonies and those who participate in them with a species of aggressive contempt. I cannot sympathise with them. Every revealed system must rest for its foundation upon either reason or faith. The former decides upon evidence, scrutinised by the light of a critical intellect; the latter seeks its "evidence of things unseen" only in the heart. How many of us have intelligence, learning, or leisure to investigate the grounds of our belief in even the simplest article of faith? What immense erudition is requisite to decide whether the gospels containing a narrative of the Saviour's life be forgeries, revelations or mere histories? How often do sects split upon the mere literal rendering of a Greek sentence? And if the learned, who have devoted their whole lives to this alone, be so feeble, how shall we expect strength of wisdom from the mass of mankind, who have not the first element of critical science? We believe in the existence of a Saviour, and denounce as infidels and horrible monsters all who refuse assent to our faith. Any why do we thus believe? Because we have been told so in our youth by persons of learning and probity, in whom we have confidence, and whose better judgment in this matter we substitute for our own. The Aragonese believes in the Madonna del Pilar for identically the same reasons. . . . The Protestant idea is, perhaps, better fitted for the affairs of this world, as it dwells more upon the fulfilment of our duties towards our fellow-man. In a word, it is a fine support for those who, in the consciousness of strength, need no assistance. But for the broken in spirit, for those who, disappointed in their hopes, and crushed beneath an unrelenting fate, would fain turn from the world and forget its pleasures and sorrows alike, I fear it offers little consolation. Even for the earth we need something more than morality, something apart from and higher than humanity or its virtues, as is proven by the small number of Protestant churches in which the Protestant idea is carried out to its legitimate deductions. It is, therefore, the height of an absurd vanity for us, with upcast eyes, to thank the Creator for not having made us like those publicans. Be all this as it may, I feel a profound respect for sincere devotion, wherever and however manifested. Not only so, but I have ever considered it consistent both with courtesy and principle to honor religious ceremonies even when they might not meet with my personal approbation. I have knelt before the Elevation of the Host and bowed my head on the Paseo at the solemn peal of the Angelus, without feeling myself the worse therefor, and some of the pleasantest recollections of my life are these Spanish cathedrals, where the sombre grandeur of the architecture and the devotion of the congregation harmonized in elevating me above the mere materiality of existence.[59]

Johnston Pettigrew was never a regular member of any church, including the one of which his grandfather had been a minister. His relatives regarded him as rather free in his religious views. Yet Pettigrew had read the Bible thoroughly, as well as much related historical and theological matter, and he was better versed in the doctrines of most churches than many of their adherents. Though his faith was not conventionally expressed, he was a reverent man. Not a Catholic himself, he admired the tenacity of the Spanish faith versus the modern world and its skepticism: "The spirit of the age is entirely against not only superstition, but, I am sorry to say, religion," he wrote, "that is a religion in the vital sense of the word, and the real ground of apprehension at present is from a deficiency, not an excess of belief."[60]

Pettigrew was aware that civilization was subsisting on the dwindling moral capital borrowed from its Christian origin. He admired the barbarians who overthrew the Roman Empire for a certain independence and dignity which saved them from Roman debauchery, "but they surely evinced little appreciation of that spirit of charity, of gentleness, of forgiving love, which it was the object of the Evangile to preach. This, the true spirit of modern civilization, is due solely to the religion of our Saviour." He penned an appreciation for the softening effect that worship of the Virgin had had upon European civilization.[61]

In his instinctive piety, transcending sectarian dogma or affiliation, Pettigrew was typically southern.

Perhaps the most significant southern development of the late antebellum period was the working back toward Christian orthodoxy, which separated the South from almost every other Protestant society. Pettigrew in his own way exemplified this perfectly. What the antebellum period began, the Civil War completed. The war years, during which death and defeat followed death and defeat, revealing ever more plainly the folly of worldly pride, drew the people back to their God. One can see this taking place very plainly in the letters of the extended Pettigrew family. William Shepard Pettigrew, in his forties, became an Episcopal priest at the end of the war. There was little formal change in Johnston Pettigrew's religion, but on his deathbed, in a scene expressive of Christian resignation, he professed himself a believer.

The analysis and quotations above, extensive as they are, do not do justice to all the subtleties of Pettigrew's worldview, but they reveal some predominant themes and something of the depth of his vision.

Johnston Pettigrew was a superior representative of late antebellum southern society, both articulating and realizing its ideals more fully than the ideals of any society or class are usually realized in the mundane world. As a definer of the South Pettigrew was a liberal in the American sense — he was opposed to artificial distinctions between men and to illegitimate control over the mind and actions of the individual. Liberty for him was a specific condition of real men in a real society at a real point in time, not a conveniently unspecific ideological construction. He was free because he was Johnston Pettigrew, because he was a Carolinian and an American, because he was the inheritor of republican institutions and of social conditions and personal virtues conducive to the preservation of those institutions.

Among the impulses of his heart and mind were localism, an instinctive recoil from the impersonal cash-nexus version of democracy rising in his time, a militant personal pride tempered by charitable ethics, and a desire to devote his life to something other than getting and spending. Given these qualities of mind and heart, Pettigrew was attracted to the Spanish, a rooted yet individualistic people, who, he perceived, placed their highest values upon qualities of character and conduct revealed in the spontaneous intercourse of man and man, not in the transactions of the marketplace or the conventions of mass politics. He used the congenial Spaniards to illustrate his own preferences for society and ways of life.

There is a widespread tendency to measure the Old South against a utopian standard rather than against the shortcomings of other real societies then and now. Historians who discuss the antebellum South often treat it as if it were to be explained only as an aberration, distinctive only by the persistence of African slavery, and important only because it offered a temporary obstacle to the upward march of industrial democracy. If that is all the Old South was, it is hard to understand why its study should continue to consume not only the intellectual but the emotional energy of so many men and women far removed in time, place, and sympathies. Could it be that there are some positive qualities in that society that arrest now and then our unwilling attention and even admiration?

The southern society which reached its premature peak in Johnston Pettigrew's generation had provided a majority of the brains and sentiment for the development of American democratic institutions and a majority of the brawn and valor for the territorial expansion of those institutions. It was dynamic enough to have adapted to the frontier more readily and to have brought under its sway a far greater portion of geographic North America than did the rival New England–generated culture. Southern society (considered apart from one of its features, plantation slavery) was in 1860 still expanding and elaborating itself into more complex forms. It had laid the foundations of the empire of Texas, planted its seeds on the Pacific shore, and begun to exhibit sophisticated expressions of culture and intellect. It was dynamic and viable, confident and proud, not anxious and obsessed, confused and crumbling. To say that southern society was confident is not to say that southerners were fatuously optimistic or that individual southerners did not feel their individual anxieties. There was decidedly a streak of subjective melancholy, produced probably by the isolation and uncertainty of life, but that did not prevent objective dynamism. A vague individual melancholy may be quite typical of expansive societies.

Nor was the South aberrant from the mainstream of the American democratic inheritance. Despite the contradiction of slavery it embodied its own particular version of that inheritance. An absence of any direct reference to black slavery will, of course, strike the modern observer forcefully in looking over the array of Pettigrew's thought, and it is admittedly a large omission. Historians are fond of quoting Alexander H. Stephens, vice-president of the Confederate States, who said that the new southern nation was established on principles opposite of those of the Declaration of Independence. Instead of equality, it was "founded upon exactly the opposite idea; its foundations are laid, its corner-stone rests upon the great truth that the negro is not equal to the white man — that slavery, subordination to the superior race — is his natural and normal condition." They are less fond of quoting President Jefferson Davis, who stated that the Confederacy fulfilled the Declaration of Independence, that it "illustrates the American idea that governments rest on the consent of the governed."

These are two contradictory positions in the modern view. By the same token Pettigrew's liberal worldview can be contrasted with that of proslavery thinkers of the late antebellum South like George Fitzhugh or James H. Thornwell, who outlined an increasingly hierarchical social philosophy, extending the logic of slavery to all of society. While all these figures tell us something about the Old South, it is entirely possible that Davis is a more representative, less eccentric figure than Stephens, and that Pettigrew, if a less systematic thinker, is a more representative figure than Fitzhugh. That southern society could embrace such wide contradictions and divergent tendencies with a common loyalty, is, indeed, evidence that the South possessed already the wide boundaries of a nationality rather than embodying a simple regional divergence.

The contrast and ambiguity is certainly a warning against too sweeping generalizations and value judgments about the knot of issues that brought on the cataclysmic American conflict of the mid–nineteenth century. If we compare Fitzhugh with the triumphant form of American nationalist democracy that emerged from the Civil War, no modern citizen will be in doubt of his preference. But that is too easy; let us compare American society in its present state with the version of the Lost Cause expressed by Pettigrew, and we may have food for serious contemplation and run the risk of forfeiting our too easy comfort. We may even be forced to make adjustments in our value judgments.

Possibly both Pettigrew and Fitzhugh were characteristic of the South. History, like life, seldom gives us pure examples of virtue or depravity or unmixed blessings in its victories and defeats. Nor are history's lessons usually clear and easy, as Johnston Pettigrew's generation of southerners learned the hard way. Similar standards should be applied to winners and losers. Those who most deplored the southern Cavalier and applauded his destruction had their eyes on the main chance. They took no thought of what would fill his place when he was gone, that without a class of honor-conscious and duty-bound leaders to give them spirit, liberty might become lubberland and democracy little more than a means of dividing the pie.

If time had been allowed for the principles which illuminated Pettigrew's slave trade report "to have been enforced and illustrated, to have been applied to the larger consideration of the whole controversy," and for Pettigrew and a few men like him to have risen to influence, William Henry Trescot reflected after the war, "I think a school of public opinion would have been formed at the South which would have ... manifested its ability to deal wisely and successfully with those issues which have just reached their bloody solution." Trescot continued:

> When I think of him, and men not unlike him, and think that even they could not save us; when I see that the cause which called out all their virtues and employed all their ability has been permitted to sink into utter ruin; when I find that the great principles of constitutional liberty, the pure and well-ordered society . . . have been allowed to perish out of the land, I feel as if, in that Southern Cause, there must have been some terrible mistake. But when I look back again upon such lives and deaths . . . I feel sure that, unless God has altered the principles and motives of human conduct, we were not wholly wrong.[62]

Like all flesh, Johnston Pettigrew was flawed. Yet his virtues outweighed his defects. He expressed and lived the conviction that honor and duty is the other side of the coin of wealth and privilege, that the function of the leader is to lead. Such qualities have lost their meaning as social values. We are scarcely able to understand what the words once meant; we doubt that the qualities they express ever existed. We do not use the words and are inclined to think that those who do are hypocrites. But in a world where creature comforts pass for community, where slogans substitute for order and publicity for honor, we may feel their lack more than we know.

"Adieu," the young southerner Johnston Pettigrew once thought as he climbed a mountain pass into Spain. "Adieu to a civilization which reduces men to machines, which sacrifices half that is stalwart and individual in humanity to the false glitter of centralization, and to the luxurious enjoyments of a manufacturing, money age." His friends did not doubt that Johnston Pettigrew would have chosen to die as he did than to live to see the sorrows ahead.[63] Although he would have done his duty, he would have been out of place in the long months of horrid, modern trench warfare that lay before the end. The new world coming had no need of Cavaliers.

Notes

Preface

1 Clement Eaton, *Freedom of Thought in the Old South* (Durham: Duke University Press, 1940), 54.

2 Comer Vann Woodward, "The Southern Ethic in a Puritan World," *William and Mary Quarterly*, 3d ser., 25 (July 1968):363–65.

3 Compare Sally Edwards, *The Man Who Said No* (New York: Coward McCann, 1970) with Lacy K. Ford, "James Louis Petigru: The Last South Carolina Federalist," in *Intellectual Life in Antebellum Charleston*, ed. Michael O'Brien and David Moltke-Hansen (Knoxville: University of Tennessee Press, 1986), 152–85.

4 Eugene D. Genovese, "Marxian Interpretations of the Slave South," in *Toward a New Past: Dissenting Essays in American History*, ed. Barton J. Bernstein (New York: Pantheon Books, 1968), 114.

5 William Garrott Brown, *The Lower South in American History* (New York: Macmillan Company, 1903), viii.

Chapter 1. The Lake

1 [James Johnston Pettigrew], *Notes on Spain and the Spaniards in the Summer of 1859, with a Glance at Sardinia*, by a Carolinian (Charleston: Evans and Cogswell, 1861), 303.

2 Manuscript notes of James Johnston Pettigrew from information given him by James Louis Petigru, who collected it from older relatives prior to 1840, in the Pettigrew Family Papers, Southern Historical Collection, University of North Carolina, Chapel Hill, N.C. (hereinafter cited as Pettigrew Papers UNC). See also genealogical chart in the same group, and James Petigru Carson, *Life, Letters and Speeches of James Louis Petigru, the Union Man of South*

Carolina (Washington: W. H. Lowdermilk and Company, 1920), 1–3. The French origin cannot be established conclusively.

3 The best short account of Charles Pettigrew's life is still that written by James Johnston Pettigrew after research in his grandfather's papers and published anonymously in *Life and Correspondence of James Iredell, One of the Associate Justices of the Supreme Court of the United States*, by Griffith John McRee, 2 vols. (New York: D. Appleton and Company, 1857–1858), vol. 2, pp. 591–93. See also Bennett Harrison Wall, "Charles Pettigrew, A Study of an Early North Carolina Religious Leader and Planter," Master's thesis, University of North Carolina at Chapel Hill, 1940, and Sarah McCulloh Lemmon, *Parson Pettigrew of the "Old Church": 1744–1807*, vol. 52 of *James Sprunt Studies in History and Political Science* (Chapel Hill: University of North Carolina Press, 1970).

4 Bennett Harrison Wall, "Ebenezer Pettigrew, an Economic Study of an Ante-Bellum Planter," Ph.D. diss., University of North Carolina at Chapel Hill, 1946, 4, 6, 10, 19.

5 Wall, "Ebenezer Pettigrew," 398; Federal Writers Project, *North Carolina: A Guide to the Old North State*, American Guide Series (Chapel Hill: University of North Carolina Press, 1939), 405. William S. Powell, *North Carolina Gazetteer* (Chapel Hill: University of North Carolina Press, 1968), 270, gives the area of the lake as 66,000 acres. Among other attractions, The Lake has become a major source of prehistoric Indian artifacts.

6 Manuscript family history by William Shepard Pettigrew, Pettigrew Papers UNC. Bonarva House was built in 1815 and burned in 1860 when it was the residence of Johnston Pettigrew's brother Charles. A picture published with the article "General James Johnston Pettigrew of North Carolina," by Ben Dixon MacNeill in the *Raleigh News and Observer*, 12 June 1927, is erroneously identified as a representation of the house in which James Johnston Pettigrew was born. Pettigrew was born at Bonarva, which is no longer extant. The picture is of another building, probably Magnolia House. See also Wall, "Ebenezer Pettigrew," 7, 47.

7 Wall, "Ebenezer Pettigrew," 2–6.

8 Manuscript family history by William Shepard Pettigrew, Pettigrew Papers UNC; Wall, "Ebenezer Pettigrew," 8, 300–321, 403–4.

9 Wall, "Ebenezer Pettigrew," 51, 160.

10 Manuscript family history by William Shepard Pettigrew, Pettigrew Papers UNC; Wall, "Ebenezer Pettigrew," 22–23, 31, 398; Federal Writers Project, *North Carolina Guide*, 495. Somerset Place is now preserved as one of the attractions of the Pettigrew State Park. Magnolia, Ebenezer Pettigrew's last residence and long the residence of his son William, is still standing. A picture of Magnolia was published with the article by Mary Winder Osborne, "The Pettigrew Family," *The State* (Raleigh, N.C.) 5 (10 July 1937):2. Ebenezer

Pettigrew to John Herritage Bryan, 14 and 16 January 1837, Pettigrew Papers UNC.

11 James Louis Petigru to Susan Petigru King, 30 September 1845, Allston Family Papers, South Carolina Historical Society, Charleston, S.C.

12 Ebenezer Pettigrew to James Cathcart Johnston, 11 July 1828, Pettigrew Papers UNC.

13 Manuscript family history by William Shepard Pettigrew, Pettigrew Papers UNC; undated manuscript sketch of John Herritage Bryan and his family in the William Shepard Bryan Papers, Southern Historical Collection, University of North Carolina.

14 In all the vast preserved papers of the Pettigrew and Bryan families at the University of North Carolina and at the North Carolina Department of Archives and History, I find no letter from James Johnston Pettigrew to Mary Shepard Bryan after he was grown and only a few businesslike letters to John Herritage Bryan. Nor was Pettigrew close in later life to any of the Bryan children with whom he grew up except the one nearest his own age, William Shepard Bryan, who resided in Baltimore and after the Civil War became a justice of the Maryland Supreme Court. Regarding J. H. Bryan's resentment, see JJP to W. S. Pettigrew, 30 December 1855, Pettigrew Papers UNC.

15 For a few examples of JJP's childhood illnesses, see Ann Blount Shepard Pettigrew to Ebenezer Pettigrew, 23 December 1829 and 16 January 1830; E. Pettigrew to James Cathcart Johnston, 9 March 1830, and to Charles Lockhart Pettigrew, 21 December 1836; all in Pettigrew Papers UNC. See also Charles Shepard to E. Pettigrew, 23 May 1836, and J. H. Bryan to E. Pettigrew, 9 June 1833, Pettigrew Family Papers, North Carolina Department of Archives and History, Raleigh, N.C. (hereinafter cited as Pettigrew Papers NCDAH). See also Cornelia Phillips Spencer, *The Last Ninety Days of the War in North Carolina* (New York: Watchman Publishing Company, 1866), 279. Mrs. Spencer's sketch of Pettigrew, published as an appendix in her book, first appeared in the *Fayetteville Observer*, 3 August 1863. It was also reprinted in *Lives of Distinguished North Carolinians*, ed. William Joseph Peele (Raleigh: North Carolina Publishing Society, 1898), 414–21, with material added by Peele, 422–35. The sketch of James Johnston Pettigrew's life was also printed as "General James Johnston Pettigrew," *University of North Carolina Magazine*, 4th ser., 2 (June 1883):154–62. In the last mentioned publication the authorship of the sketch was erroneously ascribed to Mrs. Spencer's brother, Samuel Field Phillips. Her authorship is established by the letter of Edward Joseph Hale to W. S. Pettigrew, 5 August 1863, in Pettigrew Papers NCDAH. Mrs. Spencer knew Pettigrew when he was at the University of North Carolina, and she also consulted with his brother William in writing the sketch. Many letters about JJP's health are in the Pettigrew Papers UNC. Henry Ebenezer died in 1831

at the age of seven. James died in 1833 at age eleven when he fell overboard in the Atlantic while being sent to Europe for treatment: William Shepard Pettigrew's manuscript family history, Pettigrew Papers UNC.

16 JJP to W. S. Pettigrew, 25 March 1852, and JJP's childhood letter to his father, 6 December 1836, Pettigrew Papers UNC.

17 A good description of the physical beauty of the region is in "Pettigrew Park Will Combine Famous Carolina Plantations," *Raleigh News and Observer*, 9 October 1938. See also Federal Writers Project, *North Carolina Guide*, 405.

18 This is apparent from many letters in Pettigrew Papers UNC. See also William Henry Trescot, *Memorial of the Life of J. Johnston Pettigrew, Brig. Gen. of the Confederate States Army* (Charleston: John Russell, 1870), 16.

19 John Herritage Bryan to Ebenezer Pettigrew, 9 June 1833, and Charles Shepard to Ebenezer Pettigrew, 19 June 1833, Pettigrew Papers NCDAH.

20 Charles and William Pettigrew to Ebenezer Pettigrew, 2 May 1836, and Charles Pettigrew to Ebenezer Pettigrew, 26 May 1837, Pettigrew Papers UNC.

21 Charles Pettigrew to Ebenezer Pettigrew, 12 June 1836, Pettigrew Papers UNC; Spencer, *Last Ninety Days*, 279; William James Bingham to Ebenezer Pettigrew, 30 July 1836, and Charles Pettigrew to Ebenezer Pettigrew, (March?) 1837, Pettigrew Papers UNC.

22 W. J. Bingham to E. Pettigrew, 9 May, 31 May, and 15 June 1839, Pettigrew Papers UNC; Spencer, *Last Ninety Days*, 279–80.

23 JJP to Ebenezer Pettigrew, 30 October 1838 and 12 April 1839; JJP to W. S. Pettigrew, 31 August and 3 October 1842; W. J. Bingham to E. Pettigrew, 16 June 1838, 1 July 1839, 4 April 1840, 12 and 20 July 1840; all in Pettigrew Papers UNC.

24 Many letters exchanged by Bingham and Ebenezer Pettigrew during the 1830s and 1840s are in the Pettigrew Papers UNC and the Pettigrew Papers NCDAH. Circular from trustees to patrons of Bingham Academy, 16 September 1839, and James Shepard to Ann Blount Shepard Pettigrew, 9 September 1829, Pettigrew Papers UNC.

25 Regarding the self-willedness which the father and teacher labored to put down, see W. J. Bingham to E. Pettigrew, 13 August 1839, 27 October 1840, 11 January and 31 July 1841, Pettigrew Papers UNC.

26 Letters from Ebenezer Pettigrew to JJP from 1837 to 1848 (while JJP was nine to twenty years old), Pettigrew Papers UNC; see also letters exchanged by W. J. Bingham and E. Pettigrew, 1837 to 1843, in the same group. W. S. Pettigrew to J. C. Johnston, 21 September 1848, Pettigrew Papers UNC.

27 Ebenezer Pettigrew to JJP, 2 September 1839, Pettigrew Papers UNC.

28 Ebenezer Pettigrew to JJP, 12 July 1840; W. J. Bingham to E. Pettigrew, 27 November 1841; E. Pettigrew to W. J. Bingham, 5 January 1842; W. J. Bing-

ham to E. Pettigrew, 4 April 1840; E. Pettigrew to W. J. Bingham, 5 and 22 January 1842; all in Pettigrew Papers UNC.

29 JJP to W. S. Pettigrew, 20 August 1851, Pettigrew Papers UNC.

30 W. J. Bingham to E. Pettigrew, 1 December 1841, Pettigrew Papers UNC.

31 W. J. Bingham to E. Pettigrew, 8 June 1842, Pettigrew Papers UNC.

32 JJP to E. Pettigrew, 13 June 1843, and W. J. Bingham to E. Pettigrew, 1 December 1841 and 8 June 1842, Pettigrew Papers UNC.

33 E. Pettigrew to J. C. Johnston, 5 March 1842, Pettigrew Papers UNC.

Chapter 2. The University

1 Kemp Plummer Battle, *History of the University of North Carolina*, 2 vols. (Raleigh: Edwards and Broughton, 1907–1912), 1:93, 504; Kemp Plummer Battle, "Commodore Maury and General Pettigrew," *University of North Carolina Magazine*, 4th ser., 12 (May 1893):278–79. James Louis Petigru to JJP, 5 December 1854, Pettigrew Papers UNC. *Raleigh North Carolina Standard*, 11 June 1862; see also Battle, *History*, 1:729. J. B. Allen in the *Charlotte Observer*, 5 May 1929; for a nearly identical comment from a contemporary of Pettigrew, see *Raleigh Register*, 29 July 1863.

2 Theodore Bryant Kingsbury, Untitled review of James Johnston Pettigrew's *Notes on Spain and the Spaniards*, in *Our Living and Our Dead* 3 (December 1875):784. Clipping from unidentified Raleigh newspaper (July 1863), and marginal notes in Pettigrew scrapbook, Pettigrew Papers NCDAH.

3 Daniel to JJP, 9 December 1844 and 6 January 1846, Pettigrew Papers UNC. Daniel died prematurely in 1852.

4 Philanthropic Society minutes for 26 August 1843, 21 January 1844, spring semester 1845 passim, and 3 May 1846, Philanthropic Society Records, University Archives, University of North Carolina (hereinafter cited as Phi Society Records); JJP to Bryan Grimes, 14 May 1847, Bryan Grimes Papers, North Carolina Department of Archives and History.

5 Battle, *History*, 1:566.

6 Trescot, *Memorial*, 18.

7 Minutes, Phi Society Records, 1843–1847 passim; Battle, *History*, 1:504.

8 JJP to W. S. Pettigrew, 8 March 1846, Pettigrew Papers UNC.

9 Ibid.; Mary Pettigrew to JJP, 30 April 1846, Pettigrew Papers UNC.

10 Battle, *History*, 1:552–53.

11 Library register for 1843–1845, Phi Society Records.

12 Manuscript (December 1846), Pettigrew Papers UNC; Battle, "Maury and Pettigrew," 278–79.

13 Spencer, *Last Ninety Days*, 279–80.

14 Battle, "Maury and Pettigrew," 278–79.

15 Spencer, *Last Ninety Days*, 280; Battle, *History*, 1:590.

16 John Herritage Bryan to E. Pettigrew, 5 July 1837, Pettigrew Papers NCDAH. The Bryan house had previously belonged to United States Senator George Edmund Badger and was near the house where the future bishop and Confederate general Leonidas Polk had grown up. Manuscript biographical sketch of John Herritage Bryan, William Shepard Bryan Papers; and numerous letters exchanged by JJP with his sisters, Mary and Ann, and with various classmates, 1843–1847, Pettigrew Papers UNC, mention the homes to which JJP was invited and the notables, local and visiting, whom he met.

17 John Napoleon Daniel to JJP, 21 December 1844, and Mary Pettigrew to JJP, 10 August 1843, Pettigrew Papers UNC. JJP to Bryan Grimes, 25 May 1847, Grimes Papers; see also, in the same group, JJP to Grimes, 16 and 18 June 1847, and Grimes to JJP, (?) August and 4 October 1847.

18 John Herritage Bryan to E. Pettigrew, 30 March 1844, Pettigrew Papers NCDAH; JJP to E. Pettigrew, 19 April 1844, Pettigrew Papers UNC; JJP to Bryan Grimes, 25 May 1847, Grimes Papers.

19 Norcom to JJP, 7 June 1846, and JJP to W. S. Pettigrew, 27 September 1846, Pettigrew Papers UNC.

20 JJP to Mary or Ann Pettigrew, 25 February 1839; E. Pettigrew to J. C. Johnston, 5 March 1842; E. Pettigrew to JJP, 24 April 1845; Mary Pettigrew to JJP, 13 February 1845; all in Pettigrew Papers UNC.

21 JJP to W. S. Pettigrew, 16 February 1845, Pettigrew Papers UNC.

22 John Herritage Bryan to JJP, 22 February 1845, and JJP to E. Pettigrew, 20 March 1845, Pettigrew Papers UNC; J. H. Bryan to E. Pettigrew, 18 March 1845, Pettigrew Papers NCDAH.

23 JJP to E. Pettigrew, 27 October 1845, and E. Pettigrew to JJP, 12 November 1845, Pettigrew Papers UNC.

24 E. Pettigrew to JJP, 15 August 1843 and 5 February 1844; W J Bingham to E. Pettigrew, 22 June 1846; JJP to E. Pettigrew, 9 June 1846; W. J. Bingham to E. Pettigrew, 5 January 1844; JJP to E. Pettigrew, 22 November 1845; all in Pettigrew Papers UNC.

25 W. J. Bingham to E. Pettigrew, 22 June 1846, and JJP to E. Pettigrew, 13 January (1844?), Pettigrew Papers UNC; John Herritage Bryan to E. Pettigrew, 26 November 1843, Pettigrew Papers NCDAH: Battle, *History*, 1:507.

26 *Raleigh Register*, 11 June 1847; *Fayetteville Observer*, 15 June 1847; Battle, *History*, 1:504–8, 551; JJP to Henry Wadsworth Longfellow, 21 March 1847, Henry Wadsworth Longfellow Papers, Houghton Library, Harvard University, Cambridge, Mass.; Longfellow to JJP, 27 March 1847, Pettigrew Papers UNC.

27 Battle, *History*, 1:505; Battle, "Maury and Pettigrew," 275; *Raleigh Register*,

8 June 1847; Battle, *History*, 1:557; W. J. Bingham to E. Pettigrew, 5 June 1847, Pettigrew Papers UNC.

28 JJP to Bryan Grimes, 18 June 1847, Grimes Papers.

29 David Lowry Swain to E. Pettigrew, 31 July 1847, Pettigrew Papers NCDAH. W. J. Bingham to E. Pettigrew, 5 June 1847, and Matthew Fontaine Maury to JJP, 17 and 24 June 1847, with JJP's endorsement on the latter; E. Pettigrew to J. C. Johnston, 12 June 1847; all in the Pettigrew Papers UNC.

Chapter 3. Stargazing

1 John W. Wayland, *The Pathfinder of the Seas: The Life of Matthew Fontaine Maury* (Richmond: Garrett and Massie, 1930), 55; Charles Lee Lewis, *Matthew Fontaine Maury: The Pathfinder of the Seas* (Annapolis: United States Naval Institute, 1927), 44–45.

2 Lewis, *Maury*, 44–45, 47; Wayland, *Maury*, 54–55. By the late twentieth century the Naval Observatory had become the official residence of the vice-president.

3 JJP to Ann Pettigrew, 9 July 1847, and to W. S. Pettigrew, 12 September 1847, Pettigrew Papers UNC; JJP to Bryan Grimes, 17 July and 5 September 1847, Grimes Papers.

4 Lewis, *Maury*, 46, 48, 50; Wayland, *Maury*, 55–56; United States National Observatory, *Astronomical Observations Made During the Year 1847 at the National Observatory, Washington, under the Direction of M. F. Maury, LL.D., Lt., United States Navy, Superintendent* (Washington: C. Alexander [printer], 1853); JJP to J. C. Johnston, 30 March (185?), Pettigrew Papers UNC.

5 JJP to Bryan Grimes, 17 July and 5 September 1847, Grimes Papers; David to Emily Outlaw, 9 December 1847, David Outlaw Papers, Southern Historical Collection, University of North Carolina; JJP to E. Pettigrew, 10 July 1847, Pettigrew Papers UNC. By "Eves" he may have meant prostitutes.

6 John B. Palmer to JJP, 21 October 1855, and William Lewis Herndon to JJP, 28 December 1852, Pettigrew Papers UNC; Abel P. Upshur to JJP, 11 February 1856, Pettigrew Papers NCDAH; JJP to Bryan Grimes, 8 August 1847, Grimes Papers.

7 JJP to W. S. Pettigrew, 6 November 1847, Pettigrew Papers UNC.

8 JJP to E. Pettigrew, 1 November 1847 and 7 February 1848, Pettigrew Papers UNC. See M. F. Maury to JJP, 31 January 1862, and to Mary Pettigrew Browne, 6 May 1870, Pettigrew Papers UNC; M. F. Maury to JJP, 2 and 3 February 1862, Pettigrew Papers NCDAH; Kemp Plummer Battle, "Maury's Estimate of Pettigrew," *University of North Carolina Magazine*, 4th ser., 13 (October 1893):39–40.

9 JJP to W. S. Pettigrew, 12 September 1847, and JJP to E. Pettigrew, 7 February 1848, Pettigrew Papers UNC.

10 JJP to E. Pettigrew, 1 November 1847, Pettigrew Papers UNC.

11 JJP to Ann Pettigrew, 30 November 1847, and to E. Pettigrew, 27 November 1847, Pettigrew Papers UNC.

12 M. F. Maury to JJP, 17 June 1847, Pettigrew Papers UNC.

13 Trescot, *Memorial*, 19.

14 E. Pettigrew to JJP, 11 November 1847, Pettigrew Papers UNC.

15 E. Pettigrew to JJP, 15 March 1848, Pettigrew Papers UNC.

16 The only extended secondary treatment of James Cathcart Johnston (1782–1865) of which I am aware is that incorporated in the book in hand. The sketch by Martha M. Smith, "James Cathcart Johnson," in *Dictionary of North Carolina Biography*, ed. William S. Powell, 3 vols. to date (Chapel Hill: University of North Carolina Press, 1979–   ), 3:302–4, is useful.

17 E. Pettigrew to JJP, 15 March 1848, Pettigrew Papers UNC.

18 E. Pettigrew to James Alfred Pearce, 31 January 1848; JJP to E. Pettigrew, 24 February, 10 March, 25 March, and 7 April 1848, Pettigrew Papers UNC; James Mason Campbell to JJP, 19 February 1848, Pettigrew Papers NCDAH.

19 JJP to E. Pettigrew, 26 March and 7 May 1848, Pettigrew Papers UNC.

20 JJP to E. Pettigrew, 3 June 1848, Pettigrew Papers UNC.

21 JJP to Bryan Grimes, 30 April 1848, Grimes Papers.

22 Ibid.

23 Regarding the oppressiveness of the city, see JJP to W. S. Pettigrew, 10 June 1848, and to E. Pettigrew, 6 July 1848; concerning his reaction to the urban proletariat: JJP to E. Pettigrew, 24 February and 3 June 1848; all in Pettigrew Papers UNC. See also JJP to E. Pettigrew, 26 March 1848, Pettigrew Papers UNC; and JJP to Bryan Grimes, 16 May 1848, Grimes Papers. Also JJP to J. C. Johnston, 3 April 1848, to W. S. Pettigrew, 26 March 1848, and to E. Pettigrew, 7 May 1848, Pettigrew Papers UNC. A. Beaurend (?) to JJP, 13 May 1848, Pettigrew Papers UNC; JJP to Bryan Grimes, 30 April 1848, Grimes Papers.

24 JJP to E. Pettigrew, 24 February 1848, and to J. C. Johnston, 3 April 1848, Pettigrew Papers UNC.

25 JJP to E. Pettigrew, 3 June 1848, Pettigrew Papers UNC.

26 J. C. Johnston to JJP, undated (May 1848), Pettigrew Papers UNC.

27 JJP to E. Pettigrew, 3 June 1848, Pettigrew Papers UNC.

28 J. C. Johnston to JJP, 19 June 1848, Pettigrew Papers UNC.

29 J. C. Johnston to W. S. Pettigrew, 28 June 1848, Pettigrew Papers UNC.

30 JJP to E. Pettigrew, 6 July 1848; B. Maitland to JJP, 6 July 1848; W. S. Pettigrew to JJP, 11 July 1848; B. Maitland, Baltimore, to JJP, Boston, 13 July 1848; all in Pettigrew Papers UNC.

31 Will of Ebenezer Pettigrew, and W. S. Pettigrew to J. C. Johnston, 21 September 1848, Pettigrew Papers UNC.

32 W. S. Pettigrew to J. C. Johnston, 21 September 1848, Pettigrew Papers UNC.

33 W. S. Pettigrew's book of accounts with JJP, 1848–1863, and JJP's own account book, 1847–1861, in Pettigrew Papers UNC; see JJP to W. S. Pettigrew, 25 March 1852, and Charles Lockhart Pettigrew to JJP, 26 March 1853, Pettigrew Papers UNC, regarding the Tennessee and New Bern properties.

34 JJP to W. S. Pettigrew, 6 August 1848; J. C. Johnston to W. S. Pettigrew, 18 October 1848; James Louis Petrigru to Charles Lockhart Pettigrew, 22 August 1848; all in Pettigrew Papers UNC.

Chapter 4. A City of Knights-errant

1 James Louis Petigru to Charles Lockhart Pettigrew, 22 August 1848; see also J. L. Petigru to JJP, 12 January 1849; both in Pettigrew Papers UNC.

2 No better evidence of the respect enjoyed by James Louis Petigru in South Carolina can be provided than the reaction to his death in the midst of the Civil War. The leading Confederate civil and military officials at Charleston attended the funeral despite Petigru's well-known unionism, and a memorial was published containing moving tributes from strong political opponents. "Certainly no man has lived in our day who possessed so much moral and so little official authority," Robert Barnwell Rhett said: see *Memorial of the Late James L. Petigru: Proceedings of the Bar of Charleston, S. C., March 25, 1863* (Charleston: Walker, Evans and Cogswell, 1880), 29. This is a vivid illustration of how the gentlemanly code for personal relations transcended political considerations in the Old South.

3 JJP to J. C. Johnston, 5 February 1849, Pettigrew Papers UNC. The phrases "Knight Errants," referring to South Carolinians, and "Mr. Calhoun's Plantation," referring to the state, were not coined by Pettigrew but had been used by J. C. Johnston in a previous letter.

4 J. L. Petigru to Jane Petigru North, 7 February 1849, printed in Carson, *Petigru*, 276. This is one of the few letters from J. L. Petigru to his sister, Jane North, that has not been found in manuscript. Compare Jane Petigru North to Caroline North, 19 February 1849, Pettigrew Papers UNC. J. L. Petigru to Charles L. Pettigrew, 2 August 1849, Pettigrew Papers UNC.

5 J. L. Petigru to Jane Petigru North, 7 February 1849, printed in Carson, *Petigru*, 276. Also Jane to Caroline North, 19 February 1849; Octavia M. Bryan to JJP, undated (1849); Mary Pettigrew to JJP, 25 March 1849; Caroline to Jane North, 5 February 1849; all in Pettigrew Papers UNC.

6 JJP to J. C. Johnston, 29 (May) 1849, and to Ann Pettigrew, 1 June 1849, Pettigrew Papers UNC.

7   JJP to Bryan Grimes, 27 March 1848, Grimes Papers. Caroline North to Mary LaBruce Petigru, 26 March 1849, Pettigrew Papers UNC; see also Caroline to Jane North, 2 April 1849, in the same group.

8   Carson, *Petigru*, 258–59. Henry C. King (1828–1862) was the son of Mitchell King and husband of Susan DuPont Petigru King, the novelist. In Carson, *Petigru*, 226, it is said of King: "He was a man more noted for his manliness, kindness of heart and geniality than for ambition to shine in his profession." JJP to W. S. Pettigrew, 18 October 1849, Pettigrew Papers UNC.

9   As to his youthful struggles and literary ambitions see Carson, *Petigru*, 33–36, and William John Grayson, *James Louis Petigru, A Biographical Sketch* (New York: Harper and Brothers, 1866), 42–48. J. J. Pettigrew often found J. L. Petigru perusing literary works at the breakfast table: JJP to J. C. Johnston, 16 April 1849, Pettigrew Papers UNC.

10 JJP to J. C. Johnston, 8 August 1849, Pettigrew Papers UNC; J. L. Petigru to Jane Petigru North, 23 May 1849, printed in Carson, *Petigru*, 277.

11 J. C. Johnston to JJP, 24 December 1848, Pettigrew Papers UNC.

12 J. L. Petigru to Charles L. Pettigrew, 2 August 1849, Pettigrew Papers UNC.

13 W. S. Pettigrew to Ann Pettigrew, 18 October 1849, Pettigrew Papers UNC. (W. S. Pettigrew marked this letter of misgivings "not sent.") W. S. Pettigrew to JJP, 31 May 1849, Pettigrew Papers UNC.

14 Caroline North to JJP, 29 June 1849; JJP to W. S. Pettigrew, 12 July 1849; Theodore Gaillard Barker to JJP, undated (1840), inviting Pettigrew to a supper with the St. Cecilia Society; JJP to J. C. Johnston, 20 March 1849; JJP to J. C. Johnston, 29 (May) 1849; JJP to W. S. Pettigrew, 12 July and 28 August 1849; JJP to J. C. Johnston, 9 November 1849; all in Pettigrew Papers UNC.

15 JJP to J. C. Johnston, 29 (May) 1849, Pettigrew Papers UNC.

16 Caroline North to JJP, 9 November 1849; W. S. Pettigrew to J. C. Johnston, 24 December 1849; J. C. Johnston to W. S Pettigrew, 7 January 1850; all in Pettigrew Papers UNC.

17 JJP to J. C. Johnston, 30 December 1849 and 8 January 1850, Pettigrew Papers UNC.

18 JJP to J. C. Johnston, 30 December 1849; JJP's European diary, p. 1; J. C. Johnston to W. S. Pettigrew, 7 January 1850; all in Pettigrew Papers UNC.

Chapter 5. Europe, North and South

1   JJP to Ann Pettigrew, 22 January 1850; J. J. Pettigrew's European diary, pp. 1–3 (summary entry for 9–21 January 1850); both in Pettigrew Papers UNC. Unless otherwise indicated, all unpublished sources cited in this chapter are either letters or diary entries found in Pettigrew Papers UNC. Therefore the citation of the group will not be repeated in succeeding notes.

2   JJP to Ann Pettigrew, 22 January 1850; Diary, 22–26 January 1850; JJP to J. C. Johnston, 4 February 1850; and JJP to W. S. Pettigrew, 1 March 1850.

3   JJP to J. C. Johnston, 4 February 1850; Diary, 26 and 29 January, 1 February 1850.

4   JJP to W. S. Pettigrew, 1 March 1850; Diary, 3 February, 20 February, 19 March, 30 March, 31 March, 27 May, and 8 June 1850.

5   German friends are mentioned throughout the Diary; see also JJP to J. C. Johnston, 1 December 1850, and JJP to J. L. Petigru, 2 March 1850; Diary, p. 10.

6   Diary, 13 February 1850; JJP to W. S. Pettigrew, 1 March 1850; JJP to W. S. Pettigrew, 1 March 1850; Diary, 21 March 1850; JJP to J. L. Petigru, 2 March 1850.

7   Diary, 8 June 1850.

8   George Harvey Genzmer, "Francis James Child," *Dictionary of American Biography*, ed. Allen Johnson and Dumas Malone, 21 vols. (New York: Charles Scribner's Sons, 1928–1937), 4:166–67.

9   Diary, inside cover, 27 January, 29 January, 30 January, 28 February, 6 July 1850; JJP to J. C. Johnston, 4 February 1850; JJP to W. S. Pettigrew, 1 March 1850.

10   Diary, 26 June 1850 and passim; JJP to J. C. Johnston, (?) April 1850; JJP to W. S. Pettigrew, 1 March 1850.

11   Diary, 17 February, 15 March 1850; see also 13 March. "Thayer" was probably Alexander Wheelock Thayer of Massachusetts, later biographer of Beethoven and American consul at Trieste.

12   No contemporary evidence of this incident has been found. It is recorded by Pettigrew's brother in William Shepard Pettigrew, "Biographical Sketch of General J. Johnston Pettigrew," *University of North Carolina Magazine*, 4th ser., 6 (October 1886):44–45. The manuscript of this article is in the Pettigrew Papers UNC.

13   JJP to Ann Pettigrew, 16 June 1850; Diary, 28 February 1850; JJP to W. S. Pettigrew, 20 November 1850; JJP to J. C. Johnston, (?) April 1850; Diary, passim; JJP to "My dear cousin," undated (March 1850).

14   JJP to W. S. Pettigrew, 3 January 1851; JJP to J. C. Johnston, (?) April 1850; Diary, 26 March 1850.

15   JJP to Ann Pettigrew, 16 June 1850; see also JJP to J. C. Johnston, (?) April 1850.

16   JJP to J. C. Johnston, 1 December 1850.

17   Ibid.

18   Johann Augustus Wilhelm Neander (1789–1850) was the author of a history of the Christian church and of a life of Christ. For the background and result of Pettigrew's mission see Ralph E. Luker, "God, Man, and the World

of James Warley Miles, Charleston's Transcendentalist," *Historical Magazine of the Protestant Episcopal Church* 39 (June 1970):101–36. JJP to J. L. Petigru, 2 March 1850, and to "My dear cousin," undated (March 1850); Diary, 10 March 1850, and undated entry, p. 12.

19   JJP to J. L. Petigru, 26 May 1851; Maury to JJP, 28 June 1850.

20   JJP to J. C. Johnston, 1 December 1850; see also JJP to W. S. Pettigrew, 11 August 1850, and to Ann Pettigrew, 10 November 1850; Diary, April to September 1850 passim; JJP to J. C. Johnston, 21 August 1850.

21   Diary, April to September 1850 passim; see also JJP to W. S. Pettigrew, 11 August 1850, and to Caroline North, 21 August 1850.

22   JJP to Ann Pettigrew, 10 November 1850.

23   JJP to Ann Pettigrew, 10 November 1850; see also JJP to J. C. Johnston, 1 December 1850.

24   JJP to W. S. Pettigrew, 20 November 1850.

25   JJP to J. C. Johnston, 15 March 1851.

26   Ibid.

27   Ibid.; see also Diary, 13 March 1851.

28   Diary (in Italian and French), March to August 1851 passim; JJP to J. C. Johnston, 2 April 1851, and to Ann Pettigrew, 24 May 1851.

29   "Le donne sono gia bella."

30   "Adesso comminciano le donne nen ad esser belle, ma Angela!"

31   "ah Dio! que cielo! que belle ragazze!!"

32   "Belle ragazze de pertutto. Come ho sofferto quelle giorno!! Tentazione[?]!!"

33   "Aventure avec les demoiselles; dont j'embrasse la plus jolie de 14 ans, pour un Koutze. helas quelle difference entre celle-ci celle-de Naples!!"

34   "Passé le nuit a Realf où ma belle italienne me recoit en rougissant. An mon Dieu! pourquoi es-tu fait les italiennes pour nous tourmenter?"

35   JJP to J. C. Johnston, 5 July 1851; see also JJP to J. L. Petigru, 26 May 1851.

36   JJP to J. C. Johnston, 2 April 1851.

37   Child to JJP, 8 December 1851; JJP to J. L. Petigru, (?) September 1851; [James Johnston Pettigrew], *Notes on Spain*, 47; JJP to J. C. Johnston, 22 October 1851; Diary, 30 July 1851; JJP to Ann Pettigrew, 24 August 1853; JJP to J. L. Petigru, (?) September 1851.

38   Pettigrew's general European Diary, summary entry for 14 April to 28 May 1852 and passim; also his separate diary for Spain passim. The first is the volume cited throughout as "Diary." The second volume, concerning only Spain and written in Spanish, will be hereinafter cited as "Diario," since it is entitled "Diario de un Viaje en Espana. . . ."

39   Diary, 27 January and 28 February 1850.

40   Diary, 22 January 1850; *Notes on Spain*, 168–72.

41   John Sidney Thrasher to JJP, 13 December 1852. JJP to Augustin Louis

Taveau, 24 October 1852, Augustin Louis Taveau Papers, Duke University Library, Durham, N.C.

42 JJP to W. S. Pettigrew, 16 October 1851.

43 JJP to J. C. Johnston, 11 May 1852, and to W. S. Pettigrew, 13 May 1852; Diary, 10 May 1852.

44 JJP to W. S. Pettigrew, 22 September 1851; Diario, 1 December 1851.

Chapter 6. Alas! Romantic Spain

1 JJP to J. C. Johnston, 15 December 1851, Pettigrew Papers UNC.

2 *Notes on Spain*, 352.

3 JJP to J. C. Johnston, 15 December 1851, Pettigrew Papers UNC.

4 *Notes on Spain*, 352–53.

5 Basil Lanneau Gildersleeve, *Creed of the Old South, 1865–1915* (Baltimore: Johns Hopkins University Press, 1915), the mature view of a former Confederate of great learning, is suggestive of what I am indicating here. For other intimations of the same thing see Comer Vann Woodward, *Origins of the New South: 1877–1913*, vol. 9 of *The History of the South* (Baton Rouge: Louisiana State University Press, 1951), 173–74; and Richard Mervin Weaver, *The Southern Tradition at Bay: A History of Postbellum Thought* (New Rochelle: Arlington House, 1968).

6 From Edmund Burke, *Reflections on the Revolution in France*.

7 Joseph Gregoire de Roulhac Hamilton, "Daniel Moreau Barringer," *Dictionary of American Biography*, 1:648–49; JJP to W. S. Pettigrew, 6 August 1848, to J. C. Johnston, 15 December 1851, and to J. L. Petigru, 7 January 1852, Pettigrew Papers UNC.

8 JJP to J. C. Johnston, 15 December 1851, and Diario, 11 December 1851, Pettigrew Papers UNC.

9 JJP to W. S. Pettigrew, 1 January 1852, and to J. L. Petigru, 7 January 1852, Pettigrew Papers UNC.

10 Horatio G. Perry to JJP, 12 January 1852, Pettigrew Papers UNC; JJP to Daniel Moreau Barringer, 6 March 1852, Pettigrew Papers NCDAH; D. M. Barringer to JJP, 18 March 1852, JJP to W. S. Pettigrew, 25 March 1852, and JJP to J. C. Johnston, 11 May 1852, Pettigrew Papers UNC; Horatio G. Perry to D. M. Barringer, 26 March 1852, Daniel Moreau Barringer Papers, Southern Historical Collection, University of North Carolina.

11 JJP to J. C. Johnston, 11 May 1852, Pettigrew Papers UNC. JJP to D. M. Barringer, 4 December 1852, Pettigrew Papers NCDAH; see also Barringer to William Henry Trescot, 14 October 1867, in the same group.

12 JJP to J. C. Johnston, 6 December 1853, Pettigrew Papers UNC.

13 Hamilton, "Barringer"; *Notes on Spain*, 422, 430.

14   A. Curtis Wilgus, "John Sidney Thrasher," *Dictionary of American Biography*, 18:509–10. Many letters from Thrasher to Pettigrew, 1853–1860, in Pettigrew Papers UNC, discuss Cuba, Spanish literature, and Thrasher's marriage. J. S. Thrasher to JJP, 7 December 1855, 2 and 15 January 1854, Pettigrew Papers UNC.

15   Diario passim, and JJP to J. C. Johnston, 15 January 1852, Pettigrew Papers UNC; *Notes on Spain*, 103.

16   JJP to J. C. Johnston, 15 January and 11 May 1852, and to J. L. Petigru, 7 January 1852, Pettigrew Papers UNC; JJP to D. M. Barringer, 14 January 1852, Pettigrew Papers NCDAH; *Notes on Spain*, 86.

17   *Notes on Spain*, 18.

18   JJP to D. M. Barringer, 6 March 1852, Pettigrew Papers NCDAH; JJP to W. S. Pettigrew, 8 July 1853, Pettigrew Papers UNC.

19   Diario, 8–14 April 1852; Diary, 14 April to 28 May 1852; JJP to J. C. Johnston, 11 May 1852; JJP to Ann Pettigrew, 10 June 1852; all in Pettigrew Papers UNC.

20   JJP to Ann Pettigrew, 10 June 1852, and J. C. Johnston to JJP, 3 February 1852, Pettigrew Papers UNC. There are uncomplimentary references throughout Pettigrew's diary to the Englishmen he encountered. For more examples of Anglophobia, see *Notes on Spain*, 422–28; and letters to J. C. Johnston, 21 August 1850, and to W. S. Pettigrew, 3 January 1851, Pettigrew Papers UNC.

21   JJP to W. S. Pettigrew, 28 May 1852; Diary, 14 April to 12 July 1852; JJP to Ann Pettigrew, 18 July 1852; all in Pettigrew Papers UNC.

22   Diary, 13–28 July 1852, Pettigrew Papers UNC.

23   JJP to J. C. Johnston, letter mistakenly dated 19 June 1852 (actually written 19 July), Pettigrew Papers UNC.

24   Albert Jay Nock, *Jefferson* (Washington: National Home Library Foundation, 1926), 86, 104.

25   JJP to J. C. Johnston, (19 July) 1852, Pettigrew Papers UNC.

26   Ibid.; see also Diary, 13 July to 18 September 1852, Pettigrew Papers UNC.

27   JJP to Williams and Butler, 1 January 1852, W. S. Pettigrew to JJP, 17 March 1853, and JJP's account book, all in Pettigrew Papers UNC.

28   Kingsbury, Review of *Notes on Spain*, 788.

29   JJP to W. S. Pettigrew, 20 August 1851, Pettigrew Papers UNC.

30   JJP to D. M. Barringer, 16 January 1855, Pettigrew Papers NCDAH.

Chapter 7. Kin

1   Charles L. Pettigrew to W. S. Pettigrew, 22 September 1852, Pettigrew Papers UNC.

2 Caroline North to Henry Deas Lesesne, 24 September 1852, Caroline North to Jane Petigru North, (?) October 1852, Pettigrew Papers UNC.

3 J. C. Johnston to W. S. Pettigrew, 10 November 1852, W. S. Pettigrew to J. C. Johnston, 2 November 1852, Pettigrew Papers UNC.

4 Trescot, *Memorial*, 24; JJP to W. S. Pettigrew, 8 July 1853, Pettigrew Papers UNC.

5 JJP to W. S. Pettigrew, 8 July 1853; see also JJP to W. S. Pettigrew, 8 October 1849, 16 May 1853, 17 June 1854, and 24 August 1855; all in Pettigrew Papers UNC.

6 JJP to W. S. Pettigrew, 8 July 1853, Pettigrew Papers UNC; Trescot, *Memorial*, 24.

7 JJP to W. S. Pettigrew, 8 July 1853, Pettigrew Papers UNC.

8 Ibid.; Caroline North to Jane Petigru North, (?) October 1852, Pettigrew Papers UNC.

9 JJP to W. S. Pettigrew, 8 July 1853, Pettigrew Papers UNC. The Spanish historian referred to is Pascual de Gayangos y Arce (1809–1897).

10 Arabic and Hebrew exercises, bibliography and notes for a history of the Spanish Moors in a manuscript volume, Pettigrew Papers UNC; see also W. S. Pettigrew, "Biographical Sketch," 44.

11 John Sidney Thrasher to JJP, 15 December 1852, JJP to J. C. Johnston, 4 January 1853, Pettigrew Papers UNC; Joseph Blythe Allston to Adele Petigru (Mrs. R. F. W.) Allston, 7 January (1853), Allston Papers; C. L. Pettigrew to Caroline North, 22 January 1853, Pettigrew Papers UNC; JJP to William Alexander Graham, 20 December 1852, William Alexander Graham Papers, Southern Historical Collection, University of North Carolina; J. De Choiseul, Charleston, to M. Reybaud, Havana, 7 January 1853, Pettigrew Papers UNC.

12 JJP to Ann Pettigrew, 19 January 1853, and to J. C. Johnston, 15 February 1853, Pettigrew Papers UNC; also, in the same group, see Pettigrew's "Diario de un Viaje de Charleston à Cuba y volvivendo par la Nueva Orleans," 11–28 January 1853.

13 JJP to J. C. Johnston, 15 February 1853, Pettigrew Papers UNC.

14 J. C. Johnston to JJP, 7 February 1853, JJP to J. C. Johnston, 15 February 1853, and Cuba–New Orleans diary, 3–14 February 1853, Pettigrew Papers UNC; Lincoln Lionel Levy to JJP, 8 April 1853, Pettigrew Papers NCDAH.

15 JJP to Ann Pettigrew, 8 October 1853, JJP to J. C. Johnston, 29 November and 6 December 1853, and JJP to W. S. Pettigrew, 15 August 1853, Pettigrew Papers UNC; JJP to John Herritage Bryan, 10 October 1853, John Herritage Bryan Collection, North Carolina Department of Archives and History; J. H. Bryan to JJP, 15 October 1853, Pettigrew Papers UNC.

16 JJP to W. S. Pettigrew, 10 October and 15 August 1853, and JJP to J. C. Johnston, 4 January 1853, Pettigrew Papers UNC.

17 Notation, 13 April 1853, in Pettigrew's European diary volume: "Premier appearance in the Court of Common Pleas"; JJP to J. C. Johnston, 17 May and 6 December 1853; all in Pettigrew Papers UNC. Kingsbury, Review of *Notes on Spain*, 787.

18 JJP to J. C. Johnston, 6 December 1853, and letter of 28 January 1854 (mistakenly dated 1853), Pettigrew Papers UNC; see also JJP to W. S. Pettigrew, 7 January 1854, Pettigrew Papers UNC.

19 J. L. Petigru to Caroline North, 18 February 1854, JJP to J. C. Johnston, 28 January 1854 (mistakenly dated 1853), Pettigrew Papers UNC.

20 Certificate dated 2 May 1855, along with a collection of legal briefs, Pettigrew Papers NCDAH; JJP to J. C. Johnston, 30 March (185?), Pettigrew Papers UNC; Carson, *Petigru*, 457.

21 General James Hamilton, Jr., to JJP, 3 December 1855, Pettigrew Papers NCDAH; JJP to J. C. Johnston, 2 April 1855, and W. S. Pettigrew to J. C. Johnston, 26 April 1855, Pettigrew Papers UNC; J. L. Petigru to Jane Petigru North, 2 December 1854, in Carson, *Petigru*, 30; Mary Pettigrew to William Shepard Bryan, 25 February (185?), William Shepard Bryan Papers.

22 Carson, *Petigru*, 67, 69, 226; Grayson, *Petigru*, 164. The Petigru law office is now a private residence and a registered National Historic Landmark.

23 Trescot, *Memorial*, 25–26; JJP's "obituary" in the *Charleston Courier*, 4 June 1862; James Conner to Joseph Blythe Allston, 8 August 1864, Pettigrew Papers NCDAH; JJP to W. S. Pettigrew, 23 November 1855, Pettigrew Papers UNC.

24 JJP to W. S. Pettigrew, 7 January 1854, Pettigrew Papers UNC.

25 JJP to J. C. Johnston, 14 March 1856, and receipts for dues paid, Pettigrew Papers UNC.

26 JJP to W. S. Pettigrew, 8 July 1853, J. C. Johnston to W. S. Pettigrew, 22 August 1854, Pettigrew Papers UNC.

27 J. C. Johnston to W. S. Pettigrew, 6 March 1849, Pettigrew Papers UNC; Benjamin Allston to Adele Petigru Allston, 9 November 1858, Allston Papers.

28 Mary Pettigrew to W. S. Pettigrew, 29 March 1856, Pettigrew Papers UNC.

29 Caroline North Pettigrew to W. S. Pettigrew, 12 November 1858; JJP to Henry Deas Lesesne, undated (May, 1859); and Lesesne to JJP, 31 May 1859; all in Pettigrew Papers UNC. JJP to H. D. Lesesne, 6 June 1859, Eldridge Civil War Collection, Henry E. Huntington Library, San Marino, Calif.

30 Adele Petigru Allston to R. F. W. Allston, 4 June 1850, Allston Papers; JJP to W. S. Pettigrew, 28 December 1856, and Caroline North Pettigrew to Charles L. Pettigrew, 4, 13 and 16 June 1854, Pettigrew Papers UNC.

31 Susan Petigru King to James Louis Petigru, 5 June 1862, Pettigrew Papers UNC.

32 Louis Petigru Porcher to Adele Petigru Allston, 9 October 1854, Allston

Papers; Mary Pettigrew to W. S. Pettigrew, 7–9 January 1850, Pettigrew Papers UNC.

33   JJP to W. S. Pettigrew, 7 March 1853; Caroline N. Pettigrew to C. L. Pettigrew, 10 November 1858; JJP to W. S. Pettigrew, 7 March 1853; Caroline North to Minnie North, 19 September 1852; Caroline North to Jane Petigru North, 13 September and (?) October 1852; all in Pettigrew Papers UNC. Carie and Johnston continued to exchange letters after her marriage and until Pettigrew's death in the same friendly, humorous, and intimate tone as before; letters are chiefly in the Pettigrew Papers UNC; see also JJP to W. S. Pettigrew, 16 May 1853, and to J. C. Johnston, 28 March 1853, Pettigrew Papers UNC.

34   Jane Petigru North to Caroline N. Pettigrew, 20 June 1856; Caroline N. Pettigrew to C. L. Pettigrew, 4 June 1854; Mary Pettigrew to W. S. Pettigrew, 12 August 1848; all in Pettigrew Papers UNC.

35   Almost every letter from his sister Mary and his cousin Caroline North to Pettigrew from his first meeting with Miss McDuffie in 1849 until her marriage in 1858 makes some mention of her: chiefly in the Pettigrew Papers UNC; see especially Caroline North to JJP, 7 January 1858. Pettigrew occasionally replied to these broad hints, but in a light manner. On at least one occasion he asked a friend to report Miss McDuffie's activities when she was in Columbia: see William H. Bachman to JJP, 11 June 1856, Pettigrew Papers NCDAH. See also Mary Singleton McDuffie to Martha Calhoun Burt, 18 April (1856?), Mary Singleton McDuffie Letters, Duke University Library.

36   Louise Petigru Porcher to Adele Petigru Allston, 4 December 1852, Allston Papers.

37   Pettigrew's "obituary," *Charleston Courier*, 4 June 1862, evidently written by someone who knew him fairly well.

38   Language exercises, bibliography, chronology of Arab rulers, and other notes in a manuscript volume, Pettigrew Papers UNC; W. S. Pettigrew, "Biographical Sketch," 44; receipts and correspondence with New York booksellers, 1849–1860 passim, Pettigrew Papers UNC; JJP to W. S. Pettigrew, 25 January 1858, Pettigrew Papers UNC; James Conner to Joseph Blythe Allston, 8 August 1864, Pettigrew Papers NCDAH; *Charleston Courier*, 4 June 1862; J. L. Petigru to Jane Petigru North, 27 February 1855, in Carson, *Petigru*, 313.

39   JJP to J. C. Johnston, 6 December 1853, Pettigrew Papers UNC; Leonidas W. Spratt to JJP, (?) December 1853, Pettigrew Papers NCDAH. Irregular files of the *Charleston Standard* for the period in which Pettigrew was associated with it survive in the Charleston Free Library Society and the Duke University Library. Pettigrew evidently selected the foreign news to run, chiefly from London papers and official dispatches. The editorials are anonymous

and it is impossible to distinguish in the surviving issues anything in the style that might indicate authorship. Almost all are leisurely and loquacious commentaries on foreign affairs lacking in urgency for Americans.

40 Griffith John McRee to JJP, 28 August (1855?), and 18 December (1856?); JJP to W. S. Pettigrew, 30 December 1855 and 11 November 1856; all in Pettigrew Papers UNC; JJP to G. J. McRee, (?) September 1856, Pettigrew Papers NCDAH. See also Griffith John McRee, *Life and Correspondence of James Iredell, One of the Associate Justices of the Supreme Court of the United States*, 2:591–93.

41 McRee, *Iredell*, 2:591, 592.

42 William Buell Sprague to JJP, 5 and 13 January 1858, Pettigrew Papers UNC; see also William Buell Sprague, *Annals of the American Pulpit*, 9 vols. (New York: Carter and Brothers, 1857–1869), 5:315–17.

43 *Charleston Standard*, 7 January 1854, clipping in Pettigrew Papers UNC; Samuel McGowan to JJP, 17 February 1859, Pettigrew Papers UNC; John B. Erwin et al. to JJP, 24 January 1860, Pettigrew Papers NCDAH; JJP to Committee, 18 March 1858, Phi Society Records; L. L. Fraser to JJP, 13 December 1858, Pettigrew Papers NCDAH.

44 James Warley Miles to JJP, (?) May 1854, Pettigrew Papers NCDAH; William Henry Trescot to Mary Pettigrew Browne, 27 June 1870, Pettigrew Papers UNC.

45 Receipts, Pettigrew Papers UNC; *Charleston Courier*, 23 February 1857; JJP to J. C. Johnston, 12 March 1853, Pettigrew Papers UNC; receipts, notes, accounts, and other papers concerning the Hayne lecture, 1857, Pettigrew Papers NCDAH; John Sidney Thrasher to JJP, 28 February 1854, Pettigrew Papers UNC.

46 JJP to Ann Pettigrew, 14 September 1853, and J. C. Johnston to W. S. Pettigrew, 19 September 1853, Pettigrew Papers UNC.

47 JJP to J. C. Johnston, 28 January 1854 (mistakenly dated 1853); receipts for rent and furnishings and correspondence with E. L. Whitaker, owner of the St. Michael's Alley house, 1857–1861 (scattered dates); and JJP's account book; all in Pettigrew Papers UNC. See also Carson, *Petigru*, 76. The Petigru mansion burned; the King Street house is still standing. See also JJP to J. C. Johnston, 22 June 1855, Pettigrew Papers UNC.

48 JJP to R. F. W. Allston, 21 November 1852, Allston Papers.

49 *Charleston Mercury*, 22 June 1861. J. L. Petigru to JJP, 24 June 1861; J. L. Petigru to JJP, 6 October and 30 November 1862; Susan Petigru King to J. L. Petigru, 5 June 1862; Caroline N. Pettigrew to C. L. Pettigrew, 10 November 1858; all in Pettigrew Papers UNC.

50 JJP to W. S. Pettigrew, 28 December 1856, Pettigrew Papers UNC.

51 Account book of JJP; W. S. Pettigrew's book of accounts with JJP; W. S. Pettigrew's loose accounts of January 1 of each year 1848 to 1858; W. S. Pettigrew to J. C. Johnston, 18 November 1852, and to JJP, 19 August 1854; all in Pettigrew Papers UNC.

52 JJP to C. L. Pettigrew, 4 November 1858, and W. S. Pettigrew to JJP, 10 June 1858, Pettigrew Papers UNC.

53 JJP to W. S. Pettigrew, 25 January 1858, Pettigrew Papers UNC.

54 J. C. Johnston to JJP, 22 March 1858, Pettigrew Papers UNC.

55 J. C. Johnston to JJP, 7 February 1853, and JJP to W. S. Pettigrew, 26 March 1858, Pettigrew Papers UNC.

56 JJP to W. S. Pettigrew, 16 June 1858; Wade Hampton to JJP, 19 May 1858; JJP to C. L. Pettigrew, 4 November 1858; JJP to W. S. Pettigrew, 6 February 1859; receipts for bonds, and JJP's account book; all in Pettigrew Papers UNC.

57 Copy of JJP's will and letter of instructions and W. S. Pettigrew's inventory of his estate, and letters to W. S. Pettigrew from Henry Deas Lesesne, 23 July 1863, and J. C. Johnston, 2 October 1863; all in Pettigrew Papers UNC.

Chapter 8. Of Death and Fate

1 JJP to W. S. Pettigrew, (?) May, 12 May, and 11 September 1854, and to J. C. Johnston, 9 November 1849, Pettigrew Papers UNC.

2 J. C. Johnston to W. S. Pettigrew, 19 September 1853, and W. S. Pettigrew to J. C. Johnston, 18 November 1852, Pettigrew Papers UNC.

3 JJP to J. C. Johnston, 25 September 1854, Pettigrew Papers UNC; Caroline Banks Black, "Aspects of the History of Yellow Fever Epidemics in Charleston, South Carolina," Master's thesis, Duke University, 1943, p. 16.

4 JJP to J. C. Johnston, 25 September 1854; see also JJP to W. S. Pettigrew, 11 September 1854, and Caroline N. to Charles L. Pettigrew, 3 October 1854; all in Pettigrew Papers UNC. JJP to W. S. Pettigrew, 11 September 1854, and to J. C. Johnston, 28 August 1854, Pettigrew Papers UNC.

5 JJP to W. S. Pettigrew, 11 September 1854, and to J. C. Johnston, 25 September 1854, Pettigrew Papers UNC.

6 Caroline N. to Charles L. Pettigrew, 3 October 1854, and JJP to Ann Pettigrew, 15 October 1854, Pettigrew Papers UNC; Louise Petigru Porcher to Adele Petigru Allston, 9 October 1854, Allston Papers.

7 JJP to Ann Pettigrew, 15 October 1854, and JJP to W. S. Pettigrew, 20 April 1855, Pettigrew Papers UNC; Black, "Epidemics," 16; Harriett Petigru Lesesne to Adele Petigru Allston, 5 October 1858, Allston Papers; Benjamin Allston to JJP, 1 October 1858, Pettigrew Papers NCDAH.

8   Harriett P. Lesesne to Adele P. Allston, 5 October 1858, Allston Papers; see also R. F. W. Allston to JJP, 3 and 11 October 1858, Pettigrew Papers NCDAH.

9   Caroline N. to Charles L. Pettigrew, 10 and 12 November 1858, Pettigrew Papers UNC; Ben Allston to Adele P. Allston, 9 November 1858, Allston Papers.

10 Pauline C. Fowle to JJP, 20 February 1855, Pettigrew Papers NCDAH; JJP to W. S. Pettigrew, 8 September and 24 October 1860, Pettigrew Papers UNC.

11 Memoranda and correspondence on the *Courier* affair, March 1856, Pettigrew Papers UNC. For other incidents see letters exchanged by JJP and A. C. McGillivray, 28 May 1858, Pettigrew Papers UNC; and JJP to William B. Pringle, undated (30 May 1857), Pettigrew Papers NCDAH.

12 Allen J. Green to JJP, 28 June 1858, Pettigrew Papers UNC.

13 JJP to W. S. Pettigrew, 6 October 1855, Pettigrew Papers UNC; *Charleston Mercury*, 6 November 1855; John DeCamp, *Reply of Commander John DeCamp to Aspersions upon His Character Contained in an Article Published in the Charleston Mercury of November 6, 1855* (New York: Privately printed, 1856), copy in the Pettigrew Papers UNC.

14 JJP to John DeCamp, 12 February 1856, Pettigrew Papers UNC.

15 DeCamp to JJP, 21 February 1856, Pettigrew Papers UNC.

16 *Notes on Spain*, 413.

17 Mary LaBruce Petigru to JJP, 16 July 1857, Pettigrew Papers UNC.

18 J. C. Johnston to JJP, 24 December 1848, and Susan Petigru King to J. L. Petigru, 5 June 1862, Pettigrew Papers UNC.

19 JJP to W. S. Pettigrew, 23 November 1853, and to W. S. Pettigrew, 17 June 1854, Pettigrew Papers UNC.

20 Trescot, *Memorial*, 63–64.

21 JJP to W. S. Pettigrew, 5 January 1858, Pettigrew Papers UNC; *Notes on Spain*, 111.

22 JJP to W. S. Pettigrew, 10 June 1848, and J. C. Johnston to W. S. Pettigrew, 3 November 1856, Pettigrew Papers UNC.

23 JJP to W. S. Pettigrew, 20 November 1850, Pettigrew Papers UNC.

24 *Proceedings of the Democratic State Convention of South Carolina, Held at Columbia, 5th and 6th of May, 1856* (Columbia: R. W. Gibbes, 1856), 3, 18, 27–28. See also letters to JJP from Charles Macbeath, 31 May 1856, from Nelson Mitchell, 6 May 1856, and from Preston Smith Brooks, 25 May 1856, all in the Pettigrew Papers NCDAH.

25 Pettigrew's name headed the list of five signers of a letter sent out for preliminary arrangements, undated (June 1856); see also many letters and telegrams of June 1856 in response, all in the Pettigrew Papers NCDAH; see also *Charleston Standard*, 27 June 1856, clipping in Pettigrew Papers NCDAH.

26 JJP to W. S. Pettigrew, 3 November 1856, Pettigrew Papers UNC; James Conner to JJP, 17 October 1856, Pettigrew Papers NCDAH.

27 See Trescot, *Memorial*, 29–33.

28 South Carolina General Assembly, *Journal of the House of Representatives of the State of South Carolina. Being the Session of 1856* (Columbia, 1856), 6–7, 44, 178; also papers related to the inaugural, December 1856, Pettigrew Papers NCDAH.

29 Trescot, *Memorial*, 34; *Charleston Courier*, 17 December 1856.

30 *Charleston Courier*, undated clipping (dispatch dated 3 December 1856), scrapbook, Pettigrew Papers NCDAH.

31 James Conner to JJP, 2 December 1856, and clippings in Pettigrew scrapbook, Pettigrew Papers NCDAH; S.C. General Assembly, *Journal of the House, 1856*, 127; Trescot, *Memorial*, 34.

32 JJP to William Shepard Bryan, 7 November 1856, William Shepard Bryan Papers; South Carolina General Assembly, *Journal of the House of Representatives of the State of South Carolina. Being the Session of 1857* (Columbia, 1857), 7; JJP to Caroline N. Pettigrew, 25 December 1857, Pettigrew Papers UNC.

33 S.C. General Assembly, *Journal of the House, 1857*, 5, 41; R. F. W. Allston to JJP, 29 January (1857) and 9 and 24 April 1858, Pettigrew Papers UNC; Benjamin Allston to JJP, 4 April 1858, Pettigrew Papers UNC.

34 Letters of recommendation, June 1857, Pettigrew Papers UNC; Andrew Gordon Magrath to JJP, 10 June 1857, Pettigrew Papers NCDAH; W. S. Pettigrew to JJP, 8 July 1857, Pettigrew Papers UNC.

35 The account given of the Magrath-Taber affair and aftermath is reconstructed from articles in the Charleston *News, Courier, Standard*, and *Mercury*, September–December 1856, (extensive clippings loose and in scrapbook in Pettigrew Papers NCDAH), and from the correspondence and memoranda of Conner and Pettigrew, in the same group, especially Conner's manuscript statement of 17 November 1856. All succeeding information about the affair comes from these sources unless otherwise indicated.

36 John Sidney Thrasher to JJP, 24 November 1856, Pettigrew Papers NCDAH, reporting comment in New Orleans.

37 JJP to W. S. Pettigrew, 18 August 1856, Pettigrew Papers UNC.

38 J. L. Petigru to Susan Petigru King, 28 November 1856, manuscript copy made in 1866, James Louis Petigru Papers, Manuscript Division, Library of Congress, Washington, D.C.; Robert Barnwell Rhett to JJP, 13 January 1857, Pettigrew Papers NCDAH; Carson, *Petigru*, 319–20.

39 Letters exchanged by Pettigrew and Cunningham, 22 October 1857, Pettigrew Papers NCDAH; Allen J. Green to JJP, 28 June 1858, Pettigrew Papers UNC.

40 R. F. W. Allston to JJP, 21 October 1858; JJP to W. S. Pettigrew, 24 Octo-

ber 1858; R. F. W. Allston to JJP, 21 October 1858; Franklin Gaillard to JJP, 18 October 1858; all in Pettigrew Papers UNC. See also *Charleston Courier,* undated clipping, October 1858, scrapbook, Pettigrew Papers NCDAH.

41 J. L. Petigru to Alfred Huger, 22 October 1858, manuscript copy made in 1866, Petigru Papers.

42 JJP to W. S. Pettigrew, 16 August 1860, Pettigrew Papers UNC. James Lawrence Orr to JJP, 8 February 1860; James Farrow to JJP, 5 February 1860; J. J. Pope, Jr., to JJP, 4 September 1860; all in Pettigrew Papers NCDAH; also JJP to William Porcher Miles, 4 and 13 February 1860, William Porcher Miles Papers, Southern Historical Collection, University of North Carolina.

Chapter 9. Of North and South

1 S.C. General Assembly, *Journal of the House, 1856,* 35–37.

2 James L. Orr to JJP, 30 October 1857, and S. G. Earle to JJP, 18 November 1857, Pettigrew Papers NCDAH; S.C. General Assembly, *Journal of the House, 1857,* 36; J. L. Orr to JJP, 20 April 1857, Pettigrew Papers NCDAH.

3 See James Conner to JJP, 5 December 1856, and to Joseph Blythe Allston, 8 August 1864, and JJP's scrapbook, all in Pettigrew Papers NCDAH; see also entries of 28 July and 12 September in JJP's diary, "Journal of Military Reviews in the Summer of 1857," in Pettigrew Papers UNC. Bryan Edwards's standard work is *The History, Civil and Commercial, of the British Colonies in the West Indies,* 3 vols, 3d ed. (London: J. Stockdale, 1801). Leonidas W. Spratt to JJP, 29 November 1856, Pettigrew Papers NCDAH.

4 Pettigrew's report was first printed as a public document: South Carolina General Assembly, *Report of the Minority of the Special Committee of Seven, to Whom Was Referred So Much of His Late Excellency's Message No. 1 As Relates to Slavery and the Slave Trade* (Columbia, 1857) It was next printed by Pettigrew in an edition of one hundred copies: *Report of the Minority of the Special Committee of Seven, to Whom Was Referred So Much of Governor Adams' Message No. 1, as Relates to Slavery and the Slave Trade* (Columbia: Carolina Times, 1857). The third printing, a one-thousand-copy edition paid for by Pettigrew, had the same title as the second but was published by Harper and Calvo, Charleston, 1858. This last and fullest edition will be the one cited below (hereinafter cited as Pettigrew, *Slave Trade*). The manuscript of the report is in Pettigrew Papers UNC.

5 Pettigrew, *Slave Trade,* 3–4.

6 Ibid., 5–6, 38.

7 Ibid., 5–6.

8 Ibid., 6–8, 37.

9 Ibid., 10–16.

10 Ibid., 16.

11 Ibid., 16–20.

12 Ibid., 20–21.

13 Ibid., 22–27.

14 Ibid., 28–39, quote from 35.

15 Ibid., 22–27.

16 Ibid., 29.

17 Ibid., 27.

18 South Carolina General Assembly, *Report of the Special Committee of the House of Representatives, of South Carolina, on So Much of the Message of His Excellency Governor James H. Adams, As Relates to Slavery and the Slave Trade* (Columbia, 1857); S.C. General Assembly, *Journal of the House, 1857*, 147.

19 Receipt for printing the Carolina Times edition of the minority report and cover letters, 21 December 1857, and receipt for printing the Harper and Calvo edition of the minority report, 15 February 1858, Pettigrew Papers UNC; many letters requesting copies and commenting on the report, December 1857 through May 1859, Pettigrew Papers NCDAH; Pettigrew, *Slave Trade*, 40; "Protest Against a Renewal of the Slave Trade," *De Bow's Review*, 25 (August and September 1858):166–85, 289–308.

20 Clippings, Pettigrew scrapbook, Pettigrew Papers NCDAH.

21 *New York Times*, 16 February 1858; *New York Tribune*, 7 January 1858.

22 J. L. Orr to JJP, 18 January 1858, and many other letters, 1857–1860, in Pettigrew Papers NCDAH; Matthew Fontaine Maury to JJP, 21 December 1857, W. S. Pettigrew to JJP, 16 January 1858, and Caroline North Pettigrew to JJP, 7 January 1858, all in Pettigrew Papers UNC.

23 *Charleston Mercury*, 11 January 1858; Pettigrew, *Slave Trade*, 40.

24 JJP to W. S. Pettigrew, 22 September 1851, 25 March 1852, and 30 October 1859, Pettigrew Papers UNC; J. L. Petigru to Jane Petigru North, 17 June 1859, in Carson, *Petigru*, 346.

25 J. L. Petigru to JJP, 15 November 1861; W. S. Pettigrew to JJP, 28 October 1854; JJP to W. S. Pettigrew, 11 November 1854; all in Pettigrew Papers UNC.

26 JJP to C. L. Pettigrew, 10 October 1861, Grimes Papers. Wrote Richard Benbury Creecy to W. S. Pettigrew on 27 March 1872: "I was gratified by the feeling exhibited by a servant who attended Gen. P. when he fell. . . . He has called at my office several times in my absence to see a likeness which I had sent to the engraver" (Pettigrew Papers UNC).

27 JJP to W. S. Pettigrew, 20 November 1850, Pettigrew Papers UNC.

28 For instance, see Pettigrew's comments on slavery in Moorish Spain in his *Notes on Spain*, 269.

29 JJP to J. C. Johnston, 27 October 1859, Pettigrew Papers UNC.

30 JJP to J. C. Johnston, 16 April 1849, and J. C. Johnston to JJP, 16 June 1849, Pettigrew Papers UNC.
31 J. C. Johnston to W. S. Pettigrew, 6 March 1849; JJP to J. C. Johnston, 16 April 1849; JJP to J. C. Johnston, 29 (May) 1849; all in Pettigrew Papers UNC.
32 JJP to J. C. Johnston, 3 November 1848, Pettigrew Papers UNC.
33 JJP to W. S. Pettigrew and to J. C. Johnston, both dated 8 January 1850; JJP to W. S. Pettigrew, 8 January 1850; JJP to J. C. Johnston, 1 January 1855; all in Pettigrew Papers UNC.
34 JJP to W. S. Pettigrew and J. C. Johnston, 8 January 1850, Pettigrew Papers UNC; see also James Conner to Joseph Blythe Allston, 8 August 1864, Pettigrew Papers NCDAH.
35 JJP to W. S. Pettigrew, 1 March 1850, 3 November 1856, and 20 August 1851, Pettigrew Papers UNC.
36 JJP to W. S. Pettigrew, 20 November 1850, and 30 April 1850, Pettigrew Papers UNC. The zealous antislavery man was not a New Englander, however, but a son of James Gillespie Birney.
37 JJP to W. S. Pettigrew, 3 January 1851, Pettigrew Papers UNC.
38 JJP to J. C. Johnston, 27 October 1859, Pettigrew Papers UNC.
39 Ibid.
40 JJP to Daniel M. Barringer, 15 April 1860, Barringer Papers; JJP to W. S. Pettigrew, 24 October 1860, Pettigrew Papers UNC.
41 J. L. Petigru to David Lowry Swain, 4 March 1861, Walter Clark Manuscripts, North Carolina Department of Archives and History; see also J. L. Petigru to J. H. Bryan, 15 February 1861, John Herritage Bryan Collection. *Memorial of the Late James L. Petigru*, 32–34.
42 Carson, *Petigru*, vi.
43 JJP to W. S. Pettigrew, 20 November 1859, and the reply of W. S. Pettigrew, 29 November 1859, Pettigrew Papers UNC.
44 JJP to J. C. Johnston, 14 March 1856, Pettigrew Papers UNC.

Chapter 10. Of Arms and Men

1 JJP to W. S. Pettigrew, 27 June 1856, Pettigrew Papers UNC.
2 JJP to W. S. Pettigrew, 9 May 1856, Pettigrew Papers UNC.
3 Ibid.
4 JJP to W. S. Pettigrew, 28 December 1856, and receipts for books and equipment, 10 April and July 1857, Pettigrew Papers UNC; unidentified clipping, scrapbook, Pettigrew Papers NCDAH.
5 JJP's diary, "Journal of Military Reviews in the Summer of 1857," and let-

ters to W. S. Pettigrew, 14 September 1857 and 26 April 1858, in Pettigrew Papers UNC; scattered correspondence from officers, 1857–1858, and clippings with orders issued by Pettigrew as governor's chief aide, in Pettigrew Papers NCDAH.

6 JJP's manuscript itinerary, 1859, Pettigrew Papers NCDAH; JJP to Henry Deas Lesesne, 6 June 1859, Eldridge Collection; Matthew Fontaine Maury to John Y. Mason, 25 May 1859, with Mason's endorsement of 23 June, and R. W. Bacot to JJP, 31 May 1859, Pettigrew Papers UNC; JJP to William Porcher Miles, 13 February 1860, Miles Papers; James Conner to Joseph Blythe Allston, 8 August 1864, manuscript itinerary, 1859, and undated manuscript list of equipment taken to Europe, Pettigrew Papers NCDAH; receipt for uniform, 29 June 1859, Pettigrew Papers UNC.

7 JJP to H. D. Lesesne, 6 June 1859, Eldridge Collection.

8 Manuscript itinerary, 1859, Pettigrew Papers NCDAH; JJP to W. P. Miles, 13 February 1860, Miles Papers; JJP to W. S. Pettigrew, 28 July and 9 October 1859, and Comte Bardesono to JJP (in Italian), 13 July 1859, Pettigrew Papers UNC; W. S. Pettigrew, "Biographical Sketch," 45; JJP to W. S. Pettigrew, 28 July 1859, Pettigrew Papers UNC.

9 "General James Johnston Pettigrew," in Richard Benbury Creecy, *Grandfather's Tales of North Carolina History* (Raleigh: Edwards and Broughton, 1901), 201. Creecy had his information from W. S. Pettigrew, and his sketch appeared originally in the *Elizabeth City* (N.C.) *Economist*, 16 and 23 April 1872. See also James Conner to Joseph Blythe Allston, 8 August 1864, Pettigrew Papers NCDAH; and Trescot, *Memorial*, 44. *Notes on Spain*, 10–12, 404–8.

10 JJP to W. S. Pettigrew, 28 July 1859, Pettigrew Papers UNC; *Notes on Spain*, 13–17; JJP to W. P. Miles, 4 February 1860, Miles Papers.

11 *Notes on Spain*, 51.

12 JJP to Ann Pettigrew, 11 September 1859, Pettigrew Papers UNC; see also JJP to Daniel Moreau Barringer, 15 April 1860, Barringer Papers.

13 *Notes on Spain*, 137; JJP to D. M. Barringer, 15 April 1860, Barringer Papers.

14 *Notes on Spain*, 373.

15 Benjamin Allston to JJP, 10 October 1859, Pettigrew Papers UNC.

16 *Notes on Spain*, 12–13.

17 Trescot, *Memorial*, 44; James Conner to Joseph Blythe Allston, 8 August 1864, Pettigrew Papers NCDAH.

18 James Conner to J. B. Allston, 8 August 1864, Pettigrew Papers NCDAH; Trescot, *Memorial*, 44.

19 Unidentified clipping, scrapbook, Pettigrew Papers NCDAH.

20 Mark Mayo Boatner, *The Civil War Dictionary* (New York: David McKay

Company, 1959), 28, 50; Ezra J. Warner, *Generals in Gray: Lives of the Confederate Commanders* (Baton Rouge: Louisiana State University Press, 1959), 13, 15.

21 JJP to W. S. Pettigrew, 20 November 1859, Pettigrew Papers UNC.

22 Lists of absentees from drill, 1860, Pettigrew Papers NCDAH.

23 [James Johnston Pettigrew], "The Militia System of South Carolina," *Russell's Magazine* 6 (March 1860):529–40. Although the article was published anonymously, from the style, the content, and incidental internal evidence, I have not the least doubt that Pettigrew was the author. This is corroborated by marginalia believed to have been made by John Russell in a set of *Russell's Magazine* housed in the Rare Book Division, New York City Public Library.

24 "Militia System," 530–31.

25 Ibid., 530–32.

26 Ibid., 530–32; see also JJP to W. S. Pettigrew, 20 November 1859, Pettigrew Papers UNC.

27 "Militia System," 530–31.

28 Ibid., 532–33.

29 Ibid., 533–34.

30 Ibid., 537–38.

31 Ibid., 533.

32 Ibid., 532.

33 Ibid., 535 37.

34 Ibid., 536–37, 540.

35 Ibid., 536.

36 Ibid., 539.

37 Ibid., 538–39.

38 James Conner to J. B. Allston, 8 August 1864, Pettigrew Papers NCDAH; JJP's undated manuscript notes concerning experiments with projectiles, in the same group.

39 John Gibbon to JJP, 29 February, 25 March 1860, Pettigrew Papers NCDAH.

40 Z. C. Robbins to JJP, 1 June 1860, Pettigrew Papers NCDAH; see also account of Pettigrew with Maynard Arms Company, Massachusetts, 9 October 1860, Pettigrew Papers UNC.

41 Caroline Petigru Carson to JJP, 15 November 1860, Pettigrew Papers NCDAH.

42 JJP to D. M. Barringer, 15 April 1860, Barringer Papers.

43 The sense of impending catastrophe was a South-wide phenomenon and is well known; see JJP to W. S. Pettigrew, 24 October 1860, and W. S. Pettigrew to Josiah Collins, 18 October 1860, Pettigrew Papers UNC. Caroline North Pettigrew to JJP, 12 September 1860, Caroline North Pettigrew to W. S. Pet-

tigrew, 17 September 1860, and C. L. Pettigrew to JJP, 20 October 1860, Pettigrew Papers UNC.

44 Henry Ravenscroft Bryan to JJP, 14 November 1860, Pettigrew Papers NCDAH; W. S. Pettigrew to JJP, 29 November 1859, and Caroline N. Pettigrew, Charleston, to C. L. Pettigrew, 2, 17, and 20 November 1860, Pettigrew Papers UNC.

45 Francis J. Child to JJP, 14 November 1860, Pettigrew Papers UNC.

46 Caroline N. Pettigrew to C. L. Pettigrew, 2 November 1860, Pettigrew Papers UNC.

47 *Notes on Spain*, 368–69.

Chapter 11. The Devil Unchained at Last

1 Caroline N. to Charles L. Pettigrew, 20 November 1860, Pettigrew Papers UNC. JJP to W. S. Pettigrew, 24 October 1860, Pettigrew Papers UNC, indicates a feeling that a restoration of the Union with the slavery question permanently settled was desirable and might be possible if the South acted with unanimity.

2 Manuscript, "Memoir on the Armament of South Carolina," in Pettigrew Papers NCDAH.

3 Louise North to Caroline N. Pettigrew, 24 December 1860, Pettigrew Papers UNC; Francis W. Pickens to JJP, 12 August 1862, Pettigrew Papers NCDAH.

4 Trescot, *Memorial*, 44; Caroline N. to Charles L. Pettigrew, 2 and 7 November 1860, Pettigrew Papers UNC; James L. Petigru to Jane Petigru North, 27 November 1860, in Carson, *Petigru*, 362.

5 Louise North to Caroline N. Pettigrew, 24 December 1860, Pettigrew Papers UNC.

6 F. W. Pickens to JJP, 12 August 1862, Pettigrew Papers NCDAH.

7 Elizabeth W. Allston Pringle, *Chronicles of Chicora Wood* (New York: Charles Scribner's Sons, 1922), 173–74.

8 Captain James Johnson, Jr., to JJP, 26 December 1860, Pettigrew Papers NCDAH; "Military Notes, December 1860–April 1861," diary and memoranda of Ellison Capers, major of the First Regiment of Rifles, Ellison Capers Papers, Duke University Library; muster rolls from the Fort Sumter period in the Richard Gill Mills Dunovant Papers, Duke University Library. Dunovant was a brigadier general of militia whose command nominally included the First Regiment of Rifles.

9 Capers diary, 20 December 1860, Capers Papers; *Charleston Mercury*, 28 December 1860.

10 Caroline N. to Charles L. Pettigrew, 7 November 1860, Pettigrew Papers UNC.

11 The account of Pettigrew's and Capers's interview with Anderson is from Pettigrew's report to Pickens, draft in JJP's hand, 27 December 1860, Pettigrew Papers NCDAH. A federal officer who was also present gives substantially the same account: see Samuel Wylie Crawford, *The History of the Fall of Fort Sumter* (S. F. McLean and Company, 1898), 109–11.

12 Speech by Governor Pickens, 25 February 1861, at the presentation of a flag to the First Regiment of Rifles, clipping from unidentified Charleston newspaper, scrapbook, Pettigrew Papers NCDAH.

13 F. W. Pickens to JJP, 27 December 1860, as quoted in Crawford, *Fort Sumter*, 113. Crawford had access to Pickens's papers. The order quoted, except for the first sentence, is verbatim with an order given at the same time to Wilmot Gibbes De Saussure, Colonel of the First Regiment of Artillery, for the seizure of Fort Moultrie. See Wilmot Gibbes De Saussure Order Book, Southern Historical Collection, University of North Carolina.

14 The account of the taking of Castle Pinckney is from the *Charleston Mercury*, 28 December 1860, by a reporter who was evidently there, and from the New York *Herald*, 21 January 1861, by a reporter who interviewed witnesses. Crawford, who probably had the story from Meade, agrees substantially: Crawford, *Fort Sumter*, 114–16.

15 Capers diary, entry under date 27 December 1860 (actually up to mid-January), Capers Papers; JJP to David L. Swain, 11 January 1861, David Lowry Swain Papers, Southern Historical Collection, University of North Carolina; Alfred Huger to JJP, 9 January 1861, and Louise North to Caroline N. Pettigrew, 9 January 1861, Pettigrew Papers UNC.

16 James Conner to Joseph Blythe Allston, 8 August 1864, Pettigrew Papers NCDAH; Capers diary passim, Capers Papers; JJP to D. L. Swain, 23 January 1861, Swain Papers UNC.

17 James Conner to J. B. Allston, 8 August 1864, Pettigrew Papers NCDAH; notes in Capers diary, Capers Papers.

18 Jane Petigru North to Caroline N. Pettigrew, 25 March 1861, and Louise Petigru Porcher to Caroline N. Pettigrew, 7 January 1861, Pettigrew Papers UNC; Louise P. Porcher to JJP, 12 January 1861, and James Conner to J. B. Allston, 8 August 1864, Pettigrew Papers NCDAH; Ellison Capers to Charlotte Capers, 23 January 1861, Capers Papers; Lemuel M. Hatch, quartermaster general, to Major R. Pringle, 28 February 1861, Dunovant Papers; JJP's notation on a requisition, 8 February 1861, Eldridge Collection; *Charleston Courier*, 5 February 1861.

19 R. S. Ripley to JJP, 19 January 1861, Pettigrew Papers NCDAH.

20 Letters of JJP to R. G. M. Dunovant, 10 and 13 February 1861, and to Cap-

tain George L. James, 3 February 1861, Dunovant Papers; JJP to States Rights Gist, adjutant general, 8 April 1861, to R. G. M. Dunovant, (1 or 2 February 1861), and to George L. James, 4 February 1861, in Pettigrew Papers NCDAH; JJP to S. R. Gist, 20 January 1861, and to David Flavel Jamison, secretary of war, 15 January 1861, Frederick M. Dearborn Collection, Houghton Library, Harvard University.

21 See especially the letters cited in the note above. The papers pertaining to Pettigrew's activities in Charleston harbor, January to April 1861, are widely scattered. There are many letters from Pettigrew to Dunovant and other officers in the Dunovant Papers; many letters received and drafts of letters sent in the Pettigrew Papers NCDAH; a few letters, requisitions, and morning reports in the Eldridge Collection and the Dearborn Collection; and considerable material in the Capers Papers. See also the Ellison Capers Letters, South Caroliniana Library, University of South Carolina; the De Saussure Order Book; JJP to Andrew Gordon Magrath, 15 January 1861, Pickens-Bonham Papers, Manuscript Division, Library of Congress; and JJP to D. F. Jamison, 7 March 1861, in *The War of the Rebellion: A Compilation of the Official Records of the Union and Confederate Armies*, by United States War Department, 4 ser., 70 vols. in 128 (Washington: Government Printing Office, 1880–1901), ser. 1, 1:268–69.

22 Series of Ellison Capers's letters to his wife, Capers Papers.

23 JJP to D. L. Swain, 11 January 1861, Swain Papers UNC.

24 JJP to D. L. Swain, 23 January 1861, Swain Papers UNC; J. L. Petigru to Jane P. North, 7 March 1861, in Carson, *Petigru*, 374; Pierre G. T. Beauregard to JJP, 9 April 1861, *Official Records*, ser. 1, 1:297; W. S. Pettigrew, "Biographical Sketch," 45.

25 JJP to D. L. Swain, 23 January 1861, Swain Papers UNC.

26 Capers diary, 18 February 1861, Capers Papers.

27 J. L. Petigru to Jane P. North, 19 February 1861, in Carson, *Petigru*, 369; sheet music in Pettigrew Papers NCDAH; S. R. Gist, adjutant general, to JJP, 20 January 1861, Pettigrew Papers NCDAH; Ellison to Charlotte Capers, 14 February 1861, Capers Papers; Louise North to JJP, undated (early 1861), Pettigrew Papers UNC; Louise P. Porcher to JJP, 12 January 1861, Pettigrew Papers NCDAH.

28 Clipping from an unidentified Charleston paper, scrapbook, Pettigrew Papers NCDAH, and a manuscript, evidently copied from a newspaper account, in the same group.

29 J. L. Petigru to William Carson, 2 March 1861, manuscript copy made in 1866, Petigru Papers; J. L. Petigru to Jane P. North, 27 February and 7 March 1861, in Carson, *Petigru*, 370, 374.

30 Capers diary, March to April 1861 passim, Capers Papers; David Rumph

Jones, of Beauregard's staff, to Brigadier General R. G. M. Dunovant, 12 April 1861, Dunovant Papers; D. F. Jamison to JJP, 8 April 1861, Pettigrew Papers NCDAH; Ellison to Charlotte Capers, 10 April 1861, Capers Papers.

31 Capers diary, 5 March 1861, and Ellison to Charlotte Capers, 5 April 1861, Capers Papers.

32 Jane P. North to Caroline N. Pettigrew, 17 March 1861, Pettigrew Papers UNC.

33 J. L. Petigru to JJP, 8 April 1861, Pettigrew Papers UNC; see also in the same group, J. L. Petigru to JJP, 22 and 25 March 1861. Carson, *Petigru*, 374–75; see also Jane P. North to Caroline N. Pettigrew, 25 March 1861, Pettigrew Papers UNC.

34 J. L. Petigru to JJP, 25 March 1861, Pettigrew Papers UNC; Caroline Petigru Carson to JJP, 12 March 1861, Pettigrew Papers NCDAH.

35 J. C. Johnston to JJP, 2 January 1861, and Caroline N. Pettigrew to JJP, 23 February 1861, Pettigrew Papers UNC.

36 JJP to John Herritage Bryan, 18 April 1861, Pettigrew Papers UNC.

37 The estimate of the size of Pettigrew's command is mine. Morning reports of 18 and 20 January 1861, at Fort Morris, Moultrie Island, in the Dearborn Collection, show Pettigrew commanding about five hundred men. This included only six of the nine companies of the First Regiment of Rifles. Many men must have been temporarily absent from the six companies for various reasons, and Pettigrew commanded on Sullivan's Island various artillerymen and auxiliaries as well as the regiment. J. L. Petigru to JJP, 8 April 1861, Pettigrew Papers UNC.

Chapter 12. All Quiet Along the Potomac

1 Manuscript statement of F. W. Pickens, 21 April 1861, Pettigrew Papers NCDAH; *Charleston Courier*, 22 and 26 April 1861; Theodore Gaillard Barker to Captain Robert Campbell, Pendleton Rifles, 23 April 1861, Pettigrew Papers NCDAH.

2 Many letters from applicants, April and May 1861; undated clipping (May 1861) from *Charleston Courier*, scrapbook; T. G. Barker to JJP, 11 May 1861; and John Tyler, Jr., War Department, to JJP, 14 May 1861; all in Pettigrew Papers NCDAH.

3 T. G. Barker to JJP, 11 May 1861, Pettigrew Papers NCDAH; JJP to W. S. Pettigrew, 13 May 1861, and Jane Petigru North to Caroline North Pettigrew, 15 May 1861, Pettigrew Papers UNC; undated clipping (May 1861), from *Charleston Courier*, scrapbook, Pettigrew Papers NCDAH.

4 JJP to W. S. Pettigrew, 13 May 1861, Pettigrew Papers UNC; for a similar attitude, see T. G. Barker to JJP, 11 May 1861, Pettigrew Papers NCDAH.

5 JJP to W. S. Pettigrew, 13, 18, 25, and 28 May 1861, Pettigrew Papers UNC.

6 James Conner to J. B. Allston, 8 August 1864, Pettigrew Papers NCDAH; JJP to W. S. Pettigrew, 25 May 1861, and to John Herritage Bryan, 18 April 1861, Pettigrew Papers UNC.

7 JJP to W. S. Pettigrew, 25 May 1861, Pettigrew Papers UNC.

8 JJP to W. S. Pettigrew, 28 and 18 May 1861, and memoranda and manuscripts of speeches of W. S. Pettigrew, May to November 1861, Pettigrew Papers UNC.

9 W. S. Pettigrew to JJP, 5 and 18 May 1861, Pettigrew Papers UNC. Both letters are mistakenly dated. That dated 5 May evidently should have been dated 25 May, and that dated 18 May was written about 21 May and was erroneously given the date of the letter to which it was a reply. JJP to W. S. Pettigrew, 25 and 28 May 1861, Pettigrew Papers UNC.

10 W. S. Pettigrew to JJP, 25 May 1861 (mistakenly dated 5 May), and Jane P. North to Caroline N. Pettigrew, 30 May 1861, Pettigrew Papers UNC.

11 Jane P. North to Caroline N. Pettigrew, 10 June 1861, Pettigrew Papers UNC.

12 T. G. Barker to JJP, 7 June 1861; Committee to JJP, 4 June 1861; James Conner to JJP, 12 June 1861; all in Pettigrew Papers NCDAH. J. L. Petigru to Caroline Petigru Carson, 5 July 1861, Petigru Papers.

13 J. H. Bryan to JJP, 24 April 1861, and John Franklin Hoke, adjutant general of North Carolina, to JJP, 11 July 1861, Pettigrew Papers NCDAH. For the first few months of its existence, the Twenty-second North Carolina was known as the Twelfth North Carolina, but in a general renumbering of North Carolina regiments became the Twenty-second and was so known ever after. I shall refer to it as the Twenty-second throughout. J. H. Bryan to W. S. Pettigrew, 12 July 1861, Pettigrew Papers UNC.

14 To JJP from F. W. Pickens, 15 July 1861, and from Louis Gourdin Young, 9 July 1861, Pettigrew Papers NCDAH; JJP to J. H. Bryan, 18 April 1861, Pettigrew Papers UNC.

15 Physical description chiefly from letter-of-safe-conduct to Cuba issued by United States State Department, 7 June 1854. This document describes him as fair, but many wartime descriptions portray Pettigrew as "swarthy," perhaps because of his constant sunburn. Letter-of-safe-conduct in Pettigrew Papers UNC.

16 Walter Clark, *General James Johnston Pettigrew, C. S. A.*, 6–7. This pamphlet, which contains a speech made by Clark at the unveiling of a marble tablet near the place of Pettigrew's death, has been printed on several occasions: in the *Raleigh News and Observer*, 19 September 1920; in *Confederate Veteran* 28 (November 1920):413–15; and in *North Carolina Booklet* 20 (1921):171–80.

17 Clark, *Pettigrew*, 6–7; see also J. Conner to J. B. Allston, 8 August 1864, Pettigrew Papers NCDAH.

18 Hamilton Claverhouse Graham, "Address on the Life and Services of General James Johnston Pettigrew," in *Confederate Memorial Addresses, Monday, May 11, 1885, New Bern, N.C.*, by New Bern Ladies Memorial Association (Richmond: Whittet and Shepperson, 1886), 19; Samuel Finley Harper, "Four Years in the Army of Northern Virginia," in *Lenoir* (N.C.) *News-Topic*, 5 October 1923.

19 Graham Daves, "Twenty-Second North Carolina Regiment," in *Histories of the Several Regiments and Battalions from North Carolina, in the Great War of 1861–65, Written by Members of the Respective Commands*, ed. Walter Clark, 5 vols. (Raleigh and Goldsboro: State of North Carolina, 1901), 2:161–62; W. D. Bishop (private of the Twenty-Second North Carolina) to "Dear Mother," 18 July 1861, W. D. Bishop Papers, North Carolina Department of Archives and History; description of soldiers from a series of memoranda, October to December 1861, Pettigrew Papers NCDAH, concerning members of the regiment who died of measles at Evansport, Virginia.

20 D. M. Barringer to William Henry Trescot, 14 October 1867, Pettigrew Papers NCDAH; J. L. Petigru to Caroline P. Carson, 17 July 1861, Petigru Papers.

21 Graham, "Address," 18; receipts for arms, 1 August 1861, Pettigrew Papers NCDAH; Daves, "Twenty-Second North Carolina," in Clark, *Histories* 2:163; Harper, "Four Years"; Clark, *Pettigrew*, 7; W. D. Bishop to "Dear Mother," 17 (August?) 1861, Bishop Papers.

22 Dabney Herndon Maury (staff officer to department commander) to JJP, 28 August 1861, Pettigrew Papers NCDAH; W. D. Bishop to "Dear Mother," 19 (September?) 1861, Bishop Papers.

23 JJP to W. S. Pettigrew, 20 September 1861, Pettigrew Papers UNC; Harper, "Four Years"; JJP to General Theophilus Hunter Holmes, 8 September 1861, Pettigrew Papers NCDAH.

24 Graham, "Address," 18; Daves, "Twenty-Second North Carolina," in Clark, *Histories* 2:164; Samuel Gibbs French, *Two Wars: An Autobiography* (Nashville: Confederate Veteran, 1901), 143.

25 JJP to William Porcher Miles, 19 August 1861, Miles Papers.

26 W. P. Miles to JJP, 22 August 1861, and William H. N. Smith to JJP, 24 August 1861, Pettigrew Papers NCDAH.

27 James Lowndes to "Cousin Harriet," 23 October 1861, James Lowndes Letters, South Caroliniana Library, University of South Carolina; JJP to Gen. T. H. Holmes, 8 September 1861, marked "unofficial," Pettigrew Papers NCDAH; JJP to W. S. Pettigrew, 20 September 1861, Pettigrew Papers UNC; D. H. Maury to JJP, 13 November 1861, Pettigrew Papers NCDAH; JJP to W. S. Pettigrew, 20 September 1861, Pettigrew Papers UNC.

28 JJP to Edmund Burke Haywood, 7 October 1861, Ernest Haywood Collection, Southern Historical Collection, University of North Carolina. Haywood

was an old friend of Pettigrew and was high in the wartime medical administration in North Carolina. See also memoranda of dead soldiers, October to December 1861, Pettigrew Papers NCDAH; and JJP to Mary Pettigrew, 2 December 1861, Pettigrew Papers UNC.

29 Clipping, 4 November 1861, from unidentified Petersburg newspaper, quoting *Greensboro Times* correspondent, scrapbook, Pettigrew Papers NCDAH.

30 Daves, "Twenty-Second North Carolina," in Clark, *Histories* 2:167; JJP to W. P. Miles, 24 August 1861, Miles Papers; JJP to Caroline N. Pettigrew, 15 January 1862, Pettigrew Papers UNC; also letters from privates of Pettigrew's regiment: W. D. Bishop to "Dear Mother & folks," 28 January and 16 February 1862, Bishop Papers; Calier Green Hamilton to Eli Spinks Hamilton, 30 September 1861, Oliver Clark Hamilton and Calier Green Hamilton Letters (typed copies), North Carolina Department of Archives and History; and Sion H. Oxford to Rebecca Oxford, 1 November 1861, Rebecca Mariah Oxford McCall Papers, Duke University Library.

31 JJP to E. B. Haywood, 7 October 1861, Haywood Collection; see also JJP to C. L. Pettigrew, 10 October 1861, Grimes Papers.

32 French, *Two Wars*, 140; French's and Holmes's letters to JJP, 1861–1863, Pettigrew Papers NCDAH.

33 JJP to C. L. Pettigrew, 10 October 1861, Grimes Papers; C. L. Pettigrew to JJP, 2 October 1861, and JJP to W. S. Pettigrew, 20 September 1861, Pettigrew Papers UNC; L. G. Young to W. S. Pettigrew, 8 June and 11 July 1862, Pettigrew Papers NCDAH; also W. S. to C. L. Pettigrew, 7 June 1862, and L. G. Young to W. S. Pettigrew, 2 June 1862, Pettigrew Papers UNC.

34 John S. Ryan to JJP, 14 August 1862, John S. Ryan Papers, South Caroliniana Library, University of South Carolina; receipt from General Albert Gallatin Blanchard, 14 May 1862, Pettigrew Papers NCDAH; to JJP from Rufus Lenoir, 2 December 1861, and (Mrs.) M. W. Martin, 8 March 1862, Pettigrew Papers NCDAH.

35 *Greensboro Patriot*, 9 January 1862.

36 To JJP from T. H. Holmes, 19 December 1861, from D. H. Maury, 19 December 1861, and from Secretary of War Judah P. Benjamin, 28 December 1861, Pettigrew Papers NCDAH.

37 JJP to W. S. Pettigrew, 18 February 1862, Pettigrew Papers UNC.

38 JJP to W. S. Pettigrew, 20 September 1861, Pettigrew Papers UNC.

39 W. S. Pettigrew to JJP, 1 October 1862, Pettigrew Papers UNC; Clark, *Histories* 4:539, 624; JJP to Mary Pettigrew, 2 December 1861, Pettigrew Papers UNC.

40 General James Green Martin to JJP, 25 February 1862, Pettigrew Papers NCDAH; W. D. Bishop to "Dear Mother & folks," 16 February and 4 April 1862, Bishop Papers.

41 Commission as brigadier general dated 26 February 1862; J. Conner to J. B. Allston, 8 August 1864; and JJP to General Samuel Cooper, 1 March 1862; all in Pettigrew Papers NCDAH.

42 J. Conner to J. B. Allston, 8 August 1864, Pettigrew Papers NCDAH; J. L. Petigru to Susan Petigru King, 6 March 1862, manuscript copy made 1866, Petigru Papers; and W. S. Pettigrew, "Biographical Sketch," 46.

43 J. L. Petigru to Susan P. King (copy), 6 March 1862, Petigru Papers; Mary Boykin Chesnut, *A Diary from Dixie*, ed. Ben Ames Williams (Boston: Houghton Mifflin Company, 1949), 201.

44 J. Conner to J. B. Allston, 8 August 1864, Pettigrew Papers NCDAH.

45 Graham, "Address," 19; John Withers to JJP, 3 March 1862, Pettigrew Papers UNC; J. Conner to J. B. Allston, 8 August 1864, Pettigrew Papers NCDAH.

46 French, *Two Wars*, 143; W. D. Bishop to "Dear Mother," 13 March and 4 April 1862, Bishop Papers.

47 War Department endorsement returning commission, 22 March 1862, on Pettigrew's letter to Cooper of 1 March 1862, Pettigrew Papers NCDAH; also in the same group J. Conner to J. B. Allston, 8 August 1864; see also J. L. Petigru to Jane P. North, 2 and 9 April 1862, printed in Carson, *Petigru*, 440, 441.

48 J. L. Petigru to Jane P. North, 26 March and 9 April 1862, printed in Carson, *Petigru*, 439, 441; J. Conner to J. B. Allston, 8 August 1864, Pettigrew Papers NCDAH.

49 Letters exchanged by Generals T. H. Holmes and R. E. Lee, 27 and 30 April 1862, *Official Records*, ser. 1, 9:465, 468; General T. H. Holmes to General Samuel Cooper, 26 October 1862, *Official Records*, ser. 1, 13:899; Major John Wetmore Hinsdale to JJP, 13 October 1862, Theophilus Hunter Holmes Papers, Duke University Library.

50 Douglas Southall Freeman, *Lee's Lieutenants: A Study in Command*, 3 vols. (New York: Charles Scribner's Sons, 1942–1944), 1:161.

Chapter 13. Fleeting Glory

1 *Official Records*, ser. 1, vol. 11, pt. 3, p. 484; W. D. Bishop to "Dear Mother," 26 (April?) 1862, Bishop Papers; Louis Gourdin Young to JJP, 30 July 1861, Pettigrew Papers NCDAH.

2 Daves, "Twenty-Second North Carolina," in Clark, *Histories* 2:167; Graham, "Address," 19. Daves and Graham were both present.

3 *Official Records*, ser. 1, vol. 11, pt. 3, p. 484.

4 Freeman, *Lee's Lieutenants*, 1:225ff.

5 The account of the early part of the battle comes from the official report of

General Gustavus Woodson Smith to Major Thomas G. Rhett, 23 July 1862, in *Official Records*, ser. 1, vol. 11, pt. 1, pp. 989–91.

6   The account of Pettigrew's wounding and the aftermath was pieced together chiefly from the following three sources: 1) L. G. Young to W. S. Pettigrew, 2 June 1862, Pettigrew Papers UNC; 2) Copy of undated letter (about October 1862) of JJP to Captain John Wetmore Hinsdale, Pettigrew Papers NCDAH. (I have not located the manuscript of this leter. The copy, however, is accompanied by Hinsdale's affidavit verifying its authenticity, and Walter Clark evidently saw the original in Hinsdale's possession before 1920: see Clark, *Pettigrew*, 7, and Hinsdale to Pettigrew, 13 October 1862, Holmes Papers; and 3) JJP to General William Henry Chase Whiting, 4 June 1862, published in Claude Baker Denson, "William Henry Chase Whiting, Major-General, C. S. Army," *Southern Historical Society Papers* 26 (1898):142–44. I have not located the manuscript of this letter, but Denson had access to Whiting's papers and Freeman accepts the letter as authentic (Freeman, *Lee's Lieutenants*, 1:245). For other sources of information about Pettigrew's wounding and capture, see Rev. T. W. Hooper to L. G. Young, 30 June 1862, Pettigrew Papers UNC; J. D. Edmondson to Alice [*sic*, Ann] Pettigrew, 4 June 1862, Pettigrew Papers NCDAH; and General Smith's official report cited in note 5.

7   JJP to J. W. Hinsdale, undated copy (October 1862), Pettigrew Papers NCDAH: "I subsequently received another shot in the left arm and a bayonet in the right leg," Pettigrew commented casually.

8   Ibid.; L. G. Young to W. S. Pettigrew, 2 June 1862, Pettigrew Papers UNC; report of Colonel W. Raymund Lee, Twentieth Massachusetts, 3 June 1862, in *Official Records*, ser. 1, vol. 11, pt. 1, pp. 809–10; unidentified clipping, scrapbook, Pettigrew Papers NCDAH; Oliver Wendell Holmes, Jr., *Touched with Fire: Civil War Letters and Diary of Oliver Wendell Holmes, Jr.*, ed. Mark De Wolfe Howe (Cambridge: Harvard University Press, 1946), 50. Holmes, the future Supreme Court justice, was an officer of the Twentieth Massachusetts.

9   The federal surgeon was Daniel Hand, "Reminiscences of an Army Surgeon," in *Glimpses of the Nation's Struggle. A Series of Papers Read Before the Minnesota Commandery of the Military Order of the Loyal Legion of the United States* (St. Paul: St. Paul Book and Stationery Company, 1886), 286–87. See also Francis Amassa Walker, *History of the Second Army Corps in the Army of the Potomac*, 2d. ed. (New York: Charles Scribner's Sons, 1891), 37. For information about the Austrian prisoners see *Notes on Spain*, 3.

10   JJP to J. W. Hinsdale, undated copy, Pettigrew Papers NCDAH; JJP to W. S. Pettigrew, 8 August 1862, Pettigrew Papers NCDAH; Hand, "Reminiscences," 286–87.

11 John C. Winder to W. S. Pettigrew, 3 June 1862, Pettigrew Papers NCDAH;
    Chesnut, *A Diary from Dixie*, 231, 238.
12 W. S. Pettigrew to Mary Pettigrew, 1 July 1862, Pettigrew Papers UNC; see
    also in the same group L. G. Young to W. S. Pettigrew, 2 June 1862, and
    W. S. Pettigrew to Charles L. Pettigrew, 7 June 1862.
13 Rev. T. W. Hooper to L. G. Young, 30 June 1862, Pettigrew Papers UNC;
    Richmond Dispatch, 17 June 1862, quoting a northern paper.
14 JJP to W. H. C. Whiting, 4 June 1862, printed in Denson, "Whiting."
15 W. S. Pettigrew to Ann Pettigrew and James B. Shepard, telegram, 4 June
    1862, Pettigrew Papers NCDAH. For a few examples of Pettigrew's "obitu-
    aries," see *Charleston Courier*, 4 June 1862; and *Petersburg Express*, undated
    clipping, scrapbook, Pettigrew Papers NCDAH.
16 W. S. Pettigrew to C. L. Pettigrew, 7 June 1862, and to Mary Pettigrew,
    1 July 1862, Pettigrew Papers UNC; to JJP, 10 June 1862, Pettigrew Papers
    NCDAH; *Official Records*, ser. 1, vol. 11, pt. 1, p. 990.
17 JJP to W. H. C. Whiting, 4 June 1862, printed in Denson, "Whiting."
18 *Official Records*, ser. 1, vol. 11, pt. 2, p. 506, and pt. 3, p. 484; Daves, "Twenty-
    Second North Carolina," in Clark, *Histories* 2:168 ff.
19 General John Adams Dix to General John Ellis Wool, 12 June 1862, *Official
    Records*, ser. 2, 3:678; Hardy and Brothers to JJP, 12 June 1862, Pettigrew
    Papers NCDAH.
20 Mary W. Shepard Bryan to daughter, 20 June 1862, John Herritage Bryan
    Collection; Virginia Ritchie to Ann or Mary Pettigrew, 8 July 1862, Pettigrew
    Papers UNC. To JJP from James Mason Campbell, 28 June 1862, and from
    "an Old Friend," undated; and John Williams to W. S. Pettigrew, 19 June
    1862; all in Pettigrew Papers NCDAH.
21 General Lorenzo Thomas to General J. E. Wool, 14 June 1862, *Official
    Records*, ser. 2, 4:18; see also 4:21–31 passim.
22 Susan Matilda Chisolm Middleton to Harriott Kinloch Middleton, 23–25 Au-
    gust 1862, Cheves Family Papers, South Carolina Historical Society; General
    J. E. Wool to Secretary of War Edwin McMasters Stanton, 16 June 1862, and
    General L. Thomas to Wool, 17 June 1862, *Official Records*, ser. 2, 4:25–26,
    31.
23 *Official Records*, ser. 2, 4:40; W. S. Pettigrew to Caroline North Pettigrew,
    30 July 1862, Pettigrew Papers UNC; J. M. Campbell to JJP, 28 June and
    14 July 1862, and Edward Warren to JJP, 22 June 1862, Pettigrew Papers
    NCDAH. The last letter is endorsed by a federal officer: "Gen. Pettigrew can
    avail himself of Dr. W's kindness for necessaries without reserve." A dozen
    letters offering assistance in June 1862 are in the Pettigrew Papers NCDAH.
    Pauline G. Fowle to JJP, 8 July 1862, and Caroline Petigru Carson to Captain

A. A. Gibson, 25 June 1862, Pettigrew Papers NCDAH; J. Barroll Washington to General L. Thomas, 30 July 1862, *Official Records*, ser. 2, 4:313.

24 *Official Records*, ser. 2, 4:450; JJP to W. S. Pettigrew, 8 August 1862, Pettigrew Papers NCDAH; J. L. Petigru to Susan Petigru King, 25 August 1862, manuscript copy made in 1866, Petigru Papers.

25 JJP to Samuel Finley Harper (written with left hand), 4 September 1862, Samuel Finley Harper Papers, North Carolina Department of Archives and History, in reply to Harper to Pettigrew, 28 August 1862, Pettigrew Papers NCDAH. JJP to Daniel Moreau Barringer, 6 August 1862, Pettigrew Papers NCDAH.

26 James Conner to Mary Pettigrew, 26 July 1867, Pettigrew Papers NCDAH.

27 William Henry Trescot to JJP, 7 August 1862, Pettigrew Papers UNC.

28 JJP to J. W. Hinsdale, undated copy, Pettigrew Papers NCDAH; Mary W. S. Bryan to son, 8 September 1862, John Herritage Bryan Collection; Joseph P. Carr to JJP, 8 August 1862, and JJP to W. S. Pettigrew, 8 August 1862, Pettigrew Papers NCDAH.

Chapter 14. An Interlude with Bandits

1 *Official Records*, ser. 1, 9:480; Clark, *Histories* 1:587–88, 2:336–39, and 3:64, 86–87.

2 Freeman, *Lee's Lieutenants* 2:467 ff.

3 JJP to General Samuel Cooper, 30 August (1862), draft; Charles Scott Venable (of Lee's staff) to JJP, 21 September 1862; Secretary of War George Wythe Randolph to William Porcher Miles, 6 September 1862, enclosed in Miles to Pettigrew of same date; all in Pettigrew Papers NCDAH. General Robert E. Lee to General Gustavus W. Smith, 30 October 1862, in *Official Records*, ser. 2, vol. 19, pt. 2, p. 689.

4 Louis Gourdin Young, "The Pettigrew-Kirkland-MacRae Brigade," in Clark, *Histories* 4:556.

5 Colonel W. J. Martin and Captain E. R. Outlaw, "The Eleventh Regiment," in Clark, *Histories* 1:583–86.

6 Major Charles Manly Stedman, "The Forty-Fourth Regiment," in Clark, *Histories* 3:21–24; Captain John H. Thorp, "The Forty-Seventh Regiment," in Clark, *Histories* 3:83–86; Adjutant John H. Robinson, "The Fifty-Second Regiment," in Clark, *Histories* 3:223–27.

7 George C. Underwood, "The Twenty-Sixth Regiment," in Clark, *Histories* 2:303, 308, 328, 331–35; Clyde Wilson, "Henry King Burgwyn, Jr.," *Dictionary of North Carolina Biography*, 1:276–77.

8 *Official Records*, ser. 1, 18:750, 788, 888, 901; Clark, *Histories* 2:339.

9   Clark, *Histories* 1:587–88, 2:336–39, 3:24, 86–87; extensive military correspondence of Pettigrew, chiefly messages from General Samuel Gibbs French and other officers, September and October 1862, Pettigrew Papers NCDAH; see also Clark, *Histories* 3:228–29; and the series of letters from A. C. Myers (private soldier of 52d N.C. Regiment) to Laura E. Myers, August to November 1862, A. C. Myers Papers, North Carolina Department of Archives and History.

10 JJP to Caroline North Pettigrew, 25 September 1862, Pettigrew Papers UNC; undated manuscript plan and General G. W. Smith to General S. G. French, 7 September 1862, with French's note to Pettigrew, Pettigrew Papers NCDAH. Much correspondence of Pettigrew with scouts, citizens, and other officers and also manuscript maps made in the field, 1862 and 1863, in Pettigrew Papers NCDAH; for example, see JJP to S. G. French, (?) September 1862, and letters to Pettigrew from W. B. Wellons, 1 and 5 September 1862, from P. J. Holmes, 7 December 1862, and from S. G. French, 6 December 1862. See also JJP to Captain Graham Daves, 6 October 1862, in Eldridge Collection; and Joseph Johnathan Davis to Mary Pettigrew, 24 June 1867, Pettigrew Papers NCDAH.

11 Quantity of military correspondence, much of it pencilled in the field, September 1862, Pettigrew Papers NCDAH; there is also a small amount of related correspondence printed in *Official Records*, ser. 1, 18 (see index to volume); see also A. C. Myers to Laura E. Myers, 17 and 24 September 1862, Myers Papers. JJP to W. S. Pettigrew, 23 and 29 September 1862, Pettigrew Papers UNC.

12 A. C. Myers to Laura and Joe Myers, 17 and 24 September, 4 October, 3 and 25 November, and 7 December 1862, Myers Papers; Clark, *Histories* 3:228.

13 Young, "Pettigrew Brigade," in Clark, *Histories* 4:556.

14 JJP to W. S. Pettigrew, 29 September 1862, Pettigrew Papers UNC.

15 James Conner to Joseph B. Allston, 8 August 1864, Colonel John Brown to JJP, 2 May 1863, and Elizabeth G. Richmond to JJP, 17 April 1863, Pettigrew Papers NCDAH.

16 John Cheves Haskell, *The Haskell Memoirs*, ed. Gilbert E. Govan and James W. Livingood (New York: G. P. Putnam's Sons, 1960), 41.

17 JJP to W. S. Pettigrew, 20 September 1861, Pettigrew Papers UNC.

18 Leonidas Lafayette Polk to wife, 17 October 1862, Leonidas Lafayette Polk Papers, Southern Historical Collection, University of North Carolina.

19 William J. Baker to wife, 23 October 1862, Blanche Baker Papers, Southern Historical Collection, University of North Carolina; H. L. Clay, War Department, to JJP, 7 March 1863, quoting Jefferson Davis, Pettigrew Papers NCDAH; order dated 13 September 1862, in Robert A. Patterson (surgeon) Papers, North Carolina Department of Archives and History.

20 Ten members of Congress to Secretary of War G. W. Randolph, 27 September 1862, and Randolph's memorandum on, in *Official Records*, ser. 1, vol. 51, pt. 2, pp. 627–28; Zebulon B. Vance to JJP, 21 October 1862, Pettigrew Papers NCDAH.

21 Zebulon B. Vance to JJP, 21 October 1862, Pettigrew Papers NCDAH; JJP to W. S. Pettigrew, 15 November 1862, Pettigrew Papers UNC; L. L. Polk to wife, 31 October 1862, Polk Papers.

22 Freeman, *Lee's Lieutenants* 2:420–21.

23 A. C. Myers to Laura E. Myers, 18 December 1862, Myers Papers; eyewitness account of L. L. Polk, to wife, 24 December 1862, Polk Papers.

24 L. L. Polk to wife, 24 December 1862, Polk Papers; A. C. Myers to Laura E. Myers, 18 December 1862, Myers Papers.

25 Freeman, *Lee's Lieutenants* 2:421; Clark, *Histories* 2:339; A. C. Myers to Laura E. Myers, 18 December 1862, Myers Papers.

26 Freeman, *Lee's Lieutenants* 2:422.

27 Young, "Pettigrew Brigade," in Clark, *Histories* 4:558; A. C. Myers to Laura E. Myers, 6 and 25 January and 11 February 1863, Myers Papers; Clark, *Histories* 3:232; Colonel John Brown, 42d N.C. Regiment, to JJP, 2 May 1863, Pettigrew Papers NCDAH.

28 Young, "Pettigrew Brigade," in Clark, *Histories* 4:558; inspection reports of L. G. Young to JJP, 10, 19, and 27 February and 2 and 6 March 1863, Pettigrew Papers NCDAH; *Official Records*, ser. 1, 18:865; General S. G. French to JJP, 1 February 1863, Pettigrew Papers NCDAH.

29 Inspection reports cited in note 28; A. C. Myers to Laura E. Myers, 25 January 1863, Myers Papers; Robert Bingham to Sarah Tillinghast, 7 February 1863, William Norwood Tillinghast Papers, Duke University Library; A. C. Myers to Laura Myers, 26 February 1863, Myers Papers.

30 Inspection reports cited in note 28; Robert Bingham to Sarah Tillinghast, 7 February 1863, Tillinghast Papers; communications to Pettigrew from various officers, late January and early February, 1863, Pettigrew Papers NCDAH; A. C. Myers to Laura E. Myers, 1 February, 5 and 27 March 1863, Myers Papers; L. L. Polk to wife, 27 January 1863, Polk Papers; Clark, *Histories* 2:400–401.

31 French, *Two Wars*, 152.

32 Z. B. Vance to JJP, 7 February 1863, Pettigrew Papers NCDAH; many notes from John N. Whitford in same group, mostly undated and penciled in the field; General Junius Daniel to John N. Whitford, 19 March 1863, Eldridge Collection; JJP to Z. B. Vance, 5 February 1863, Zebulon Baird Vance Papers, North Carolina Department of Archives and History.

33 JJP to Z. B. Vance, 5 February 1863, Vance Papers.

34 Mary Pettigrew to JJP, 28 March 1862, W. S. Pettigrew to JJP, 14 October

1862, and Caroline N. Pettigrew to JJP, 13 October 1862, Pettigrew Papers UNC.

35 James C. Johnston, Jr., to JJP, 23 August 1862, JJP to W. S. Pettigrew, 15 November 1862, and JJP to Ann Pettigrew, 26 November 1862, Pettigrew Papers UNC; Edward Stanly (Lincoln's appointed "governor" of North Carolina) to General John Gray Foster, 20 January 1863, in *Official Records*, ser. 1, 18:525–26.

36 J. C. Johnston to W. S. Pettigrew, 22 June 1863, Pettigrew Papers UNC.

37 Carson, *Petigru*, 226, 466.

38 J. L. Petigru to Jane Petigru North, 7 November 1861, printed in Carson, *Petigru*, 411–12; J. L. Petigru to JJP, 6 October 1862, Pettigrew Papers UNC.

39 JJP to Henry Deas Lesesne, 27 February 1863, and P. G. T. Beauregard to JJP, 28 February 1863, Pettigrew Papers NCDAH.

40 *Charleston Courier*, 11 March 1863; Minnie North Allston to Louise North, 11 March 1863, and to JJP, 22 March 1863, Pettigrew Papers UNC; Grayson, *Petigru*, 169–70; J. L. Petigru to JJP, 21 October 1862, and JJP to Jane Petigru North, 19 May 1863, Pettigrew Papers UNC.

41 JJP to W. S. Pettigrew, 23 September 1862, and W. S. Pettigrew to JJP, 1 October 1862, Pettigrew Papers UNC.

42 JJP to James Petigru Carson, 17 December 1862, Pettigrew Papers NCDAH.

43 JJP to W. S. Pettigrew, 24 April 1863, Pettigrew Papers UNC.

44 General S. G. French to JJP, 12 and 14 February 1863, Pettigrew Papers NCDAH.

45 Freeman, *Lee's Lieutenants* 2:470, 473–74.

46 General Daniel Harvey Hill to JJP, 10 March 1863, Pettigrew Papers NCDAH; same printed in *Official Records*, ser. 1, 18:195.

47 Official reports of JJP to D. H. Hill, 17 March 1863, and of J. C. Haskell to Captain Nicholas Collin Hughes, 16 March 1863, both printed in *Official Records*, ser. 1, 18:190–94; Haskell, *Memoirs*, 40–41. The account of Pettigrew's part of the battle of New Bern is pieced together chiefly from the three sources just mentioned. The manuscripts of Pettigrew's and Haskell's reports can be found in the Daniel Harvey Hill Papers, Virginia State Library, Richmond, Virginia, and there is a draft of Pettigrew's in the Pettigrew Papers NCDAH. I also used for details and corroboration the following: A. C. Myers to Joe Myers, 25 March 1863, Myers Papers; Clark, *Histories* 2:339–40; message to JJP from J. N. Whitford, undated, and from D. H. Hill, 11, 12, 14, and 17 March, in Pettigrew Papers NCDAH; and messages from Pettigrew to Hill in *Official Records*, ser. 1, 18 (see index of volume).

48 D. H. Hill to JJP, midnight 21/22 March 1863, Pettigrew Papers NCDAH; D. H. Hill to General James Longstreet, 16 March 1863, *Official Records*, ser. 1, 18:188–89; D. H. Hill to JJP, 22 March 1863, Pettigrew Papers NCDAH.

49 Haskell, *Memoirs*, 43.

50 For Pettigrew's reasoning see his official report cited above; as to the vague objectives of the campaign see Clark, *Histories* 4:557, and John Gilchrist Barrett, *The Civil War in North Carolina* (Chapel Hill: University of North Carolina Press, 1963), 155–56.

51 JJP to D. H. Hill, official report, 17 March 1863, *Official Records*, ser. 1, 18:192–94.

52 Barrett, *War in N.C.*, 156, 160.

53 JJP to W. S. Pettigrew, 24 April 1863, Pettigrew Papers UNC; Clark, *Histories* 3:233–34, 4:557; Collett Leventhorpe to Mary Pettigrew, 14 May 1867, Pettigrew Papers NCDAH; A. C. Myers to Laura E. Myers, 8 April 1863, Myers Papers.

54 Barrett, *War in N.C.*, 161–62.

55 This incident is related in Haskell, *Memoirs*, 44–45.

56 General D. H. Hill to General Samuel Cooper, 1 May 1863, *Official Records*, ser. 1, 18:1034; A. C. Myers to Laura E. Myers, 3 May 1863, Myers Papers; Freeman, *Lee's Lieutenants* 2:710.

57 To JJP from Major T. O. Chestney (Elzey's staff), 3 May 1863, from Samuel Cooper, 3 May 1863, from James Longstreet, 6 May 1863, Pettigrew Papers NCDAH; Arnold Elzey to R. E. Lee, 3 May 1863, *Official Records*, ser. 1, vol. 51, pt. 2, p. 701; R. E. Lee to Secretary of War James Alexander Seddon, 3 May 1863, and John Withers to JJP, 5 May 1863, *Official Records*, ser. 1, vol. 25, pt. 2, pp. 768, 778; A. C. Myers to Laura E. Myers, 9 May 1863, Myers Papers; Clark, *Histories* 3:235.

58 Freeman, *Lee's Lieutenants* 2:711. Freeman gives no source for this statement.

59 Armistead Lindsay Long (Lee's staff) to JJP, 19 May 1863, *Official Records*, ser. 1, 18:1065; Freeman, *Lee's Lieutenants* 2:710–11; Clark, *Histories* 3:235.

60 Clark, *Histories* 3:235; R. H. Finney (Heth's staff) to JJP, 13 June 1863, Collett Leventhorpe to Mary Pettigrew, 14 May 1867, Pettigrew Papers NCDAH; Clark, *Histories* 3:235; diary of Henry Clay Albright, captain in 26th N.C. Regiment, 15–25 June 1863, Henry Clay Albright Papers, North Carolina Department of Archives and History; Clark, *Histories* 3:24–26; Robert Bingham Reminiscences (typed copy), in the Southern Historical Collection, University of North Carolina, describe the action at Hanover Junction in detail.

61 JJP to Z. B. Vance, 22 May 1863, manuscript copy in Governors' Letterbooks, vol. 50.1, pp. 255–56, North Carolina Department of Archives and History; also in *Official Records*, ser. 1, vol. 51, pt. 2, pp. 712–13.

62 JJP to Jane P. North, 19 May 1863, Pettigrew Papers UNC.

63 Typed manuscript of Lane's speech given at Gettysburg on 3 July 1903, in the John Randolph Lane Papers, Southern Historical Collection, University of

North Carolina; this speech was published in the *Raleigh News and Observer*, 5 July 1903. See also Joseph Jonathan Davis to Mary Pettigrew, 24 June 1867, Pettigrew Papers NCDAH. See also Clyde Wilson, "John Randolph Lane," *Dictionary of North Carolina Biography*, vol. 4, forthcoming.

64   H. C. Albright diary, 20–28 June 1863, Albright Papers; Clark, *Histories* 2:342.

65   Clark, *Histories* 2:342; Collett Leventhorpe to Mary Pettigrew, 14 May 1867, Pettigrew Papers NCDAH.

66   John Hughes to Mary Pettigrew, 12 June 1867, Pettigrew Papers NCDAH.

Chapter 15. Falling Waters

1   Henry Heth, "Letter from Major-General Henry Heth, of A. P. Hill's Corps, A.N.V.," *Southern Historical Society Papers* 4 (October 1877):157; entry for 30 June 1863, Albright diary, Albright Papers; also, Harry H. Hall, *A Johnny Reb Band from Salem: The Pride of Tarheelia* (Raleigh: North Carolina Confederate Centennial Commission, 1963), 46. This work contains abstracts from the diary of a bandsman in Pettigrew's brigade, Julius Augustus Leinbach, the manuscript of which is now lost but which was published in part in newspapers ca. 1905.

2   Heth, "Letter," 157; Louis Gourdin Young, "Pettigrew's Brigade at Gettysburg," in Clark, *Histories* 5:115–16. Young's account was also published in essentially the same form in a pamphlet, *The Battle of Gettysburg, An Address by Captain Louis G. Young* [Savannah: Privately printed, 1900].

3   Heth, "Letter," 157; Young, "Gettysburg," in Clark, *Histories* 5:116–17.

4   Clark, *Histories* 2:342; Young, "Gettysburg," in Clark, *Histories* 5:117.

5   Young, "Gettysburg," in Clark, *Histories* 5:117; also Clark, *Histories* 1:589, 2:343.

6   Heth, "Letter," 158–59; Clark, *Histories* 2:344–46.

7   Speech of Lieutenant Colonel John Randolph Lane of the 26th North Carolina Regiment, at Gettysburg, 3 July 1903, Lane Papers; to Mary Pettigrew from Captain Joseph Jonathan Davis, 24 June 1867, and from Colonel Collett Leventhorpe, 14 May 1867, Pettigrew Papers NCDAH.

8   Clark, *Histories* 2:345–46; Lane speech, Lane Papers.

9   This account was constructed from several sources: Lane speech and letter of Captain Taylor J. Cureton to J. R. Lane, 15 June 1890, Lane Papers; Albright diary, 1 July 1863, Albright Papers; Clark, *Histories* 2:346–55; Young, "Gettysburg," in Clark, *Histories* 5:119–20; and the official report of General Henry Heth in *Official Records*, ser. 1, vol. 27, pt. 2, p. 638.

10   Heth, "Letter," 158; Clark, *Histories* 2:357–58, based upon a letter written by an officer to Governor Zebulon Baird Vance on 4 July 1863; William F. Fox,

Regimental Losses in the American Civil War, 1861–1865, 4th ed. (Albany: Joseph McDonough, 1898), 556, 569; Clark, *Histories* 1:590, 2:348; T. J. Cureton to J. R. Lane, 15 June 1890, Lane Papers; L. G. Young to Major William J. Baker, 10 February 1864, in Francis Donnell Winston Papers, North Carolina Department of Archives and History. The letter of Young to Baker has been published at least twice, both times under the title "Pettigrew's Brigade at Gettysburg," the first time in the *Richmond Enquirer*, 18 March 1864, and the second in *Our Living and Our Dead* 1 (February 1875):552–58. T. J. Cureton to J. R. Lane, 15 June 1890, Lane Papers; Clark, *Histories* 2:358ff.; Young, "Gettysburg," in Clark, *Histories* 5:131.

11 T. J. Cureton to J. R. Lane, 22 June 1890, Lane Papers; Albright diary, 1 July 1863, Albright Papers.

12 Heth, "Letter," 158; Freeman, *Lee's Lieutenants* 3:147–50, 181.

13 Clark, *Histories* 2:362; T. J. Cureton to J. R. Lane, 22 June 1890, Lane Papers.

14 Albright diary, 2 July 1863, Albright Papers; T. J. Cureton to J. R. Lane, 22 June 1890, Lane Papers; Clark, *Histories* 2:362.

15 Freeman, *Lee's Lieutenants* 3:147–50.

16 Ibid.

17 Young, "Gettysburg," in Clark, *Histories* 5:124; Birkett Davenport Fry, "Pettigrew's Charge at Gettysburg," *Southern Historical Society Papers* 7 (February 1879):92.

18 Fry, "Gettysburg," 92; T. J. Cureton to J. R. Lane, 22 June 1890, Lane Papers.

19 Fry, "Gettysburg," 92.

20 T. J. Cureton to J. R. Lane, 22 June 1890, Lane Papers. This letter is the source for the same incident in Clark, *Histories* 2:365. The physical description comes partly from my imagination, incorporating details known on other occasions.

21 Fry, "Gettysburg," 92; Young, "Gettysburg," in Clark, *Histories* 5:124–25; Clark, *Histories* 5:104.

22 This account of the Pickett-Pettigrew charge was constructed from the following sources: Freeman, *Lee's Lieutenants* 3:157–86; Young, "Gettysburg," in Clark, *Histories* 5:124–29, 132; Fry, "Gettysburg," 92–93; T. J. Cureton to J. R. Lane, 22 June 1890, Lane Papers; Clark, *Histories* 2:362–66; L. G. Young to W. J. Baker, 10 February 1864, Francis Donnell Winston Papers; Captain George M. Whiting, 47th North Carolina Regiment, to John Paris, 18 March 1867, John Paris Papers, Southern Historical Collection, University of North Carolina; and T. M. R. Talcott (of Lee's staff), "The Third Day at Gettysburg," *Southern Historical Society Papers* 41 (September 1916):44.

23 Clark, *Histories* 2:365–66; T. J. Cureton to J. R. Lane, 22 June 1890, Lane Papers; Charles Scott Venable, of Lee's staff, to Joseph Jonathan Davis, 12 August 1889, printed in *Raleigh News and Observer*, 27 November 1889.

24   T. J. Cureton to J. R. Lane, 22 June 1890, Lane Papers; Albright diary, 4 July 1863, Albright Papers; Clark, *Histories* 3:92.

25   For a review of the controversy see "North Carolina at Gettysburg," collecting statements of many eyewitnesses, in *Raleigh Observer*, 18 September 1877; Clark, *Histories* 2:367–68.

26   Young, "Gettysburg," in Clark, *Histories* 5:130.

27   Clark, *Pettigrew*, 10–11. For a Virginian view sympathetic to the North Carolina position, see General Fitzhugh Lee's letter in an undated clipping from *Philadelphia Times*, Pettigrew Papers NCDAH.

28   Major Francis W. Bird, 11th North Carolina Regiment, to Mrs. Patrick Henry Winston, 6 August 1863, Robert Watson Winston Papers, Southern Historical Collection, University of North Carolina; Major John Thomas Jones, 26th North Carolina Regiment, to Edmund Walter Jones, 17 August 1863, Edmund Walter Jones Papers, Southern Historical Collection, University of North Carolina; Young, "Gettysburg," in Clark, *Histories* 5:131; Clark, *Histories* 2:358; Clark, *Pettigrew*, 9.

29   Clark, *Histories* 2:357–58.

30   *Official Records*, ser. 1, vol. 27, pt. 2, pp. 329–34; Clark, *Histories* 2:367; Clark, *Pettigrew*, 9; Fox, *Regimental Losses*, 555–56, 569.

31   Manuscript copy of "Pettigrew's Old Brigade," by Colonel George H. Faribault (written ca. 1867), Paris Papers; Clark, *Pettigrew*, 10; Fry, "Gettysburg," 93.

32   W. R. Bond, *Pickett or Pettigrew? An Historical Essay* (Weldon, N.C.: Hall and Sledge, 1888), 10–11.

33   Albright diary, 4 July 1863, Albright Papers; *Official Records*, ser. 1, vol. 27, pt. 3, p. 994; Clark, *Histories* 2:358; biographical sketch of Pettigrew, quoting a manuscript diary of Dr. W. H. Lilly who was present, in *Lives of Distinguished North Carolinians*, ed. William Joseph Peele (Raleigh. North Carolina Publishing Society, 1898), 423; Albright diary, 4–14 July 1863, Albright Papers.

34   Albright diary, 4–14 July 1863, Albright Papers; Hall, *Johnny Reb Band*, 56, quoting Leinbach diary; John Wilson, Jr., to Mary Pettigrew, 22 June 1867, Pettigrew Papers NCDAH.

35   Albright diary, 7–9 July 1863, Albright Papers; JJP to Zebulon B. Vance, 9 July 1863, Zebulon Baird Vance Papers, North Carolina Department of Archives and History; Albright diary, 10–14 July 1863, Albright Papers; Clark, *Histories* 3:239–40.

36   Pettigrew's wounding at Falling Waters is amply documented by eyewitnesses who agree in most respects: W. J. Baker to wife, 15 July 1863, D. G. Cowand to wife, 20 July 1863, George Pettigrew Collins to Mary Pettigrew, 18 August 1863, and William B. Shepard to W. S. Pettigrew, undated, all in the Pettigrew

Papers NCDAH; L. G. Young to Major Joseph Englehard, 17 August 1874, in "Death of Brigadier General J. Johnston Pettigrew, of North Carolina," *Our Living and Our Dead* 1 (September 1874):29–32; Clark, *Histories* 2:376, 3:110, 240, 4:559–61; J. T. Jones to E. W. Jones, 17 July 1863, Jones Papers; Albright diary, 14 July 1863, Albright Papers; and Sion Harrington Oxford to Rebecca Oxford, 17 July 1863, McCall Papers. Freeman, in *Lee's Lieutenants* 3:192, erroneously puts the time of Pettigrew's wounding at around midnight on 13/14 July. This error is copied from Heth's official report, *Official Records*, ser. 1, vol. 27, pt. 2, p. 640. The sketch of James Johnston Pettigrew in the *Dictionary of American Biography* 14:516, by Donovan Yeuell, is inaccurate in several respects and inexplicably states that Pettigrew was wounded on the night of 14 July.

37 Major J. T. Jones to E. W. Jones, 17 July 1863, Jones Papers; Clark, *Histories* 3:110, 4:560.

38 J. T. Jones to E. W. Jones, 17 July 1863, Jones Papers; S. H. Oxford to Rebecca Oxford, 17 July 1863, McCall Papers; Clark, *Histories* 3:241.

39 W. J. Baker to wife, 15 July 1863, and W. B. Shepard to W. S. Pettigrew, undated, Pettigrew Papers NCDAH; Peele, *Lives*, 424, quoting the diary of Dr. W. H. Lilly who was present.

40 L. G. Young to Mary Pettigrew, 1 August 1863, Pettigrew Papers UNC; Paul E. Steiner, M.D., "Medical Military Studies of the Civil War," pt. 6: "Brigadier General James Johnston Pettigrew," *Military Medicine* 130 (September 1965):935–37; Peele, *Lives*, 424; Clark, *Histories* 2:376–77.

41 Clark, *Histories* 2:376–77; W. B. Shepard to W. S. Pettigrew, undated, Pettigrew Papers NCDAH; L. G. Young to Mary Pettigrew, 1 August 1863, Pettigrew Papers UNC; C. S. Venable, Lee's staff, to J. J. Davis, 12 August 1889, *Raleigh News and Observer*, 27 November 1889; G. P. Collins to W. S. Pettigrew, undated, Pettigrew Papers NCDAH; Mrs. G. P. Collins to Mary Pettigrew, 30 July 1863, Pettigrew Papers UNC.

42 W. B. Shepard to W. S. Pettigrew, undated, Pettigrew Papers NCDAH; L. G. Young to Mary Pettigrew, 1 August 1863, manuscript memoranda of W. S. Pettigrew, (1863?), and W. B. Shepard to Mary Pettigrew, 18 September 1866, Pettigrew Papers UNC. See also John Wilson, Jr., to Mary Pettigrew, 22 June 1867, Pettigrew Papers NCDAH; Mrs. G. P. Collins to Mary Pettigrew, 30 July 1863, Pettigrew Papers UNC.

43 Joseph Pere Bell Wilmer to Ann Pettigrew McKay, 24 October 1863, and L. G. Young to Mary Pettigrew, 1 August 1863, Pettigrew Papers UNC; Clark, *Histories* 2:376–77 (eyewitness). Wilmer later became the Episcopal bishop of Louisiana.

44 L. G. Young to Mary Pettigrew, 1 August 1863, Pettigrew Papers UNC; W. B. Shepard to W. S. Pettigrew, undated, Pettigrew Papers NCDAH. See

also David Alexander Barnes to James B. Shepard, 17 July 1863, James Biddle Shepard Paper, North Carolina Department of Archives and History. The last words come from Young, "Pettigrew Brigade," in Clark, *Histories* 4:561.

45 L. G. Young to Mary Pettigrew Browne, 27 March 1899, Pettigrew Papers UNC; James Conner to J. B. Allston, 8 August 1864, Pettigrew Papers NCDAH.

46 *Charleston Courier*, 4 June 1862, "obituary" evidently written by someone who knew Pettigrew well; Matthew Fontaine Maury to Mary Pettigrew Browne, 6 May 1870, Pettigrew Papers UNC.

47 Cornelia Phillips Spencer, "General Pettigrew's Book," *University of North Carolina Magazine*, 4th ser., 6 (March 1887):263; *Charleston Courier*, 4 June 1862; Jane Petigru North to Louise Petigru Porcher, 21 July 1863, Pettigrew Papers UNC.

48 Trescot, *Memorial*, 38.

49 W. B. Shepard to Mary Pettigrew, 18 September 1866, Pettigrew Papers UNC; Collett Leventhorpe to Mary Pettigrew, 14 May 1867, Pettigrew Papers NCDAH.

50 To Mary Pettigrew from Anne S. Bryan, 1 August 1863, and from Mary W. Shepard Bryan, 4 August 1863, Pettigrew Papers UNC; *Raleigh North Carolina Standard*, 28 July 1863; clippings from unidentified Raleigh newspapers, 24 and 25 July 1863, scrapbrook, Pettigrew Papers NCDAH; W. S. Pettigrew, "Biographical Sketch," 50.

Chapter 16. The Mind and Heart of a Carolinian

1 JJP to W. S. Pettigrew, 18 June 1861, Pettigrew Papers UNC.

2 Ibid.; Receipts for printing and binding, 15 June 1861 and 1 March 1862.

3 Minnie North Allston to Caroline North Pettigrew, 17 July 1861, and J. L. Petigru to JJP, 24 June 1861, Pettigrew Papers UNC.

4 Ludwig Lewisohn, "A History of Literature in South Carolina," chap. 11:Pettigrew and Trescot, *Charleston News*, 30 August 1903.

5 Kingsbury, Review of *Notes on Spain* 784–85.

6 Ibid., 785–86.

7 Nathan Wilson Walker, "James Johnston Pettigrew," in *Library of Southern Literature*, ed. Edwin Anderson Alderman and Joel Chandler Harris, 16 vols. (Atlanta: Martin and Hoyt Company, 1908–1913), vol. 9, p. 3984. Walker was a professor at the University of North Carolina.

8 Trescot, *Memorial*, 42–43.

9 *Notes on Spain*, 132–36. For another example of his etymological skill see 238–39.

10 Ibid., iv.

11 Ibid., 108–14, 187–89, 200–227.
12 Ibid., 54.
13 Ibid., 57–58.
14 Ibid., 186–87.
15 Ibid., 247.
16 Ibid., 316–17.
17 Ibid., iii.
18 Ibid., 16.
19 Ibid., 140, 152.
20 *Charleston Courier*, 24, 27, and 31 October 1857. Pettigrew's authorship of these anonymous articles is deduced from the content and from evidence in his scrapbook in the Pettigrew Papers NCDAH. JJP to J. C. Johnston, 22 June 1855, Pettigrew Papers UNC.
21 *Notes on Spain*, 418.
22 Ibid., 422–28.
23 Spencer, "General Pettigrew's Book," 263–64. Mrs. Spencer was a southerner in situation and sentiment, though her father was from England and her mother from New Jersey.
24 *Notes on Spain*, 31–34, 63.
25 Ibid., 55–56.
26 Ibid., 376–77.
27 Ibid., 419.
28 Ibid., 420.
29 Ibid., 415–16.
30 Ibid., 417; for the sins of England in general, see 416–22. JJP to J. C. Johnston, 1 January 1855 (mistakenly written 1854), Pettigrew Papers UNC.
31 Pettigrew, *Slave Trade*, 18.
32 *Notes on Spain*, 377; see also 418.
33 Ibid., 378; see also 374–82 for extended discussion of Spanish history in connection with the concept of constitutional government.
34 Ibid., 63; regarding decrying the urban proletariat, see 391.
35 JJP to Ann Pettigrew, 11 July 1849, Pettigrew Papers UNC.
36 JJP to J. C. Johnston, 10 June 1853, Pettigrew Papers UNC.
37 *Notes on Spain*, 418, 429.
38 Ibid., 418.
39 Pettigrew, *Slave Trade*, 5.
40 *Notes on Spain*, 24–25.
41 Ibid., 385–86.
42 Ibid., 374–78, 80.
43 Ibid., 392.
44 Ibid., 375.

45 Ibid., 339; p. 29: "One must travel in Europe to appreciate the unspeakable blessings of American liberty."

46 Ibid., 58.

47 Ibid., 388–91.

48 Ibid., 153–54.

49 Ibid., 153–54; Pettigrew, *Slave Trade*, 17–18.

50 *Notes on Spain*, 386.

51 Ibid., 395–96.

52 For one of many examples that might be cited, see William Cullen Bryant's comments upon meeting some planters on a train in *Prose Writings of William Cullen Bryant*, ed. Parke Godwin, 2 vols. (New York: D. Appleton and Company, 1884), 2:4.

53 *Notes on Spain*, 405, 243–44, 261.

54 Ibid., 330–32.

55 Ibid., 168–72, 242–63, 247–62.

56 JJP to J. C. Johnston, 15 February 1853, Pettigrew Papers UNC.

57 Undated clipping from *Charleston Courier* in Pettigrew's scrapbook with indication of his authorship, Pettigrew Papers NCDAH.

58 Ibid.

59 *Notes on Spain*, 76–79; for other observations on Catholicism see 402–4.

60 Louis G. Young to Mary Pettigrew, 1 August 1863, and Caroline N. Pettigrew to Jane Petigru North, (?) October 1852, Pettigrew Papers UNC. J. C. Johnston, in a letter to W. S. Pettigrew, 19 September 1853, Pettigrew Papers UNC, says of JJP: "He appears to have read the Bible with great attention. Altho not an admirer of the doctrines of the Church he is well-versed in Biblical history & reading." *Notes on Spain*, 403.

61 *Notes on Spain*, 258.

62 Trescot, *Memorial*, 62–64.

63 *Notes on Spain*, 51; J. J. Davis to Mary Pettigrew, 24 June 1867, Pettigrew Papers NCDAH.

Sources

The materials most pertinent to re-creating the life and mind of James Johnston Pettigrew are found in the preserved papers of his family, an estimated 17,500 manuscripts, which are divided between the Southern Historical Collection of the University of North Carolina at Chapel Hill and the North Carolina Department of Archives and History, Raleigh.

These collections include Pettigrew's own papers: letters received, travel diaries, manuscript writings, business papers, clippings. They include as well his many letters to his father, brothers, sisters, and other kinfolk and the many letters about him exchanged by his relatives with each other and with other people.

The Pettigrew Family Papers, which reflect the life of three generations of an extended planter family in both Carolinas, are unique in volume, depth, completeness, time span, and articulateness. The North Carolina Department of Archives and History has published two volumes of *The Pettigrew Papers*, edited by Sarah M. Lemmon (1971, 1988), though the published papers have not yet reached the active years of James Johnston Pettigrew.

In addition, there are letters written by Pettigrew and other pertinent manuscripts in the papers of relatives, friends, and political and military associates preserved in various collections and valuable materials in his own published writings and in the publications of contemporaries.

Where a source is printed in more than one version, as is often the case with soldiers' recollections and memorials, entries have been provided in this bibliography for all versions, but the most readily available version has been cited in the Notes.

Primary sources are subdivided into Manuscripts, Published Writings of James Johnston Pettigrew (omitting newspaper material), Biographical Treatments of James Johnston Pettigrew by Contemporaries, Other Published Accounts by Contemporaries, Government Documents, Newspapers and Periodicals, and Miscellaneous Printed Primary Sources.

The accounting of secondary sources is narrowly focused on materials directly relevant to this study and obviously omits a vast amount of background literature on the southern mind, the Civil War, and the various public events and social trends in which Pettigrew was involved. I also omitted some two dozen twentieth-century articles which have been located that deal with Pettigrew. These are mostly entries in biographical collections or popular treatments of his military career. While often slight, derivative, and containing inaccuracies, they do indicate a continuing substantial interest in the historical figure.

One other type of source is not accounted for: the physical remains of Pettigrew's world, including the great battlefields. Except for the J. L. Petigru law office in St. Michael's Alley, most of the Charleston structures with which Pettigrew was most intimately associated are no longer standing, but Charleston is still Charleston. The Pettigrew State Park in eastern North Carolina, under the devoted superintendence of Sidney H. Shearin, preserves some of the physical atmosphere of The Lake and also hosts annual reunions of the descendants of the families of black Carolinians who made up an indispensable part of that life.

Primary Sources

Manuscripts

Duke University, Perkins Library. Durham, North Carolina.
　　Ellison Capers Papers
　　Richard Gill Mills Dunovant Papers
　　Theophilus Hunter Holmes Papers
　　Rebecca Mariah Oxford McCall Papers
　　Mary Singleton McDuffie Letters
　　Augustin Louis Taveau Papers
　　William Norwood Tillinghast Papers
Harvard University, Houghton Library. Cambridge, Massachusetts.
　　Frederick M. Dearborn Collection
　　Henry Wadsworth Longfellow Papers
The Huntington Library. San Marino, California.
　　Eldridge Civil War Collection
Library of Congress, Manuscript Division. Washington, D.C.
　　James Louis Petigru Papers
　　Pickens-Bonham Papers
New York City Public Library, Rare Book Division. New York, New York.
　　John Russell's annotated set of *Russell's Magazine*
North Carolina Department of Archives and History. Raleigh, North Carolina.
　　Henry Clay Albright Papers
　　W. D. Bishop Papers
　　John Herritage Bryan Collection

Walter Clark Manuscripts
Governors' Letterbooks: Zebulon B. Vance
Bryan Grimes Papers
Oliver Clark Hamilton and Calier Green Hamilton Letters
Samuel Finley Harper Papers
A. C. Myers Papers
Robert A. Patterson Papers
Pettigrew Family Papers
James Biddle Shepard Paper
David Lowry Swain Papers
Zebulon Baird Vance Papers
Francis Donnell Winston Papers
University of North Carolina at Chapel Hill. Chapel Hill, North Carolina.
North Carolina Collection:
University Senior and Junior Orations, 1842–1846
Southern Historical Collection:
Blanche Baker Papers
Daniel Moreau Barringer Papers
Robert Bingham Reminiscences
William Shepard Bryan Papers
Wilmot Gibbes De Saussure Order Book
William Alexander Graham Papers
Hayes Collection (microfilm)
Ernest Haywood Collection
Edmund Walter Jones Papers
John Randolph Lane Papers
William Porcher Miles Papers
David Outlaw Papers
John Paris Papers
Pettigrew Family Papers
Leonidas Lafayette Polk Papers
David Lowry Swain Papers
Robert Watson Winston Papers
University Archives:
Philanthropic Society Records
South Carolina Historical Society. Charleston, South Carolina.
Allston Family Papers
Cheves Family Papers
University of South Carolina, South Caroliniana Library. Columbia, South Carolina.
Ellison Capers Letters

James Lowndes Letters
John S. Ryan Papers
Virginia State Library. Richmond, Virginia.
Daniel Harvey Hill Papers

Published Writings of James Johnston Pettigrew (except newspaper articles)

"Biographical Notice of the Rt. Rev. Charles Pettigrew, First Bishop of the Diocese of North Carolina." Appendix to *Life and Correspondence of James Iredell, One of the Associate Justices of the Supreme Court of the United States,* by Griffith John McRee. 2 vols. New York: D. Appleton and Company, 1857–1858. Vol. 2, pp. 591–93.

"The Militia System of South Carolina." *Russell's Magazine* 6 (March 1860):529–40.

Notes on Spain and the Spaniards in the Summer of 1859, with a Glance at Sardinia. Charleston: Evans and Cogswell, 1861.

"Protest Against a Renewal of the Slave Trade." *De Bow's Review* 25 (August and September 1858):166–85, 289–308.

Report of the Minority of the Special Committee of Seven, to Whom Was Referred So Much of Governor Adams' Message No. 1, as Relates to Slavery and the Slave Trade. Columbia: Carolina Times, 1857. Rev. ed. Charleston: Harper and Calvo, 1858.

Biographical Treatments of James Johnston Pettigrew by Contemporaries

Battle, Kemp Plummer. "Commodore Maury and General Pettigrew." *University of North Carolina Magazine,* 4th ser., 12 (May 1893):273–80.

———. "Maury's Estimate of Pettigrew." *University of North Carolina Magazine,* 4th ser., 13 (October 1893):39–40.

Clark, Walter. "General James Johnston Pettigrew, C.S.A." In *North Carolina Booklet* 20 (1921):171–80. Published by North Carolina Society of the Daughters of the American Revolution, Raleigh, North Carolina.

———. *General James Johnston Pettigrew, C.S.A.: Address by Chief Justice Walter Clark of the Supreme Court of North Carolina at Bunker Hill, West Virginia, September 17, 1920.* N.p., n.d.

———. "General Pettigrew." *Confederate Veteran* 28 (November 1920):413–15.

———. "James Johnston Pettigrew." *Raleigh News and Observer,* 19 September 1920.

Creecy, Richard Benbury. *Grandfather's Tales of North Carolina History.* Raleigh: Edwards and Broughton, 1901.

———. "Sketch of the Life of General J. J. Pettigrew." *Elizabeth City (N.C.) Economist,* 16 and 23 April 1872.

"General J. Johnston Pettigrew." *Charleston Courier,* 4 June 1862.

Graham, Hamilton Claverhouse. "Address on the Life and Services of General James Johnston Pettigrew." In *Confederate Memorial Addresses, Monday, May 11, 1885, New Bern, N.C.*, New Bern Ladies Memorial Association. Richmond: Whittet and Shepperson, 1886. Pp. 9–27.

Kingsbury, Theodore Bryant. Untitled review of James Johnston Pettigrew's *Notes on Spain and the Spaniards*. In *Our Living and Our Dead* 3 (December 1875): 783–89.

"The Late General Pettigrew." *Raleigh Register*, 29 July 1863.

Peele, William Joseph, ed. *Lives of Distinguished North Carolinians*. Raleigh: North Carolina Publishing Society, 1898.

Pettigrew, William Shepard. "Biographical Sketch of General J. Johnston Pettigrew." *University of North Carolina Magazine*, 4th ser., 6 (October 1886):43–50.

[Spencer, Cornelia Phillips.] "General James Johnston Pettigrew." *Fayetteville Observer*, 3 August 1863.

——. "General James Johnston Pettigrew." *University of North Carolina Magazine*, 4th ser., 2 (June 1883):154–62.

Spencer, Cornelia Phillips. "General Pettigrew's Book." *University of North Carolina Magazine*, 4th ser., 6 (March 1887):262–68.

——. *The Last Ninety Days of the War in North Carolina*. New York: Watchman Publishing Company, 1866.

Trescot, William Henry. *Memorial of the Life of J. Johnston Pettigrew, Brig. Gen. of the Confederate States Army*. Charleston: John Russell, 1870.

Young, Louis Gourdin. "Death of Brigadier General J. Johnston Pettigrew, of North Carolina." *Our Living and Our Dead* 1 (September 1874):29–32.

Other Published Accounts By Contemporaries

Battle, Kemp Plummer. *History of the University of North Carolina*. 2 vols. Raleigh: Edwards and Broughton, 1907–1912.

Bond, W. R. *Pickett or Pettigrew? An Historical Essay*. Weldon, N.C.: Hall and Sledge, 1888.

Carson, James Petigru. *Life, Letters and Speeches of James Louis Petigru, the Union Man of South Carolina*. Washington: W. H. Lowdermilk and Company, 1920.

Chesnut, Mary Boykin. *A Diary from Dixie*. Edited by Ben Ames Williams. Boston: Houghton Mifflin Company, 1949.

Clark, Walter, ed. *Histories of the Several Regiments and Battalions from North Carolina, in the Great War 1861–'65, Written by Members of the Respective Commands*. 5 vols. Raleigh and Goldsboro: State of North Carolina, 1901.

Crawford, Samuel Wylie. *The History of the Fall of Fort Sumter*. New York: S. F. McLean and Company, 1898.

Denson, Claude Baker. "William Henry Chase Whiting, Major-General C. S. Army." *Southern Historical Society Papers* 26 (1898):129–81.

French, Samuel Gibbs. *Two Wars: An Autobiography*. Nashville: Confederate Veteran, 1901.

Fry, Birkett Davenport. "Pettigrew's Charge at Gettysburg." *Southern Historical Society Papers* 6 (February 1879):91–93.

Grayson, William John. *James Louis Petigru, A Biographical Sketch*. New York: Harper and Brothers, 1866.

Hall, Harry H. *A Johnny Reb Band from Salem: The Pride of Tarheelia*. Raleigh: North Carolina Confederate Centennial Commission, 1963.

Hand, Daniel. "Reminiscences of an Army Surgeon." In *Glimpses of the Nation's Struggle. A Series of Papers Read Before the Minnesota Commandery of the Military Order of the Loyal Legion of the United States*. St. Paul: St. Paul Book and Stationery Company, 1887. Pp. 276–307.

Harper, Samuel Finley. "Four Years in the Army of Northern Virginia." *Lenoir* (N.C.) *News-Topic*, 5 October 1923.

Haskell, John Cheves. *The Haskell Memoirs*. Edited by Gilbert E. Govan and James W. Livingood. New York: G. P. Putnam's Sons, 1960.

Heth, Henry. "Letter from Major-General Henry Heth, A. P. Hill's Corps, A.N.V." *Southern Historical Society Papers* 4 (October 1877):151–60.

Holmes, Oliver Wendell, Jr. *Touched with Fire: Civil War Letters and Diary of Oliver Wendell Holmes, Jr.* Edited by Mark De Wolfe Howe. Cambridge: Harvard University Press, 1946.

"North Carolina at Gettysburg." *Raleigh Observer*, 18 September 1877.

Pringle, Elizabeth Allston. *Chronicles of Chicora Wood*. New York: Charles Scribner's Sons, 1922.

Talcott, T. M. R. "The Third Day at Gettysburg." *Southern Historical Society Papers* 41 (September 1916):37–48.

Venable, Charles Scott. Letter to Joseph J. Davis, 12 August 1889. In *Raleigh News and Observer*, November 27, 1889.

Walker, Francis Amassa. *History of the Second Army Corps in the Army of the Potomac*. 2d ed. New York: Charles Scribner's Sons, 1891.

Young, Louis Gourdin. *The Battle of Gettysburg, An Address by Captain Louis G. Young*. [Savannah: Privately printed, 1900].

——. "Pettigrew's Brigade at Gettysburg." *Our Living and Our Dead* 1 (February 1875):552–58.

——. "Pettigrew's Brigade at Gettysburg." *Richmond Enquirer*, 18 March 1864.

Government Documents

South Carolina General Assembly. *Journal of the House of Representatives of the State of South Carolina. Being the Session of 1856*. Columbia, S.C., 1856.

———. *Journal of the House of Representatives of the State of South Carolina. Being the Session of 1857.* Columbia, S.C., 1857.

———. *Report of the Minority of the Special Committee of Seven, to Whom Was Referred So Much of His Late Excellency's Message No. 1 As Relates to Slavery and the Slave Trade.* Columbia, S.C., 1857.

———. *Report of the Special Committee of the House of Representatives, of South Carolina, on So Much of the Message of His Excellency Governor James H. Adams, As Relates to Slavery and the Slave Trade.* Columbia, S.C., 1857.

———. *Reports and Resolutions of the General Assembly of the State of South Carolina, Passed at the Annual Session of 1856.* Columbia, S.C., 1856.

———. *Reports and Resolutions of the General Assembly of the State of South Carolina, Passed at the Annual Session of 1857.* Columbia, S.C., 1857.

United States National Observatory. *Astronomical Observations Made During the Year 1847 at the National Observatory, Washington, under the Direction of M. F. Maury, LL.D., Lt., United States Navy, Superintendent.* Washington: C. Alexander [printer], 1853.

United States War Department. *The War of the Rebellion: A Compilation of the Official Records of the Union and Confederate Armies.* 4 ser., 70 vols. in 128. Washington: Government Printing Office, 1880–1901.

Newspapers and Periodicals

Charleston Courier, 1853–1863.

Charleston Mercury, 1853–1863.

Charleston Standard, 1853–1857. (Irregular files survive in the Duke University Library and the Charleston Free Library Society.)

Fayetteville Observer, 1847–1863.

Raleigh Register, 1847–1863.

Russell's Magazine. 6 vols. Charleston, 1857–1860.

Miscellaneous Printed Primary Sources

Capers, William Henry. *Rifle Regiment Quickstep. Composed and Respectfully Dedicated to Col. J. Johnston Pettigrew, the Officers and Members of the First Rifle Regiment.* Charleston: George F. Cole, 1861.

DeCamp, John. *Reply of Commander John DeCamp to Aspersions upon His Character Contained in an Article Published in the Charleston Mercury of November 6, 1855.* New York: Privately printed, 1856.

Epitaphs in the Grave-Yard at Bonarva, Lake Phelps, North Carolina. New York: Protestant Episcopal Press, 1834. (Manuscript additions in the copy in the North Carolina Collection, University of North Carolina at Chapel Hill.)

Memorial of the Late James L. Petigru: Proceedings of the Bar of Charleston, S.C., March 25, 1863. Charleston: Walker, Evans and Cogswell, 1880.

Proceedings of the Democratic State Convention of South Carolina, Held at Columbia, 5th and 6th of May, 1856. Columbia: R. W. Gibbes, 1856.

Sprague, William Buell, *Annals of the American Pulpit*, 9 vols. New York: Carter and Brothers, 1857–1869.

Secondary Sources

Barrett, John Gilchrist. *The Civil War in North Carolina*. Chapel Hill: University of North Carolina Press, 1963.

Black, Caroline Banks. "Aspects of the History of Yellow Fever Epidemics in Charleston, South Carolina." Master's thesis, Duke University, 1943.

Boatner, Mark Mayo. *The Civil War Dictionary*. New York: David McKay Company, 1959.

Brown, William Garrott. *The Lower South in American History*. New York: Macmillan Company, 1903.

Davis, Archie K. *Boy Colonel of the Confederacy: The Life and Times of Henry King Burgwyn, Jr*. Chapel Hill: University of North Carolina Press, 1985.

Easterby, James Harold, ed. *The South Carolina Rice Plantation as Revealed in the Papers of Robert F. W. Allston*. Chicago: University of Chicago Press, 1945.

Eaton, Clement. *Freedom of Thought in the Old South*. Durham: Duke University Press, 1940.

Edwards, Bryan. *The History, Civil and Commercial, of the British Colonies in the West Indies*. 3 vols. 3d ed. London: J. Stockdale, 1801.

Federal Writers Project. *North Carolina: A Guide to the Old North State*. American Guide Series. Chapel Hill: University of North Carolina Press, 1939.

Fox, William F. *Regimental Losses in the American Civil War, 1861–1865*. 4th ed. Albany: Joseph McDonough, 1898.

Freeman, Douglas Southall. *Lee's Lieutenants: A Study in Command*. 3 vols. New York: Charles Scribner's Sons, 1942–1944.

Genovese, Eugene D. "Marxian Interpretations of the Slave South." In *Toward a New Past: Dissenting Essays in American History*. Edited by Barton J. Bernstein. New York: Pantheon Books, 1968.

Genzmer, George Harvey. "Francis James Child." *Dictionary of American Biography*. Edited by Allen Johnson and Dumas Malone. 21 vols. New York: Charles Scribner's Sons, 1928–1937. Vol. 4, pp. 166–67.

Gildersleeve, Basil Lanneau. *Creed of the Old South, 1865–1915*. Baltimore: Johns Hopkins University Press, 1915.

Hamilton, Joseph Gregoire de Roulhac. "Daniel Moreau Barringer." *Dictionary of American Biography*. Edited by Allen Johnson and Dumas Malone. 21 vols. New York: Charles Scribner's Sons, 1928–1937. Vol. 1, pp. 648–49.

Kennedy, Fronde. "Russell's Magazine." *South Atlantic Quarterly* 18 (April 1919): 125–44.

Lemmon, Sarah McCulloh. *Parson Pettigrew of the "Old Church": 1744–1807*. Vol. 52 of *James Sprunt Studies in History and Political Science*. Chapel Hill, University of North Carolina Press, 1970.

Lewis, Charles Lee. *Matthew Fontaine Maury: The Pathfinder of the Seas*. Annapolis: United States Naval Institute, 1927.

Lewisohn, Ludwig. "A History of Literature in South Carolina." Chapter 11: Pettigrew and Trescot. *Charleston News*, 30 August 1903.

Luker, Ralph E. "God, Man, and the World of James Warley Miles, Charleston's Transcendentalist." *Historical Magazine of the Protestant Episcopal Church* 39 (June 1970):101–36.

Pettigrew Folders, Clipping File, North Carolina Collection, University of North Carolina Library, Chapel Hill, N.C.

Powell, William S. *North Carolina Gazetteer*. Chapel Hill: University of North Carolina Press, 1968.

Smith, Martha M. "James Cathcart Johnston." *Dictionary of North Carolina Biography*. Edited by William S. Powell. 3 vols to date. Chapel Hill: University of North Carolina Press, 1979– . Vol. 3, pp. 302–04.

Steiner, Paul E., M.D. "Medical Military Studies of the Civil War," pt. 6: "Brigadier General James Johnston Pettigrew." *Military Medicine* 130 (September 1965):930–37.

Walker, Nathan Wilson. "James Johnston Pettigrew." In *Library of Southern Literature*. Edited by Edwin Anderson Alderman and Joel Chandler Harris. 16 vols. Atlanta: Martin and Hoyt Company, 1908–1913. Vol. 9, pp. 3981–4001.

Wall, Bennett Harrison. "Charles Pettigrew, A Study of an Early North Carolina Religious Leader and Planter." Master's thesis, University of North Carolina at Chapel Hill, 1940.

——. "Ebenezer Pettigrew, an Economic Study of an Ante-Bellum Planter." Ph.D. diss., University of North Carolina at Chapel Hill, 1946.

Warner, Ezra J. *Generals in Gray: Lives of the Confederate Commanders*. Baton Rouge: Louisiana State University Press, 1959.

Wayland, John W. *The Pathfinder of the Seas: The Life of Matthew Fontaine Maury*. Richmond: Garrett and Massie, 1930.

Wilgus, A. Curtis. "John Sidney Thrasher." *Dictionary of American Biography*. Edited by Allen Johnson and Dumas Malone. 21 vols. New York: Charles Scribner's Sons, 1928–1937. Vol. 18, pp. 509–10.

Wilson, Clyde N. "Henry King Burgwyn, Jr." *Dictionary of North Carolina Biography*. Edited by William S. Powell. 3 vols to date. Chapel Hill: University of North Carolina Press, 1979– . Vol. 1, pp. 276–77.

——. "John Randolph Lane." *Dictionary of North Carolina Biography*. Vol. 4. Forth-coming.

——. " 'The Most Promising Young Man of the South': James J. Pettigrew." *Civil War Times Illustrated* 11 (February 1973):12–23.

Woodward, Comer Vann. "The Southern Ethic in a Puritan World." *William and Mary Quarterly*, 3d ser., 25 (July 1968):343–70.

Index

Trescot, William Henry, 14, 77, 169, 205, 208, 236
Twenty-second North Carolina Regiment, 152–57, 158, 162, 269
Twenty-sixth North Carolina Regiment, 171–72, 192, 193, 194, 199–200, 201

Uncle Tom's Cabin, 107, 110–11
University of Berlin, 39–40
University of North Carolina, 12–20

Vance, Zebulon Baird, 171, 175, 178, 201

Walker, Leroy P., 149
Warren, Edward, 274

Washington Light Infantry, 116, 121–22, 136, 140, 149, 151
Whitford, John N., Maj., 178
Whiting, William Henry Chase, Gen., 162, 163, 166, 183, 184
Williams, John, 25, 167
Wilmer, J. P. B., Rev., 204
Wilmot Proviso, 109
Winnsboro Register, 105
Wool, John E., 168

Young, Louis Gourdin, 162, 169, 173, 183, 203, 204

Zouaves, 136
Zumalacarregui, Tomás de, Gen., 132–33, 158, 187, 198